PILOTS' GUIDE TO THE LESSER ANTILLES

Also by Paul Fillingham

Basic Guide to Flying
The Balloon Book
Complete Guide to Canoeing and Kayaking
Basic Guide to Soaring

PILOTS' GUIDE TO THE LESSER ANTILLES

Paul Fillingham

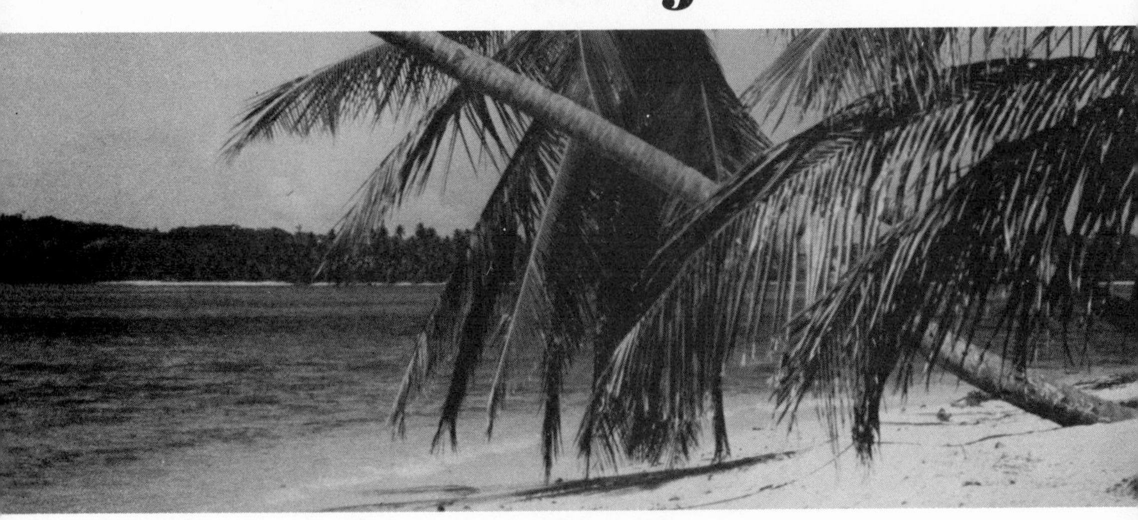

McGRAW-HILL BOOK COMPANY
New York St. Louis San Francisco
Düsseldorf London
Mexico Sydney Toronto

Photo Credits Air France: pp. 147, 154, 158, 160, 171, 186, 191, 193; Antigua Tourist Board: pp. 130, 134, 140, 144, 204; Barbados Tourist Office: xiii, 16, 241, 254-255, 264, 270; BVI Tourist Information Office: p. 80; Caribbean Tourism Association: pp. 56, 234; Club Mediterannee: pp. 154–155, 165, 187; Defense Mapping Agency Aerospace Center: pp. 11, 22–23, 25, 45, 86, 102, 105, 114, 173, 176, 185, 199, 244, 274, 337–366; Eastern Airlines: pp. 196, 201, 204; Eastern Caribbean Travel Association: pp. 124, 129, 174, 179, 215, 217; French West Indies Tourist Office: pp. 107, 111, 164, 169, 171, 182; Rose Fujimoto: p. 110; Grenada Tourist Office: pp. 226, 229; Judy Gurovitz (courtesy Clement-Petrocik Company): p. 168; Fritz Henle: pp. 43, 62; Hill & Knowlton, Inc.: p. 271; Charles R. Mayer for BVI Tourist Information Office: pp. 65, 70, 74, 81; New York Public Library: pp. 5, 73, 121, 132, 142, 149, 177, 184, 198, 216, 231, 235, 299; Puerto Rico Tourism Company: pp. xvi, 3, 24, 26, 28, 30, 33, 34, 35, 39, 41, 59, 76; St. Vincent Tourist Board: p. 211; Sint Maarten, St. Eustatius & Saba Tourist Office: pp. 84, 88, 94, 98, 101, 103; Martin Stansfeld: p. 221; The Travel Agent: p. 117; Trinidad & Tobago Tourist Bureau: pp. 9, 14, 19, 21, 209, 218, 224, 233, 273, 279, 284, 285, 287, 289, 290, 291, 293, 295, 297; U.S. Virgin Islands Tourist Bureau: pp. xvii, 64, 301.

Printed in the United States of America.

1 2 3 4 5 6 7 8 9 D O D O 7 8 3 2 1 0 9

LIBRARY OF CONGRESS CATALOGING IN PUBLICATION DATA
Fillingham, Paul.
Pilots' guide to the Lesser Antilles.
Bibliography: p.
1. Air-pilot guides—Antilles, Lesser. I. Title.
TL726.5.L47F54 629.132'54'729 78-27491
ISBN 0-07-020815-8

Book design by Gloria Gentile

This is for James the Elder,
Jonathan the Belonger and
for F-W.W., R.W., A.W.,
and W-D.v.H., S.v.H.
and Mister Bautz

Contents

How to Use This Book

For the purpose of this handbook, the Lesser Antilles (or Eastern Caribbean archipelago) is that extended range of islands running east, then south of the island of Puerto Rico all the way down to Trinidad & Tobago. This myriad-island archipelago has great attraction to the private pilot in that it is possible to compress the many varieties of the Caribbean experience—with its glamorous mix of different cultures—into one visit, or expand it into several. The distances between the islands are seldom more than 100 NM and variety is, after all, the spice of life.

The first section of this book is called Preview, and gives you a brief overview of what you may expect to find when you get to the islands. It's intended as a sampler to provide orientation on a basis from which you can make your choice.

Getting to the islands is described only briefly here, since the coast of Florida provides numerous points of departure, many of which have overwater equipment for rent (albeit costly), several with Customs, and a whole host of radio navaids to fly in and out on.

The only thing you'll have to check locally is the current status of flying in the ADIZ (Air Defense Identification Zone), though Part 99 of the FARs prescribes the rules for operating civil airplanes in a Designated Defense Area and through an ADIZ. This is usually accomplished by filing either an IFR or DVFR

Flight Plan. The latter will often include the point of penetration. Usually you're required to be no faster than 180 knots and at or below 10,000 feet. The rules change locally from month to month, so before you file your flight plan, query to learn the current status.

For your actual flight planning there are a number of charts available, including the ONC and WAC series. The former are good on the living-room floor, the latter better in the cockpit. Also, and not normally noted for VFR flying of the Bahamian chain of islands, is V30-35, prepared and published by the Defense Mapping Agency Hydrographic Center. It starts at Grand Bahama Island and takes you all the way down to St. Lucia/Martinique. Also good is V30-35P, which includes the entire area, published by the US Naval Oceanographic Office.

For radio aids, the Department of Defense Enroute Low Altitude Caribbean and South American charts are invaluable, as they're updated every 56 days throughout the year. There's also an airport guidebook called *Caribbean Flite Guide* that gives you fairly essential data about most of the airports in the area. Published out of Port of Spain, Trinidad, it's updated quarterly, and is noted in the Further Reading section at the back of the book.

When making your flight plan—and make a point of having one, even if you'll be line-of-sight between points—figure for some sort of wind component and note the above-surface winds rather carefully. Make a practice of checking this wind factor while en route.

One cardinal rule about flying the islands: Remember that gasoline may not be available, for one reason or another. Sometimes the pumps are closed down, other times there's simply no gas (and occasionally no oil). So always rely on having an hour's fuel in the tanks when you land at your destination. (And carry a few spare quarts of oil.)

Fuel is almost always available at one of the Turks & Caicos Islands, nevertheless check with MIAMI Flight Service for the latest information. Do not rely on refueling in the out islands of the Bahamas unless you've checked ahead of time—and even then, be sceptical, and pleasantly surprised if you find that the fuel is available.

Current best buys on fuel are, at the time of writing, in Trinidad (a producer) and Antigua (a refiner).

The majority of FAA-approved repair facilities are to be found within the island chain. Most are clustered within the USVI (U.S. Virgin Islands) and Puerto Rico. A list is provided in the Appendices.

You'll be charged a small landing fee at several airports, and others will try to take you for a departure tax. However, you can avoid this by listing passengers as crew on the General Declaration form. Thus you can have co-pilot, radio operator, and navigator in a small four-place machine.

File a flight plan wherever you go. This is for your own safety, and also it will help you avoid Customs overtime charges, since when you file you can check whether overtime rates will be in effect when you arrive at your destination.*

This information is provided in check-list format within the appendices, but is also given here so you'll know what to expect.

Following Preview, we come to the islands themselves. Each section begins with a brief note on Flying In, which is provided to give you some orientation, plus any notes on fields that may require some additional skills—such as Melville Field, Dominica, where a ridge must be crossed on base leg before a rather steep descent down a valley. In certain places you'll find a note: "For local tourism queries call" and then a telephone number. These are special phones manned by the local tourism people who are there to untangle any problem you may have. Don't use them to inquire about local excursions. Keep them strictly for real problems. Also note that not all territories provide this service.

The reason the islands have been listed as "Territories" is that their political status varies from nation-states to de facto departments of European countries. Thus an omnibus word to cover them all.

*The worst offenders are, typically, the US Customs Service, who enjoy high pay for their work and look for bonuses for overtime, a practice introduced with "prohibition."

Introduction

This book had its beginning in early 1966 when the author began his collection of notes on flying the Antilles. In those days, LIAT had just taken delivery of its first two Avro 748s, and were using Bonanzas and the early model De Havilland of Canada Twin Otters (since phased out of operation in favor of Britten-Norman Islanders).

Several of the airfields described here were still at the dream stage, while others hadn't even been thought of. Tourism, too, was only just beginning to gear up, with the completion of a number of Rockresorts' properties representing the upper end of the trade; the emphasis was on the small, self-funded and self-run operation that has been giving ground ever since to sophisticated, cost-procedured businesses that for the most part are better geared to separating the tourist from his dollar while offering more in the way of amenities and comfort.

Then, political development has occurred in the islands, with still-effective colonies moving into associated status and in some cases (St. Lucia is the most recent) to full independence within the Commonwealth of Nations. The French islands are fully parts of metropolitan France, and the Dutch islands are part of the

Kingdom of the Netherlands. (Interestingly, Puerto Rico and the territory of the US Virgin Islands have still to be accorded full representation by the colonising power—the United States.)

Yet despite political advancement and the significant upgrading of a number of aviation facilities, the Lesser Antilles—or Eastern Caribbean archipelago—is still very much virgin territory to the vast majority of US pilots. On the whole, it is easier for European pilots to accept the change of pace and style and culture that occurs when island-hopping here, for in Europe, nation-states change language and culture only too rapidly for those of us born in the midwest. There, a pilot might fly an afternoon's flight point-to-point and remain in his or her home state. In the Eastern Caribbean, an hour's flight or less can have you moving from a Netherlands' environment, to a British West Indian, to a French, and then to a French-patois-speaking former British colony.

Fortunately, English is the language of aviation, and while you'll hear controllers speaking their own local language to local pilots, they'll come in with English when you need them. Incidentally, you may care to note that there's direct communication at the push of a button from Antigua all the way down (and up) the islands to Trinidad.

A synthesis of the material presented here originally appeared in the September 1970 issue of *Private Pilot* magazine, for which thanks must be rendered to Don Typond, then editor, and Leslie Smith, then publisher of the paper. Since that time, there have been several articles about Caribbean vacationing from stateside by private airplane, and an increasing number of pilots adventurous enough to try it.

Following the Territories are the Appendices. The first appendix is an itemized Pilot's Briefing. This covers aircraft checks before leaving, radios and navigation, emergency procedures, standard maneuvers, weight and balance, bureaucratic and IFR procedures, weather, ditching technique, and some odds and ends of experience-grown advice. It's mostly common sense and is there to remind.

The Check Lists mentioned earlier and some helpful Tables follow the Pilot's Briefing. The Appendices also include a brief note about the Club Mediterranee organization and a brief history of the Caribbean's own home-grown airline, Leeward Islands Air

Transport (LIAT), whose Avro 748s and Britten-Norman Islanders you're sure to see on your peregrinations. Some very nice people work for this outfit, and their pilots—if they are not busy pursuing their incredible 98-percent on-time record—will be happy to swap notes with you. Also included are the FAA listings of Certified Repair Stations and Authorized Inspectors. For quick reference there's a table of ICAO weather symbols, plus an ICAO flight plan and a General Declaration form.

In point of fact, the private aircraft comes into its own in territory like this. Scheduled services are few and far between, and while there are an increasing number of firms offering airplanes for charter, it's simply easier to fly yourself. If there is one cardinal rule down here, it is always to have plenty of reserve fuel on board; so, despite the temperature, keep the tanks topped up. There's a lot of water around here between islands, and the aircraft engine that will run on sea-water has yet to be made.*

Among the nicest items to report about the Lesser Antilles is the professionalism of the FAA's outpost at San Juan, Puerto Rico, whose activities I've studied for a period of more than ten years. If prizes were awarded to bureaucrats, these people would steal it year after year for their unfailing good will, efficiency and help to pilots who visit the region they supervise. No names, no packdrill.

The same goes for the various tourism associations with whom I've been privileged to work in the past and who provided considerable input and assistance in putting this book together. These include both the Eastern Caribbean Tourism Association—and its several founding members, who will know who they are, and the Caribbean Travel Association, as well as the various tourism bodies associated with the individual states and territories in the area.

I'd like to acknowledge the help and assistance of Air France, American Airlines, British Airways, Eastern Airlines and Leeward Island Air Transport and their unfailing courtesy to me, and the help—and permission—of *The Travel Agent News Magazine* for

*Those interested in the less happy statistics of fliers should note that prominent among cause of mishap is fuel mismanagement; single-engine pilots should take heart by a look at twin statistics and remember that starting with the Bleriot Channel crossing and continuing with Lindbergh through today, almost routine crossings of the Atlantic are made on one fan.

use of material which first appeared there. I should also like to thank Jack Fones, of BVI (British Virgin Islands) in New York, for his assistance, and Mort Sondheimer, who does legion work—as do his minions—for his clients. Special thanks, too, are due Doel Garcia and Juan Santoni, Jr., in Puerto Rico, Mrs. Gertrude Protain in Grenada, Roddy Grant, Peter, Yvonne, Sonny, Ralph, Ruth, Jacqueline Mayers, Mitchell Coddrington, Pearl, a certain magistrate who taught me more about law than I ever knew existed, Kenneth Fields, Raymond Rodriguez, Clara Schwabe and family, plus many, many more, including my editor, Mrs. Lou Ashworth.

But perhaps the true hero of this book is that wonderful creator of sound you're going to hear when you sojourn in these islands. (See above.) He and she are known colloquially as "coqui" in the Spanish-speaking islands, and they are the prince and princess of the night with their happy talk. Their gossip, their love words to one another as the stars light up the night sky and as the moon shines down onto these happy shores and wave-washed beaches are the real elixir of life that Ponce de Leon never found.

Enjoy!

PILOTS' GUIDE
TO THE
LESSER ANTILLES

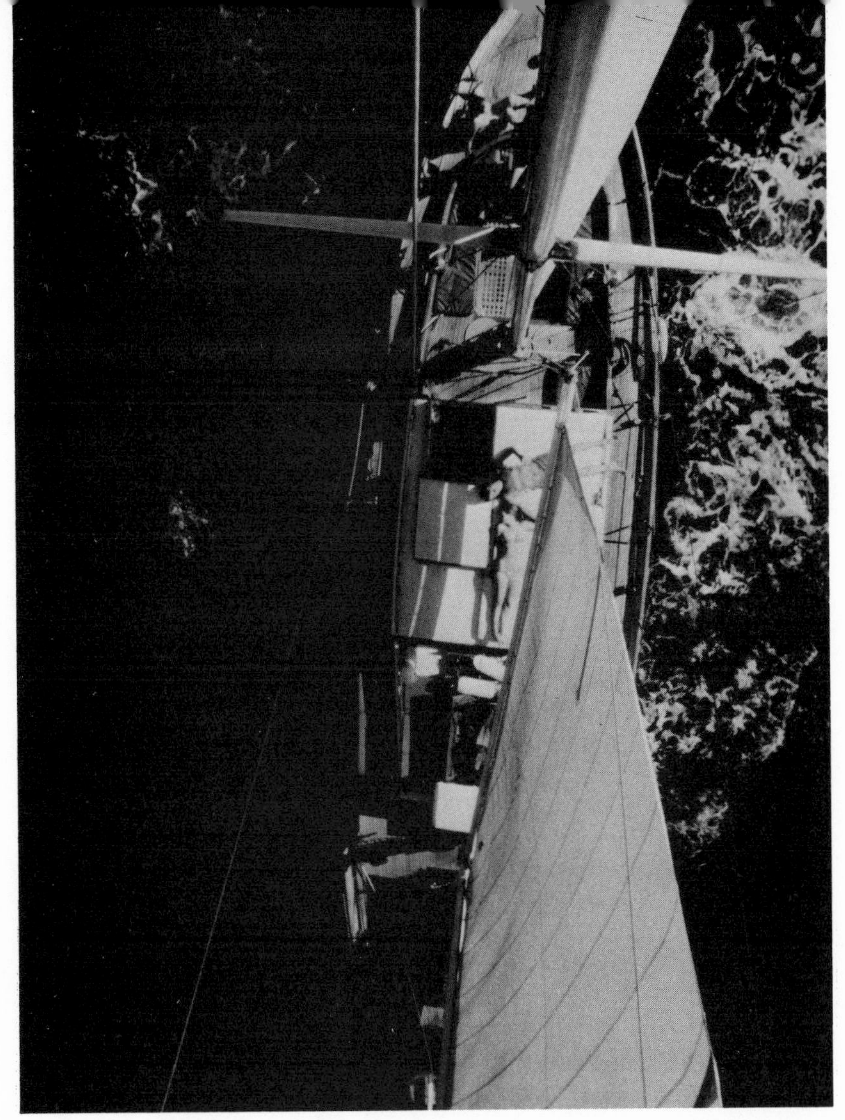

FLIGHT AND EN-ROUTE PLANNING

Preview

The sea really does get bluer as you move down toward the sun, and the sands get whiter, as more and more adventurous pilots are beginning to discover.

While it's quite a way to go, the flight can be made safely in even quite small single-engine aircraft. For one thing, the longest over-water hop is not much more than 100 NM at any point on the way there, and while you may obviously prefer to make more direct point-to-point routings, there's no reason to think you need to do it in a twin, provided you're up-to-date on your maintenance and carry the appropriate safety equipment on board.

In the islands themselves, single-engine pilots routinely make inter-island trips for shopping, business, or pleasure, and from time to time to take on more fuel, as supplies of gasoline and oil can be a someday occasion from time to time, island to island. (It's for this reason that local pilots recommend you always have a spare hour's worth of gas in your tanks when you land anywhere, and that you carry several spare quarts of oil when you fly here).

You'll most probably be able to make the journey more cheaply than on commercial flights if you're traveling with family or friends. And if they fly too, then you've solved the problem of a co-pilot to take control while you lazily look down at those fronded palm trees along the beaches below.

In terms of distance, the archipelago that makes up the Lesser

Antilles (or Eastern Caribbean) is rather more than 800 miles long, and for this reason it can take time to get around—especially if you're flying in the teeth of a tradewind that may be pushing 20 knots or more. However, venerable Cessna 150s and 172s are to be found locally, and while the going is just a little slow, the view from these high-wingers is spectacular.

With few exceptions—the island of Anegada in the British Virgins, Anguilla, and parts of Barbados—the islands of the Lesser Antilles are the result of volcanic action in the distant past. Several still boast semi-dormant volcanoes; some, like Guadeloupe's Soufriere,* threaten eruption from time to time, causing people to make precautionary evacuations. Others, like those on St. Lucia, are basically drive-in type features, where the hot spring baths originally founded in Napoleonic times are still functioning.

VORTAC and DME have been making their way into the region, but NDBs are still favored here. Collectors of aviation minutia will be interested to know that the original radio range is still operating down here, though most people are equipped with VOR receivers. Instrument landing facilities are available in the Bahama Islands at Nassau International, Freeport International, Grand Bahama, and at Eleuthera NALF, on the way down, and at Grand Turk in the Turks & Caicos Islands. Miami has remote stations at Grand Bahama (126.9), Nassau (124.2), and at Grand Turk (118.4).

You'll need to file a DVFR flight plan if you're flying VFR since you'll be penetrating the ADIZ but, provided you will not be going faster than 180 kts or higher than 10,000 ft, you'll have no problems and don't require permission.** If you're flying IFR, then there's no problem at all since ATC takes care of all of that.

The Turks & Caicos Islands make a good stopping-off point on the way down or back. Depending on your route, it's anything from around 560 NM to 660 NM from landfall to landfall, so if you can manage 120 kts cruise you should take about 4.6 hours the shorter way around. (Obviously, it's nice if you can go faster, since it becomes a snap with a cruise of 150 kts or better.)

For your flight planning there are several charts to choose from.

*The term *soufriere* actually means "sulphur mine" but is used in many of the French (and formerly French) islands to mean volcano.

**As mentioned, check FSS for current status.

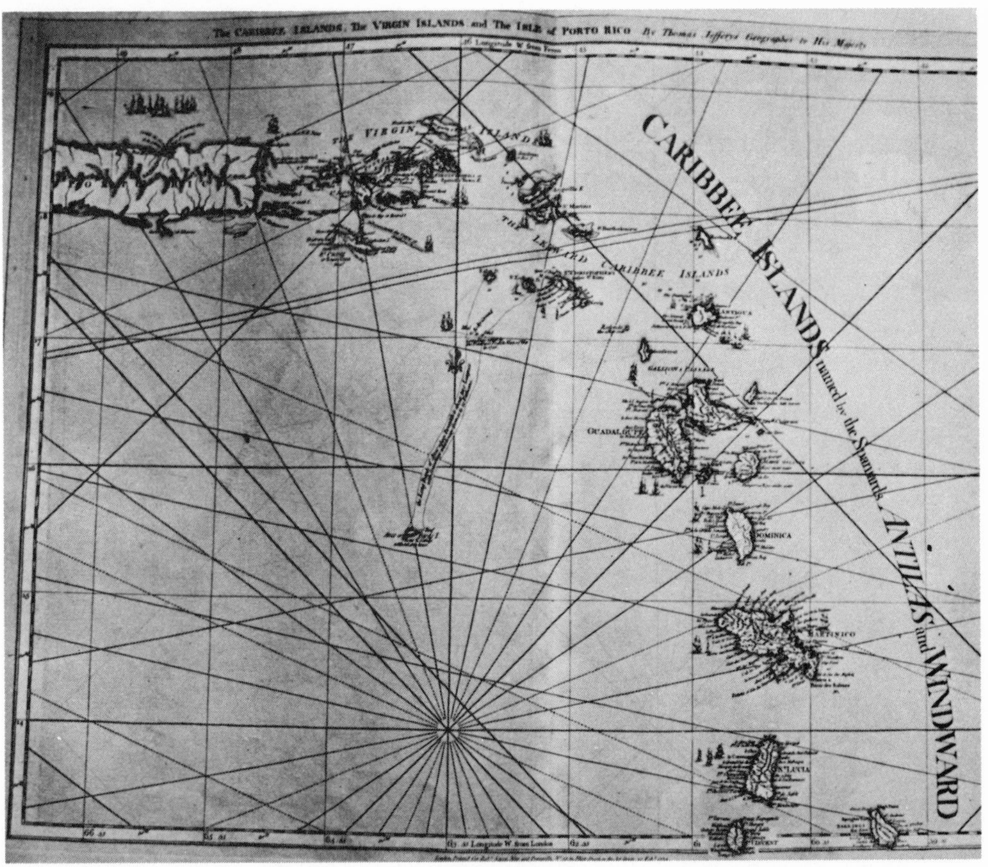

Detail of section from an early map by the famous English cartographer, Thomas Jefferys.

Good for out-of-the-cockpit work are the ONC series ONC J-27 and K-27, while for in the cockpit you'll find WAC series CJ-27 and CK-27 the best. For the Bahama Islands down to Puerto Rico, Air Navigation Chart V30-35 (North Atlantic Ocean *Bahama Islands–Leeward Island*) is also good, and there's a very useful Local Aeronautical Chart covering Puerto Rico and the Virgin Islands. DOD Flight Information Publication En Route Low Altitude Caribbean and South America charts are published every two months. The ones to include are L-3 (covering Miami coast), L-5 and L-6 (one chart, covering the Eastern Caribbean) plus Area Charts A-1 and A-2 (one chart, covering Miami-Nassau and Puerto Rico) and provide essential electronic aid data.

Two publications are also useful: the (En Route) Supplement

Caribbean and South America, and Low Altitude Instrument Approach procedures. The former is more useful than the latter, since it's mostly strictly CAVU in the islands, but the latter is nice to have aboard anyway. (Instrument Approaches are available in Puerto Rico at Borinquen, Puerto Rico International, Mayaguez, Ponce, and Roosevelt Roads; at St. Croix and St. Thomas, USVI; Coolidge, Antigua; Le Raizet, Guadeloupe; Le Lamentin, Martinique; Grantley Adams, Barbados; and Piarco, Trinidad & Tobago.)

Because you'll want to increase your gliding distance and improve your range you'll tend to fly high, using 9,500 as a cruise altitude on the way down. An additional advantage is that those VOR needles start twitching an unbelievable distance away, which'll please you.

While a lot of the fun is in being able to get around the area, it's a mistake to hurry too fast. Get to enjoy the relaxed and low-key lifestyle, because there's no real urgency to rush on to the next place. Each island is marvelous in its own individual way, and there are no real clinkers. Just plan ahead, decide where you think you'd like to go to, and take it from there.

Ideally you'll want to make some sort of blend of what there is culturally, which is American, Spanish, French, Dutch and English. But there's much more than immediate heritage. For example, islands with an American tradition include Puerto Rico (which is really Spanish—just the first of a hundred-and-one contradistinctions you're going to enjoy) and the US Virgin Islands (which were Danish until 1917).

As mentioned, your flight to the islands will take you out over the Bahamian chain with innumerable small fields almost everyplace if you have to come down for a rest. (Don't rely on gasoline's being available, however). The Bahamas, which have numerous sun-drenched beaches of their own, have been an independent nation since July 1973, but retain ties with Britain as a member of the Commonwealth of Nations.

The Turks & Caicos Islands offer some excellent snorkeling and scuba diving, and because tourism is a relatively new industry in these parts, there are still many areas in which wildlife and undisturbed scenery abound. Local guides are available and can provide boats and equipment. You might consider breaking your journey here for a day or two.

Although many Americans are familiar with the beaches of Isla Verde and San Juan, Puerto Rico, the interior of this island offers a breathtaking variety of scenes and views. The new expressway between San Juan and the south coast has dramatically opened up the island, cutting the journey time by car from seven or eight hours to little more than an hour and a half (less if you don't observe the speed limit). Car rental costs about the same as in US metro areas, with branches of Avis, Hertz, National, and Thrifty, plus Borinquen, Executive, and Atlantic Dollar-A-Day.

The local Tourism Company, a government tourism development organization, has fostered the building of *paradores,* or small country inns. These, like their counterparts in Spain, are local hostelries providing accommodation, good food and cheer in traditional island settings. A week's stay using the parador system and a rental car would give you an in-depth experience of what it is to enjoy traditional Puertorriquenian hospitality and charm, plus the opportunity to visit the many attractions that most American visitors miss—including a tropical rain forest, prehistoric caves at Camuy, and a traditional coffee plantation in the mountains.

The US Virgin Islands are a brief hop from San Juan. En route you'll fly over the Loiza river, just 15 NM east of Puerto Rico International (SJU). You may like to note that this is a traditional local reporting area for aircraft inbound to SJU. The distance to St. Thomas is not quite 80 NM and to St. Croix is just over 100 NM.

The traditional duty-free stores of St. Thomas still provide an astonishing range of good buys, and the duty-free allowance has just gone up to $600 for items purchased in the United States Virgin Islands.

It may be worth noting also that the Federal Government recently raised to $300—formerly $100—the value of articles other than tobacco or liquor products that may be brought home duty-free. Not so widely known is that under the *generalized system of preferences* a wide range of articles made in developing countries may be imported duty-free over and above the $300 allowance. They include such items as candy, china and porcelain, field glasses, furs, jade, motorbikes, stereo records, wood carvings and so on. US Customs Service, Washington, D.C. 20229, can provide up-to-date details of the do's and don'ts.

Also worth noting is that states even get into the act on bringing liquor back. Florida, for example, allows you up to 5 gallons, one quart duty-free, 3 quarts subject to Federal duty only, the remaining 4 gallons being subject to both Federal and state taxes. Texas allows one quart only and charges 50¢ on that, while New York allows two quarts but doesn't tax it. The Federal regulations at the time of writing insist that the traveler be 21 years of age. Above the duty-free allowance, one is assessed at 10 percent of purchase price plus $10.50 per gallon.

Sailing in the British Virgin Islands is some of the best in the entire Caribbean, with only the Grenadines offering comparison. US currency is used, though to celebrate 300 years of constitutional rule, the government issued their own currency on June 30, 1973. You should have proof of citizenship; a passport is best.

Thanks to a decision to maintain the islands as a specialized vacation area, it is still possible to enjoy a quiet, somewhat rural holiday; the majority of visitors fortunately still continue to be sailors who stay aboard their chartered sailing boats. Beef Island is the Airport of Entry, and there are landing strips on Virgin Gorda and Anegada. Beef Island is little more than 25 NM from St. Thomas, and about 50 NM from St. Croix.

100 NM from Beef brings you to Princess Juliana airport, the Airport of Entry for St. Maarten. Some 10 NM north is the island of Anguilla, where some of the finest lobster in the entire Caribbean is still to be enjoyed. A small field (not an A.E.) at Grand Case exists on the north (French) side of St. Martin; the island is jointly governed by France and Holland. Just 20 NM south and east is the island of St. Barts, which is French. The strip used to be very short but is now 2,100 ft long. It's still for the more experienced pilot, as you must perform some contour flying on final. The same must be said of Saba (Dutch), a small island some 25 NM just north of west of St. Maarten. Here the strip is only 1,700 ft long, so your short field technique had better be good.

Naiads are sometimes to be found even in tropical mountain streams and rills.

Oranjestad's F. D. Roosevelt Field on St. Eustatius is 2,000 ft long, some 40 NM due south of St. Maarten. The island itself enjoys an attractive isolation; there are peaks for climbing, and some beaches. Interestingly, St. Eustatius was the first foreign state to recognize the new American flag. It was on November 16, 1776, that the *Andrew Doria,* a brig-of-war, under Captain Isaiah Robinson, sailed into harbor. A plaque at Fort Oranje commemorates the national gun salute fired that day, by order of then-Governor Johannes de Graaff.

Another short hop of just 20 NM brings one to Golden Rock airport in St. Kitts. Mt. Misery, an imposing 4,374-ft crag at the north end of the island, will occasionally blanket radio transmissions to the tower.

St. Kitts itself came a long way in terms of economic development under the leadership of the late Premier Robert Bradshaw. His philosophy was that tourism should move slowly but surely along, and that the associated state "should not dress up in a garb we cannot wear."

The result is a still pleasantly old-fashioned and leisurely atmosphere, with colonial-style buildings. The charm of the old-time West Indian inns will intrigue. The Fairview Inn maintains the 18th-century warmth of the Colonial Great House it once was, and is worth the ten-minute drive from Basseterre. The food is Kittician style and excellent. The Golden Lemon, to the north of the island and small—just 7 rooms, four-poster beds, numerous local antiques—and is delightful, as is nearby Rawlin's Plantation—an operating plantation until 1974, when it was opened to guests. Accommodations are in 6 double rooms in and around the 17th-century buildings.

A quick trip across The Narrows—the strip of water that separates St. Kitts from neighboring Nevis—brings you to Newcastle's 1900-ft field. It's about 12 NM from Golden Rock airport. Once again there are a number of colonial places, and the food at Rest Haven Inn, near Pinney's Beach, is worth the detour.

Some 50 NM east of Newcastle is Coolidge, Airport of Entry to the Associated State of Antigua. With its dependency of Barbuda, and the small island of Redonda, it lies 250 miles as a crow flies southeast of Puerto Rico.

Antigua is an unusually attractive island with rolling terrain, lushly green when rains have fallen, but an arid brown in times of drought. An important water conservation project, the Potsways Dam, has improved matters considerably. Tourism has recently replaced agriculture as the mainstay of the island's economy. There are many attractive beaches and good hotels, and there is

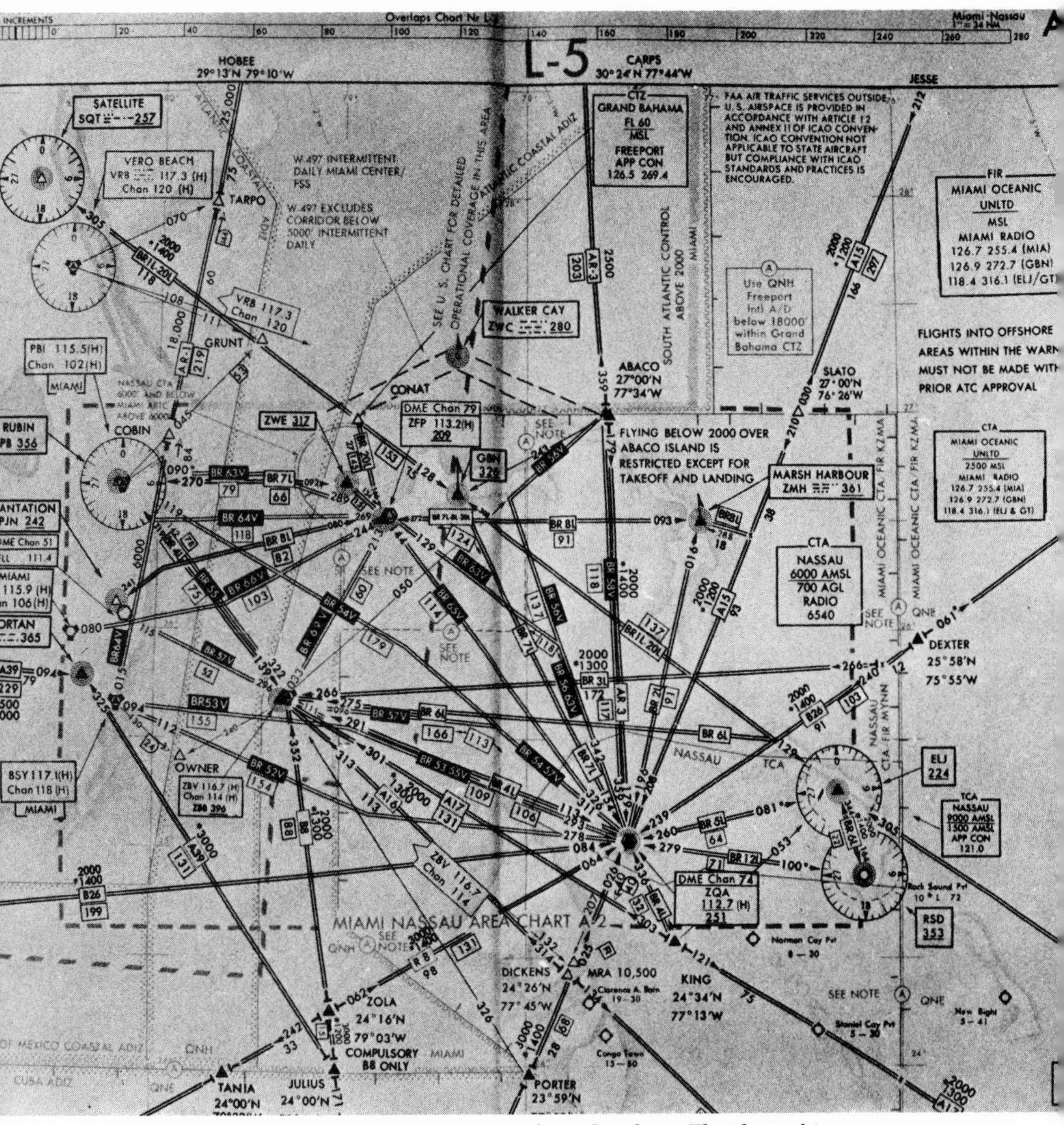

There are a plethora of ways to move out from Southern Florida as this extract from the En Route chart shows, with plenty of aids to guide you on your way. *(Not to be used for navigation.)*

the fabulous English Harbor, a center for sailors from all over the world.

Nelson's Dockyard at English Harbor was originally built in 1784 within this almost landlocked and protected bay. Much Nelsonian memorabilia is to be found in a small museum in Nelson's former home, and the entire area undergoes constant restoration and repair.

Two landing strips are to be found on Barbuda, one at Cocoa Point, some 27 NM from Coolidge, the other at Coddrington, a further 7 NM further north. The Coco Point Lodge is costly but offers considerable privacy and an exquisite beach. Management has a policy of aggressive pricing to discourage day visitors.

Antigua produces a surprisingly good rum—surprising, only because the island of Barbados has been (with famed Barbancourt) the best-known producer in the Lesser Antilles until Antiguan production began. Planter's Punch is a staple at all hotels and bars and should be treated with some respect.

Not quite 40 NM southwest of Coolidge Airport is Blackburne Field in Montserrat. There are two volcanoes, the island is covered with rich vegetation—and there's an attractive nine-hole golf course. Not too many tourists visit the island, which is what makes it so attractive to those who do—there is none of the hustle and bustle that some of the other islands experience. Cedric Osbourne, who runs Vue Pointe, is one of the kindliest island hosts you'll ever meet. A curious feature here is that the powdery sand of the beaches is black. Horseback riding is a fine way to get around.

For a total change of pace, there's Guadeloupe, which recently received a four-power summit accolade (and a US President in his running togs harried by his wife) some 55 NM on to the south. Le Raizet is the Airport of Entry at the island's capital of Pointe-a-Pitre. Both Guadeloupe and Martinique (further down the island chain) are *departements* of France; their citizens are French, there is no color bar, and there are no "natives." Indeed, the mingling of African and French blood has produced incredible beauties—both male and female—in both these islands. As might be expected, the food in both islands is of exceptional quality, a happy blend of traditional *haute cuisine de France* and the zesty Creole specialities. There are a number of excellent hotels, and two Club Med establishments, one with an airport nearby.

Landing strips are to be found at Guadeloupe's out islands, La Desirade, Marie Galante, and Terre de Haut. The latter is one of the three places here that "naturists"* have made their home, and is possibly the best.

A further 50 NM south of Le Raizet is Melville Hall field in Dominica—beautiful, mountainous, with a lush rain forest. A word of caution: Do not attempt to make a downwind landing from the sea, although the field has been lengthened to 4,800 ft. The trade wind funnels the air towards the mountains at speeds of up to 40 kts on occasion. The technique here is to overfly the airport so that you can see the terrain you'll be contour flying over as you make your downwind, base leg and final approach. You climb inland on the downwind, make a short base over a ridge, then drop full flap to give you a steep descent over the palm trees, using power to bring you down.

If you think you're going to land halfway down the runway, clean her up, go around, and try it again. There's plenty of room. One pilot in a Mooney went around three times, according to a local tale, and made it on the fourth with a perfect squeaker.

Although English is the official language, a beautiful form of French patois is spoken by almost everybody. The last remaining Caribs have a reservation area around Salybia, a small town not far from the airport. Two local specialties not to be missed are the "mountain chicken" (delicious giant frogs' legs) and the Dominican version of *calaloo*, the West Indian crab stew.

Martinique's Le Lamentin airport at Fort de France is not quite 70 NM from Melville Hall. The island has been called, with some justification, the Pearl of the Antilles and many Caribbean residents come here just to get away from it all. Josephine, the wife of Napoleon Bonaparte, originally came from this island, from the village of Trois Ilets. (She later lived in St. Lucia for some years.)

Apart from excellent food, pleasant hotels, and the almost cognac quality of the island rum, Martinique is the inventor of the *beguine*, the island's traditional dance. If you have an opportunity

*The "au naturel" crowd. No swimsuits. Naked. Definitely an "R" rating. PG if you're an adult.

There's an astounding range of religious expression in the islands, which, while including most of the various forms of Christianity, also encompasses Buddhism, Hinduism, Islam, and Judaism, together with several varieties of earlier Afro-religious practice.

to catch one of the performances of the *Ballets Martiniquais*, you should do so. They occasionally perform on visiting cruise ships, and it's worth checking with the local Tourist Office to find out their schedule.

You'll get a 20 percent discount on your traveler's checks if you're shopping for luxury items.

Vigie Airport at Castries is the northern Airport of Entry for St.

Lucia, a 40-NM hop from Fort de France. The old (World War II) USAF base at Vieux Fort at the south of the island has been reopened for some time now as Hewanorra International, and there is a private strip (1,500 ft) at Grand Anse.

As in Dominica, the official language is English, but most St. Lucians converse in French patois. St. Lucia is coming into its own as a tourism center and as a sailing base. The delightful Marigot Bay harbor has new company with Rodney Bay Development, whose marina is now the home of Stevens Yachts.

Arnos Vale is the Airport of Entry for the island of St. Vincent and its Grenadine islands, which, thanks to an enlightened approach to tourism, have become over the years among the most truly West Indian in hospitality and fare. The main island itself is attractive, the people friendly, and there's plenty to do. New airstrips have opened up four Grenadine islands to air traffic: Mustique, Palm Island (officially Prune Island), Union Island, and Carriacou. A boat ride from nearby Prune Island will get you to Petit St. Vincent, with its 113-acre resort. The food here is excellent, and it has become a traditional gathering place for sailors at Thanksgiving.

About 115 NM due east of Arnos Vale lies Seawell International, as Grantley Adams Field is best known outside of Barbados. Barbados has become the leading country in the Eastern Caribbean, providing not only superior cricketers—the sport of the British islands—but academic leadership in world forums, from the active campuses of the University of the West Indies, plus advanced planning in Third World economics.

The Bajans are some of the most sophisticated people in this part of the world, but still enjoy such British traditions as afternoon tea and grass-court tennis. They are also the most politically literate, with a predominantly black Cabinet and Senate.

The island offers some of the finest hotels on the Caribbean coast. Apartment hotels also offer savings for groups, as do home rentals.

A nearly perfect island, Barbados has plenty of activity, if that's what you like, or peace and serendipity, if you prefer. Mount Gay

While cargo is increasingly freighted by air between major points within the islands, the island schooner is still the backbone of maritime trade. Seen here, on old-style harbor patrol, two Bajan constables at Bridgetown, Barbados.

rum is still one of the Caribbean's best. Flying fish is the local delicacy, as is *oursin*, a local sea urchin (also found in the French islands). Roast suckling pig is occasionally offered at barbecues. The Ocean View in Hastings is noted for its island fare.

Grenada's Pearls Airport is 155 NM from Seawell, 75 NM from Arnos Vale, and just 25 NM from Carriacou. The island enjoyed a fine reputation for many years, as a tourism center and for the relaxed and pleasant lifestyle of its people. Serious political squabbles during 1973–74 nipped tourism and, while the situation has much improved locally, visitors have remained cautious.

Grenada has its own special charms, however, which range from some of the most beautiful beaches in all the Caribbean, at famed Grand Anse, to some of the best West Indian fare to be found anywhere in the islands, at the Ross Point Inn. As in Barbados, a number of apartments and cottages are available for rent.

Piarco, Trinidad & Tobago's Airport of Entry, is 93 NM almost due south of Pearls. Trinidad & Tobago is one of the more unusually interesting countries in the world in that it consists of two islands and has a rare double name. It also has a unique multiracial society, and, on account of recent offshore oil strikes, it is well on the way to becoming one of the world's richest small nations. The two islands are entirely different, with commercial interests, some fine architecture (both religious and lay), industrious people, a sugar industry, an asphalt industry, and the crude oil industry typifying Trinidad; Tobago is rural, relaxed, with verdant mountains and shining beaches, and, of course, the resort hotels.

There are the usual duty-free stores, but good local buys are in East Indian filigree jewelry, Indian silver and ivory, and in men's tailoring. Duty-free cameras are also attractively priced here and include the world's top makes.

Because of its multiracial nature you can dine well on Chinese, Indian, Indonesian, and Creole fare. Local specialties are the mangrove oyster, a small kidney-sized shellfish that tastes delicious, and the cascadura fish, which comes from the freshwater streams of Trinidad. If you are a hunter, the season runs from October 1 through March 31, and there's a surprising variety of quarry. Some fine horse racing takes place at Queen's Park Savannah in Port of Spain and at the Arima Race Club in the city of San Fernando. And there is Carnival, with calypso and steel band, whose only rival in terms of music and color is Rio's.

On tranquil Tobago there are a number of fine hotels and resorts, but one of the better ways to enjoy your vacation here is to take a "cottage." These range in size and price, frequently include maid service and sometimes even cooks and gardeners. Night life is limited here, certainly when compared to Trinidad.

During the season, each of the leading hotels takes one night a week for putting on a show, a dance, a movie performance, or an old-fashioned barbecue party—which can be lively. Music and dancing can be found at the *Club La Tropicale* (at the *Della Mira*

Hotel in Scarborough) or at the *Cellar Pub* (at *Mount Irvine Bay Hotel*).

One final word: FORMS.

There are two forms you'll need. An ICAO flight plan form—which is slightly different from the normal FAA format—and a pad of General Declaration forms, plus carbon paper. In most territories you need to have two copies going in and two going out, and you should spray the interior of your aircraft with an approved insecticide twenty minutes before arrival at a new airport. (Obviously if you're hopping between St. Thomas and St. Croix you won't spray and you won't have to fill out forms.)

You'll find a copy of each of these in the Appendices. The ICAO form is provided so that you can use it for telephoning in your flight plan. The General Declaration form you'll have to buy.

And now to the individual territories.

THE TERRITORIES

Turks & Caicos Islands

Flying In

The islands lie some 500 NM southeast of Florida and approximately 80 NM north of the island of Haiti/Santo Domingo. Providenciales Airport is Airport of Entry for Caicos Islands only, and is known in the area as Provo. Fuel is usually available. Don't forget to ADCUS your flight plan, as a minimum of half an hour is required.

North Caicos, South Caicos, and Grand Turk are also Airports of Entry, and fuel will usually be available at one or more of these airports.

What to Do

There are numerous beaches and some tennis courts; scuba and snorkeling are the big attractions. Boat charters are also available for fishing from all the islands.

Food

Specialties include conch chowder and fritters, lobster, turtle steak, whelk soup, and other types of fresh fish.

One of the great attractions in these neighborly islands is the pristine nature of the area, and the extraordinarily good scuba (and snorkeling) to be experienced. (*photo*)

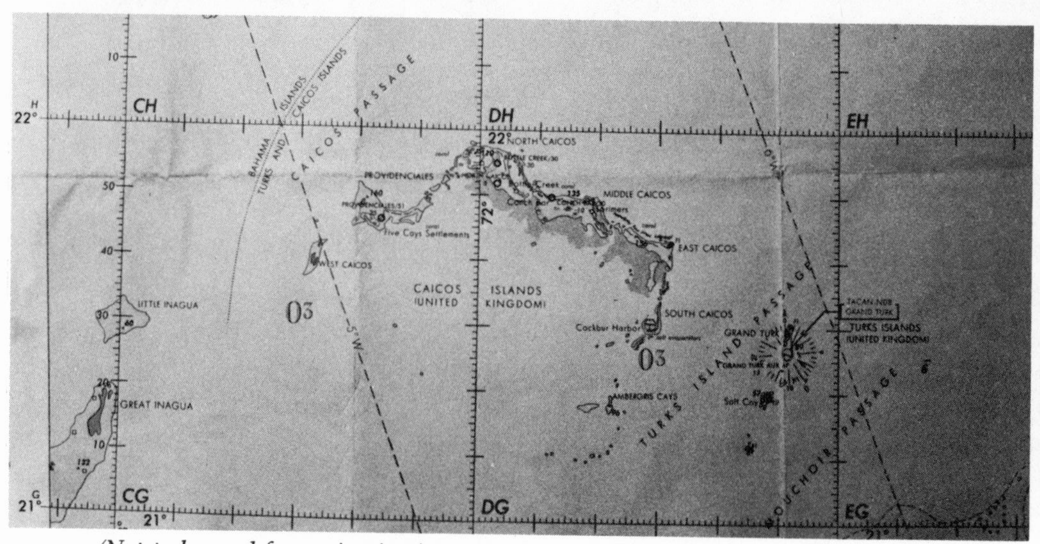

(Not to be used for navigation.)

Hotels

Hotels tend to be small, with twenty rooms or less, and offer very personalized service. Among the more popular with aviators are *The Admiral's Arms Inn*, South Caicos; *The Prospect of Whitby*, North Caicos; *The Meridian Club* at Pine Cay; and the *Salt Raker Inn* at Grand Turk. For further information, contact the Turks & Caicos Island Tourist Board, 777 West Talcott, Chicago, Illinois 60631; [312] 763-2008.

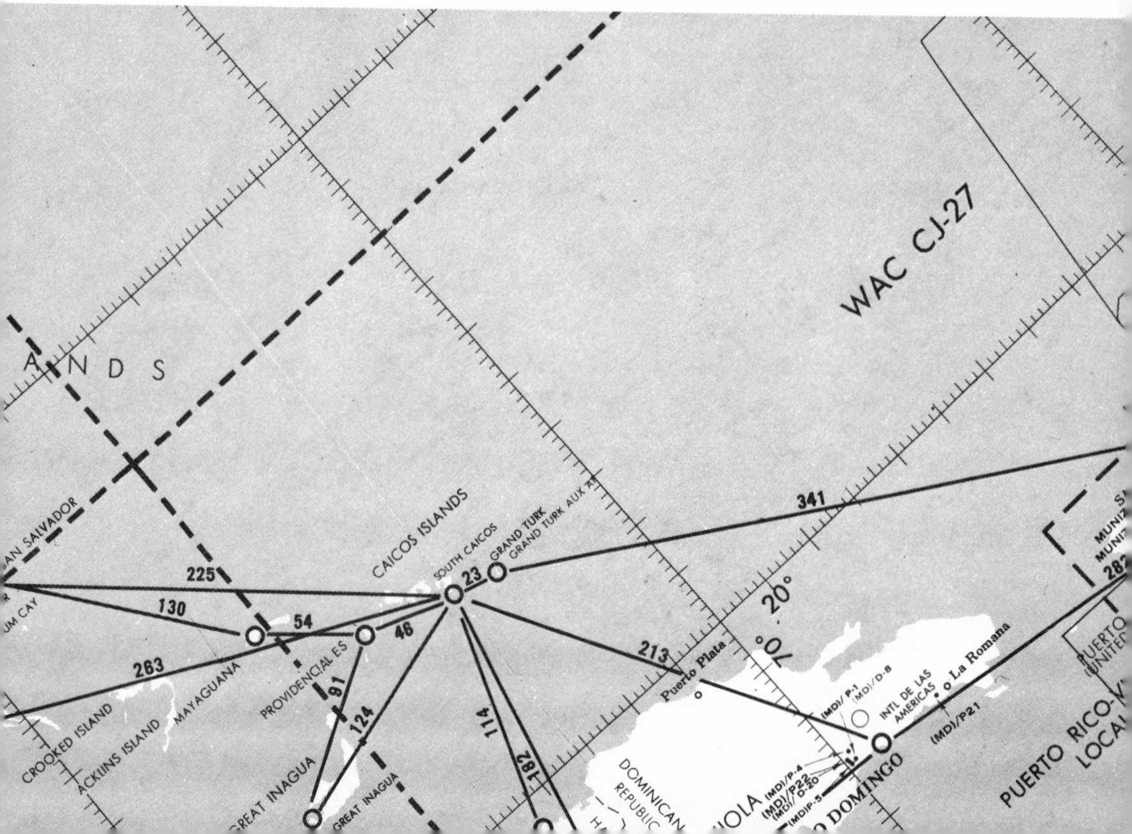

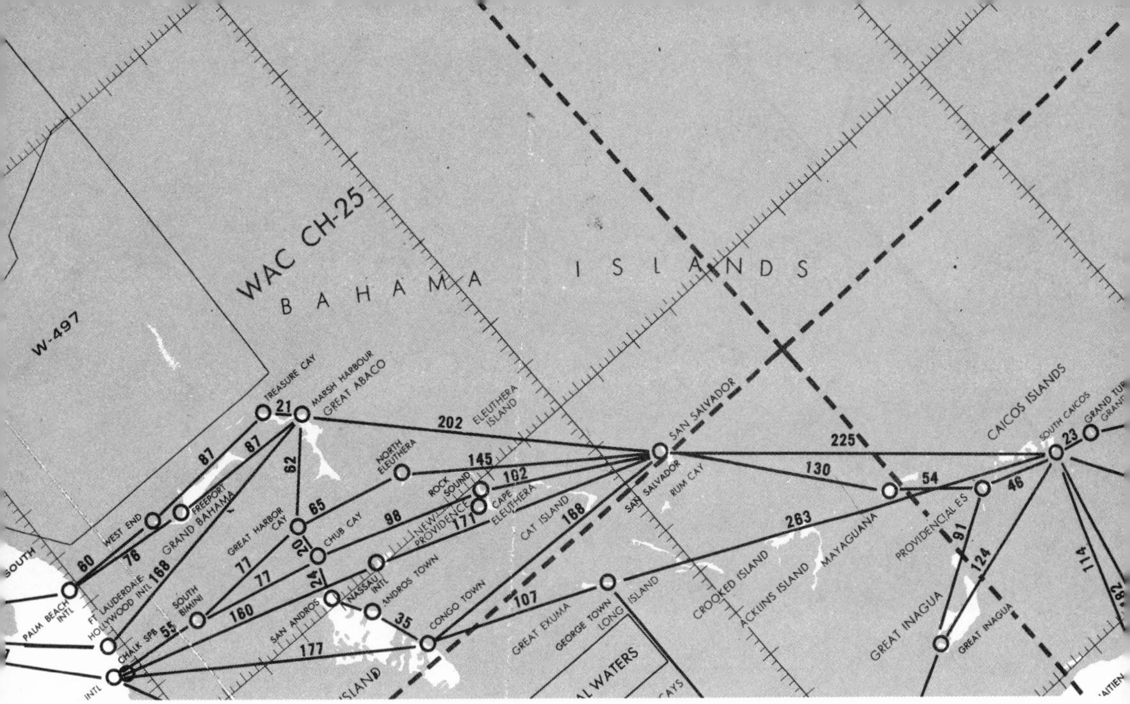

Detail from the Gulf of Mexico and Caribbean Planning chart (reverse side of the Puerto Rico & Virgin Islands Local Chart).

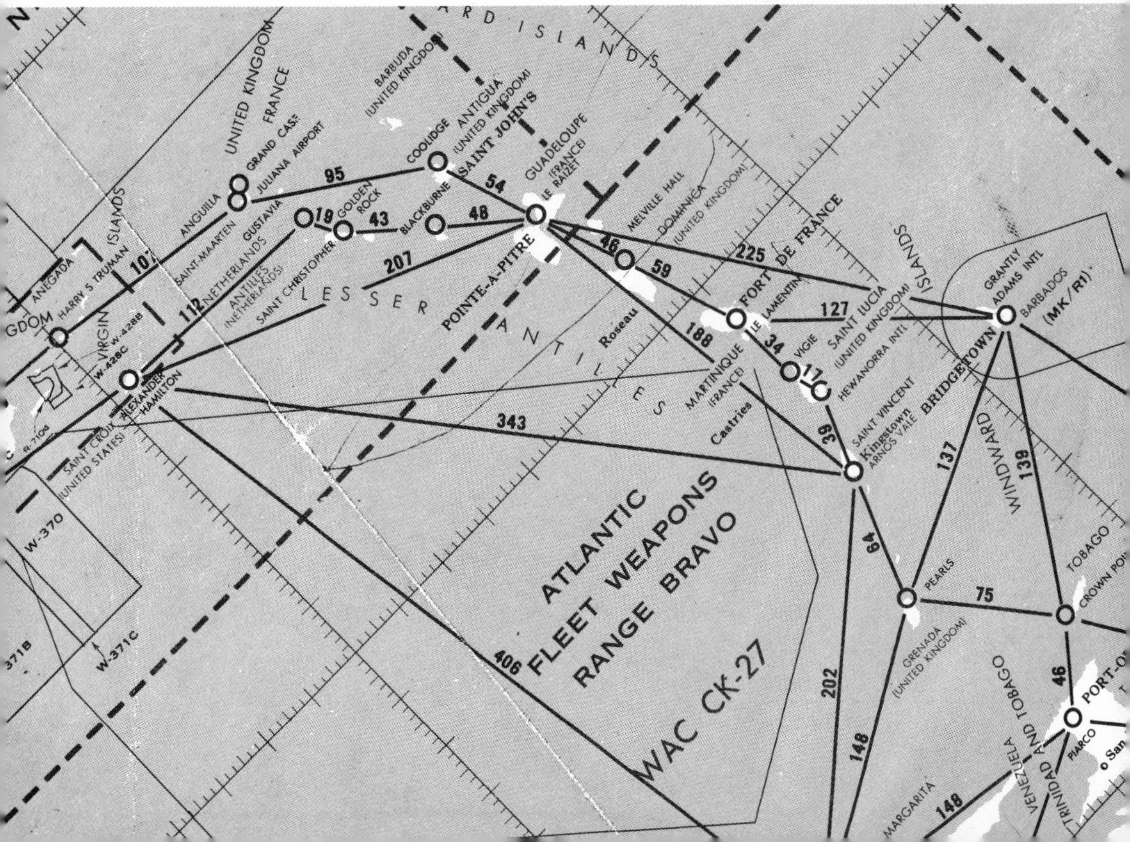

Puerto Rico

Flying In

Approaching eastward toward *Puerto Rico International* airport, you'll be monitoring San Juan Center on 120.3 and you can request traffic advisories. The harbor entrance and the famous old Spanish castle of El Morro are the alerting point for International's control tower on 118.3. This gives you an approach to the main field of not quite 10 NM. Down to your right across the water you'll see the airfield of Isla Grande. This is now an Airport of Entry and is operational (with Customs) from 0800 through 1900 except on Sundays and holidays. Their tower is on 118.7 and keep your eyes moving, since the International airport is pretty busy. Jet transports, DC-3s, and other machinery all use the approach to PR International, so watch for wake turbulence if there are any other aircraft in sight.*

If you're coming in westbound for any reason, the reporting

*Borinquen, the former Ramey Air Force Base near Aguadilla, has recently been listed in charts as an Airport of Entry. Check whether full customs service is now available.

The imposing presence of the El Morro Fortress, which guards the San Juan harbor entrance, makes it a useful reporting point when approaching either Puerto Rico International (El Morro abeam) or the Isla Grande field in downtown San Juan. (*photo*)

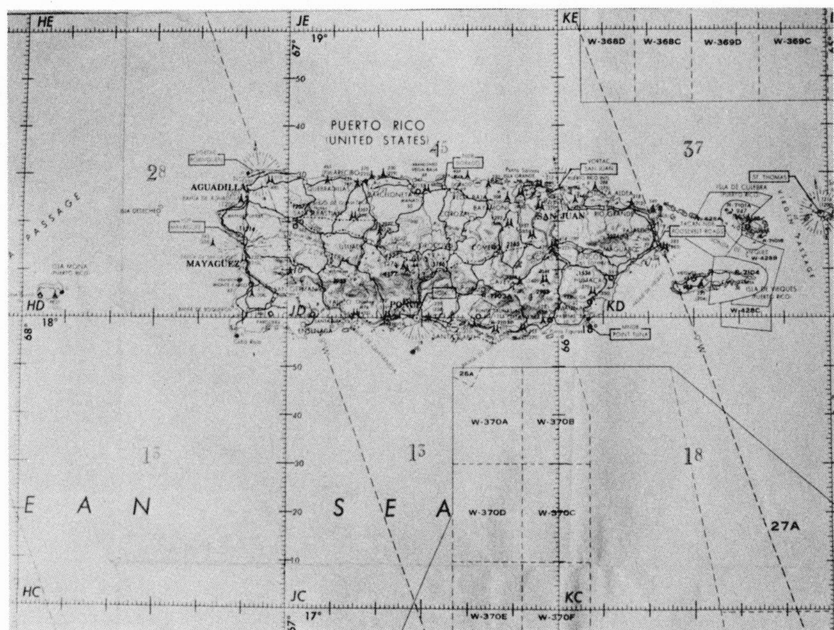

(Not to be used for navigation.)

point is the *Loiza River*, an enormous piece of water that looks as if it had been sculpted into the land. You can't miss it.

Once you get down, ground control on 121.9 (Isla Grande is 121.7) will direct you to the general aviation ramp, which lies in back of the main commercial loading bays. You'll share ramp space here with several air taxi and third-level carrier operations while you check with Customs and Immigration. Tie-downs and hangarage are available at the field if you want to keep your airplane here, or you can land at the Isla Grande airport, which may be more convenient if you're staying in downtown San Juan or the old city.

The hotels in the San Juan area are to be found close by the main airport on a stretch of strand known as Isla Verde, and in the main city in the Condado Beach area. *The Hotel Pierre*, which adjoins the famous Swiss Chalet restaurant, is favored by business visitors; it's in Santurce, just a few minutes' walk from Ashford Avenue (Avenida Ashford), which parallels the city's main beach. There's a pool, a small bar, and all rooms are air-conditioned with private bath.

The Loiza River is still forded the old-fashioned way. The river is another reporting point for aircraft west of SJU.

Background Briefing

The island enjoys a Spanish cultural background dating from 1508 when Juan Ponce de Leon, in his search for the Fountain of Youth, established the first settlement here. (His remains are buried in the San Juan Cathedral.) In spite of continual fighting, Spain managed to hold on to the island for three centuries, despite attempts by Sir Francis Drake and Sir Harry Morgan to change its status. For the next couple of centuries all was relatively peaceful, and a number of Europeans from countries other than Spain emigrated to these shores. Finally, Luis Munoz Rivera—who has been called the George Washington of Puerto Rico—obtained a Charter of Autonomy from the Spanish government in 1897, which gave the territory dominion status, with effective local self-government.

Alas, it was all too short-lived. The following year the United States went to war with Spain and landed troops on the south coast of the island on July 25, 1898. The Treaty of Paris the following year ceded the island to US sovereignty. Puerto Ricans were eventually granted US citizenship in 1917.

The twenties were a bad period for islanders, and Luis Munoz Marin, who in 1948 would become the territory's first elected governor, was agitating for independence. But his Popular Democratic Party decided the way ahead was through land reform and laws protecting workers rather than independence and, following World War II, under the guiding hand of David Ogilvy, Operation Bootstrap was put into effect.

Because of its Commonwealth status, the island pays no federal taxes and local taxes are used only locally. Under Bootstrap, tax exemption and deferral provided the impetus for new investments, which by 1971 had resulted in $2 billion and 2,000 new plants. Income from manufacturing is today nearly four times that from agriculture, though sugar, corn, tobacco, and rum are still exported.

During the sixties—and continuing today—the debate on the choice of independence, statehood, or the current commonwealth status continued. A plebiscite held in 1967 found only 38.9 percent of the voters favoring statehood, but the following year—to the surprise of many—the pro-statehood party, the New Progressives, brought a Ponce industrialist to the governor's house. Luis A. Ferre, although an advocate of statehood, had said that the matter would be resolved through a special plebiscite outside of the general election.

Ferre was defeated at the end of his fourth year, to be succeeded by Rafael Hernandez-Colon of the Popular Democrats. Colon was instrumental in revitalizing the Bootstrap operation, and arranged for the purchase of ITT's PR subsidiary, the Puerto Rico Telephone Company, in order to provide better telephone service in the island. A similar scheme was undertaken to develop the island as a center of containerized shipping, and the Tourism Development Company—now called the Tourism Company—was formed to foster and promote tourism.

All this was insufficient to keep Governor Hernandez-Colon in

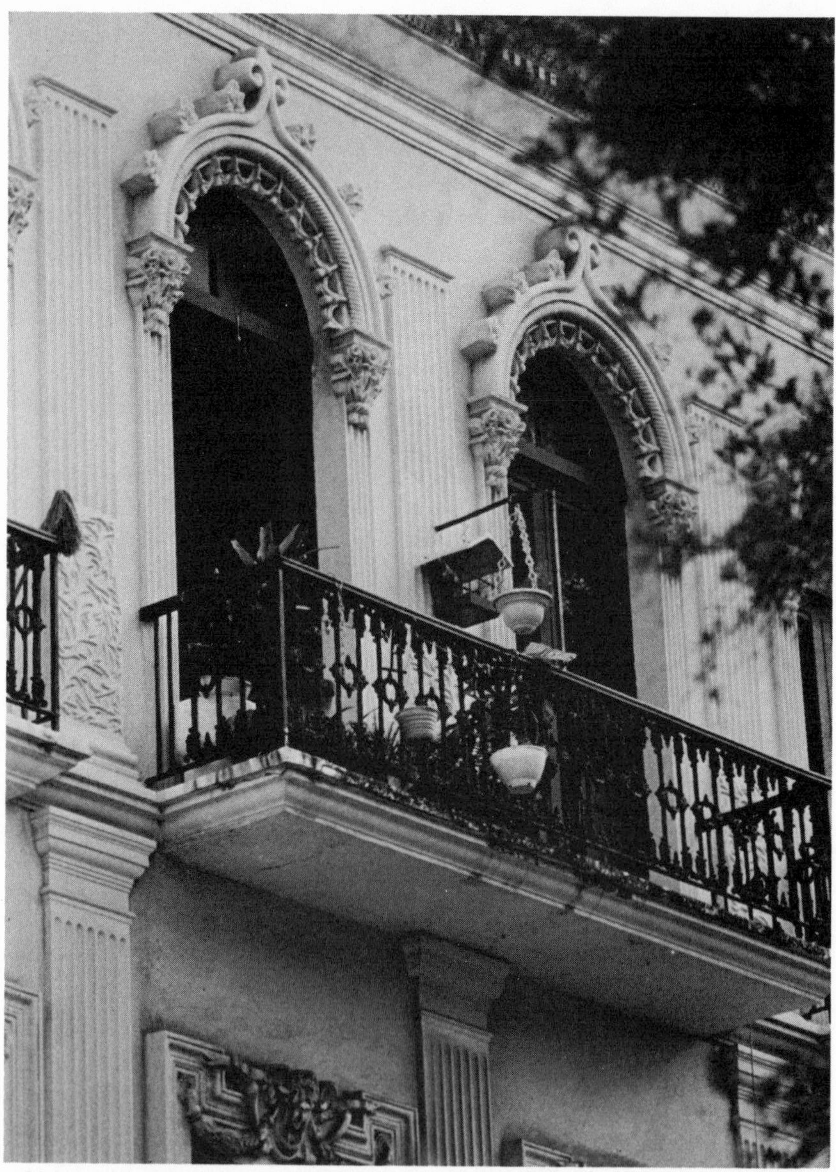

Old San Juan boasts some of the finest examples of Spanish colonial architecture, and work is in progress on the restoration of whole areas of the original inner city.

office, and in 1976 the election of Carlos Romero Barcelo saw a return of the Statehood party to power.* As far as tourism is

*If re-elected in 1980, Governor Barcelo is on record as stating that he will hold a further plebescite on the issue of commonwealth status, independence or statehood. Should statehood win, he would immediately ask Congress to grant it.

concerned, since 1976 there has been a regrowth overall, and both the Tourism Company and the newly named Hotel and Tourism Association are working to maintain and improve the already high standards that now obtain.

What to Do/Hotels/Food

With an area some 30 percent smaller than Connecticut (3,435 square miles) and a population in excess of 3 million, Puerto Rico is one of the more densely populated communities on the planet yet offers some of the more interesting contrasts, ranging from the industrial to the idyllic, to be found anywhere in the Caribbean. There are wild mountain ranges, calm, palm-fringed white beaches, surf and calm waters, rain forest, luxury resorts, night life ranging from disco to sedate dancing, plus the usual entertainment circuit, deep-sea fishing, horseback riding, cockfighting, concerts—the Casals Festival brings musicians from all over the world—art museums, Arawak artifacts and sites, and, of course, the universities.

A good way to get the lay of the land is to tour the island by air—there are airports dotted around at convenient intervals (eleven on the island itself), and available on the smaller islands of Culebra and Vieques. The *Seafarer's Inn* on Culebra offers some of the finest seafood in the area, and is worth the detour.

Once you've made your aerial check, leave the airplane either in San Juan, in Mayaguez, or in Ponce, and rent a car.* The south coast still has some of the better beaches and the most tranquil seas. Unfortunately, careless industrialization has spoiled many of the views, and insufficient attention to landscaping and the lack of clean air requirements cause blight. Still, the *Hotel Copamarina*, Guanica—right where US troops landed in 1898—is popular with families, and is on its own private beach. Meals are a la carte and include local and international dishes.

Another way to get the feel of the area is to make an island tour, staying at the *paradores*. Like their counterparts in Spain, the paradores emphasize local conditions and culture, and vary from a delightful old-style plantation home on a coffee estate to the *El Verde*, situated near the rain forest, and the excellent beach resort

*Get air-conditioning: it costs an extra $4 to $5 per day and is worth every additional cent.

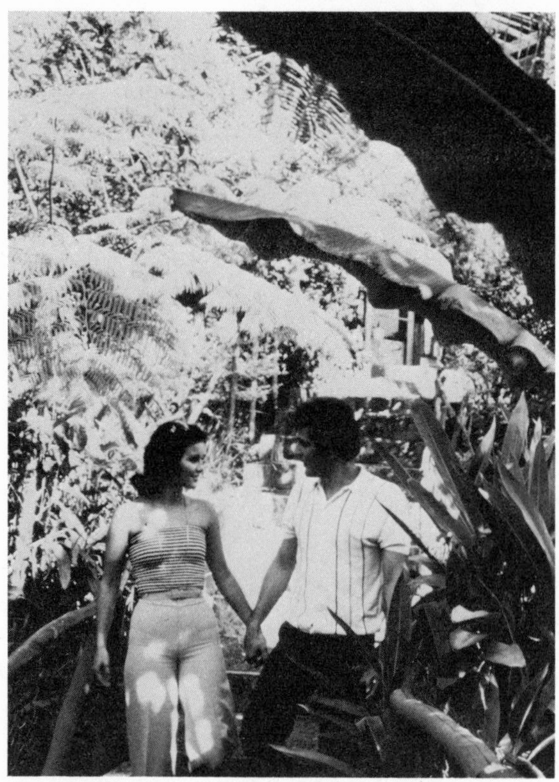

Typical of the lush foliage to be found in the rain forest, this picture was shot within the grounds of the Parador El Verde.

at *Quadrebrillas,* near the former Ramey Air Force Base at Borinquen.

Tourism-savvy visitors have been making use of the paradores for several years, and you'll get a much quicker feel of what Puerto Rican culture is really all about by staying at these hostelries. Obviously it will help if you have some Spanish, but *gracias* (thank you) and *por favor* (please) will go a long way in making your English understood with the help. All management, desk, and supervising personnel speak English.

The standard of food at most ranges from very good to excellent.

For inexpensive resort living, the new *Punta Borinquen**

*Interestingly, Borinquen was the name by which the island was known to its original Indian inhabitants, while Columbus named it San Juan. The current name was due to a confused cartographer who mistook the name of the main port (Puerto Rico-Rich Port) with the name of the island.

complex—the aforementioned former, Strategic Air Command Ramey base—now rents three-bedroom homes to vacationers at moderate rates. There's a golf course, and the attractive Las Playuelas beach is close at hand. Tie-downs and fuel are available at the local aero club, which offers a warm welcome to visiting pilots.

More sophisticated resort living is to be found at the *Dorado Beach* complex, also with its own private airport. Originally founded by Laurance Rockefeller, the complex has swimming, tennis, and golf—the *Dorado Beach Hotel* and the *Cerromar Beach Hotel* have no fewer than four Robert Trent Jones golf courses between them.

If you prefer the northeast of the island, near the magnificent and much-photographed Luquillo Beach, there's the new (opened January 1976) *Hyatt Rio Mar* on its 523-acre site with 7 tennis courts, an 18-hole golf course, plus pool and beach.

Finally, there's the super-deluxe *El Conquistador* complex on a 400-acre site near Las Croabas, with its championship 18-hole golf course, marina, casino, and much, much more. Published rates are super high, and if this is for you you'll save money by taking one of the several package arrangements they offer.

For a different type of resort living there's *Humacoa*, at the 2,800-acre *Palmas del Mar* resort. You can fly directly to this resort and leisure community. The airport monitors Unicom-1, on 122.8. Or you can drive—about forty-five minutes from San Juan. The resort includes 220 condominium apartment units all with kitchen, four swimming pools, numerous tennis courts, a golf course, plus villas, a botanical garden, horseback riding, deepsea fishing. Rates are highish, around $60 per person for the one- to three-bedroom units. If you prefer the 23-room Palmas Inn figure about double the price, extra for food. Quality is excellent.

You can still enjoy the beach scene either in the heart of downtown San Juan—even in Puerta de Tierra, near the old Fort San Jeronimo at the *Caribe Hilton*—or at the several hotels on Condado Beach, such as the *Condado Holiday Inn*, linked to its completely refurbished *Laguna Wing* with a brand-new enclosed bridge crossing Avenida Ashford. Then there's the *Condado Beach* and *La Concha*, in the midst of the Convention Center, the *Da Vinci*, the *Puerto Rico Sheraton* and the *Howard Johnson's Nabori*

Lodge, to name the better known. More modest but still good beach-front values continue up through Ocean Park to Punta Las Marias.

Out toward Isla Verde, there are a number of choices. If you prefer to be in the old city itself, best choice here is the 300-year-old *El Convento*, now managed by the Venetian hotel chain CIGA. The building was originally a Carmelite convent, and recent restoration makes it once again one of the island's show-places, with heavy, carved wooden furniture, magnificent paintings, rich carpeting, and fine tapestries. There's a small lighted pool, and the Ponce de Leon dining room is hung with tapestries, giving a remarkably European feeling to the hotel.

OLD SAN JUAN

The old city was founded in 1521, and the principal tourist attraction is the El Morro fort over which you flew in. It was possession of this enormous castle at the harbor entrance that enabled the Spanish to maintain control of the island. Initial construction took over forty-seven years, from 1539 to 1586. The English managed to capture the fort from the landward side in an attack in 1598 but held it only briefly. Work continued on the fortifications until, in 1776, nearly 200 years later, it was declared complete. The National Park Service provides conducted tours, or you can wander alone with a cassette narrated by Jose Ferrer.

Near the Castle entrance is the Church of San Jose, reckoned to be the oldest place of Christian worship still in use in the western hemisphere. Founded by Dominican monks in 1523, the church offers the chance to view increasingly rare medieval architecture, with Gothic roofing rarer still in the New World. Ponce de Leon's body was originally buried here, and his family coat of arms still hangs beneath the ceiling over the main altar. A statue fashioned from the bronze of British cannon captured in 1797 stands outside on the Plaza.

Numerous other buildings are to be found, and the entire area of Old San Juan is undergoing painstaking restoration, using original documents and plans. Undoubtedly the work will take many years to complete, but the dedication of the workers involved on this project makes a tour of this early New World city an adventure in time.

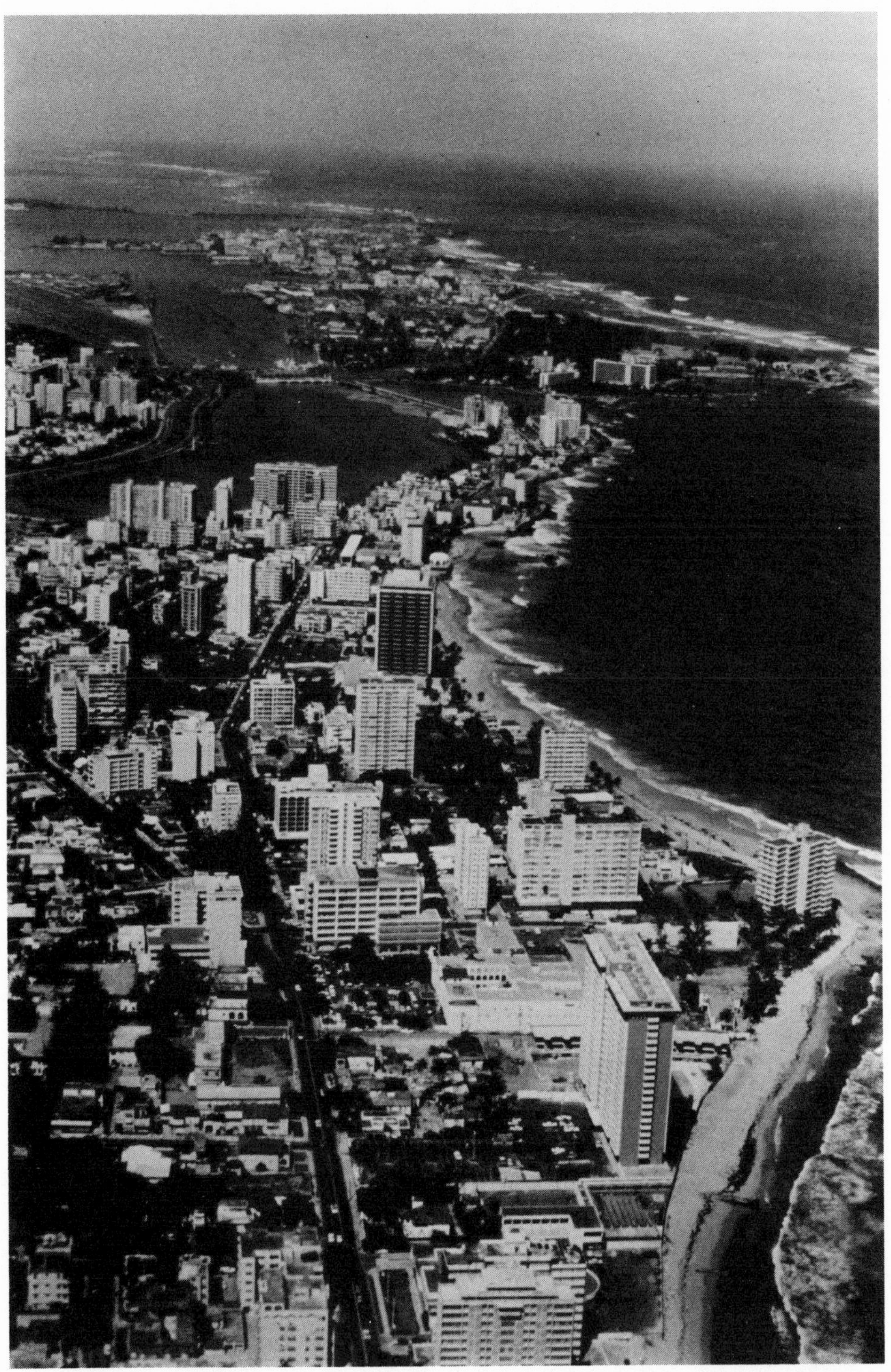

Aerial view of the newer—Condado—section of the City of San Juan. Road at center of picture nearest shoreline is the Avenida Ashford, with top hotels between it and the sea. At upper left the runway at Isla Grande can be noted.

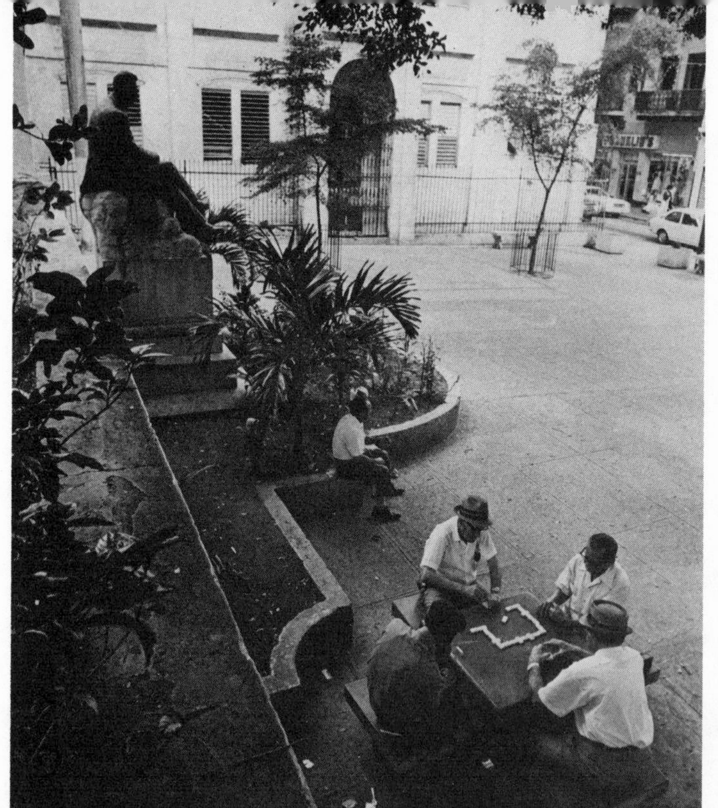

A friendly game of dominoes (top).

The Institute of Puerto Rican Culture is responsible for the restoration of the Spanish colonial houses seen here on Calle Christo, Old San Juan (above).

ɪnce's Museum of Art, designed by lward Durell Stone, is well worth the tour for one of the finest collections in ɜntral and Latin America. You'll find ɔrks by Gainsborough, Reynolds, Van ɣke and Velazquez, and others (above).

La Torre—the Tower—at the University of Puerto Rico, Rio Piedras. Founded in 1903, UPR is fully accredited, and handles some 30,000 students at three campuses, which include a medical school.

Ballet, opera, and music are part of the cultural scene in Puerto Rico, and the Casals Festival brings music lovers (and players) from around the world (left).

The Santo Domingo Convent, adjacent to the Church, is of typical Spanish colonial architecture, and is today used by the Institute of Puerto Rican Culture as a showplace for local art. Concerts are occasionally held here. There are a number of parks and plazas, the most attractive of which are the Plaza de Armas, Parque de las Palomas, and the Plaza de San Jose, by the church. The Governor's mansion, La Fortaleza, completed in 1540 and modernized a hundred years ago, is open to the public from 9:00 AM to 4:30 PM Monday to Saturday, and on Sundays between 9:00 AM and 12 noon. The Casa Blanca, begun in 1521 as the official residence of the first governor, Ponce de Leon, is also worth a visit, as is the San Juan Cathedral. Musicians and music lovers should not miss the new Pablo Casals Museum, next door to the San Jose church.

Book-lovers should check La Casa del Libro at 225 Cristo Street, a museum and library devoted to the "art of the book." Situated in an 18th-century colonial home, it houses frequent special exhibitions of local treasures. Open daily, 11:00 AM to 5:00 PM, except Sundays. Next door is the Museum of Puerto Rican Art, with collections of paintings and sculpture from the 18th–century to the present. Open 9:00 AM to 5:00 PM. Just up the block on the corner of San Franscisco and Cristo streets (or calles) is the famous Casa Don Q. An elegant 18th-century Spanish colonial townhouse, beautifully restored by the Serralles family, which owns the Don Q distilleries, visitors are invited to stop by for a complimentary drink in true old Spanish atmosphere while exploring the old city. Open 10:00 AM until noon, 1:00 to 4:00 PM Monday through Friday, and from 9:30 AM to 11:30 AM on Saturdays.

Students of military and naval architecture should inspect El Arsenal, originally constructed as a naval station in 1800; the San Cristobal fort, completed in 1772; and the Military Museum at Fort San Jeronimo—away from the old city—open 9:00 AM to 5:00 PM and free on Sundays. It houses collections of Spanish weapons and armor.

Excursions "Out on the Island"

Roads have improved enormously "out on the Island," as the locals say. Apart from Route 52, as the expressway that joins Ponce and San Juan is called, even the smaller highways and byways have been getting their share of maintenance and improvement. This is not to say that everything is perfect, but it is a lot better than it used to be and there are now some 4,000 miles of good roads available to drivers.

An easy day excursion is El Yunque, the tropical rain forest and bird sanctuary that is under the jurisdiction of the US Forestry Service. Either arrange to drive yourself, from one of the several car rentals listed in the monthly *Que Pasa* (the official visitors guide to the island), or hire a *publico* for your group.

If you decide to do it yourself, leave San Juan on Route 26 as if you were going to the International Airport, but continue on past the airport to Las Cruces, where you catch up with Route 3. You skirt Carolina and Loiza and Rio Grande on your way to Mameyes (or Palmer), where you make a right onto Route 191. The road climbs up into the rain forest, the air becomes more humid, and the vegetation gives way to tree ferns and orchids, tropical vines, and mountain rivulets and falls. If you are lucky you may catch sight of the indigenous but all-but-extinct Puerto Rican parrot. You'll almost certainly be entertained by the little tree frog who sings his own name, *coqui*, in a plaintive two-note cry.

It may well rain (well, what did you expect in a rain forest?), since the area receives some 200 inches per year. Still, there's plenty of shelter, an observation tower from which to look down to the sea, and fine local foods and Spanish wine at the *El Yunque* restaurant, which also features Spanish fare.

For your return route, you may like to continue through the rain forest via the *Parador El Verde*—keep going uphill through Florida until you make a right on Route 31, then on into Juncos where you make another right on to Route 185/953. About four miles down the road is another right turn, on 953, which takes you to Route 186. Yet another right on 186 will bring you shortly to the Paradore.

To return by the shore, go downhill on Route 186 toward Rio Grande, where you pick up 187. This brings you down to the sea and eventually to the colorful town of Loiza Aldea, where you may admire the first church to be dedicated to Ireland's patron saint, Patrick. The annual *festa* or *fiesta* in late July is more African than elsewhere in Puerto Rico. There was still a hand-poled ferry across the Loiza River at time of this writing, and the coastal road will bring you back through the Bosque Estatal de Pinones and so into town.

There are a number of other excursions around the island, but for the best views you will want to take to the mountains. Check the current issue of *Que Pasa*, available free in your hotel room or from the offices of the Tourism Company. It contains mountains of useful information about what is currently going on, including the month's events, various festivals, informative items about some of the more unique fauna and flora (such as the *dinoflagellate*, which causes the phosphorescent effect at nearby Parguera's Phosphorescent Bay), basic facts about the island, a guide to the old city, and more. The best part about it is that it is written and published in the island and the information is usually right-up-to-the-minute. Consult it also for current hotel rates. If you are planning ahead, query the Tourism Company's offices in New York, Chicago, Los Angeles, Atlanta, Washington, DC, Toronto, Canada and Frankfurt-am-Main, West Germany.

There is a remarkable array of locally made goods, including fashions with original designs available in clothes for the beach, the street, for cocktail parties, and even the most formal affairs. Local art is worthy of your time, including paintings, sculpture, and graphic arts. The island is quite well known for its local cigars, stringed instruments, items made from tortoise shell and horn, and jewelry. There are a number of good buys in imported goods, some of which are, curiously, below freeport prices. Make sure you know what the discount price at home is for items you might want before you set out.

Also, check prices in the neighboring Virgin Islands before making your purchase, as these could be cheaper. You could also shop in PR on your way home.

THE PARADORES OF PUERTO RICO

The *parador* system—the word dates back to 16th-century Spain—was reborn under the tourism development efforts of modern Spain. It was designed to provide

*Collectors of aviation minutiae will be interested to note that in this corner of the world one or two LF/MF aids are still to be found in which the NDB transmitter will send its ident for 50 seconds to be followed by a 10-second dash.

This is a sign to look out for it you're looking for good value for money in the island—the parador system started in 1974.

travelers with comfortable, basic accommodations at reasonable prices, while maintaining the cultural ethos of the region.

The original paradores were usually inns or hostelries situated at convenient way points where travelers could change horses and catch a nap and a meal before continuing on their way. Modern paradores are usually situated at places that are of cultural or historic interest but that were unlikely to justify the building of a large scale hotel. Frequently, existing structures have been converted to provide accommodations, as at the city of Ciudad Rodrigo, a key battle scene in the Napoleonic Wars in Spain.

The system of paradores in Puerto Rico is very new, having gone first into effect here in 1974. And while the emphasis on reasonable rates remains, the paradores boast an excellence of service and a diversity of activities and entertainment, set within the bounds of a friendly and cordial atmosphere—all designed not merely for visitors from outside of Puerto Rico, but also so that its many lesser-pursed urban citizens can experience the gracious hospitality, the customs, and the traditions of the people of the land.

For the visitor from outside the island, the parador system here makes a unique way to vacation if exploring the island by car.

These hostelries are always in accessible places, frequently offering unusual attractions. A good example is the *Parador El Verde*, mentioned earlier, which nestles amid the incredibly luxuriant foliage of the tropical rain forest that runs across the range of the Luquillo Mountains. This is raw jungle, stacked with giant vines, enormous tree ferns, numerous rare shrubs and plants and flowers, plus a range of birds and frogs that sing like birds—you'll seldom have an opportunity to experience anything like this.

El Verde has eighteen rooms and cabanas, all with bath, a little cocktail bar, plus an informal dining room. Cuisine is international with native specialties. There are two pools (one for the kids) and incredible views from the extensive grounds. On Sundays there's live local music plus a festive family-style buffet luncheon.

Down the mountain at the world-famous Luquillo Beach is the tiny *Parador Martorell*—six rooms with only semi-private facilities plus one with its own private bath. The parador provides packed lunches, great for easy excursions—to the colorful town of Loiza Aldea, for island folk art and a look at the historic Fajardo railroad; up to the Rain Forest; or to La Charca de Las Pailas swimming hole.

Or how about a coffee plantation? The parador *Hacienda Gripinas* was formerly just such a plantation, high in the hills of the Cordillera Central, just five minutes from the picturesque mountain town of Javuva. The gardens here are beautiful and constantly cared for, and all nine rooms have private bath and plantation-style noiseless ceiling fans. (Because you're in the hills, you don't need air conditioning, and you may want a sweater for those cooler evenings.) The restaurant features a number of native Creole dishes plus international fare. And those surroundings: the 20 acres remaining are still planted with coffee bushes, which are harvested each year.

At the time of the Spanish conquest, a group of Taino Indians lived in this area. Local excursions from this parador include a visit to the Borinquen Indian Monument in Javuva, the Indian Ceremonial Ballpark at Utuado, and also to the Piedra Escrita (Written Stone) and Charca de los Petroglifos (Pool of the Petroglyphs) for the stones carved by these lost tribes.

And just thirty minutes away there's boating and fishing on Lake Caonillas.

Coffee is still cultivated in the island, and is a delicious beverage when prepared Puerto Rican style.

The *Hacienda Juanita* is also situated in Taino country, near the Monte del Estado, just outside of Maricao. It has 11 rooms, a restaurant featuring Creole and international food, horseback riding, and a pleasantly Spanish ambiance.

Big attraction is the *Banos de Coama* (Coama Hot Springs), a modern 46-room hotel built in 19th-century style in aromatic woods. Named for an original hotel built here in 1847, the spas have been known to Americans for a long while and, back in 1933, Franklin D. Roosevelt himself took the cure.

If you use the new motorway, you're not much more than half

an hour from Caribbean beaches. Horseback riding is available also.

Two more paradors are to be found at the tiny seaside (and fishing) village of Quebradillas, which has one of the finest beaches in the island. These are the *Parador Vistamar,* set up on a hill overlooking the sea, with a profusion of rich purple bourgainvillea, 26 rooms—some with kitchen—and an excellent dining room and bar. Horseback riding and tennis. The beach is about five minutes' walk down the hill, and about ten minutes' back up; the road is steep so you may want to use your car.

And finally, there's *Parador El Guajatica,* right alongside that beach; the grounds are attractively landscaped with palm trees, bougainvillea, and hibiscus and other tropical flowers and shrubs. There are 38 air-conditioned rooms, each with balcony facing the ocean, each with private bath. Kind of cozy. There are two pools, one for adults and a dunking pool for children. During weekends it can get noisy by the poolside as teenagers gather around for sport and to impress one another.

There's a pleasant, airy restaurant serving Puerto Rican specialties, plus such international favorites as filet mignon and lobster thermidor. The fresh seafood is excellent. Unusual among the paradores, this one has a conference room available for those who want to combine business with leisure.

Other special features are live music at weekends and, on Sundays, a magnificent buffet luncheon. Golf addicts can play at the Punta Borinquen links originally built for the US military. It's a fine 18-hole course.

For up-to-date details call, toll free, (800) 241-5054 (the Paradores Reservation System) or write Tourism Company of Puerto Rico, Paradores Puertorriquenos Program, 1290 Avenue of the Americas, New York, N.Y. 10019. Tel: (212) 582-5652.

U. S. Virgin Islands

As you fly eastward from Puerto Rico, the first Virgin Islands you encounter are those claimed as unincorporated territory of the United States. United States travelers who are venturing outside the continent for the first time just love these islands because American is spoken (albeit with a Caribbean lilt), the currency is the US dollar, and there is a pleasant mix of mainstream American hotel accommodations alongside a more exotic indigenous mix.

Much is made of the extraordinary tax-free gifts you can purchase here, and it is true—provided that you know what discounts are available to you in your own hometown at the discount stores. Then there's the Customs concession, which permits you to bring six hundred dollars' worth of items duty-free (based on the wholesale value of the products, about 40 percent less than the retail price) if you're a US resident, mentioned earlier.

These Virgin Islands are also an excellent place to experience that typical tropical vacation you've always wanted. The islands have been American since 1917—they were Danish for a long while before that—and if development has been somewhat haphazard in places, with one or two ugly sores upon the horizon, that's somewhat down-home too. But there are also some beautiful

Famed Whim Greathouse in St. Croix, USVI. (Photo by Fritz Henle.)

resorts and some excellently constructed restorations. In any case, the superb geophysical structure of the islands is difficult to disguise.

Depending on whose count you take, there are more than 40 islands. The three best known are St. Thomas (where all the heavy action is), St. John (a still nearly pristine tropical beauty where more than three-fifths of the island is National Park) and St. Croix (where a young Alexander Hamilton spent some formative years and where the original good old boys ran profitable plantations).

Both St. Thomas and St. Croix have Airports of Entry.

Flying In

Your flight path to St. Thomas from Puerto Rico takes you over the formerly restricted area of Culebra. The Local Chart still shows it as restricted; the San Juan–area FAA says it isn't and doesn't know why it continues to be so labeled.

Harry S. Truman Airport at Charlotte Amalie (pronounced Charlotte Amahl-ya) is the Airport of Entry at St. Thomas for the USVI, with a single runway 09/27 and a usually bobbly approach over the water using runway 09. Length is a comfortable 4,600 ft with strip lighting, VASI, and threshold strobes.*

While you won't have a problem flying in with communications, communications beneath 4,000 MSL are restricted in the northern arc from 270° to 090°. Normal tower frequency is 118.1, with 118.8 used for arrivals and departures in an arc running 240° thru 120°. The broadcast VOR/DME is located 3 NM west of the field, frequency 108.6 Ch 23. (Ident is STT.) There's an ILS approach, and in addition to that bobble effect there are sometimes clusters of seabirds just to the south of runway 09.

For local tourism queries in St. Thomas, call 774-9493.

If you are going directly to St. Croix (pronounced Saint Croy), you'll overfly the island of Vieques, which was in the headlines for some time owing to military operations here. Peace has descended, but check with the FSS to make sure the status still obtains. *Alexander Hamilton* is the Airport of Entry in St. Croix, but if you are simply flying from St. Thomas to St. Croix you don't have to go through the paperwork hassle.

*There's a hill at the end of Runway 09 and if you're flying a twin you may want to do as the airlines do, i.e., don't leave at gross weight.

There's an ILS,* and the runway lighting includes sequence flashing and high intensity approach lights plus a VASI system. Length is 7,600 ft.

The broadcast VOR/DME's ident is COY at 108.2 Ch 19, broadcast on 123.6, the frequency of San Juan Area radio. St. Croix tower is 118.6 and ground control is 121.7. You may want to note that Buck Island, which lies off the northeast shore of the main island, is a national monument and overflight should be at not less than 2,000 ft above the terrain.

Note also that the VOR is unreliable in the arc from 035°

*Localizer only

The short hop from San Juan to St. Thomas takes you abeam the island of Culebra, where the *Seafarer's Inn* is noted for its lobster. To St. Croix you'll pass close by Vieques. (*Not to be used for navigation.*)

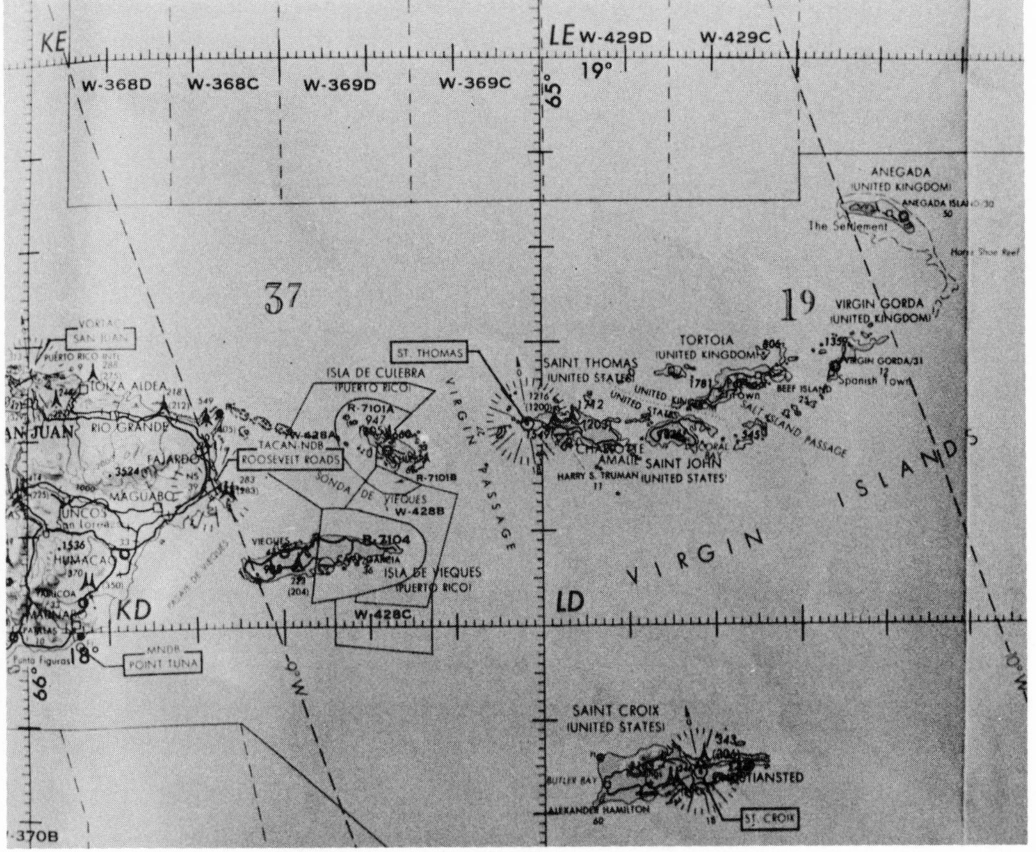

through 065° and again from 155° through 225°. The VOR/DME becomes unusable from 115° through 155° beyond 20 NM, below 5,000 ft. As at St. Thomas there are birds in the vicinity of the airport. Both fields can usually supply 100 octane.*

For local tourism queries, call 773-4470.

Background Briefing

Like most of the islands in the Lesser Antilles or Eastern Caribbean, the Virgin Islands are of volcanic origin. They were created millennia ago by the same system that produces new islands off Iceland and, quite recently, in the Galapagos. This is not to say their volcanos do not erupt—witness the recent scare when St. Vincent's Soufriere started rumbling. It may be of interest to examine briefly just how these volcanic islands occur.

The earth's crust—the relatively solid structure that covers the highly compressed, turgid mixture of hot rocks called the *mantle*—is anywhere from two to 35 miles thick, somewhat less under the oceans. The mantle that the crust covers is relatively solid under the pressure, but appears to enjoy a slow movement of its own, with convection cells bringing heated material from the earth's super-hot liquid core toward the crust—an almost identical phenomenon to the way air behaves when it is heated, except that we're dealing with relatively solid rocklike material.

Meanwhile, the earth's crust consists not of one vast solid plate but of a number of plates, which move around relatively slowly. Off the California coast, for example, the oceanic plate is buckling under the continental plate at the rate of 3 centimeters, or 1.18 inches, per year. Meanwhile, this pressure is causing movement along the San Andreas Fault at an astonishingly speedy 3.5 *inches* per year, according to latest calculations using lasers and satellites for accuracy.

As a result of this constant working, an enormous energy is built up, which, when released, will produce either a shattering earthquake or, where the crust is both thin and soft (as under the ocean floor) volcanic eruptions. When there is an eruption, the crust opens up allowing for a local release of pressure, which permits the mantle material to liquefy. This hot magna and sea-water mix combines explosively and, if the sea water doesn't slow everything

*On Sundays, it can be difficult to obtain fuel in St. Thomas.

down, there's a tense buildup of ash and lava beneath the surface. Often there will be secondary discharges from side vents, and sometimes, if the crust's weakness doesn't heal, an island will be formed.

A place where there is a weakness and where this activity takes place sporadically is called a "hot spot." Typical hot spots include the Hawaiian Islands, where the movement of plates has permitted the creation of islands in a nearly straight line; the Galapagos Islands, with a slight curve; and the arc known as the Lesser Antilles. (There are some 120 hot spots around the planet, of which Yellowstone Park and Greenland are two of the best known).

Of course, the basic island is just volcanic rock, in its pristine form, but, as studies by the Darwin Station in Santa Cruz, G.I., have shown, the lava is quickly weathered and in the space of about 50 years begins to support some primitive forms of life—an incredibly short space of time in terms of the planet's age. First to appear are small plants such as *coldenia,* which you can still find in the more rocky parts of the islands. These are very ancient little plants in terms of evolution, highly resistant to heat and drought, which perform the backbreaking work of transmuting the lava into a soil more easily colonized by other life.

No one knows for sure quite how long all this takes, but eventually other plants and grasses take root.* And subsequently animal species appear.

The lush rain forests that are to be found in Puerto Rico and Dominica, with some remnants in Tortola in the BVI, have long since disappeared from the US Virgin Islands, over which, in recent times, no less than seven different flags have flown claiming sovereignty.

The first people here, to the best of current knowledge, were the Arawak Indians, who successfully pioneered the region, and who reputedly ventured as far north as mainland Florida from what is believed today to have been their homeland in the Guajiro territory of Colombia. Theirs was a relatively peaceful culture that appears to have existed over a period of some three hundred years,

*The Agricultural Station in St. Vincent some years ago discovered some prehistoric varieties of wheat grass seed possibly half a million years old. They successfully germinated some.

from around 1000 AD through about 1350, when it was vigorously overthrown by Caribs who followed the journeyings north of the pioneers. The Caribs were good at fighting, though their culture was less skilled. As warriors they were more than a match for the Arawaks who fought a slow, losing retreat northward.

The Caribs' methods were remarkably simple: Kill off all the men and boys and then mate the women. They maintained their warlike nature long after they'd taken over these mini-colonies. Interestingly, during Columbus's second voyage in 1493, his landing party in the USVI had a disagreement with these Indians and was set on by a canoeful of warriors. They managed to shoot fire arrows at the Spanish ships even after their own canoes had been sunk by gunfire.

It is not known what happened to these natives, who had vanished by 1625 when both the Dutch and British made settlements here. Possibly the Spanish killed them; possibly they caught European diseases and being unresistant died, or possibly they were taken to work the gold mines of Santo Domingo.*

The Dutch and British were none too friendly during these early years. Matters came to a head in 1645 when the Dutch governor of the territory managed to kill his English counterpart. This produced an immediate counterattack in which the Dutch governor and a number of settlers were killed by the Brits.

A new Dutch governor was appointed, and on his arrival the British played one of the games that caused them in earlier times to be labeled "perfidious Albion." In a show of friendship they sent envoys to invite the new governor to visit their town. He graciously accepted and on his arrival was chained, tried, and shot.

Since they were outnumbered, the Dutch sensibly left the islands and sailed off to St. Maarten and St. Eustatius, where they remain to this day.

Then, in 1650, the Spaniards landed a 1200-man squad from neighboring Puerto Rico and proceeded to wipe out the British garrison. Those who were not killed and who didn't die of their wounds were given three weeks to leave by these gallant conquistadores. The news soon traveled down-island and the Dutch thought to return.

*There's a Carib Reserve in Dominica.

They sent a small invasion force. It was massacred.

The French, who had until now taken no active part in this territorial imperative, now landed a small force, and by cunning and trickery persuaded the Spanish garrison to surrender. Incredibly, for reasons best known to the garrison commander, the Spanish did, and their 1200 men set sail back to Puerto Rico. The French force was just 65 strong.

Less than a year later, in 1651, the French king sold the islands to a Monsieur De Poincy for a private kingdom. De Poincy in turn ceded them two years later to his religious order, the Knights of Malta, whose first group of settlers, while nominally Maltese, were actually French. They had a bad time of it. They sent messages for assistance back to France and a Chevalier de la Mothe was sent out with a shipload of provisions for the distressed settlers.

In a manner that seemed to be becoming a tradition of welcome in the territory, the settlers gave him brief welcome, locked him in irons, and took off with the ship and provisions for Brazil.

A second Chevalier, the Chevalier de Bois, was sent out in 1659 to restore order and did quite well. But times were changing and the Knights of Malta felt they'd had enough. In 1665 they sold the territory to the French West India Company.

Due to bad management and misfortune, this new corporation became so riddled with debt that the French king decided to take over the islands again. Some twenty years later, all inhabitants were ordered moved to Santo Domingo and the islands returned to a (relatively) primal status, with only freebooters, pirates, and privateers using their shores. (In 1720, a French fleet captured half a dozen British merchantmen in harbors here, and the king "confiscated" them for being in "his" islands. *Force majeure!*)

Then the Danes decided they wanted in on the Caribbean game, and in 1733 the Danish West India and Guinea Company purchased the islands from the King of France.

Danish settlers were promptly recruited and instructed to get on with the bonanza. This they did surprisingly well, though they experienced considerable difficulty in collecting taxes and duties from the freebooters who'd traditionally used the place on a no-cost basis. So it came about that the Danish King in 1755 declared the islands a Crown Colony, and then, in 1764, a free port for all.

This move almost doubled prosperity overnight, and the islands became an important center for all trading, legal and illegal, in the Caribbean. Slave trading, sugar, rum were all big business, but arms to be used in the War of Independence against Britain also filtered through.

Fort Christian in St. Thomas, which survives to this day, was built by the Danes. A number of pirates were hanged here, and although the place is still used mostly as a police station, it has a small museum housing Carib and Arawak artifacts discovered in the area.

The Danes stayed and built houses, but by the 1830s it was said you could find more than a hundred different nationalities here, including numerous Britishers who'd left their own islands as slavery was about to be abolished. (The Danes abolished slavery in 1848, some sixteen years before the Civil War brought it to an end in the USA.)

The islands were bought, for some $300 an acre, by the United States in 1917 primarily because it was thought that German submarines would use them to launch attacks on US shipping during World War I. Today these Virgins are an unincorporated territory of the United States.

Despite modern development, some three-fifths of the buildings in downtown St. Thomas are more than a hundred years old. The local Masonic Lodge, which maintains its affiliation with Grand Lodge of London, England, was founded in 1818. Here too is the second-oldest Jewish synagogue and Jewish cemetery on American soil. Then there is the 18th-century Lutheran church, second-oldest in the Western Hemisphere; the Dutch Reformed Church is also one of the first built in this hemisphere. Rebuilt after a recent disastrous fire is the 17th-century Nisky Moravian Mission building.

Over on St. Croix at Christiansted is Fort Christiansvaern, which was originally constructed in 1744 (primarily for harbor defense) and added to in the following century. Today you can wander around old-time bastions and cannon and even investigate its cool dungeons.

Currently undergoing restoration is the Danish Customs House. It was completed about 1830, though the original one story structure was built in 1751.

The Government House's West Wing goes back to 1747, and is one of several buildings on the island worth a visit. The second-floor ballroom is a real showpiece.

Frederiksted was almost totally wiped out by a fire in 1879, but the enterprising townspeople decided to restructure the buildings by using wood on top of the stone structures that survived. The result is surprisingly pleasing. There are a number of late-18th-century buildings including Holy Trinity Lutheran Church (Hospital Street), Apothecary Hall (Queen Street), and the old Customs House.

St. Paul's Anglican Church (Prince Street) was originally founded in 1772, but the new structure was completed around 1815. Fort Frederik has been restored and supposedly dates from around 1760.

One of the great showplaces on St. Croix is an estate located some 2 miles to the east of Frederiksted. Formerly known as John's Rest and now called the Whim Greathouse, the building is of neoclassic design, some 95 feet long and 35 feet wide, with ceilings more than 16 feet high. The building was restored under the direction of William G. Thayer, Jr., who still lives in Frederiksted, and consists of 3 large rooms, a small wing at the rear, and a gallery. John's Rest was built around 1794 by one Christopher MacEvoy, Jr., (a Dane despite his Scottish name—his father had become a naturalized Danish citizen). MacEvoy made a great deal of money from the plantations he'd inherited from his father (who had founded the original estate in 1751). Apparently he made so much money that in 1811 he moved to England; he later bought a sugar refinery and a castle in Denmark, where he resettled to become Chamberlain to King Frederik VI. They still tell a tale about how he appeared one day (following his appointment) in the streets of Copenhagen in a magnificent coach drawn by 4 white horses.

The problem was that only the Danish nobility were entitled to use white horses and MacEvoy was a parvenu cad and nouveau riche to boot. MacEvoy was severely rebuked and in a huff resigned his post and returned to St. Croix, where he made even more money.

Still, St. Croix must have seemed exceedingly parochial after the bright court scene. And, having refilled his coffers, he returned to

Denmark. This time it was to appear in an even more magnificent coach drawn by no less than 8—count 'em—white . . . mules. No rules were transgressed, and the Danish nobility could see the joke was on them and relented. MacEvoy was reappointed Royal Chamberlain.

The interior of the Greathouse has been restored and contains household furnishings typical of MacEvoy's era, though none is identified as belonging to him. There's a sectional sofa from Copenhagen's Royal Palace, a breakfront from the Government House in Christiansted containing Danish (Bing & Grondahl) and Richaud of Paris chinaware. Friends of the late Frances Van Riper were responsible for the donation of the chandeliers in the East Room and the Dining Salon; they originally hung in the Lutheran Church in Frederiksted.

There are a number of rare prints depicting the sugar and rum-making business as it was in those days, and in the West Room you can view the tester bed that once belonged to the wife of Danish Governor Limpricht. And there are the sugar mill and Plantation Museum, the Boiling House, Cook House, Bath House, and more. There's even—inevitably—a gift shop, with unusual basketry and planter's chairs, which can be made to order.

This stepping back in time will cost you one buck.

Over on Northside Drive is *Sprat Hall*. Now a restaurant best known for its varieties of island fare—breadfruit, kingfish in orange sauce, chayote, plus excellent seafood—it dates back to around 1670 and is unique in that it survives exactly as when it was built. There's a pleasantly informal atmosphere, but reservations are preferred for dinner which is served at 7:00 PM.

ST. JOHN

If you are in search of a place to get away from the pressures of the high-speed rat-race, then St. John is the island for you. Unless you have a seaplane, you'll have to get there by boat. Most of the island is National Park, and there's even a camp at *Cinnamon Bay* in the heart of it, right on the beach. You can rent fully equipped tents from $10.50 per day for two ($3 extra per person per day and there's room for four, though that's cozy). If you bring your own gear, bare sites cost $2 a day single with an extra buck for each additional person.

If you prefer a more solid roof over your head, one-room beach units, which come with four beds, an outside terrace, plus all the essentials, will run you an extravagant $18.50 per day for two people ($3 extra per person per day). There's a commissary on site that can provide you with basics, but you'll be better off stocking up with your favorites at a St. Thomas supermarket before you leave.

Drinking water, a bath house with flush toilets, and fresh-water showers are provided by the Park Service. Cafeteria food is available three times a day and reservations (made well in advance; two weeks is the *maximum* stay) are absolutely vital either in writing or by phone.*

Also for camping out but more spaciously are the three-room canvas cottages at *Maho Bay*. With a spectacular and different view from each cottage in the hills above a lustrous white beach, you have your own screened living and sleeping areas and an open porch. There's a central bath house and commissary, and two adults per cottage will run you $150 a week plus $35 additional per child (limited to three children).**

If you want to get away from it all but prefer to do it in style, then it's *Caneel Bay Plantation* for you. A former 18th-century Danish sugar plantation, Caneel Bay is known for having provided refuge to plantation owners during a slave revolt in 1733. French soldiers from Martinique had to be brought in to crush the rebellion; many of the slaves preferred to leap to their deaths from the cliffs at Mary's Point rather than face recapture and punishment. Virgin Islanders will tell you that their ghosts still haunt the area.

The abolition of slavery in 1848 spelled death to these smaller plantations on St. John, and the planters left. On trails through the island you'll come across the brush-covered ruins of some of these old estates and at Annaberg Mill—now well cleared and in the process of restoration—you can, with the help of a Forest Service guide, explore for yourself the former workings of King Sugar.

Today's Caneel Bay Plantation is totally devoted to satisfying its visitors. Originally opened as an inn during the nineteen-thirties, it was acquired by Laurance Rockefeller during the fifties together with some 6,000 adjoining acres, which now form the National

*Cinnamon Bay Camp, Box 120, St. John, VI. Tel: (809) 776-6330.
**Maho Bay Camps, Box 113 Cruz Bay, St. John, VI. Tel: (809) 776-6240, or in New York: 17 East 73rd Street, N.Y., N.Y. 10021 Tel: (212) 472-9453

Park. There are more than 150 superbly landscaped acres with 146 guest rooms on, or just steps away from, seven beautiful beaches. Luncheon is served at the sugar mill, with a vista of Virgin Islands, or you can make a reservation for lunch at the beach terrace dining room.

There are three categories of accommodation: deluxe beach front, beach front, and beach view. It's expensive, but the scuba and snorkeling are wondrous. There are seven tennis courts, with the Rockresorts–Sports Illustrated Tennis Clinic plan in operation. The hotel provides its own transportation from St. Thomas and some packages are offered giving you a chance to split your vacation between here and *Little Dix Bay* (another Rockresort) on Virgin Gorda, BVI.

If you're planning a day visit to St. John and want to visit the hotel, be sure to make a reservation for a meal. Better check whether they still require a jacket at lunch, which they've been known to do. The pleasant outdoor bar requires no reservation and no jacket, if you want to drop by for a drink.

An all-day excursion from St. Thomas to St. John with transportation and visiting the Annaberg ruins and Caneel Bay Plantation runs, with lunch, around $20 per person (children $15). Ferries leave St. Thomas on the hour, fare $1.50 each way. There's regular taxi service plus taxi buses (scheduled) from the Cruz Bay dock to the beaches. Rental cars cost $25 per day by advance reservation only. Caneel Bay Plantation also offers lunch plus ferry ride at $15 inclusive.

The National Park service offers one of the best buys of them all on Wednesdays: a hike with a Ranger through the Reef Bay Plantation with only a $3.50 charge for the boat ride back to Cruz Bay.* You get a thorough nature tour with plants and trees identified, and stops at the ancient Indian petroglyph carvings above the bay, an old sugar mill, and a greathouse. Reservations are advised.

Water Sports

Virgin Islands waters have produced no less than eighteen International Game Fishing Association records during the last ten years.

*You can walk back up the trail you hiked down at no charge. It's a mostly uphill climb of about three miles, so wear good hiking shoes.

And while many of the catches have been boated in waters technically belonging to the BVI, most of the fishermen's boats are USVI–based with skippers who've been doing this over the years.

These old tars practically know by the amount of salt that's in the air on a particular morning and the shade cast by the early sun where the fish'll be found. And you can find year round such fighters as Allison Tuna, Bonito, Blue Marlin, Sailfish, and Wahoo that'll give you sport and a fight for your money. (Wahoo is particularly delicious to eat if you don't choose to mount it as a trophy.)

One of the best fishing areas—Lang Bank—is but a short run from St. Croix. It's a reliable fishing ground and you'll be really unlucky if you don't manage to boat either dolphin (the fish, not the mammal, and as tasty a surf food as you'll eat when fresh) or kingfish—that is, if you don't find wahoo. The wahoo is a delight for sports fishermen, especially if you don't mind taking your chances with testline of less than 80 pounds. (Ms. Pauline Stewart over at Tortola's Fort Burt Hotel once held a record Wahoo catch on 10-pound test.) Most hotels will cooperate with the cooking of your catch.

In St. Croix, shore fishermen can fish from the rocks near Clover Crest, Frederiksted. And again, sport fishing is to be found just a short ride from the harbor.*

The Buck Island water garden is great for visiting snorkelers and scuba divers, and the waters around all the islands abound in underwater treasures like natural corals, with their sea urchin protectors, and other sea denizens including doctor fish, the brightly colored moray eel, and the intrepid but increasingly rare slipper lobster.**

Over on St. Thomas the emphasis has been more on sailboat cruising with crews. These range from the down-home to the deluxe, and include Nautilus Virgin Charters' Morgan 49, for luxurious vacations with captain, mate, and provisioning inclusive. For those who want to learn, Water Island Charters offers a split land/sea deal that includes either three or four nights at *Sugar*

*St. Croix has followed the Bermuda story in terms of getting around and mopeds rent from $13 per day. These come with a full tank of gas, safety lock, and basket. Great unless it rains.

**It is the only lobster/crawfish without claws.

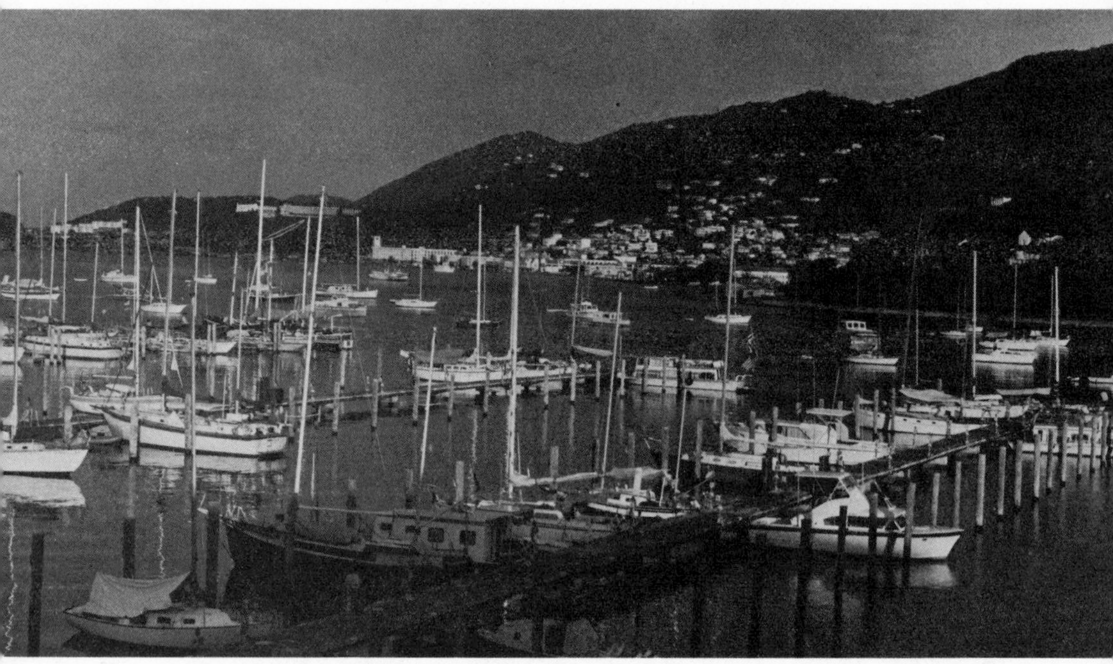

This marina in Charlotte Amalie, St. Thomas, U.S. Virgin Islands, provides safe anchorage for many of the sailing boats that make these waters the hub of marine activity in the northern Caribbean.

Bird Hotel, reputed to be the model of Herman Wouk's novel *Don't Stop de Carnival*, plus four or three days of spectacular cruising among the islands, with skipper.

For an excursion that's likely to be totally different from anything you've seen before, add Captain Cook's Glass Bottom Boat excursion around the now extinct volcano that is Charlotte Amalie's harbor. Then there's the new Coral World Underwater Observatory, a hundred feet offshore with a three-story tower that lets you view just about everything. It cost a cool $2.5 million and is the only one of its kind in the Western Hemisphere. A tank in the round lets you view shark, stingrays, barracuda, and more. Meanwhile, from the top level—a geodesic dome—there's a lounge and bar with panoramic views of St. John and the BVI.

If you choose to stay out of town (or if you want to be mobile), one of the better rates can be obtained from Sun Island Car Rentals. They've a fleet of more than one hundred Datsun B210s and cost around $19.95 per day or $125 per week with unlimited mileage.

ST. THOMAS

Hotels/Accommodations

There's an incredible range of accommodations in the island, which means there's something for everybody, ranging from the most casual of guesthouses to fine American modern.

For tops in quality there's *Frenchman's Reef Holiday Inn Beach Resort*, with three night clubs, three restaurants (Friday night is West Indian Buffet dinner night), no fewer than seven bars, four tennis courts, a fresh-water pool, water sports, discotheque, supper club, and so on. It offers gourmet-style dining plus shows nightly, and the steel band plays three nights a week. A new addition is the exotic Persian Room with authentic belly dancing. Frenchman's Reef might be described as an ultimate beach resort.

On a somewhat smaller scale is the *Limetree Beach Hotel*, just ten minutes from town at Frenchman's Cove. All 84 air-conditioned rooms are just steps from the palm-fringed shore. There's a fresh-water pool, lighted courts for tennis, sailing, scuba (with instruction available), and nightly entertainment. The food rates high.

And then, of course, there's *Bluebeard's Castle*, with the traditional comforts of a fine hotel. Originally a historic stronghold overlooking the town, it now has attractive landscaped grounds with an interesting collection of indigenous flowering plants, trees, and shrubs. The Terrace Restaurant offers a choice between West Indian and continental specialties. And there's nightly entertainment. Alas, no beach, but the hotel does provide regular transportation at a small charge to the beach at Magen's Bay. Tennis courts and pool.

If you want something different, like your own little island, the aforementioned *Sugar Bird Beach and Tennis Club* on Water Island may be for you. There are villas and apartments for rent by the day, with 66 sea-view rooms. (The villas and apartments are fully equipped for light housekeeping and include maid service but not laundry or dishwashing.) There are a number of beaches and a pool; instruction's available for tennis, sailing and scuba; and there are a variety of power and sailing vessels for charter. Typical summer rate for a 2-bedroom/2-bath unit for one to four persons is $65 per day, while a 3-bedroom/3-bath unit runs $75 per day for occupancy by one to six people. There are some branches of shops, but the ferry ride across to the former Sub Base takes only five minutes.

At the eastern end of St. Thomas is the *Sapphire Beach Resort*, with spectacular views and a sparkling beachfront. It's grown from the original 40 beach-front rooms, and now has more than 100 additional deluxe apartments. Their honeymoon and water-sports packages are good value, and Thursday night is their West Indian barbecue.

Right by the airport is the *Carib Beach Hotel.* Despite the noise from aircraft—and there's plenty of activity during the day—the Carib Beach Hotel gets numerous repeat business. There's the usual entertainment, Saturday being their West Indian evening with steel band and limbo. Snorkel equipment available.

Because of the original tentative and occasionally sporadic development of the islands, there are a number of smaller establishments that provide a range of attractive and pleasing accommodations. Typical is the *Hotel 1829*, a quiet old-world retreat where you can experience the old-fashioned comfort if not the original elegance of the West Indian townhouse. There's backgammon nightly, and the cuisine is very good—so good, in fact that Chef Gerhard Hoffman's recipes have turned up in *Gourmet* magazine. Meals are served either on the beautiful bougainvillea'd balcony or in the former living room of this attractive home. Hotel 1829 is quite a gathering place for island regulars who live here year-round. It's on Government Hill within easy walking distance of town. Also in the same area are *West Indian Manner*, another typical West Indian townhouse, and *Galleon House*, also a guesthouse with a highly convivial atmosphere.

Over on the sea on the far side of Frenchtown, up on Frenchman's Hill, is the *Harbor View*, another attractive 19th-century manor house, with the best food on the island—according to *Harper's Bazaar.* There are 10 rooms only, and a pool.

Over on Denmark Hill is the *Villa Santana*, formerly the mansion of Mexican General "Alamo" Santa Ana. There are three housekeeping cottages and five twin efficiency apartments. There's also an attractive view of the town and harbor, which are within walking distance.

Mafolie is an apartment hotel that looks like a Mediterranean villa transported to the tropics. It's on Mafolie Hill—hence the

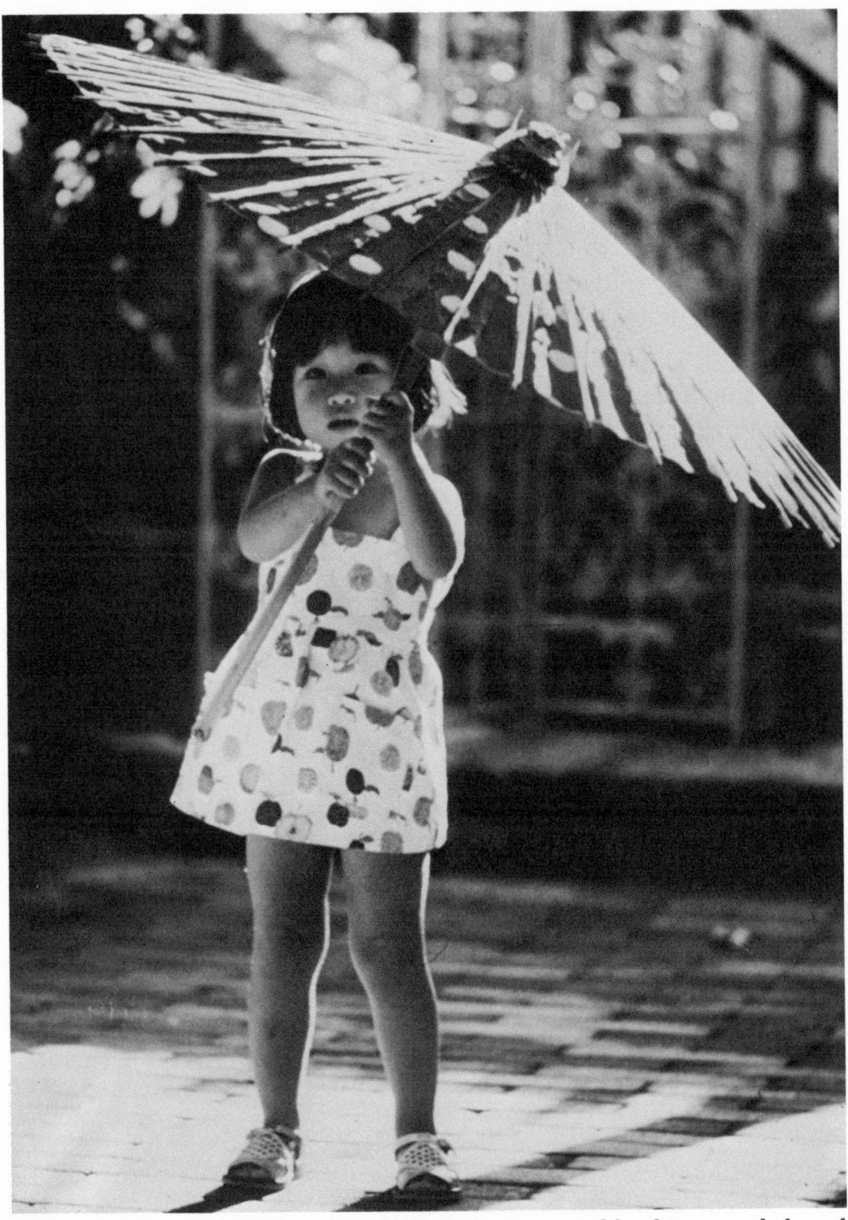

One way to keep out of the tropical sun is demonstrated by this young lady and her parasol.

name—and has about 23 rooms, some with kitchenette. There's a pool and a sundeck, and free transport to Magen's Bay. Car is recommended if you stay here.

Then there's *Magen's Point Hotel*, about ten minutes' drive up and over the hills to the north shore on beautiful Magen's Bay. Under the same ownership as the Anchor Inn of Christiansted, St. Croix, there are spacious hillside rooms with views of the ocean, an attractive restaurant, plus pool. Transport to the beach is available, and for gourmets, the *Lobster Pot* restaurant is one of the better places on the island to eat dinner. Dishes include lobster (of course!) served in a variety of ways, plus local red snapper and other seafood, plus steak, chicken, and veal cooked enticingly. Classical guitarist Larry Carsman is on hand at dinner from Tuesday through Saturday to complete your evening.

For something different and more self-sufficient you may like to consider the *Sea Horse Cottages* at Nazareth Bay.

At the east end of St. Thomas, and not far from the apartment complex of *Secret Harbor*—definitely worthwhile—there's a small beach with reasonably good snorkeling. Some newer townhouse-type units, suitable for four, have been added. Secret Harbor features one- and two-bedroom apartments with maid service. There's an attractive beach and the living-room terraces give you a true island feeling as you sip your sundowner cocktails.

Similar are the Japanese cottages of the *Shibui* complex on Constance Hill, just ten minutes from town, where you'll overlook the flight path of aircraft taking off from Runway 09. There are maid service and pool at this hillside location, and each cottage comes with living room, bedroom, and luxurious bath—sunken tubs—plus kitchen. No beach, but beach privilege available. The *Bali Ha'i Hotel*, with studio accommodations—you'll need a car—is just four miles out of town, with restaurant providing lunch and breakfast; it's another in the good-value category, as are the duplex villas at *Mandahl Estate*. *Cowpet Bay Villas* are somewhat more expensive, but the quality is matched, and *Point Pleasant*, with its view of the BVI and St. John, offers good weekly rates.

Consult the tourist board for current data.

ST. CROIX

Hotels/Accommodations

If you want to stay in Christiansted, say old-time visitors, there's no better place than the *Anchor Inn*. Owned by the same people who operate Magen's Bay Hotel (St. Thomas), it overlooks the harbor, and most of the attractively furnished air-conditioned rooms have sea-view balconies. Others will tell you that *Charte House*, built around an old Danish courtyard with freshwater pool, is a wonderful little hotel to put on your list. (The Anchor has a pool, too). Still others will suggest you list the *Phoenicia Hotel* with its Lebanese delicacies, or the *King Christian*, housed in a rebuilt and redecorated old Danish building. (King Christian also has a pool.) All are in the heart of town and all have merit. And if you're looking for efficiency, then you'd better add the *Royal Scotia Hotel* to your list for apartment living with hotel services. Efficiency kitchens in every room.

As in St. Thomas, so at St. Croix, for that island holiday in reach of it all: and that's to be found at the *Jockey Club on the Cay*, just minutes offshore by boat in the outer reaches of Christiansted Harbor. At Jockey Club you've a 7-acre beach (for swimming use the Olympic-sized freshwater pool), four brand new tennis courts, and a fabulous view of that harbor and its activities.

For more luxurious living just a little bit farther away from it all, consider the north shore's *Gentle Winds* resort with its first-class condominia plus tennis courts and nightly entertainment. Accommodations here include 1-, 2-, and 3-bedroom villas, and excellent restaurant plus pool.

Slightly closer to Christiansted is St. "C"—as the *St. Croix by the Sea* resort is known to repeat visitors. Overlooking Long Reef and Christiansted Harbor, it's also north shore, but for a different change of pace offers a delightful and old-fashioned Danish buffet(*smøre*) come Sunday night. It's the near-perfect total resort experience with tennis courts, swimming pool, and a variety of accommodations, and if rates tend to be on the high side, the hotel does offer a number of package arrangements that bring those back to earth. Consult your local travel agent for details.

The *Buccaneer Hotel* is a bit like Topsy, in that it has grown and grown and grown from its inception on this former Knights of Malta settlement. This private estate offers no fewer than three beaches, an 18-hole golf course, and several restaurants, and is generally considered to be the creme-de-la-creme of resorts in the island. And yet, and yet: Despite the fact that it's attractively landscaped, provides comfortable service, and for the most part seems to be genteelly well run, something's sometimes missing. Still, that seems a little ungenerous for an hotel that offers as

Music is an important part of people's lives in the islands, and the Virgin Islands are no exception.
Picture by Fritz Henle.

much as the Buccaneer, and you should definitely keep it on your list if you play golf or tennis.

Sprat Hall, noted for its food, also offers accommodations that give you a chance to experience the charms of Greathouse living. A 200-acre estate with its own beach, it's less than two miles to the north of Frederiksted at the west end of the island. There are stables nearby, and horseback riding is as spectacular a way to see a tropical island as any. Comfortably informal atmosphere, which you'll either enjoy or loathe.

The Great House is the oldest in the island—it dates from 1670 or thereabouts.

The *Frederiksted Hotel* provides air-conditioned units with twin double beds in the heart of town, plus free transport to La Grange Beach and the Tennis Club. You can golf at the classic Fountain Valley links some fifteen minutes away. The nearly 50 units are balconied and built around a large pool and there are attractive harbor views. Breakfast is moderately priced but rates do not include meals.

Just outside of Frederiksted is *La Grange House*, an attractively furnished old house with a dozen rooms and some waterfront cottages. Pleasant atmosphere and local cooking.

Situated between the Cruzan Rum distillery and the Whim Great House is *Estate Carlton*. Old-time visitors will remember this as a hotel plus condominia based on a 100-acre estate. At the time of writing the hotel part is closed, though the approximately 200 accommodation units are for rent. It can be a spectacular place to stay when everything is running, so a check with the Tourist Board is a good idea. There are tennis courts, pool, and a 9-hole golf course.

Moving back to the north shore, the former *Caribbean Reef Club* has now become the *Pelican Cove Beach Resort* and continues to offer good value—especially in packages. There are some 50 beach-front studio apartments with restaurant and bar. Swimming is good and the reef, while not the most spectacular in these waters, provides interesting snorkeling.

Cane Bay Plantation was once described in the Chicago *Tribune* as "a charming country inn with epicurean food." The description is apt; the food is good and the specialties have become something of a Cruzan thing when dining out.

The accommodations are divided between cottages and pleasant apartments on this 30-acre estate. Interestingly, the cottages were once the slave quarters on the plantation, but you'd never guess it from the restoration that's been done. And if you don't like the idea of living in former slave accommodations, there are those pleasant apartments with balconies and beach view. Freshwater pool and, for golfers, just a short drive to the Fountain Valley links.

Cane Bay Reef Club offers accommodations with two rooms, kitchen, and balcony and, for honeymooners, flowers and champagne. Snorkeling equipment's available and if you're not sure how to use it you can get instruction. Check your travel agent for some of the inexpensive packages offered by this hotel.

The *Grapetree Beach Hotels* are on the southeastern shore of the island at the east end of St. Croix. This is a relatively complete

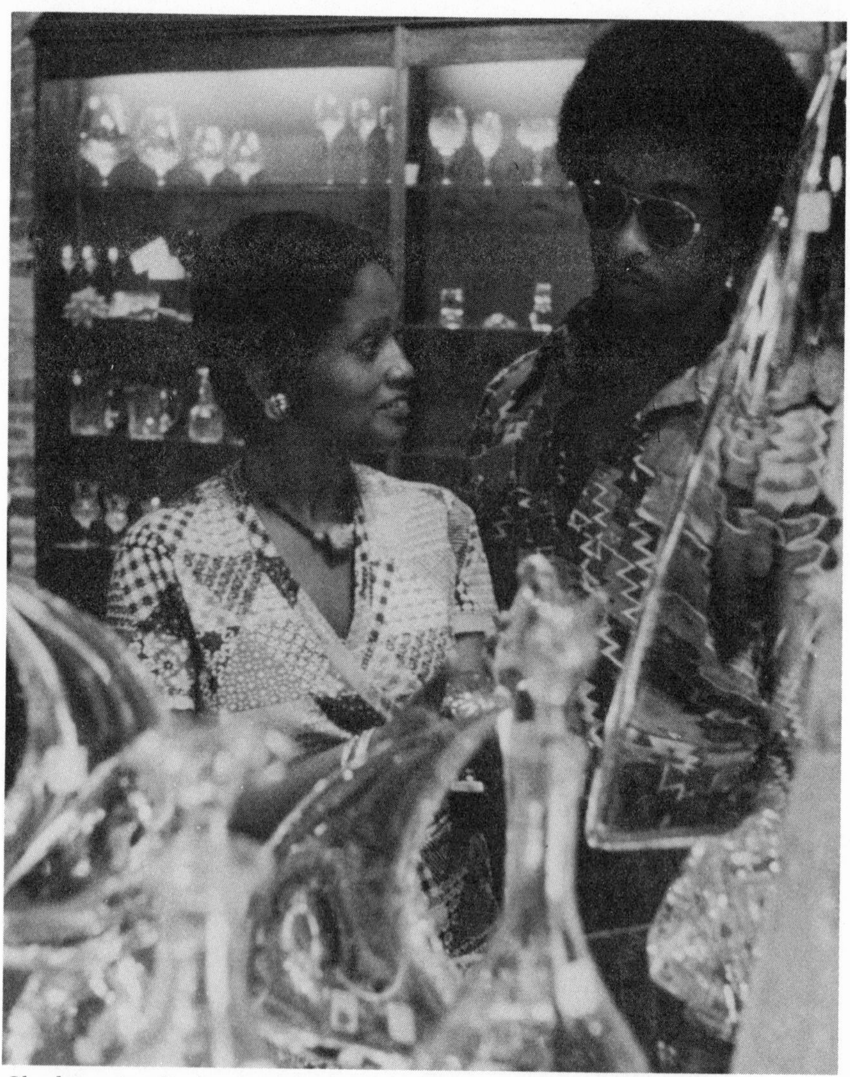

Charlotte Amalie has long been a favorite with bargain hunters for the rich selection of goods to be found, and the special status the territory rates with the U.S. Treasury Department.

resort (though for golf you have to drive to Fountain Valley), offering tennis, water sports, swimming pools, and so on. Food tends to be good and there's entertainment. If you stay here a car is a must, though the hotel does provide transportation between the two wings of the hotel.

For current data consult: Virgin Islands Government Tourist Office, 10 Rockefeller Plaza, New York, N.Y. 10020, or telephone (212) 582-4520.

British Virgin Islands

Until 1966, the British Virgin Islands were possibly the most underdeveloped of all territories in the entire Caribbean. There were few places to stay and most were difficult to reach, requiring a mix of boat and jeep. But thanks to the Queen Elizabeth bridge, which was dedicated that year and which now links Beef Island (where the former dirt strip has graduated to principal airport of the territory) to Tortola (main island and seat of government), it suddenly became much simpler for visitors to get where they were going.

Inevitably, many of the visitors were business people and, liking what they saw of the unspoiled charms of the territory, many returned with plans and schemes for the future development of the BVI. Island chic did the rest and a number of people, ranging from senior statesmen to the Beatles (and, more recently, Wings), spent time in these tranquil surroundings.

The islanders themselves are familiar with tourism, though mostly in the US Virgin Islands where formerly many worked in tourism-related industry. In 1968 the Royal Engineers (the British equivalent of the Corps of Engineers) were invited to plan and build an airfield more suited to the needs of the future. The result has been a slow but steady growth that has avoided—for the most

Beef Island airport's terminal buildings seen from Sea Apple bay. (*photo*)

part—some of the more epic disasters that have occurred in other potential paradisia. One method has been to use sailboats to house the visitors, and the BVI is possibly bareboat capital of the world today.

Still, it was no easy task. Many of the early planners and entrepreneurs have gone, though, for the most part, the best parts of their varying philosophies have been retained. One consequence is that today tourism accounts for some $10 million of the $20 million GNP, and a standard of living for the native islander that is second only to the USVI in the entire Caribbean.

From a visitor's point of view, the territory is still very virgin, yet one can find some of the best-planned luxury resorts in addition to modest, no-frills accommodation for those who just want to get away from it all—and the BVI is where you do go to get away from it all. There are usually—depending on the season—a fair number of attractive homes and apartments available for those who prefer to be self-contained when vacationing.

Background Briefing

Although there are more than 60 islands, islets, rocks, and cays, the total combined area of the BVI is only 59 square miles, about three times the size of Bermuda, or about the size of Martha's Vineyard.

Like the USVI, the BVI shares a long history of piracy and buccaneering. Dutch, French, and British privateers used Tortola and other islands as sallyports to plunder Spanish treasure ships returning to Europe. Later, attacks were made against Danish settlements. And there were the real pirates, who regarded any ship that could be disadvantaged in a fight as potential booty. Norman Island—where real treasure was discovered by the local Creque family in the past—was the model for Robert Louis Stevenson's famed *Treasure Island.* A look at a nautical chart and the salty flavor of many of the place names will confirm a colorful if sometimes bloody past.

It should not be forgotten that a no less distinguished personage than Sir Francis Drake—for whom the main channel dividing the two main groups of islands here is named—was himself a privateer. That is, he held a royal warrant from good Queen Bess permitting him to go forth and rob Spanish vessels, for in those days as in these, war was frequently conducted with the aid of mercenaries who took a percentage of the loot they obtained, plus expenses for equipping and refitting.

It is therefore not too surprising to find, among the few remains that survive, several early fort structures, built to defend local citizenry against the more lawless of seafarers.

For most of its history the territory has been British. A group of Dutchmen made the settlement near Road Town in about 1648, and were responsible for the foundations of old Fort Burt, now completely refurbished as an hotel. In those days, the Fort could guard the somewhat tricky entrance to Road Harbor, preventing surprise attack on an anchored fleet. (The Harbor today holds few surprises and there is now a deep-water harbor for larger vessels).

But this was insufficient to deter one group of pirates, reputedly some of Harry Morgan's men, and possibly including Morgan himself (who was later to become Lt. Governor of Jamaica). By 1666 the settlement was a privateer's encampment, and although the French moved in briefly—ostensibly to get rid of the privateers—they in their turn were replaced by the British who then launched a series of coordinated attacks (which were beaten off) against Danish settlements in what is now the USVI.

War gave way to sugar and a surprisingly busy commercial trade with the colonies in New England, whose whaling crews were already beginning to run somewhat far afield from their native shores. And there was slavery. Plantations flourished, rum being traded for more slaves, and blackbirding became a lively business—you can still see the slave auction market in neighboring St. Thomas—with traders exchanging human bodies for liquor and spice, which in turn would be traded for furs and other products in the north.

Then came the Society of Friends. Formed originally by George Fox in England in 1650, the Quakers could be said to be archetypes for the Wesleyans and Methodists who would follow them. They held that plainness in dress and speech and manners and religious worship, plus a civilized approach to living, were all that God asked of any human. Military service and the taking of oaths were anathema to these folk.

One of the Friends, Joshua Fielding, established a settlement in Tortola in 1727, with another in Virgin Gorda soon after. A big boost to the Quaker cause was the conversion of John Pickering, then Governor, a short time later. (Pickering is still used as a last name by a number of native islanders. In slave times, it was the custom for a slave to bear the surname of his master.)

The Quakers did introduce a certain religious feeling to the slaves, though they had less success with their masters. Interestingly, although a number of religious denominations now flourish here, the Society of Friends itself is gone.

The BVI has other claims to fame. For example, the designer of the Capitol building in Washington, DC, William Thornton, was a native British Virgin Islander. And a contemporary of his, John Lettsome, born in 1774 in Jost van Dyke (or Long Look, East End, Tortola, according to some) was to go to England to found the Royal Humane Society and the London Medical Society. (Lettsome is another last name still in use with local families.)

Abolition of slavery in British territories around the world brought a quick end to the sugar barons' and plantation owners' wealth. The recession that followed saw some estates abandoned. A couple of hurricanes and, finally, a native uprising in 1853 completed the process of disintegration. Most of the white people who'd escaped murder and fire simply left, and the former slaves allowed the old properties to waste away.*

Some of the more enterprising hoteliers have partially restored former plantations and these are undeniably attractive. One such is the more recently completed *Sugar Mill Estate Hotel* by Leonard and Joan Kushins, with a setting worthy of a botanical garden in its beauty. Another—long in the making, and one of the earliest hostelries in Tortola—is *Long Bay Hotel*, where the sugar mill serves as an attractive focal point to the garden and beach area.

Flying In

There are three airfields in the territory, at Beef Island, at Virgin Gorda, and at Anegada (the one coral-based island in the group, which lies some distance to the northeast of Tortola).

*Some idea of the quality of these earlier properties can be gauged by examination of a number of their wells. The masonry in their construction is unbelievably good, with fine brickwork, precision laid, and in some instances, relatively intact.

All flight operations are supervised from Beef Island tower, which is operational 1130–2200Z (the BVI is −4 GMT, making this an 0730–1800 local-time operation). There are a VASI system and runway lighting, but night operations require prior permission and notification. Beef's 3,600-ft asphalt strip mostly faces the prevailing trade wind, though be prepared to crab or dip a wing on short final as the apparent wind sometimes shifts. Flight information service is on 124.9, 122.8, and 118.4—the last frequency is the tower and is *advisory only* when the airport is closed.

Over at Virgin Gorda there's a 3,100-ft strip and at Anegada it's 2,500 ft. The 028 radial of the St. Croix VOR (COY 108.2 DME Ch 19), which takes you to Anegada, also passes extremely close to the strip in Virgin Gorda. The DOD Flight Information Publication A-2 (Puerto Rico Area) shows local electronic navigational aids.

The Virgin Gorda strip is parallel to the shore and it's a good idea to inspect the windsock at the southern end of the runway carefully before deciding which way you'll land. Generally required is a south-to-north landing—make a right-hand pattern to avoid contour flying your downwind and base. The hillside to the west of the runway is usually good for some marginal lift, but don't rely on it. In fact, stay away from it. And if you've any doubts about the field, overfly it a couple of times to study the layout. It's not really tricky but it has caught some less-than-wary aircrews. For this reason the local Director of Civil Aviation is supposed to be contacted for prior approval of single-engine aircraft.

On takeoff, especially if you're making that north-to-south run with more than a marginal downwind component, track toward the shore once you've built flying speed to avoid the gentle—but *deadly*—escarpment at the far end of the field. Acceptance of some crosswind component and a south-to-north takeoff is usually best policy here.

There are few tricks about landing at Anegada, home of its own indigenous iguana, which will usually hiss politely if you invade its territory and come too close. (You will be unlikely to see one, however, since the local dogs have all but finished them off.)

The 2,500-ft runway is mostly aligned with the prevailing tradewind—unusual in the Caribbean, where all too often the only piece of land suitable for a strip has a built-in crosswind—and apart

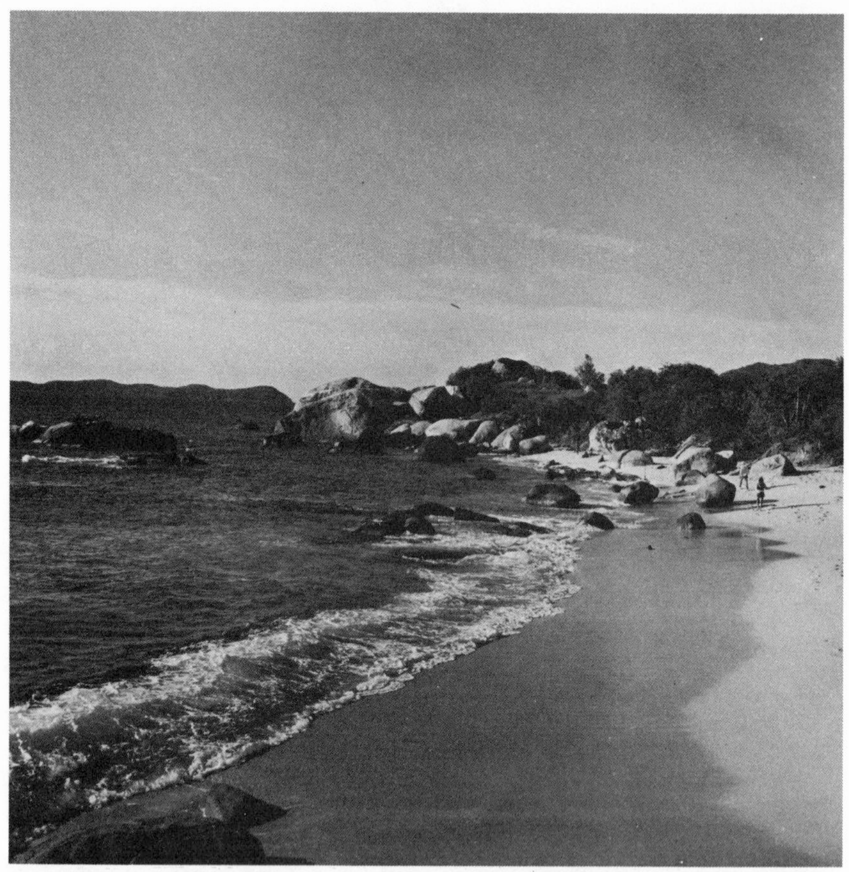

The Baths at Virgin Gorda. To appreciate this unusual formation of rocks you need to go inside. Watch your purse at this beach, however, as a local enchantment has been known to cause the disappearance of valuables.

from moderate to strong thermal activity, it's quite straightforward. Tighten your own belt, and tell the crew to tighten theirs, as you approach the island, and keep one hand on the throttle for landing and takeoff. Oh, and you'll definitely need those *astrolon* blinds to protect your avionics if you plan to park here any length of time. And yes, watch out for goats on the runway—a clearing pass is sometimes needed.

For local tourism queries, call 43134 during office hours and 42831 evenings.

Exploring the Territory

Because it consists of numerous islands in the midst of blue seas, one of the best ways to vacation here is in a boat. There are a number of firms in Tortola specializing in bareboat charter, the best known of which is perhaps Jack Van Ost's *Caribbean Sailing Yachts;* they have even developed their own craft, of which the CSY 44 has already established a reputation of excellence. *Fleet Indigo,* based at West End, Tortola, has a smaller fleet of some thirty boats varying in size from their Bombay 31s to 37s and 44-footers. *The Moorings Ltd.* established by Charlie and Ginny Cory (now owner-managers of the 24-room Mariner Inn) offers Gulfstar 37s and Custom 50s (with no less than three cabins and three heads) plus Morgan Out Island 36s and 41s. These are available with or without skipper and crew. *Latitude 18° 25' Charters* offers the incredible Cheoy Lee series Midshipmen 40s at the Marina in Road Town.

If you're bareboating, you should check *The Ample Hamper* for quality provisioning. They have food, food and more food. It's one of the specialties of this incredible grocery, which you'll find near The Moorings on Wickham's Cay II at the Village Cay Marina. They also stock more than two hundred liquor items, which run the gamut from low-priced to deluxe, with champagnes, wines, and spirits. The edibles are outstanding, and include the best that Europe can supply, including Italian cold meats, English pies, and an incredible collection of cheeses. They even can supply you with Cuban cigars.

Carib Casseroles specializes in some twenty-five gourmet dishes, ready cooked and frozen, plus such items as fish chowder (creamy), gazpacho (piquant and delicious), beef provencal and stroganoff, Bahamian conch fritters for cocktail fare, curries, and even the traditional Trinidadian *roti,* made fresh on Fridays and available frozen the rest of the week.

Since you'll most likely do a land tour out of Beef (the port of entry), let's take the trip into Road Town (fare now about $7.00).

That Queen Elizabeth bridge, you'll find, is somewhat small to have had so great an effect on development. You'll also note that the island of Tortola is strangely beautiful with numerous contrasts in scenery; indeed, as you flew in, you'll have spotted the remnant of rain forest on Tortola's Mt. Sage. There are numbers of sandy bays, with palm trees of course, and other more scenic coves with outcroppings of stone and reefs where the pelicans fish.

The roads in Tortola are comparatively good for the most part, and the route from Beef Island to Road Town as it winds round the cliffs and into valleys is a delight for most of the way. You'll quickly develop a feel for the island as you ride through the villages of Long Look and East End where wandering chickens and the occasional goat help slow down the traffic.

Your driver will possibly point out the former *Colonial Manor Hotel,* recently taken over by the Prospect Reef people for a new venture, before the road winds down toward the marina area at Maya Cove—one of the sailing centers here, and a noted hurricane "hole" when the winds start to blow. The road continues toward Road Town via Baugher's Bay (the radio station ZBVI is here), where an old fort's ruins can be found on a hill and where a rum distillery was in business until a few years ago, and so past the deep-water harbor, where you'll find another marina, The Moorings, and the Mariner Inn.

On your right, just a short step down the road, is the *Treasure Isle Hotel,* now run by Peter and Mary Wimbush, long popular with business people, and rebuilt some years back by a Bermudian syndicate. It is currently merging with the aforementioned Mariner Inn. If you wanted to head north to the other shore, you'd make a right turn just a short step farther along. Staying with the shore road brings you on to Wickham's Cay I, a land reclamation project that was a source of much discussion before it began. The shore road runs parallel to Main Street, and is called Wickham's Cay Road. Main Street has shops and stores—and still a few chickens, the *Island Sun* newspaper office (editor/publisher Carlos Downing is a good source of local gossip), and eventually the government buildings and post office. Just beyond is the Tourist Office, where they're delighted to help with almost any query.

Leaving town and continuing westward brings you past Peebles Hospital—medical services in the BVI are very good—and the Government House, an attractive and solid building set in its own gardens. If you want, you can still sign your name in the book at the gate.

Yet another marina is to your left as you pass by the *Sea View* and *Fort Burt* hotels. And there are also some apartments in the marina area, known as *Moorings Dockside.* The *Prospect Reef Resort* lies next on your left. This is an ambitious project, and the owners are planning a windsurfing center based at the former Colonial Manor Hotel. They also have some other acreage in the

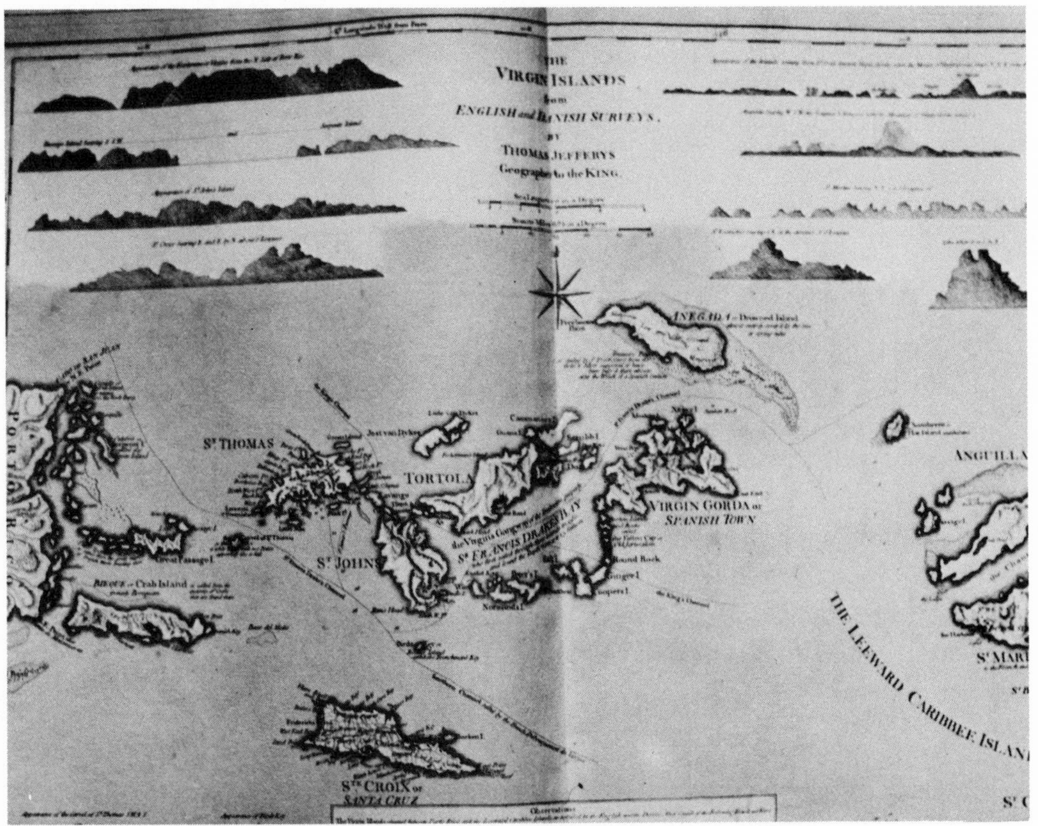

The Virgin Islands, according to Cartographer Royal Thomas Jeffreys.

Paraquita Bay area, and are determined to be an important part of the tourism effort of these islands. Their *Road Town Resort* consists of luxury units of cottages and villas, suites and condominia. The restaurant is spoken of highly—as is that at Fort Burt.

The road continues west through Sea Cows Bay and on to *Nanny Cay* where you'll find reasonable apartments with view for rent. Down toward the western end of the island is Frenchman's Cay, and the home of the *Blue Indigo Fleet* at West End. Over at Belmont Bay lies *Smuggler's Cove Hotel*, with housekeeping cottages, an attractive beach—one of the best in the territory—and a pleasant informal atmosphere. Then comes *Long Bay Estate* and its hotel, with reasonable rates (housekeeping if you prefer) and an attractive and charming setting. The road continues around the shore to Little Apple Bay where you'll find *Cliff Houses, Sebastians-on-the-Beach*—founded by the widow of the once famous St. Thomas Sebastians, now run by a new group—and the *Sugar Mill Estate*.

Wild limes grow by the roadside, and beautiful oleanders as you continue on to Cane Garden Bay, where there's an authentic old-fashioned rum distillery. You should not miss that chance to sample this local brew—it's rum, all right, and will probably rejuvenate the hairs on your chest. *Jill's Beach Bar*, simple but inviting, is open daily for lunch and dinner, breakfast by advance reservation only.

The road now climbs steeply over a saddle, and brings you back to Road Town on the southern side. On the center of the ridge of the mountain is the scenic Ridge Road by which you can reach Brewers Bay,* Josiahs Bay, and eventually the east end of Tortola in one direction; in the other it will take you to Sage Mountain, where wild lemons and lemon grass scent the air as you approach the forest. You'll find stands of mahogany and teak in addition to white cedar on the slopes, and you'll pass the Cable & Wireless communications center on your way.

*Site of the only campground in the BVI; $10 per night includes tent.

The Spanish Copper Mine at Virgin Gorda, worked by Cornishmen during the Napoleonic Wars and again assayed in the late Sixties (our time, that is).

VIRGIN GORDA

The flight from Beef to Virgin Gorda takes but a few minutes but gives you a chance to inspect the islands around. Virgin Gorda was originally settled by the Spanish who searched for gold, found copper, and after a brief while closed down shop, all in the early 1500s. The name means Fat Virgin. The copper mines were worked by Cornishmen for about twenty years around the turn of the 18th–19th century, and briefly inspected in the 1960s for significant deposits of nickel, bauxite, molybdenum, and other useful minerals. While traces were found, they were in insufficient quantities to satisfy either the needs of the prospectors or the local government.

It was Laurance Rockefeller who was to put the island on the tourist map. Until the opening of Rockresort's Little Dix Bay, the only places for visitors to stay were the former *Lord Nelson's Inn* now extensively refurbished and known as *Bluebeard's Tavern* near the rock formation known as The Baths; and a small local hostelry. Today there is more competition with a variety of accommodation plans available.

In the southern half of the island, there are housekeeping arrangements available at *Guavaberry Spring Bay*, run by old-timers Charles and Betty Roy, and *Fischers Cove Beach*, owned by Andy and Norma Flax, plus accommodations at the *Olde Yard Inn, Ocean View Hotel* and, of course, Little Dix Bay and Bluebeard's Tavern. A marina provides a yacht harbor—shopping center plus a traditional English pub, the former *Bath and Turtle*, now known as the *Olde Yard Inn*, with 10 rooms, where your hosts are Joseph and Ellen Devine. Here you'll find DIVE BVI, which runs daily dive trips, and provides Scuba Pro and Ducor diving equipment for sale or rent. Owner-manager is Joe Giacinto, an old BVI hand who has done much in discovering interesting wrecks in the region's waters.

Here also are *The Spouter*, still the only ice cream parlor in Virgin Gorda; *Gorda Paco*, which offers an interesting line of jewelry featuring stones found in the old copper mine; the *Wine Cellar*, which features homemade breads, cheeses from all over the world and a full selection of liquors. A beauty salon, a craft shop, a laundromat, plus a supermarket and *O'Neal and Grandson's* store complete the picture. At O'Neal's you can arrange horseback riding, and they can also supply you with underwater cameras.

The northern half of the island is mountainous but it's here you'll find the fabled small *Biras Creek Resort*, which offers incredible food and Norwegian-modern accommodations in 30 suite-cottages. Jorgen and Libby Thoning have managed this elegant operation since it began in 1975. The rates are high—just slightly less than at Little Dix Bay—but definitely worth it if you enjoy a vacation that has just about everything, including peace.

Just slightly lower in price is the *Bitter End Yacht Club* run by Don and Janis Neal, another home away from home (Biras Creek has a marina, too) for sailing folk in these waters. Only nine rooms, to be sure, but there's an excellent beach with good snorkeling and scuba close by. Your hotel rate here includes use of the hotel's Laser, Cal 27s, and Rhodes 19s.

Just to the north, on Mosquito Island, is *Drake's Anchorage*, another of the early established hideaways in these islands, found-

The upper slopes of Mount Sage are still unspoiled and include stands of mahogany, some citrus, and wild avocados.

ed in the days when there was no telephone in the islands and everyone tuned in each day at noon on the medium wave band for "children's hour" in which gossip and news, arrival times of visitors and boats were exchanged. The beachfront restaurant is popular with the sailing crowd, as is the Wrecked Virgin bar, and there's a private beach for the *au naturel* folk.

ANEGADA

This northeasternmost of the Virgins has long been known to sailors for its reefs, which have claimed more than three hundred ships since the 1500s. The island lies low, coral on limestone, the highest point a scant thirty feet above sea level. Consequently, it is almost invisible, and since there is sparse vegetation, few clues warn the approaching mariner, which explains how those reefs still manage to continue to trap the unwary.

Horseshoe Reef—which is where you'll find some of the finest scuba diving in the area—sweeps round southeast then south for almost two-thirds the way back to Virgin Gorda. Add to all this a strong tidal set that draws vessels toward their graves, and you'll understand why the local bareboat companies refer to it as the forbidden island. Most will refuse to let you visit without a pilot.

The sailors' navigational trick is to go in and out of harbor when the sun is at its highest. This means anytime from around 10:30 AM to about 2:30 PM. Even the government boat tends to observe this schedule, since the coral heads that can trap the unwary can best be seen then.

Still, if you look at the sailing chart you'll note (1) there are no aids to navigation, and (2) there are no soundings for a three-mile area to the south.

There's a local population of around 290, and there are vast expanses of deserted beaches on the northern and western shores. Accommodations are available at the *Reefs Hotel* in air-conditioned units available for housekeeping. There are a restaurant and a commissary, but if you plan on living it up just a little, stock up in the Ample Hamper before you leave Tortola.

The Soares family, who own *Neptune's Treasure*, a bar and restaurant on the water, were originally Bermuda fishing people of Portuguese extraction. Old man Joe is an archetypal patriarch who supervises his family, finds time to raise goats and pigs—and pigeons—and a garden, and with his wife, Grandma, helps Vernon and wife and daughters run this incredible restaurant. The speciality of the house is the local lobster, really a crayfish, of which the Soares family manage to find a supply that, in size and weight, eludes almost all other restaurants.

Tuck in and enjoy!

JOST VAN DYKE

Still one of the least spoiled islands in the entire Caribbean, Jost van Dyke is relatively hilly, with two incredibly lovely beaches at White Bay and Great Harbor, plus numerous smaller ones. For your private Swiss Family Robinson vacation there are two housekeeping arrangements: at *White Bay Sandcastle*, owner-managed by George and Marie Myrick, there are four cottages with basic services only, ideal for families or couples. You'll provision either from St. Thomas or from Tortola. At *Sandy Ground* there are eight homes for rent, and again, you'll have to do your own provisioning (remember the Ample Hamper, please; you'll be glad you did). For additional information, contact the BVI Tourist Board in Road Town, Tortola, BVI.

Jost van Dyke is best known to visiting yachtspeople, who still make a point of whooping it up on the weekend (and other nights) at *Foxy's Tamarind Restaurant*. Foxy is a thin, medium-tall "barnya"* Virgin Islander with street smarts culled from most points north and west. He's an interesting guitarist/singer and is the focal point of entertainment at this tropic isle encounter point. The food ranges from the okay to the delicious, depending on who's in charge; the drinks are predictably strong.

A relaxed atmosphere prevails at Foxy's—if you're really *bad* he'll probably include you in one of his extemporaneous calypsos. There are usually maracas, drums of various sorts, and other temporary instruments on which visitors—if they have rhythm—can join in. (A pocketknife against a Heineken bottle qualifies as an "instrument.")

*"barnya"—approximate pronunciation of island dialect phrase meaning "born here" of significance since certain privileges obtain to native born children, i.e. born in the BVI.

ACROSS THE CHANNEL

A string of islands runs down from the south end of Virgin Gorda to the southwest. The first is Fallen Jerusalem, a delightful little spot where the skinny-dipping crowd used to gather. Separated from Ginger Island by several clumps of reef and islet (including Round Rock), Fallen Jerusalem actually has a forlorn air about it, as if it had once had the makings of a great island but got changed at the last moment into an afterthought.

Worth the visit—by boat—if only to say you've been there.

Cooper Island, like Ginger Island, is believed to have been named by former mariners for what it could produce. In the case of Ginger Island, wild ginger is supposed to have grown, and there are some rootlike plants that have a ginger flavor, though they may be a tropical species of mandrake. Cooper Island had trees once upon a time, but over the years most were used for coopering—the making of barrels—for fresh water supplies. Until a few years ago it was to this island that local boatbuilders came for frames for the vessels they were building. And until recently, the old system was used to make boats. You went about until you found a tree that had a limb approximately the shape you wanted, and then you cut off the limb—or, if you needed the wood, you took out the entire tree.

Salt Island is named for its salt ponds, which formerly supplied the Royal Navy with salt for brining meat and other produce, and was for a while—in the late 17th and early 18th centuries—a useful export under the British Crown. The salt evaporation ponds (three) have not been put to commercial use as yet, but could probably justify a small packaging operation to be sold via health-food stores and to the carriage trade.

Cooper Island has a pleasant snorkeling beach near the boat jetty, close to the *Cooper Island Beach Club*. The land is privately owned, but you can use the beach if you come in from the sea. Salt Island has a small settlement on the north side, and once a year has a small festival and barbecue to which everyone is invited. On the eastern shore is a beautiful reef-protected lagoon, great for marine enthusiasts.

A small moundlike island known as Dead Man's Chest (or Dead Chest) separates this group from Peter Island, site of another of the

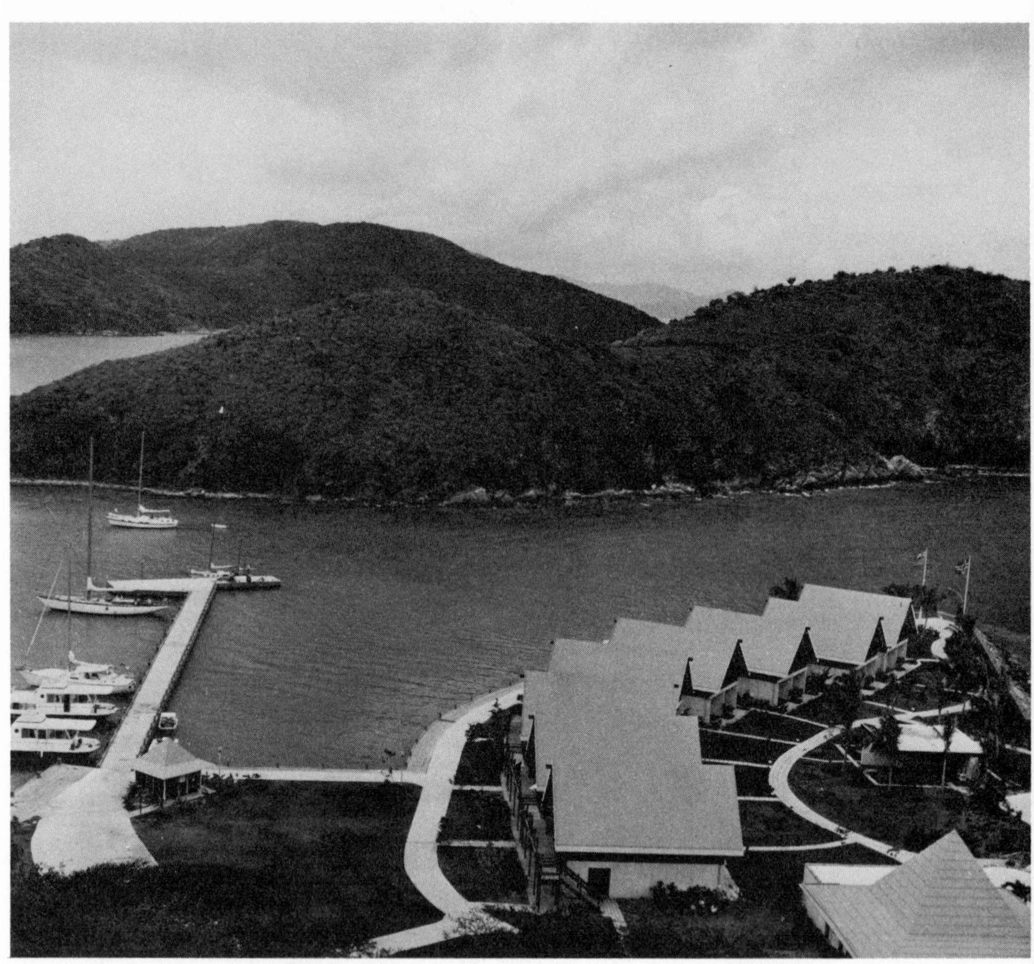

Peter Island Yacht Club—ideal for the sybarite who wants to get away from it all.

BVI's deluxe resorts. This is the resort that Peter Smedvig, the Norwegian shipman entrepreneur, has built with classic Scandinavian good taste. There are a swimming pool, tennis, air conditioning, telephones in rooms, room service, and anchorage with marine facilities—reservations preferred if you want to stern/bow dock in—plus fueling, and shower rooms (the Clubhouse bar is open until 6 PM to non-dinner guests). The restaurant is worth the detour here, with traditional Norwegian-flavored dining and numerous delicacies flown in.

Last but not least is Norman Island, the treasure island, with some caves you can boat into and a pleasantly sheltered anchorage. No people aboard, but numerous goats. Rumor has it that some get barbecued for feasts 18th-century style on the beach. Bring your own grog.

AND THE OTHERS

Well, yes, there are indeed more. There's *Marina Cay*, for example, one of the archetypes of all Virgin Island vacations, originally built by Alan Batham, and now a home away from home for the knowledgeable. It's not, to be sure, the last word in luxury or elegance, but it maintains a delightful out-island charm that is hard to beat. Especially recommended to those who are interested in diving (full range of equipment and air), or who are looking for a slightly slower-paced holiday.

Yes, that's Jacqueline Bisset, seen here on location for an underwater sequence from "The Deep," at the Rhone wreck.

Marina Cay is its own island, just a few minutes from Beef Island airport to its own dock. Meet the fleet for Happy Hour nightly at the *Banyan Tree Bar*, live music Wednesdays. Dinner for galley slaves includes fresh grouper, half a lobster, or filet mignon with complimentary wine, at 7:30 PM. Reservations preferred.

The *Last Resort Hotel* is another self-contained island resort. It's the smallest in the region on Bellamy Cay and run today by Tony and Jackie Snell. Like many other ventures in the area it has had an on/off reputation that goes back in time.

At time of writing, this friendly small island hotel *is* in operation and in no way is it to be thought of as a Last Resort. The natives are friendly and entertaining (Tony is a former show person), and if you don't mind confining yourself to a tiny island for overnight sleeping, the rest of the islands are yours to enjoy.

And then there's *Little Thatch.*

At time of writing, this (often a port of call in stormy weather for visitors returning from Jost van Dyke to West End, Tortola) is not operating. When it is, this is a neat, rustic, low-keyed, charming small hostelry that is definitely worth the visit. Check with BVI Tourist Board for state of play.

Dining Out

For the most part, this usually means—for visitors—dining in, since the locals and visitors while meeting, seldom meet for the same reasons. Thus it is a little unlikely that you'll be swept off to a dinner engagement aboard a yacht or at some fine mansion.

On the other hand, the people who elect to live in the BVI have, for the most part, an interest in matters *gastronomique* even if on occasion their better intentions on the subject have become waylaid by Colonel Saunders and the Big King (though, as yet, none of these fast-food merchants has appeared).

Little Dix Bay has always attempted to do well by its visitors, including those who came to dinner. *Biras Creek* and the *Bitter End* have both built a substantial following with the sailing fraternity. All are on Virgin Gorda.

On Tortola, *Long Bay Hotel* has for years been a friendly standby producing mostly good value for money (depending mostly on the manager), while *Prospect Reef*—new and bidding for nonpareil status—tries very hard, as do *Treasure Isle* and the *Sugar Mill Estate Hotels.*

Ali Baba, a recent Mid-Eastern spot in Road Town, offers Lebanese and other specialties, while *Cell 5, Maria's,* the venerable *Poop Deck,* and *Upstairs, Downstairs* provide occasionally effulgent concurrence.

What the British Virgins Are—and What They Aren't

Numerous resorts and other enterprises have appeared and then disappeared or been sold to new owners, primarily because outsiders didn't understand that life in the Caribbean is slow and easy. It doesn't lend itself to production-line speed-up to achieve economy.

This kind of life is a particular characteristic of the British Virgins. The first visitors to the area in modern times recognized it as a uniquely beautiful region that needed to be protected against big real estate developers more interested in money than the islanders' quality of life. For the most part, protective efforts have been successful. The return of the Scandinavians has been particularly beneficial. They are cosmopolitan, people of taste and discernment, and capable of giving Americans a wide-world view of tourism.

If you enjoy sailing, but are not too experienced, this is where you'll vacation.

If you're up for something that includes sand and sea, you'll check this out.

If you're a captain of industry—anywhere in the world—try a weekend at Peter Island or Biras Creek for the time of your life. Rent a Boston Whaler to visit the rest of the islands. You deserve it.

To check for current data: British Virgin Islands Tourist Information, 515 Madison Avenue, New York, N.Y. 10022, or telephone (212) 371-6759. *The Welcome,* a bimonthly magazine published by the BVI tourist board, is also available from BVI Information Service at 801 York Mills Road, Don Mills, Ontario M3B1X7 Canada; also available at BVI hotels and stores.

Sint Maarten [Saint Martin]

Flying In

The flight from the Virgin Islands to Sint Maarten (Saint Martin) is around 100 NM depending on which airport you fly from. It's farthest from St. Thomas (about 115 NM) and closest to Beef or Virgin Gorda (about 85 NM), but it is across the Anegada Passage and there's usually a subtle trade-wind component you'll want to figure into your calculations.

Pilots of single-engined aircraft will tend to take time to climb to a reasonable cruise altitude for this flight over water. There's an NDB at *Princess Juliana Field* (308 PJM), but for much of the way you can fly a back course on either the St. Thomas or the St. Croix VOR (approximately 110° and 87° respectively). Since there are no checkpoints below, monitor your flight very carefully. Occasional rain squalls and small clouds can make it difficult to find St. Maarten if you're not checking, but on a clear day you'll be able to discern it—and neighboring Anguilla to the north—from way out.

In addition to monitoring your flight instruments, keep an eye on the swells below to give yourself a secondary check on your heading. Don't forget to reset your gyro every ten minutes or so.

The tower at the airport also provides approach service, and it's sensible to tune in (tower is 118.7) some way out since the airport can get quite busy at times, as it's the Airport of Entry to the island. The runway is 09/27 and tower will almost certainly instruct you to use 09 unless there's an unusual downwind component (almost never); the runway is a healthy 7,050 ft long.

Background Briefing

For local tourism queries on the Dutch side, call 2337 during the day and 2293 evenings; on the French side, 87-50-36 and 87-50-60.

Carib artifacts and the ruins of rudimentary dwellings near Moho Well and Billy Folly confirm the earlier habitation of St. Martin by these Amerindian cannibals. The island's name was originally Italian—San Martino—for St. Martin of Tours because it was this saint's name day when Columbus (second voyage) sighted it, back in 1493.

That the island's name is spelled either Sint Maarten (Dutch) or Saint Martin (French) is because this 37-square-mile piece of real estate enjoys dual ownership. The French part is a *commune* of the *departement* of Guadeloupe—itself one of four overseas departments of France (the others being Martinique, Guyane-Guyana and Reunion). The Dutch part of the island is, with Saba, St. Eustatius (or "Statia" as it's more popularly known), Aruba, Bonaire, and Curacao, known as the Netherlands Antilles which are (at time of writing) an autonomous part of the Kingdom of the Netherlands.

It wasn't until the 1620s or '30s that French and Dutch settlers began to make their presence felt here, adding to the occasional privateer and buccaneer. The Spanish made a brief foray in early 1640 but didn't stay, and it was left to the legendary "Silvernails" (peg-legged Peter Stuyvesant) to start the real rush to the island in 1644. The story goes that he lost his leg in defending the local settlement against a Spanish army.

Then, in 1648, so the same story continues, a group of French and Dutch prisoners of war were able to turn the tables on their Spanish captors, who were decoyed elsewhere, and they found that through the success of their joint operation there was an island up for grabs.

The romantic tale goes on to the effect that, unwilling to turn upon each other, the Dutch and French decided to define their respective territories by a walking match. The French won the

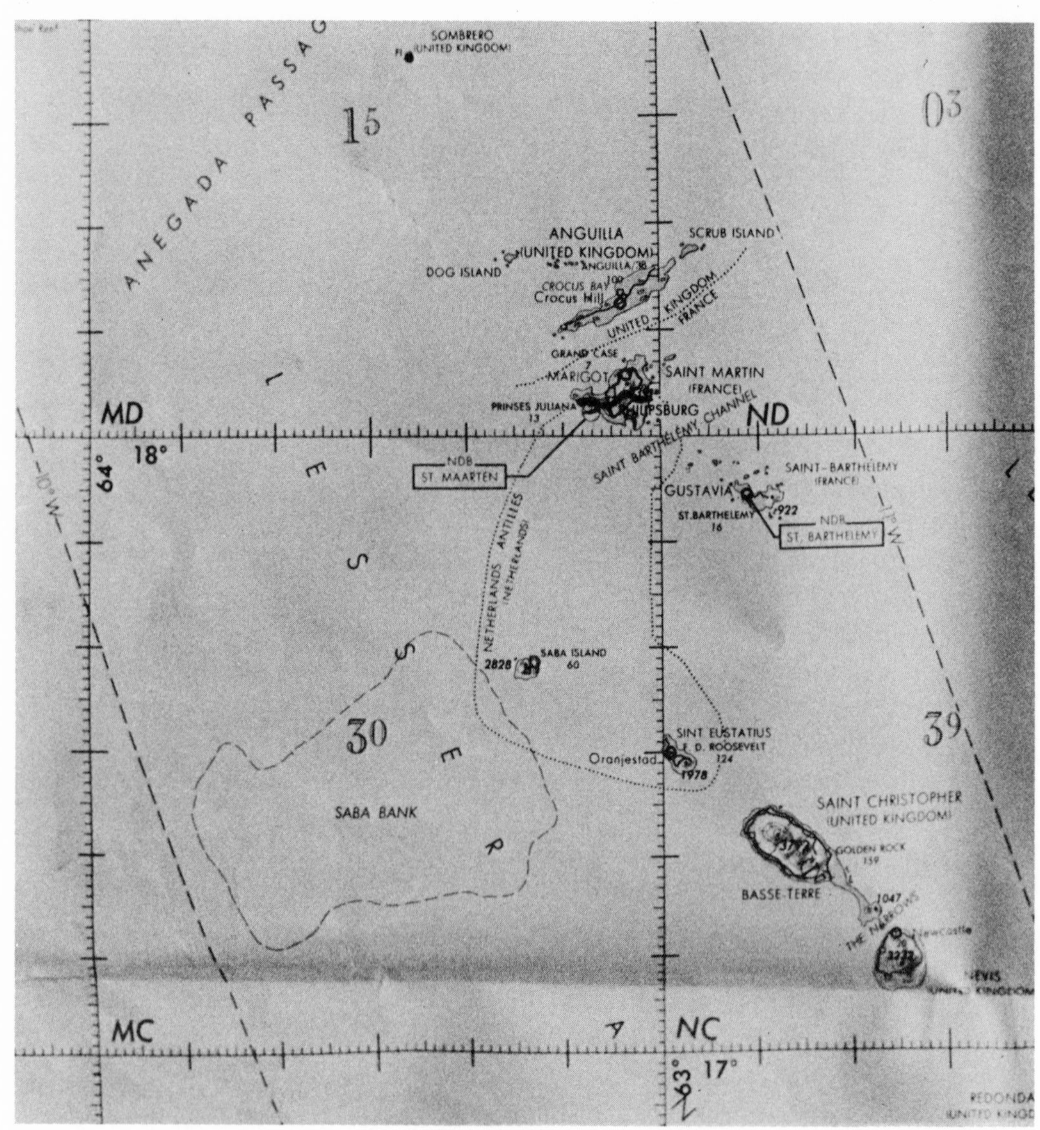

Detail from chart showing St. Martin in relation to Anguilla, Saba, Sint Eustatius, and Saint Christopher (St. Kitts).
(Not to be used for navigation.)

greater half (21 square miles), but the Dutch part turned out to be more valuable on account of the salt pond. Since there was a lot more arguing over the next several years (one report has it that the Dutch side may have changed hands as many as sixteen times after the original accord), the story's unlikely to be true. What is true is that today the islanders *do* live in complete harmony, and the name "The Friendly Island" is well deserved.

There's no Customs, no Immigration, no bureaucracy at the mutual frontier. Just a simple sign welcoming you to the French (or Dutch) side of the island. World leaders would do well to visit this little haven of peace and learn how these representatives of two totally different cultures and heritages have managed to make their island a harmonious place to be.

The south side of the island—where the main airport is—is Dutch, and most days in early morning or late afternoon you can see the neighboring islands of Saba, Statia, St. Kitts, and St. Barts. Saba's nearly 3,000-ft silhouette can be made out quite easily, some 27 miles to the south. The volcanic "Quill" of Statia is half the height but can be seen from the shore on fairly clear days, while St. Kitts—forty-four miles distant—is usually only visible when it's CAVU. From Pointe Blanche, St. Bart's is easily seen—just 14 miles off.

Philipsburg is the capital of the Dutch side, and it stretches out across Great Bay with the Great Salt Pond behind it.

Located on this narrow sand isthmus, Philipsburg was officially founded in 1763 by one Commander John Philips, a Scotsman in Dutch employ. Philips was also responsible for restoring Fort Amsterdam during his stay.

Architecturally, the town is interesting for the use of shingles almost everywhere. And because it's strung out in a line it's easy to move around. There are two main streets—Voorstraat, or Front Street, and Achterstraat, or Back Street. Some reclamation work was recently completed to provide space for a ring road.

On the airport side of the bay are the ruins of Fort Amsterdam, while on the other is the well-known *La Panoramique* restaurant, where chef Felix Teisseire and maitre d' Daniel combine to put you at ease with some of the best French food on the island.

There are more than thirty beaches on the island, but you'll have to take small tracks, often rutted and bumpy, to get to them. Once there you'll frequently be all by yourself. Another way to find your own private beach is to take a small boat and approach from the sea.

The roads are mostly good on the Dutch side, and fair on the French side, and one of the best values for the money is the bus

Fort Amsterdam, from the battlements which guarded against the former hosts of Spain.

ride from Philipsburg to France. This $1.00 round-trip experience enables you to enjoy many miles of attractive island scenery and two noticeably different cultures. A good place to catch the bus is in front of the post office on Front Street. If you sit on the right side of the bus, you'll get some interesting views of the maze of little courtyards and alleys that are part of this island's appeal.

The bus heads out toward Marigot via a fertile mountain valley known in the 18th century as Dutch Cul de Sac, which used to be the home of a number of sugar plantations. One of these former plantations has been restored the way it might have been some 300 years ago, and is now a small 9-room hotel called *Mary's Fancy*; it's set in extensive grounds and the well-known *Gianni's Restaurant* is on the premises. The landscaping is delightful, and the interior decoration seems authentic.

Next stop is along the road between Cole Bay Hill and Cay Bay Hill where Stuyvesant lost his leg in 1644. You can change buses just a bit further on for the ride past Juliana Airport (another 50 cents); or, if you stay on your original bus, you head toward the small border monument that was erected in 1948 to commemorate 300 peaceful years. Even if you miss it you'll quickly notice the change in ambiance—and not just from the road itself. Everything spells "French" from the sounds and smells to style of the architecture.

If you did change buses, you'll first pass the *Oasis Rendez-Vous* restaurant, part of the *Simson Bay Beach Hotel*, and then the charming *La Pavillon* restaurant. Owned by Max Petit, a chef superieur in his own right, this is the place for those who are looking for excellent French food cooked to order. There's a fixed-price menu in the French style, or an extensive a la carte offering.

Simson Bay Village is a pleasantly quaint fishing hamlet that you drive through on your way to *Mary's Boon* (near Runway 27 at Juliana). Mary's Boon was started by Mary Pomeroy—herself a pilot and a descendant of a Knight of Malta. The name's on the roof and there are ten large bed-sitting rooms with kitchenette. The beach here has powdery white sand and this special is for the young and young at heart. Looking across toward Mullet Bay, you can see numerous resort hotels to fit just about every taste from the *Concord* (transplanted from the Catskills with its own casino) to the *Caravanserai* and the *Summit*. Down at Baie Longue, on the other side of the frontier, is the Moorish Mediterranean mini-village La Samanna, on its own four thousand feet of white beach. You can stay either in the twin-bedded rooms in the main buildings or in the suites in the villas.

As the management advises; "It's not for everyone," but if you are looking for something that is untypical, informal, peaceful, and somewhat exclusive, this is very possibly the place for you. The food here—there are kitchens in the villas if you want to do it yourself—is some of the finest French and Creole in the island.

There are a fresh-water pool, tennis courts, snorkeling, water skiing, sailing, and island excursions—all included in the relatively high rates.

Back on the bus, the road continues around the enormous Simson Bay Lagoon via Baie Rouge, from where you can see the site of what was to have been one of the finest resorts in the world, La Belle Creole at Pointe du Bluff. Innumerable legal hassles, in which several banks played a part, brought this dream-world creation to an abrupt halt some years ago.

Just by the Marigot bridge—which occasionally opens for sailboats—at Nettle Bay Beach, is *Le Santal,* where Jean and Evelyne Dupont provide seafood delicacies (their fresh red snapper is flambeed and filleted right at your table) while you enjoy the view of Anguilla.

And so to Marigot, capital of the French side of the island.

If you're into French and Creole cooking you will find Marigot a gastronome's delight. There are a number of excellent French bistros including the noted *Beausejour,* and the authentically Provencal restaurant *La Calanque,* where the Bertets, a French couple, provide a gourmet menu that includes such items as escargot de bourgogne (snails bourgogne style), crepe de langouste (crepe with lobster), canard aux bananes (duck cooked with plantains), and so on. There's also an excellent wine cellar.

Also worth noting is *Le Caraibe,* in the inner court of the new-world *Hotel Patio.* The cordon-bleu chef here provides such items as blanquette de veau (delicious veal), lobster thermidor, plus other fare that comes with quality French cooking. And there's *L'Aventure Restaurant and Bar,* said to be the most recommended restaurant in the entire island. Their red snapper with fresh vegetables and oranges has earned praise in Europe, as have their Creole conch stew and chicken Florentine. Others speak highly of the fettucine and pesto alla Genovese. Claims the *Miami Herald*: "Nowhere else in the universe can you find such Continental delights." Check this one out for yourself.

Proceeding onward out of Marigot you come to *Le Grand Saint Martin Beach Hotel,* another first-class resort, with many rooms furnished with antique-style four-posters. Fresh-water swimming pool, enormous beach, and evening activities at the Hibiscus Club discotheque. Meanwhile, the road continues onward to the picturesque village of Grand Case where if it's time for food you should check out *Le Fish Pot*. As its name implies, this is the place for *fruits de mer*, all caught fresh daily and prepared according to your pleasure either *a la creole* (island style) or *a la francaise* (French style). There's meat and poultry if you don't much care for fish, but fish is the house specialty.

You are now in the neighborhood of the island's other airport, known locally as *Esperance Airport*, but listed officially as *Grand Case*. It's not an Airport of Entry and the runway is only 1,900 ft, but if you want to hop over the island—and have lunch at the Fish Pot—you might like to check it out.

From here it's less than five miles to Anguilla.

The road meanders around the airport toward Baie de l'Embouchure where the *Galion Beach Club* is to be found; the *Coralita Hotel* is nearby. A detour toward the coast brings you to *Oyster Pond Yacht Club*, and via Naked Boy Hill back to Philipsburg.

The Dutch Side

Accommodations

If you want a self-sufficient vacation in St. Maarten, you may do well to check the fairly extensive listing of individual homes available for rent provided by the Tourist Board. These range from simple 1-room furnished apartments on the beach to some quite luxurious villas with spectacular views, maid service, and so on. It depends on how much you want to spend.

At the top end of the scale, there's no doubt that the *Caravanserai* still leads, though its proximity to the airport means noisy days. There are some 60 air-conditioned rooms, pool, water sports available, even shops and beauty parlor. And the beach is perfect. Dining by candlelight, on the point between Maho and Burgeux bays.

Little Bay Beach Hotel, near Cay Bay Hill and just outside of Philipsburg, offers fun, glamor, excitement, and a private beach that's nearly a mile long, plus a casino. With 120 air-conditioned rooms it enjoys a year-round occupancy rate of around 80 percent, which means you should check out some of the packages offered or book well in advance. There's a pool, tennis, water sports, evening entertainment, plus a daily activities program and a beauty parlor.

The Concord Hotel is located just to the left of the approach path to Runway 09, and while you won't hear much airplane activity inside the hotel, outside is another story. Still, people keep on flocking back. There's the usual pool and beach, plus tennis courts, floor shows and dancing and, of course, a casino. This is a good place to check out package arrangements, which can reduce your bill very pleasingly.

In the same vicinity, at Mullet Bay is the *Mullet Bay Beach Hotel* with an incredible 600-plus condominium units spread around the 170-acre site. There are golf, 20 tennis courts, water sports, several restaurants, even its own medical unit and a number of stores. Noted as a convention hotel, you'll need to check early for this one despite its size. Mullet Bay has everything—and a casino.

The *Oyster Pond Yacht Club*, with its Moorish-style architecture is a pleasantly quiet and somewhat exclusive resort. One of the reasons is that it takes quite a while to find the place—nearly half an hour from the airfield by car. There are a couple of tennis courts, swimming pool, and the hotel is known locally as "splendidly chic." This is the winter-only retreat—bar and restaurant only, during the summer—that *Town & Country* magazine has rated as one of the best resort hotels in the world. There are only 20 rooms, so book early.

Next door to the Mullet Bay Beach is the *Summit Hotel*, with 68 air-conditioned rooms, pool, water sports, tennis, casino, nightly entertainment and dancing, and a daily activities program. Once again, package rates are offered and should be checked.

Around the Philipsburg area there is, of course, the *Great Bay Resort Hotel*, with 175 air-conditioned suites and cottages plus the inevitable casino. There's a large pool, all the water sports including glass-bottom boats, and a supper club with nightly shows and French cooking. Packages are usually available.

Of the island's inns possibly the best known is *Pasanggrahan* ("guest house" in an Indonesian dialect), with 24 air-conditioned rooms on the beach and some shops. Long popular with Caribbean residents who have business or pleasure to attend to in St. Maarten, the word got around the world, with the result that repeat business here is phenomenal. Situated next door is the Windward Islanders Shop—a very good store to visit for something rather different in the way of souvenirs or just plain tasteful merchandise.

Captain Hodge's Inn has a certain following (it's almost as pleasant as its neighbor), as does the *Tamarinde Guest House* at Pointe Blanche.

The *Prince Quarter Hotel* also offers reasonable accommodation and reasonable rates. On a hill above town, it has its own pool and has served the best *rijsttafel** in St. Martin. If you've never experienced this Indonesian feast you really should try it.

Notes about Philipsburg would not be complete without reference to the *West Indian Tavern.* Built on the 150-year-old site of St. Maarten's first (and only) synagogue, the Tavern is owned and operated by Irishman Stephen Thompson. There are slow-turning ceiling fans, antique nautical prints, ferns and tropical plants, and Long John Silver, the occasionally blasphemous parrot, and of course, the restaurant itself. Fresh fish and lobster daily, good Madras curries, and plenty of beef for the carnivores make this a delightful place to stop. There are also astonishingly good pina coladas at the bar, and backgammon all day through 2:00 AM.

The French Side

Accommodations

La Samanna Hotel, noted in the Background Briefing, has to rate highly among the choice of hotels in the French part of the island. And not merely for its beach, which is a beauty. It's the incredible quality and thoughtfulness with which everything's been put together, to give the guest a unique experience of what gracious tropical living can be all about. Even the sunsets seem magical here, and the landscaping with oleanders and hibiscus and cactus plants and palms will make your stay here a magic memory.

La Samanna is the epitome of informal, comfortable good times.

For a different style of tropical comfort, the *St. Tropez Beach Hotel* on Marigot Bay offers 130 air-conditioned rooms, each with

**rijsttafel,* literally, rice table. Usually several types of rice are served together with up to 50 side dishes. You can make so many permutations with the varieties of food that are offered that there's always your favorite available. Check current status with Tourist Board.

balcony overlooking the bay, beach, or lagoon and the mountains beyond. The rooms have a pleasantly airy atmosphere and a singular Mediterranean charm. There is, as you might expect, one of the finest beaches in the island for your pleasure, plus the usual aqua sports which here include glass-bottom boats, pedal boats, and fishing.

The food is good standard French fare, and informal island entertainment is provided nightly, or you can dance in the discotheque. The ocean-front rooms are the best, and consequently cost more. Some shops. A number of package arrangements are offered, so check your travel agent.

Still in the luxury category though on a smaller scale is *Le Pirate Inn*, with its fabled cuisine that brings in its numerous fans year after year. Highly casual, the accommodations (10 rooms) are basic, but you have to eat the food to understand the enthusiasm of the gastronomes. Rates include two meals and are very expensive (the meals that is), but in the opinion of many are worth it. Le Pirate is right on the water on the outskirts of town.

Up at Grand Case are the *Hodge Guest House*, with 3 apartments in a beach house, and the *Goetz House* with a similar arrangement. As for Le Pirate, book well ahead for accommodations at these.

A former plantation house awaits restoration.

Mentioned earlier also is *Le Grand St. Martin*—again check for packages for though this is a contemporary modern seaside hotel with the traditional high rates, the discounted prices make this place a worthwhile buy.

Baie de L'Embouchere is where the naturists prefer to sun themselves without benefit of top or bottom. It is also home to *Le Galion Beach Hotel & Club* with spacious suites of comfortable rooms. One of the beaches (there are two) is where the naturists gather. The other is the preserve of the more traditional. Just a little further on, near Oyster Pond Yacht Club, is the *Coralita Beach Hotel* and restaurant.

The hotel is set in 60 tropical acres with views of Caribbean beaches and the sea. The restaurant is generally reckoned to be one of the more beautiful on the island and the seafood comes fresh daily from the ocean under the supervision of the hotel's own fishermen. The hotel also has its own Island group to provide music for dancing nightly and at the Sunday buffet luncheon. Friday is the French West Indian night with bouillabaisse creole, mechoui, and lobster provencal.

Before leaving St. Martin for the other islands of these parts, it's worth mentioning that because St. Martin is virtually a duty-free port, it's often worth purchasing goods for more than your $300.00 allowance, and then paying the duty. To see what's currently available consult *St. Maarten Holiday!*—the monthly guide available in hotel rooms throughout the island and available from the tourist office. Because of these freeport prices, St. Maarten shoppers do surprisingly well on any number of items even when duty has to be paid. Check for details and don't forget to consult US Customs.

Deep-Sea Fishing

There are several good boats available for deep sea-fishing and the fishing grounds are close by. Dolphin (the fish) are generally around from the middle of the high season, in February, through August. September seems to be the best month for bonito and marlin, with wahoo showing from October through January.

Golf

Pro Ron Hallett's team assistants Chuck Frithson and John Montgomery are on hand at the Mullet Bay Beach Hotel's 18-hole course. There's the usual putting green and driving range, plus pro shop, locker rooms, and cocktail lounge. Be sure to reserve a starting time.

Sailing

A number of cruises under sail are available, and for those who want to take the time out to learn to do it for themselves, there's even a sailing school here. Or if you prefer to learn it all on your own, you can start out with a Sunfish, the tyro sailor's basic trainer. Check with your hotel.

Motor Launch

Launch excursions are available to both St. Bart's and to Saba if you'd prefer to make the ride this way to inspect their respective landing strips. Details on times available at your hotel.

Scuba

These are fine waters for scuba diving, with reefs aplenty and the *Prostellyte* man o' war that's as big a fish here for enthusiasts as the *Rhone* is in the BVI. Most hotels have scuba facilities; equipment's available for underwater tours, photography, and night diving, and there are quite a number of NAUI instructors here. If you haven't done it before, you can start under supervision after the basic three-hour course.

If the scuba is good the snorkeling has got to be better, and that's the way it is here. You'll have a chance to clear out those lungs of their pollution as you build your way up to the four-minute dive. And you'll be amazed at how much you can do once you've learned to control your breathing. And how deep you can go once you learn depth control.

And if you simply don't want the hassle, glide gently along the surface and study what's underneath, the water gardens and the creatures of the sea.

For further information about St. Maarten, contact the St. Maarten, St. Eustatius & Saba Tourist Office, 445 Park Avenue, New York City, New York 10022; (212) 688-8350. And for further information about St. Martin, contact French West Indies Tourist Board, French Government Tourist Office, 610 Fifth Avenue, New York City 10020; (212) 757-1125.

Your short field technique should be on the numbers every time if you plan to drop in at this near-aircraft carrier-type landing spot.

Saba

Flying In

There's a 1,700-ft strip that's fine if your own short-field performance is up to it. And that means landing right on the numbers on your way in behind the power curve in most aircraft, and good takeoff technique, where the idea is to get the aircraft flying as soon as possible to build up speed faster, and then get on and up and out.

Low-wingers will be able to put their faith in ground effect to a welcome test—it works—while high-wingers will keep the nosewheels on the ground just a tad longer while the ASI accumulates a little more increase on takeoff.

Still, if you're not sure about what's going on, take a ride over from St. Maarten by boat and go have a look. If you like what you see, ride right on over by air, because Saba is one of the most unusual islands to fly into in the entire length of the Eastern Caribbean.

It's a 5-square-mile cone-shaped dome of rock, a typical magmatic belch from the bowels of the earth, which leads the local tourist board into some predictable jokes. E.g., Bottom, which is up, is not a crater, but rather a bowl-shaped valley (anatomically similar to The Boss) and the principal village of the island. The island's single road is a virtual miracle of willpower on the part of one J. Lambert Hassell, who went so far as to take a correspondence course on road-building from Holland and who then went ahead with the road despite the word of the experts who said "It can't be done."

But it could, and he did it, and so you can today drive across island parkway Saba-style. This allows relatively easy access to other settlements on the island.

At Windwardside you'll find the *Captain's Quarters* with its 10 rooms and a Modified American Plan system (breakfast plus one meal) in operation. There's a swimming pool, and the food is Creole or Continental. If you want to be really private, there's *Bessie's Cottage*, which basically gives you your own home. The food here is served on the best plate and your wine is poured into crystal goblets. Enjoy.

Cranston's Antique Inn is a relative newcomer to the Saba circuit with six rooms, three with shared bath and three with private bath. Situated at the Bottom, mountain-climbing activities are on the day's activity schedule.

Back again up the hill from the Bottom* at Windwardside is *Scout's Place*, which sounds camp but really isn't, considering its former name was *Windwardside Guest House*. Five rooms, two with shared bath and three with private bath. Also at Bottom is the *Caribe Guesthouse* with five rooms, which offers to those interested deep-sea and cliff fishing, swimming, and generally messing around in boats.

For further information, contact the St. Maarten, Saba and St. Eustatius Tourist Office, 445 Park Avenue, New York, New York 10022; [212]. 688-8350.

*Bottom is up, at least 900 feet above sea level from where you come ashore if you arrive by boat—as many visitors do—at Ladder Bay, where you must climb some 525 steps up the mountain to Bottom.

However, Windwardside is—at 1,900 feet—some 1,100 feet higher than Bottom, so Bottom is both up *and* down, depending on your positional relativity.

St. Eustatius

Flying In

Known as Statia, or frequently/formerly the Golden Rock (a name stolen for St. Kitt's airport), St. Eustatius has its own 2,000-ft strip just outside Oranjestad, capital of the island. This area is the loping lowland of the island between the two extinct volcanoes known as The Quill and The Little Mountain. The island measures slightly more than 8 square miles. At the western edge of the plain is the principal town.

For all its present sleepiness, St. Eustatius was once a major mercantile center in the Caribbean. And its nickname, Golden Rock, had more to do with the potential wealth that could be earned here than anything else. Right up until and through Prohibition it was earning money for American customers—which was perhaps its due, since it, first among nations, not merely shipped the bulk of the weaponry used in the War of Independence to the would-be USA, but was one of the first to recognize the former colonies' new nationality.

Five years after her recognition of the United States as a sovereign nation, the British fleet captured and totally destroyed

The guns at Fort Oranje were first to salute the U.S. colors in November, 1776. (*photo*)

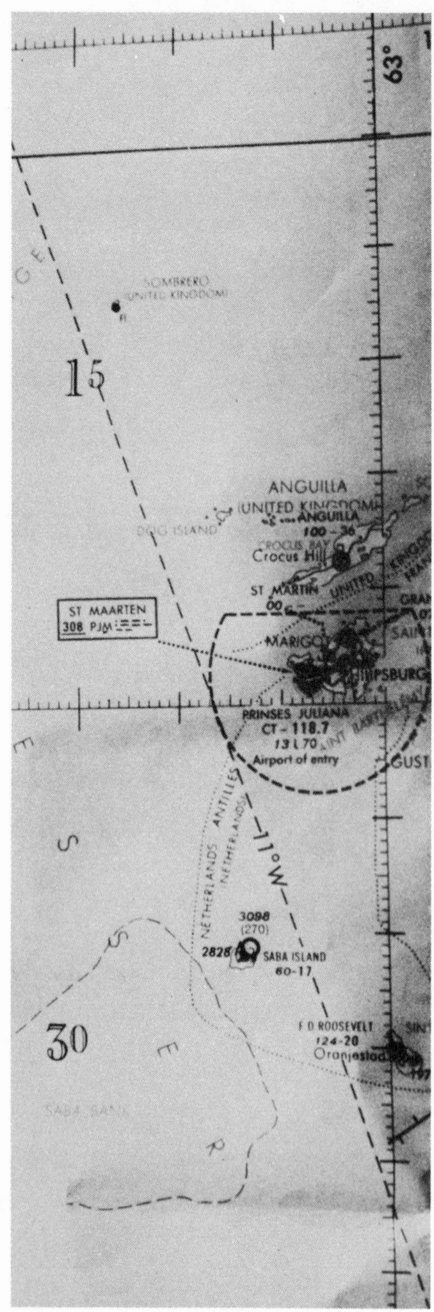

Just a short southerly hop takes you from St. Martin to Saba.
(Not to be used for navigation.)

the agricultural economy of St. Eustatius, a trauma from which it has never really recovered. The Admiral in charge of the operation was Baron George Bridges Rodney.

The island is of interest to field archeologists who can visit the 18th-century forts and the Upper and Lower Towns of Oranjestad, while field botanists can inspect the miniature rain forest in the volcano's crater. It's an extraordinary example of how quickly plant life can reconquer the soil for its own ends, and in some of the more recent lava you can still find traces of *e. coldenia*, the original groundbreaker of them all.

Some real estate is available if you want to purchase your get-away-from-it-all home, but prices are high.

Accommodations

Golden Rock Resort has reopened with its 10 rooms with private bath, swimming pool, bar, restaurant, and outdoor dining terrace. It provides free transport to and from the airport.

It's on the Atlantic side of the island, somewhat breezy, and

Turks' Head cactus frame one of the Golden Rock's attractive beaches.

suites are arranged in cottage units, two at a time. The sea view is great, as is the wind.

Mooshay Bay has 14 rooms in an old cotton gin just across the street from the Old Gin House. Rooms are with private bath. There's a cocktail lounge/tavern and swimming pool. It's in Old Oranjestad, down by the water.

Old Gin House started out life as a restaurant that just grew into nine rooms and has become a popular center of island life here. Good value for money if there are two of you, and the food is good, too. In fact, if you want to dine out from somewhere else, there's only the *Old Gin House* that matters.

Last but not least is *Ocean View Guesthouse* in Oranjestad, with 8 rooms with private bath, some dancing, billiards, bar and restaurant.

Alternative places for food—if you discount the local ice cream parlor—are the *Talk of the Town* and *Paramira Restaurant* (Chinese).

For shopping, Mazinga is still the best place. A sort of miniature Fortnum/Jackson/Statia-type place, there are one or two items you'll not find elsewhere for the money. The real bargains are still to be found in St. Maarten, however.

For further information, contact the St. Maarten, Saba and St. Eustatius Tourist Office, 445 Park Avenue, New York, New York 10022; [212]. 688-8350.

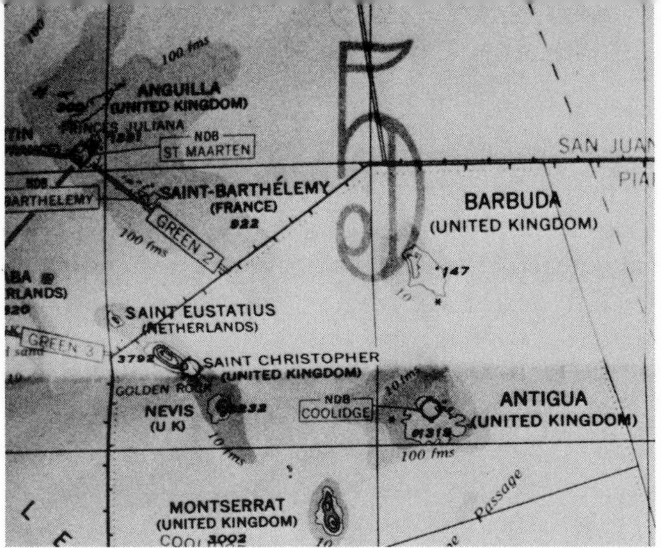

Anguilla

Flying In

Logically, Anguilla ought to get it together with the people of St. Maarten and the surrounding islands and form a unique federation of independent peoples and set an example to the rest of the world.

The fact of the matter is that most people down here do know each other, at least by sight, and most relationships are pretty friendly ones. If only by trade.

Anguilla, you see, has the cream of the crop when it comes to the local lobster, and unlike greedier cousins elsewhere they have taken the trouble to see that overfishing of these creatures has not occurred. The result is, as with OPEC oil, that there are still fine lobster to be had for not too much work on the part of the fisherman, if you don't mind paying the price.

But the Anguillans are smarter than that.

Some years ago, they decided they didn't want to be part of a Kittician Empire and ran ads in US newspapers suggesting that a revolution was brewing. Arms caches were discovered under the noses of journalists; a British paratroop team, dropped in to subdue the natives (only to find everything cool and under the islanders'

Section from aviation chart shows the close proximity of Anguilla to neighboring St. Martin. (*photo*) control), turned it all over to some British bobbies (who discovered that once they'd shed their serge in the noonday sun, it was a good place to be); and everyone had a good laugh about it all.

But the bureacrats in Whitehall got the message quickly enough and allowed Anguilla the privilege of returning to good old colonial status under the benign government of a locally elected House of Assembly supervised by a British Administrator (read Commissioner).

The island is a big 35 square miles, almost entirely fringed with white beaches. It's known locally as the Snake or Snake Island.

Places to Stay

This is no place to come if you're looking for the plush Little Dix type resort—this is strictly informal, for those who don't have to be waited on.

Mrs. Gumbs' *Rendez-Vous Bay* is well liked by visitors because of the efficiency with which it's run, and though small—only 20 rooms for guests, but the beach is at your doorstep—everyone tries to make you feel at home, and they do.

Another favorite is *Lloyds* out at The Valley, favorite with the bobbies when they were here. Just 10 rooms.

At Blowing Point is the *Cul de Sac Hotel*—shades of St. Maarten?—with a small pool and 10 rooms, and a beach nearby.

For the more self-sufficient, especially those interested in aqua sports, this is one of the least spoiled places to get it on. However, you should either bring your own gear or make arrangements to rent from St. Maarten. You'll have to recharge tanks in St. Maarten, but if you've your airplane, that's not going to be a problem, is it?

There are cottages. At Sandy Ground find *Bayview House* and *Seaside Cottage*. And *Maunday's Bay Beach Hotel* has 10 rooms. Anguilla is moving toward tourism development, but it's here you'll still be able to enjoy the original pioneering spirit along with those who live here.

St. Bart's [Barthelemy]

Flying In

Although the strip here has been lengthed from the original 600 ft of concrete plus 800-ft packed-earth overrun to 2,000 ft, it's as well to exercise some caution before making your landing approach. Overfly the field at least a couple of times so that you can check how you'll fly base and final, and be careful of wind shear, which has been known to cause problems for the less experienced.*

St. Bart's is French, and like St. Martin, a commune within the *departement* of Guadeloupe. It shares some history with the Virgin Islands (US) in that the flag of the Knights of Malta once flew here. It is also unusual in that it enjoyed Swedish sovereignty from 1784 until 1878, the only such island in the Caribbean to have come under the Swedish flag. A plebescite held in 1878 recommend-

*There are reports that a check ride plus annual proficiency certificate are now required. Get the local poop at St. Maarten.

Flight time from neighboring St. Martin to St. Barts is about eight minutes, but some care is needed for the landing, which involves contour flying on final. (*photo*)

ed a return to France and last year the islanders held a big celebration marking their centenniel.

The island is still very much the unspoiled tropical paradise, with not much nightlife, but with pleasant people who get along with each other. Everyone's simply too busy taking care of his or her own business for there to be time for political quarrels, and that's nice for visitors too. It helps if you know some French here, for the islanders still speak a nice old-fashioned 17th-century patois, which some find reminiscent of the Norman patois still used by the old people in the British Channel Islands. If you don't have French, take a small phrase book, for while most people have some English, the French respond better to those who make an effort to speak their tongue.

As might be expected, St. Bart's has been discovered by the very rich. David Rockefeller had a secret retreat here—inaccessible except from the sea—for a number of years, as have Edmond de Rothschild and the Biddles of Philadelphia. Until quite recently, the best way to enjoy a vacation here was to rent a home, preferably with maid service, and relax and pretend you also belonged to the idle rich. You can still do that, of course, though some new hotels have sprung up.*

Because St. Bart's is a completely duty-free port, there are bargains in liquors and perfumes that'll be hard to beat anywhere else in the islands. But don't expect to find regular department stores. Most business is exporting to other islands and to yacht people, and you'll find the stores set alongside the waterfront in the capital town of Gustavia. Gustavia's not even really a town; it's more a sort of overgrown fishing village. Only to be found here are the numerous garments made from the hand-block-printed material produced by Jean-Yves Froment. It's very "in" in chic circles to have resort wear from his patterns—and you can either buy the material and have it made up yourself or buy readymade goods at his store.

Despite the duty-free shopping, St. Bart's is relatively expensive for a vacation, and while some hotels do offer package arrangements, most don't for the simple reason that they're much smaller

*Write Sibarth Rental, BP 55, Gustavia, St. Barthelemy, French West Indies, for information on homes to rent.

scale. It's really only quite recently that significant numbers of people have discovered this island, and the lack of accommodations, which has permitted it to maintain its relatively pristine ambiance, is one of the nicer features—as you'll no doubt agree.

For local tourism queries, call 87-63-28.

Accommodations

The *Baie des Flamands* hotel is about ten minutes from the airfield and is a comfortable, informal, resort with 24 air-conditioned rooms with balconies and an 80-seat French/Creole restaurant, with glass doors that open onto a terrace. There's a salt-water pool, an attractive white beach, and facilities for most water sports are available.

Its sister hotel, the *St. Barth's Beach*, is about five minutes farther along on a narrow strip of land at Anse du Grand Cul-de-Sac. Here are 36 air-conditioned rooms, a spacious beach, with tennis courts on the property and aqua-sporting nearby. The snorkeling over the reef is good, and the two hotels allow guests to make use of their respective amenities.

Castelets, at Mt. Lurin, is luxurious and exclusive, and you'll need a rental car to get back up that hill. The hotel does provide transportation to the beach, but there are only nine rooms, so if you want to stay you need to book early. Even if you can't get a reservation, it's worth the visit for dinner, for the food is excellent.

Over at St. Jean Bay is the *PLM Jean Bart*, a new resort hotel facing the beach with 50 air-conditioned rooms with kitchenettes. It's slightly away from the beach itself on the hillside, and it's about a ten-minute walk to La Plage. It has a very good reputation.

The *Village St. Jean* offers similar accommodations, some 20 rooms in several buildings, again with kitchens for do-it-yourselfers.

The *Eden Rock* was, until some years ago, about the only place to stay in the island, but while the view is magnificent, the restaurant has been closed, and it's really a better place to visit for a drink than a stay. It has seven rooms, and you may want to check its current status.

On the beach just below Eden Rock is the *Emeraude Plage* with 14 rooms in seven cottages. Sandflies have been a problem here at dusk, but if you've some bug repellent—or don't mind rubbing

In St. Bart's one can still see the wearing of the old-fashioned and traditional *quichenotte*, or sunbonnet. This old lady is patiently braiding long strands of straw which will eventually be fashioned into a ladies' handbag.

Picture by Rose Fujimoto.

your body with a slice of lime (yes, it works!)—you'll enjoy a housekeeping holiday here.

Right in the heart of Gustavia is the *Presquile*, with 13 rooms. Rates are usually Modified American Plan (that is, breakfast plus dinner). Good value.

Gastronomy

Not surprisingly where there is so little to do, there is an interest, very Gallic, in good food. Long a special favorite of the locals is the *Cafe Select*, which at the time of writing is moving to new premises around the corner from its present home.

New is *La Cremaillere*, for country-style dining, with a chef hot from La Belle Patrie. Also *Le Sapotillier* (the word means sapadilla tree), which features French specialties. *L'Entrepont, Au Port*, and the *Auberge du Fort Oscar* continue to satisfy their fans.

Those interested in some occasionally outstanding Creole fare should try *Chez Cocotte*.

The above are all in Gustavia.

Over at the St. John beach area are two new restaurants that feature grilled fishes and meats. These are the garden restaurant

The port of Gustavia is an important transshipment point for numerous products, despite its apparent small size.

Chez Francais, which has a prix fixe menu, and the *Chez Francine*, which is on the beach.

And for hamburger freaks, note the *Santa Fe* up near Castelets.

Aqua-sports

While St. Bart's is not yet all well organized in this department as other islands, there are deep-sea fishing, water skiing, boat excursions, and scuba (no instructor/supervisors, however).

For further information, contact the French West Indies Tourist Board, French Government Tourist Office, 610 Fifth Avenue, New York, New York 10020; [212]. 757-1125.

St. Kitts

Flying In

Not quite 20 NM to the southeast of St. Eustatius lies the island of St. Kitts, whose *Golden Rock Airport* nestles behind the enormous peak that dominates the northern half of the island. Open from sunrise to sunset—other times on request—there's a jet-length 7,600-ft runway with runway lights and VASI. There's an NDB at the field (325 SKB), but pilots in the know generally tune to Radio Paradise whose 50,000 watts on 1260 KZ can be picked up at South Caicos, some 800 miles away. Local communications can be blanketed by Mount Misery when you fly in from the north. The mountain seems to deserve its name, for it is frequently hung about by seemingly doom- (and rain-) laden clouds.

General aviation aircraft are quite at home at Golden Rock field, with travelers arriving from the Midwest as well as from the eastern seaboard of the US. Tie-downs are usually available, and most pilots will be very glad to give you suggestions on local conditions. The local government people are also generally most helpful.

Both 100 octane and jet fuel (ASTM Type A-1 without icing inhibitor) are usually available, though 100 octane requires eight hours' notice and is more expensive here than at St. Maarten or Antigua, where it is readily available. Tower frequency is 118.3.

For local tourism queries, call 2620.

Carnival is as lively, colorful and joyous an occasion in St. Kitts as one could wish.

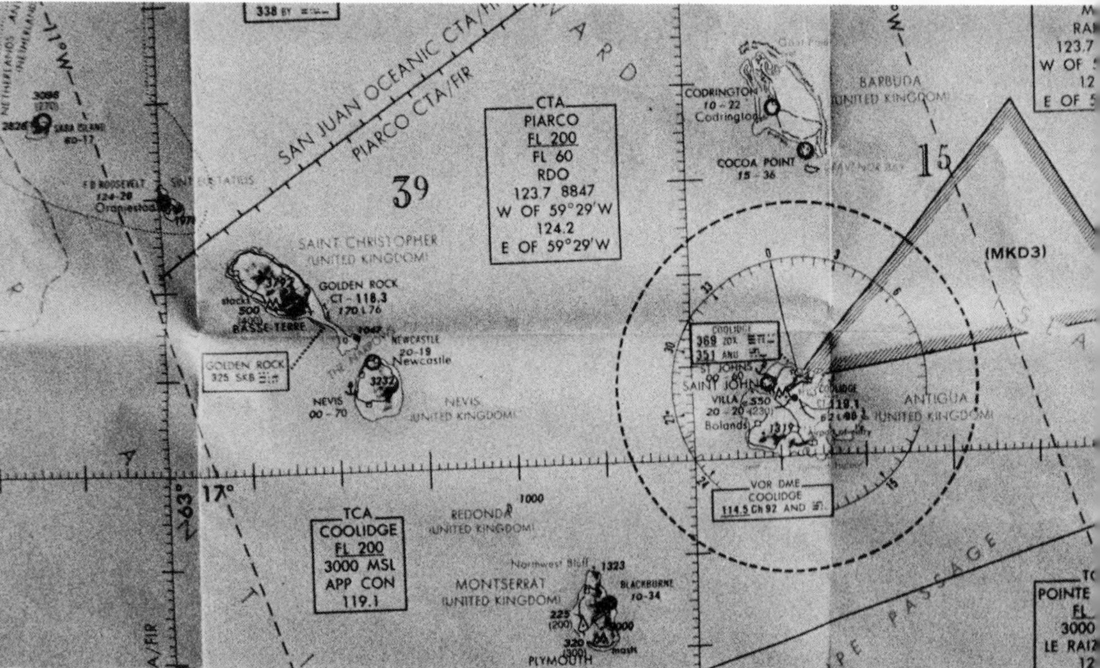

(Not to be used for navigation.)

Background Briefing

The Caribs, who were the first colonizers of this charming island, called it Liamuiga, the "fertile isle," and, from the upper reaches of the mountains, where traces of virgin rain forest may still be found, through the cane fields and to its shore, St. Kitts lives up to its former name.

The rain forest is alive with hummingbirds and the chattery shrills of green-backed monkeys (not indigenous: they were imported by early French colonists). You can still find wild lemon trees, other fruits, and orchids. There are ravines, secret crater lakes, and mountain streams.

Lower down the slopes, there is still sugar cane, though many of the old mills and plantation houses are now little more than picturesque ruins. Occasionally you'll see a line of royal palms, tall and seemingly unbending in the trade winds, their brilliant silvery green contrasting sharply with the red of the flamboyant trees.

Here lilies grow wild in the hedgerows and in the fields. Bourgainvillea—deep mauve, red, orange—and the bright hibiscus bloom year round, as does the red jasmine-like frangipani. Little geckos (house lizards) maintain an effective insect control, their long tongues shooting out to impale the unwary mosquito or fly.

At the shore you'll find a number of species of crab including the pretty Sally Lightfoot.

Columbus noted the island during his second voyage, naming it St. Christopher after his patron saint, while the cloud-ringed peak he called La Nieves after a snow-capped mountain in Spain.

The English arrived here in some force in 1623 when Sir Thomas Warner, knowing the island to be "fertile, watered and forested," established the colony with his wife and a party of fourteen settlers, intent on farming. Later in 1625, Lt. Pierre Belain d' Esnambuc and Lt. De Roissey of the French Navy put in for water with 35 men* and decided to join Sir Thomas's group, thereby setting the stage for the massacre of the indigenous Carib Indians.

With these new arrivals suddenly upon them, the Caribs got restive and made plans to mass their men for a pre-emptive strike. But one of the Carib women got wind of this and warned the settlers, who immediately launched their own attack. After the massacre, they went back to their farming, and four years later decided to divide the island between the two groups. This alliance continued till the end of the century, by which time Spain's influence was diminishing, and France and Britain had begun to vie with each other for territory.

Meanwhile, both groups sent out parties elsewhere. St. Kitts proved to be an effective home base, the British sending parties hence to Antigua and Montserrat, Barbuda and Tortuga. The French, meanwhile, went off under De Poincy's** guidance to St. Martin and St. Bart's, Guadeloupe, Desirade and Les Saints, and also to St. Croix.

The early settlers grew ginger, tobacco, indigo, and cotton, but the development of sugar as the major island crop in the middle of the 17th century saw the earlier products diminish in importance. Sugar is still the prime agricultural export of the island.

*Their own ship had foundered after being worsted in combat with the Spanish.

**It was Count Phillippe de Lonvilliers de Poincy who cultivated his famous poinciana, in the island, sending out cuttings and saplings elsewhere in the Caribbean.

Most of the early sugar estates are gone, buried under tropical vegetation, but some greathouses offering elegant accommodation remain. Windmills and steam chimneys stand in silent evidence of what once was a most prosperous land.

The English settled Nevis in 1628 and Anguilla in 1650. Nevis during the 18th century enjoyed the title of Queen of the Caribbees on account of its glamorous social life.

In Europe the politicians of France and England were feuding for overseas territory, and the alliance between the settlers eventually broke down. One of the sites to include in your list of places to go is the fort at Brimstone Hill, a staggering edifice that dominates the southwestern end of the island. In 1782 the famous siege of Brimstone Hill took place. The French attacked the fort, which was defended by a small group of 950 Scots and English. On their surrender, the French permitted them to march from the fort in full formation, out of respect for their bravery. The following year it was the Britons' turn to afford this same honor to the French.

A hurricane in 1834 badly damaged the fort but it was not evacuated until 1852. The Citadel has been partly reconstructed and its guns remounted, while the remains of the redoubts, the great cistern, barracks, ordnance store, officers' quarters, and cemetery are clearly to be seen. The Prince of Wales Bastion was restored in 1972, and reopened by HRH Prince Charles, the Prince of Wales, the following year. For the occasion the UK government presented the Restoration Society with ten oak plaques, bearing the crests of ten of the regiments that have served here, including the West Indian Regiment.

There's a souvenir store and restaurant, and on a clear day there is a fantastic view to be had of Nevis and Montserrat to the southeast, Saba and Statia to the northwest, and St. Barts and St. Maarten to the north.

The island itself is about 65 square miles, with a population of around 40,000. To the southeast, the island narrows to a five-mile-long beak of land with low hills. Here the twin gold beaches of Frigate Bay are to be found—there's talk of a new 300-room hotel to be sited at one of them—plus the secluded beaches of Cockleshell and Banana Bays on The Narrows facing Nevis.

You can drive around the island in about four hours, but there are a number of other worthwhile excursions. A day's visit to the slopes of Mount Misery is a rewarding experience. The guided tour takes you through virgin forest with bright wild orchids up to a crater's edge. On the Atlantic Coast is Black Rocks, formed by prehistoric lava flows, much modified by the ceaseless turbulence of the ocean's waves. Here the annual Guy Fawkes Day (November 5) picnic is held. Then there is Old Road Town, where Sir Thomas and his men first stepped ashore, site of the first settlement. Sir Thomas Warner's Tomb, with a fine inscription that will amuse, is at Middle Island churchyard. At Half Way Tree stands an ancient tamarind that once marked the old boundary between the French and British parts of the island, and Bloody Point, where the two groups of colonists gathered to slaughter the Caribs. The Chateau de M. de Poincy, once the colonial home away-from-home of the French Governor in the 17th century, is also worth a visit.

Then there is the capital itself, Basseterre, the name deriving from the French. Pall Mall Square has a number of interesting colonial English homes. The Treasury Building and Customs Building and the former Government House are interesting examples of the old colonial style. At the center of town is the Circus, with a Victorian clock tower, a fountain and more tall and elegant royal palms.

The Old Court House on Pall Mall Square occasionally has exhibitions of local historical artefacts in the second floor library.

Where to Stay

Under the leadership of the late Premier Robert Bradshaw, St. Kitts made haste slowly in the development of tourism. One reason it was able to afford this luxury was the importance of agriculture in its GNP, since it is a luxuriant and fertile island and good crops progress bountifully with the helping hands of people.

The result is a pleasant sort of old-fashioned hospitality that abounds in the hotels and inns of the island. And careful attention to good foods and wines, although Carib lager and rum-based Plantation Punch have their admirers. You can still eat turtle steak here, and roast sucking pig is also popular. There's not too much nightly entertainment, though some hotels have local bands for you to hop to. And there's usually backgammon or bridge.

Close to Basseterre is the *Fairview Inn,* about twelve minutes from town, with luxurious cottages set around a delightful 18th-century Greathouse. The gardens are charmingly landscaped, and there are great views from the hillside location. The 33 double rooms with private patios make this a pleasant place to relax, as does the pool, where you can cool yourself and improve your tan.

Regular entertainment is provided by island groups, and this is where the locals gather, on account of the delicious island food served at the restaurant. These include a variety of Caribbean delicacies plus local seafood. If you'd like to enjoy the comfort of West Indian atmosphere, this is as good a place as any to get used to just how good it can be.

Up at the north end of the island at Dieppe Bay is the internationally known *Golden Lemon,* a 7-room guesthouse that sits on its own palm-fringed beach. It's a bit like finding a sort of Pennsylvania Black Bass Inn in the Caribbean, for there are four-poster beds, numerous local antiques, and the owner-manager is the former decorating editor of *House & Garden.* The dining room has magnificent candelabra and elegant flower settings—but it's the food that gets the most acclamation.

There's a swimming pool for those who shun the ocean, and spacious gardens. Since the management occasionally lets the entire Inn plus pool and maid service to jaded capitalists and spymen, for long-term during summer and fall, check with your local Kittician Tourism representative if you'd like to stay here out of season.

At the present time the Golden Lemon is adding 10 more rooms to cope with its popularity rating among the cognoscenti.

If you'd like to spend time on what was once an original muscovado sugar factory, then it's the *Rawlins Plantation* for you. Most of the buildings date from the 17th century, though newer ones have been added, including two new suites. There are seven delightful acres of gardens planted with tropical shrubs, flowers and trees, and cactus. There's also excellent snorkeling close by and the owner's trimaran yacht is available for charter.

Because it is set some 350 feet above sea level, there's a near-permanent breeze to keep you cool.

For resort living, the *Royal St. Kitts Hotel and Golf Course* at

Frigate Bay is a 100-room hotel just a stone's throw from beaches on both the Atlantic and Caribbean, with snorkeling and fishing. The 18–hole golf course is reputedly designed with championship matches in mind; there's a pool, casino, and fine public rooms.

The hotel has recently taken over management of the 64–room *Fort Thomas Hotel*, just outside Basseterre on the water's edge, the site of an old historic fort. Rooms have private balconies looking either over the ocean or toward the mountains, and are air-conditioned with twin double beds, radio, and telephone.

The hotel originally opened as part of the Holiday Inn chain, so the design is modern, with a fresh-water swiming pool, spacious sundecks, and attractively landscaped gardens. There are also amenities for conference and convention business.

People in the know who enjoy St. Kitts make a point of staying at OTI, or *Ocean Terrace Inn*, which effusively welcomes its guests to the World of Island Living, with large air-conditioned rooms and a commanding view of the harbor and capital, and the island of Nevis. Accommodations, since the addition of a recent dozen, now amount to 30 doubles, all with private bath. There are ocean-front verandahs, a swimming pool, the Carnival bar, and a discotheque. The restaurant serves Creole and international fare, and OTI is a home away from home for many who have business and leisure on the island.

Accessible only by boat and at the southern tip of the island is *Banana Bay Beach* resort hotel. It's pleasantly secluded with a fine curved white sand beach with magnificient views of Nevis. There are 12 large luxurious double rooms just a few steps from the sea, each with its own bath and terrace. The food is good, and informality is generally the order of the day. Locally caught lobster is frequently featured, and wine is included in the price of accomodations.

Similarly reached by boat is *The Cockleshell*, another charming hotel for escapists located at the southeastern tip of the island. Management will meet you with their boat if they know you're coming; it's about forty-five minutes from Basseterre, so let them know.

The atmosphere is much like a pleasant houseparty, with good food, casual dress, and an informal self-service bar. All rooms are twin-bedded, with bath and verandah overlooking the sea. There's a lot of repeat business at this getaway haven, and there's fishing, snorkeling, water skiing, sailing, and tennis for the energetic.

For those who prefer to do-it-themselves, the *Tradewinds* is a group of fully equipped, self-contained cottages set in its own private coconut plantation at Conaree Beach. Management will meet you at the airport and then drive you to your cottage, where a hot meal will be waiting for you, as well as small supply of groceries to start you off.

Good snorkeling for enthusiasts, and the sea is almost at your doorstep. Behind are some pleasant mountains. Tennis, golf, fishing, and mountain climbing can all be arranged.

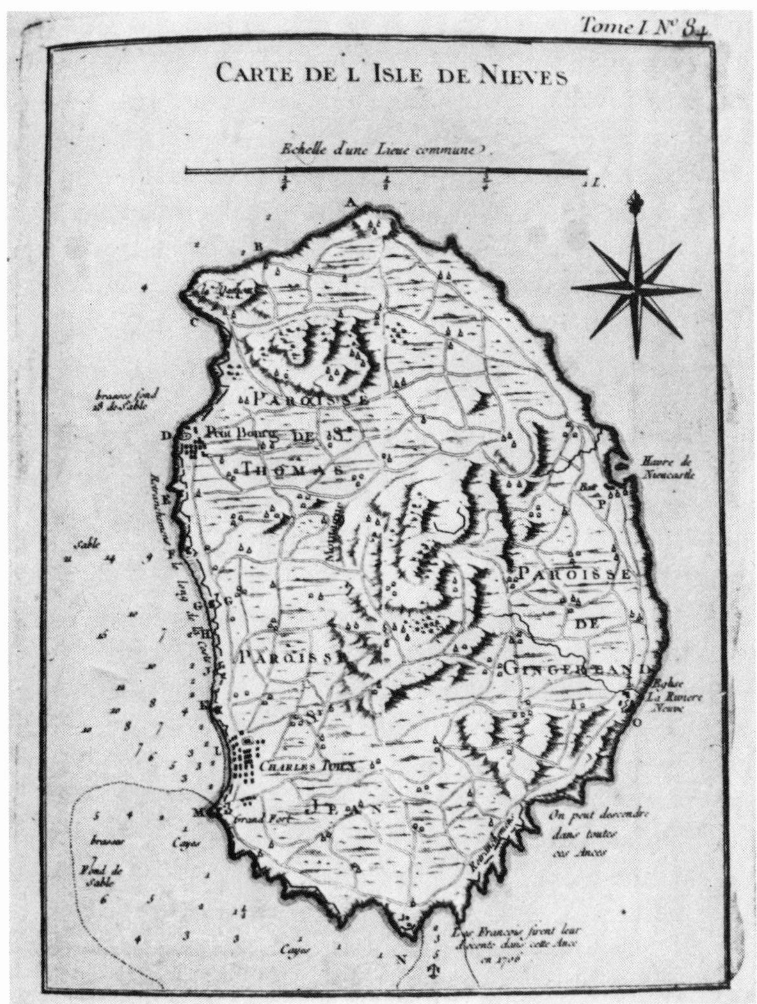

Nevis

Flying In

The strip at Nevis is 1,900 ft long and is located just outside the town of Newcastle. There's no fuel here.

Background Briefing

This volcanic island is approximately 36 square miles in area, rising from sea level to Nevis Peak, some 3,232 feet above sea level. (If

Famed French cartographer Bellin's version of the island of Nevis. (*photo*)

you fly over the peak, you may find you need carb heat as there is usually a lot of moisture in the air here.) The mountain includes two lesser heights known as Hurricane Hill and Saddle Hill.

But it's not so much the forest-clad hills that bring the visitor to Nevis as its miles and miles of golden beaches, fringed with palm trees. Charlestown, the island's capital, was in 1757 birthplace to Alexander Hamilton, reputedly the bastard son of one James Hamilton, a Scot, and Rachael Lavien, a resident of the island.

St. John's Church at Fig Tree Village has the records of Lord Nelson's marriage at Montpelier to the rich young widow Fanny Nisbet. The church is a charming reminder of England. Best man at the wedding was the Duke of Clarence who would eventually succeed George IV and become King William IV of England.

Ashby Fort to the west of Nelson's Spring—where ships were watered prior to their departure for the American War of Independence—is a point of call to include in your sightseeing, as are the remains of Jamestown, which was destroyed and submerged by a tidal wave in 1680, a fate shared by the former Port Royal in Jamaica.

The Bath House was a fashionable 19th-century center and will give you some idea of life in earlier times.

Nevis became a very "in" health resort during the 18th century thanks to its sulphur springs.

Where to stay

Golden Rock Estate is an attractive small hotel that has superseded a sugar estate. There are a swimming pool and tennis court, and transport to two beaches. It's expensive and very pleasant.

Nisbet Plantation was long ago owned by a Nisbet relative and legend has it that Fanny played here as a little girl. The hotel enjoys a considerable amount of repeat business, so you should book well in advance. Horseback riding is available, and you can relax in a pleasantly sedate and comfortable plantation atmosphere. Expensive and good.

Pinney's Beach Hotel is situated about a mile north of Charlestown on what has to be one of the finest beaches in the entire Caribbean. It also offers reasonably priced accommodation in either family cottages or double rooms with private bath and terrace.

Nearby is *Rest Haven Inn*, with a small fresh-water pool, excellent food, and accommodations that include a number of efficiency units. Reasonable prices and good value.

For further information on St. Kitts/Nevis, contact International Travel and Resorts, 39 West 55th Street, New York, New York 10019; [212]. 586-2955.

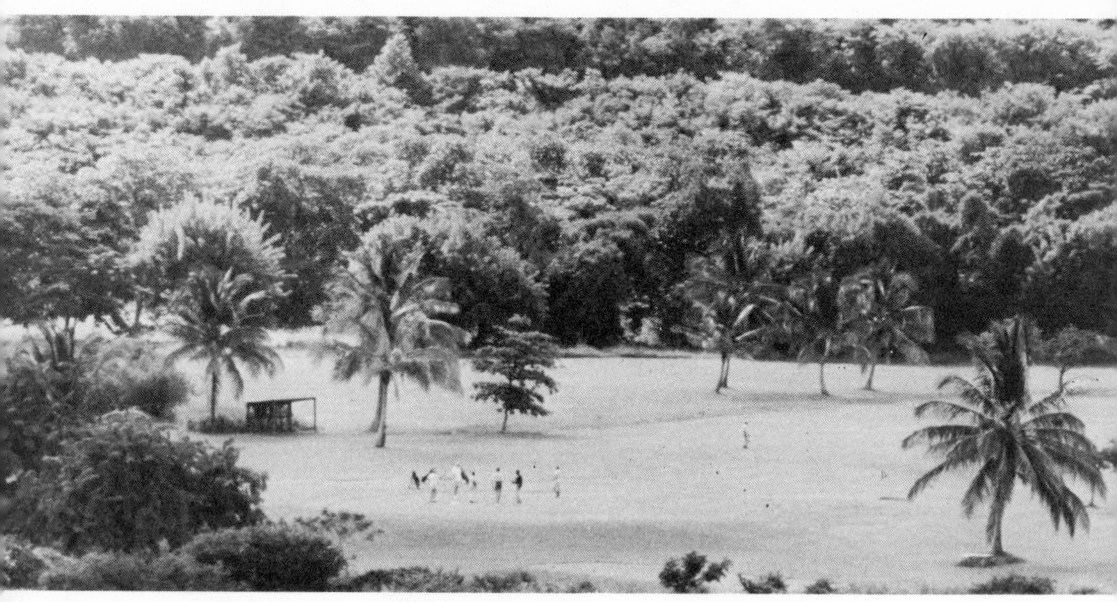

Montserrat

Flying In

Blackburne Airport is one of the few historic airports in the Caribbean because it was from this grass strip—now asphalted—that the eastern Caribbean's only home-grown airline was birthed. That airline, called LIAT (Leeward Islands Air Transport), was the original brainchild of a Kittician, Frank Delisle.

It all started off very simply, but it was immediately successful and Frank one day found he had a real airline on his hands. A brief story of LIAT is to be found in the appendices.

Today at Blackburne, there's a 3,400 ft. runway and strip lighting should you be late in arriving, plus an identifying rotating beacon. The airport's strictly VFR—you'll see why when you come in, for there's a whole heap of mountain waiting to getcha; the airport's operational from 0600 through 1800 local time. No fuel. Tower: 118.8.

For local tourism queries, call 2230 during office hours; in emergency only, after working hours at 2211.

Background Briefing

The so-called Emerald Isle of the Caribbean has long since lost its connections with Erin, save in the minds of local poets and copywriters who'll point to the small carved shamrock nestling atop the Governor's Mansion (you may look at but not go inside), the Malones, Mahoneys, and Ryans whose clans still seemingly abound here in family names and a touch of Blarney in the Irish lilt of the local speech and storytelling.

Yet in times past there was indeed an Irish connection, even though it was Sir Thomas Warner (of St. Kitts) who originally settled Montserrat. For like most Caribbean islands, Montserrat, too, was discovered by Columbus in 1493. The name derives from a mountain in Spain though to resemble the silhouette of this island. It lies approximately 50 miles north of Guadeloupe and is mountainous.

The original settlement was supposedly seven men with a longboat, who stayed at their posts for thirty-two weeks before requesting assistance. A small new group of settlers moved in thereafter and the island received a sizeable reinforcement soon after the succession—in 1653—of Oliver Cromwell as Lord Protector (for which read Dictator) of Britain.

The possibility of achieving a West Indian Empire at the expense of Spain had been under discussion by the British since the times of Good Queen Bess. The changes in monarchy, once the Tudor line ended, meant an immediate brief return of Papism, even though the monarchs couched this belief later on under the heading of the Divine Right of Kings. King Charles I took his belief in this right somewhat too seriously, misreading the feelings of his subjects, which led to civil war. The Ironsides were more than a match for the dashing Cavaliers, and Charles lost his head in 1649.

On his accession, Cromwell gave orders for a fleet to be assembled under the command of Admiral Sir William Penn (father of the Penns of Pennsylvania, and their successors in the British Virgin Islands) and an army under the command of General Robert Venables. This expedition of nearly 3,000 men was landed in Barbados (where it made off with some 4,000 "volunteers" and thus nearly ruined the local economy) and was accompanied by a sizeable number of indentured men, which included a relatively large percentage of protesting Irish.

Meanwhile, the aforementioned entente between the French and British was already beginning to break down, and the new arrivals proved helpful allies in defending Montserrat against the skirmishing attacks of the French. Then, in 1664, the French successfully captured the island; it was restored to England four years later, recaptured by the French in 1782, and finally ceded to Britain the following year. The shamrock and the distinguishable Irish brogue of the locals' speech serve merely as reminder of an earlier (and probably formidable) Irish presence here.

For those who prefer to vacation just a little bit off the beaten track, Montserrat has much to offer—as more than 3,000 North American retirees who have built homes here have discovered. (A number of these homes are usually available for rent, either with or without maid service). Like the other Caribbean islands, mean maximum temperature is in the mid-80s, mean minimum in the low 70s, and the trade winds blow throughout the year.

Despite its airport, the island has an air of the unspoiled, almost of wilderness country, with waterfalls and bubbling sulphur springs, untainted by crass commercialism.

Yet the amenities are present.

For golfers, the Montserrat Golf Club offers special rates for visitors at the Belham River Valley Golf Course, where the Club House was built almost 200 years ago by a British plantation owner, and where the course itself runs from the coastline into the hills. Designed by Edmund Ault, there are 11 holes playable as two 9-hole courses, in an area of nearly 100 acres, for a distance of 3,222 yards. Green fees are around $6.00 per day, or $30.00 for the week. Annual dues are $133.00.

The *Vue Pointe Hotel* has two lawn-tennis courts, and other activities include the full range of water sports, mountaineering—Chance Peak's 3,000 feet is a pleasant climb—horseback riding, and just plain hiking.

There are approximately 130 miles of surfaced road in the island (it's 11 miles long by about 7 miles wide) so that it's fairly easy to get almost every place. Population is around 13,000, and Plymouth, the island's capital, is supposedly one of the cleanest towns in the entire Caribbean. Saturday is Market Day and it's a must for your calendar of events. There's the usual hustle and bustle of every market, to be sure, but there's an incredible array of really fine local produce—avocados, mangoes, tomatoes, limes, peppers, soursop, dasheen, plus fresh doctor fish (delicious, fried, for breakfast), parrot fish, and so on—and the local people are always ready for a gossip.

If you're planning on doing your own housekeeping, a copy of *The Montserrat Cookbook*, recently reissued, will give you some idea of how this indigenous produce may be used to good effect. If you're looking to eat out, there are several good restaurants, despite the small size of the island. In Plymouth, there are *The Cellar* and *Cynthy's*. The *Wade Inn*—a small, informal guesthouse with 10 rooms—offers West Indian fare including that Montserratian specialty "goat water," a delightfully spicy goat stew that's lip-smacking good. *The Quarter Deck* is also popular for lunch.

As in Dominica, the other specialty is the "mountain chicken," as the frogs' legs are called. You'll usually be able to find *callalloo*, a stew made of land crab and dasheen, which is a meal in itself. At Wapping, the *Rose and Compass* offers lunch and dinner; their Planter's Punch is delicious and packs a deceitful strength.

Drunk as a liqueur is Montserrat's Perks Rum Punch, made from the recipe of Mr. J. W. R. Perkins. If you'd like something different to offer your Stateside guests, a quart brought home is sure to please.

For sightseeing there are a number of interesting places to note, such as the 18th-century ruins of the Fort on St. George's Hill. Then there's Galways Soufriere, an open crater from which spews forth molten sulphur and which can now be reached quite easily by road; in the old days you hiked in through giant tree ferns and rain forest. There's also the Great Alps Waterfall, where icy water plunges some 70 feet down into a mountain pool—great to cool off in after the walk to get there. And there's a small museum in an old sugar mill tower at Richmond Hill, Plymouth. Also in Plymouth is St. Anthony's Church, which has been rebuilt several times but which was originally consecrated in the early 17th century.

Runaway Gut (or Gaut, or Ghaut) is the site of one of the skirmishes between the French and English, and makes one wonder how they managed to fight, so steep are the sides. And if you tire of the black sand—though it feels much finer to the feet than white sand and is less glaring for the eyes—you can always go out to Carr's Bay, which is a popular "resort" for the locals.

It's worthwhile renting a car, but even better is to spend a day with a taxi driver to get oriented. Your drive from the airport will bring you to the west coast via Harris Village. Harris Lookout is worth a pause—you'll get a good view of Chance Mountain and you can decide whether it's worth the long walk up. If you like ecclesiastical architecture, you may want to stop for a quick inspection of the Anglican church (originally built in 1900 and survivor of hurricane and earthquake). Bethel Church is also worth a visit.

Where to Stay

If you're planning to stay at a hotel, remember that this is in no way your typical "resort island." Rather, it's for that old-fashioned, comfortable, get-away-from-it-all vacation.

Both *Vue Pointe* (Old Towne and about 5 miles from Plymouth) and the *Emerald Isle* are highly recommended and have been in business for many years. The latter is the nearest you'll find to a resort hotel in the island. There are 16 attractive rooms, pool—with beach view—and some form of entertainment most nights during the season, rather less in summer. Good West Indian Food.

Vue Pointe, slightly more expensive, is near the golf course, and accomodations are in comfortably furnished cottages with large bedroom, bath and total privacy. Excellent West Indian fare, and the Osborne family, who own and manage the hotel, are delightful and helpful hosts. Swimming pool, beach (with beach bar), and pleasant landscaped grounds, with a profusion of oleanders and hibiscus and hummingbirds.

Coconut Hill Hotel, just outside Plymouth, is a pleasant West Indian house. Excellent West Indian cuisine, cheerful informal atmosphere. Rates are moderate.

Also moderate are the Wade Inn in Plymouth and the *Hideaway Hotel* at Rocklands. *The Hideaway* is one of the better night spots on the island, as is the *Nep-Co-Den,* just 2 miles out of Plymouth.

Shopping

Montserrat was once a large exporter of limes and Sea Island cotton, and the locally made clothing is still worth checking out, as is the Montserrat Bay Rum. Clothes made by Kitty Barzey, Verna White, and Adolphus Tuitt are very attractive, some available stateside, according to recent reports, while Sea Island goods can be obtained from the *John Bull Shop. Cottage Crafts Shop* and *Montserrat Crafts* both offer a good selection of souvenir items, including calico scatter rugs and both locally made and Dominican-imported sisal rugs. For quality imports, try *Gifts of Quality* or *The Sugar Mill.*

Ruins of sugar mills from earlier times add to this island's considerable charm.

Further information from: Eastern Caribbean Tourist Association, 220 East 42 Street #411, New York, N.Y. 10017, Caribbean Tourism Association, 20 East 46 Street, New York, N.Y. 10017, or Montserrat Tourist Board, P. O. Box 7, Plymouth, Montserrat.

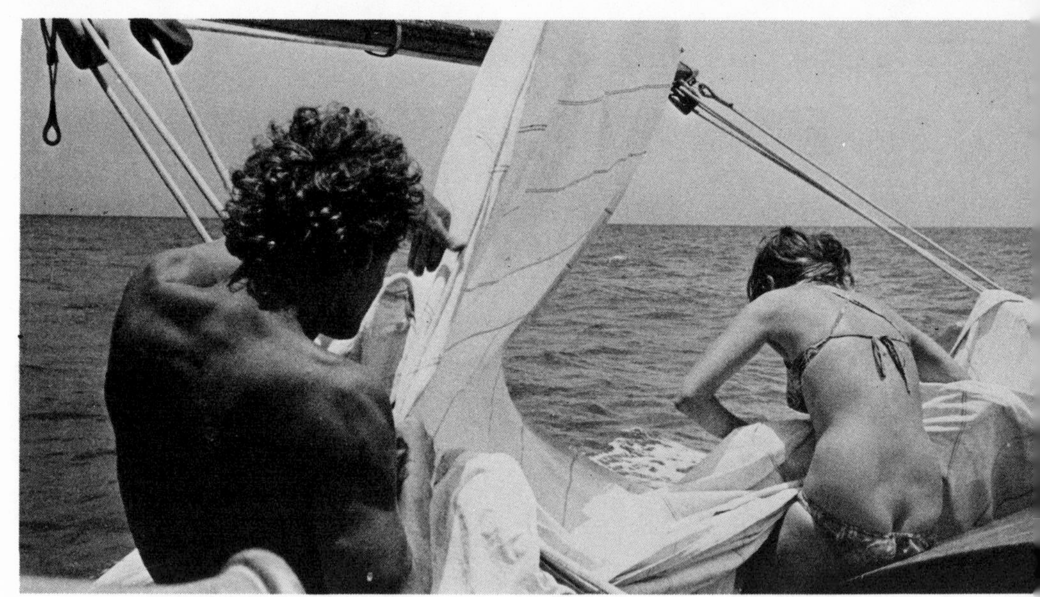

Antigua

Flying In

Coolidge Airport, Antigua, lies some 93 NM southeast of St. Martin, 52 NM east of St. Kitts, and some 166 NM to the east of St. Croix. It's a busy international airport and the home base of the LIAT fleet. There are high-intensity approach and runway lights, plus VASI. The runway's 9,000 ft long, field elevation 62 ft, and fuel is available at reasonable rates.

The Piarco control area begins just south of St. Eustatius, and includes St. Kitts, Nevis, and Barbuda. Coolidge represents the northern end of a communications link that goes all the way down to Trinidad.

Coolidge Approach is at 119.8 and the Tower is 119.1, with Ground Control on 121.9. Piarco Radio likes to be appraised of aircraft entering their zone and, at the time of writing, the frequency for aircraft approaching from west of 59° 29′ W is 123.7. Coolidge is a TCA, so you'll also want to call Approach to inform them, too.

In addition to the LIAT 748s and Islanders, numerous jet aircraft use Coolidge, so be alert for any possibility of wake turbulence.

The VOR DME is situated away from the field but will get you to the island, 114.5 Ch 92 AND. The VOR is unusable below 1,500 ft.

There are two NDBs, 369 ZDX 1.2 NM from the field and 351 ANU at the field itself. You pay your landing fee at the Tower.

For local tourism queries, call either 20029 or 20490—the Tourist Board here is first-rate.

Background Briefing

People come to Antigua for its sunshine, its fine white sandy beaches, and its water sports. Recently, agriculture—Antigua's former leading export—has had to take a back seat to tourism, which has moved up to number one.

One of the larger islands, Antigua is approximately 108 square miles in size with a population in excess of 70,000. Development here has been careful, and while the island is an important transshipment point—the new deep-water harbor has meant several real benefits to the community, as has the West Indies Oil Refinery—the fact that materials can be easily imported has meant the fairly rapid development of hotels over the past ten years.

From a tourist's point of view the island is full of surprises, extraordinary scenery, and memorable views. Its former inhabitants, the Arawaks and Caribs, have left more than 30 archeological sites, the two most interesting being Indian Creek and Mill Reef. Then there are the megaliths at Greencastle Hill and the Devil's Bridge at Indian Town, the latter a natural bridge with blow-holes spouting surf.

In more recent times have come the fortresses and other 18th-century buildings, from the time when Antigua was a British bastion against the French and one of the few islands the French were unable to conquer during the power struggles of that era.

Nelson's Dockyard, named for Admiral Horatio himself, was originally commissioned in 1755 by the British. Considerably restored, it is a fascinating look at maritime life of the 18th century. It and English Harbor were chosen because they provided considerable protection from hurricanes, and because the harbor itself is all but invisible from a seaward approach. At the end of each April the most exciting of world regattas takes place here during Antigua's sailing week.

Tennis enthusiasts will already have heard of the Lionel Tennis Week, which attracts pros from all over the world to the island just following the Christmas holidays.

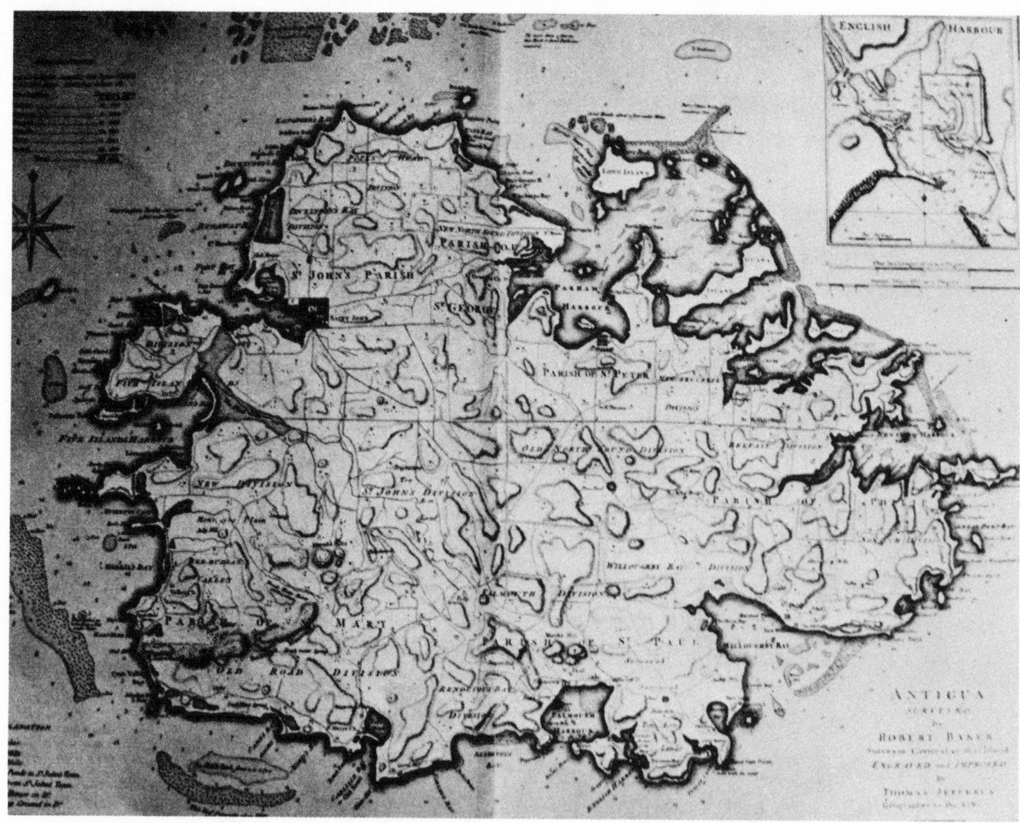

Thomas Jeffery's version of the island.

And then there is Carnival, which here in Antigua is celebrated during the ten days preceding the first Monday and Tuesday in August. It's a joyful riot of color and sound and radiant and happy people. While it may not have the exotic polish of the Carnivals of Rio and Port-of-Spain, it has an enthusiasm and freshness all its own. Musicians from all over the Caribbean are beginning to make a point of including Antigua's Carnival in their circuit, so that the visitor gets an opportunity to hear many different sorts of music including the famed Trinidadian steel band sound and the wailing strains of reggae.

Deep-sea fishing is growing in popularity and boats are available to take you to the wahoo, which is increasingly being found near by. Also a good game fish is the dolphin (not to be confused with the mammal), whose gray scales make a gorgeous troop through the colors of the rainbow as it dies, before returning to the original gray. You won't feel so sad when you taste it, since it is one of the finest of tropical fish for the table.

Most hotels have other fishing gear available, either for shore fishing or spear fishing with snorkel—parrot fish, ground feeders who enjoy coral, are a surprisingly difficult prey with a speargun. Or you can spin for amber jack and baby barracuda—surprisingly tasty fare.

Water skiing is available and a bargain at most places for the low hourly rates, and then there are cruises, either sail or cruiser, which include barbecue and cocktail cruises, plus glass-bottom boats, or just get-away-from-it-all cruises day and/or night.

If you want to catch up on your own sailing technique, the ubiquitous Sunfish is available by the day or the hour, or—if you're energetic—you may want to try your hand with a rowboat.

Then there are the beaches. The promotional literature swears there's at least one for every day of the year and it's probably true. Almost all the hotels have their own private beach and those that don't have beaches near at hand. Antigua now begins to rival Barbados in good hotels at attractive places, but unlike Barbados, there's plenty of distance between most of them. Each hotel is reasonably self-sufficient in nightlife, and guests at one hotel can usually visit another for dinner and entertainment during the season.

There are numerous taxis—don't forget to include Eastern Caribbean dollars in your pocket since the rate is cheaper than if you pay in US currency—and cars can be rented for around $20.00 per day with unlimited mileage. No faster than 40 mph on the open road and 20 mph in towns, please, and remember to drive on the left. Numerous unpaved roads will help keep your speed down and many are worth exploring since they can bring you to lesser known and attractively deserted strands.

Food in the island varies from somewhat bland American and Continental cuisine upward and includes various West Indian and Creole foods. Mostly it is pleasantly varied, sometimes spicy, and usually good. Antiguan hotels seem to be moving in the direction of gastronomic quality—there always were some outstanding chefs—and you'll be pleasantly surprised at just how good that usually is. There are a number of restaurants in St. John's, the

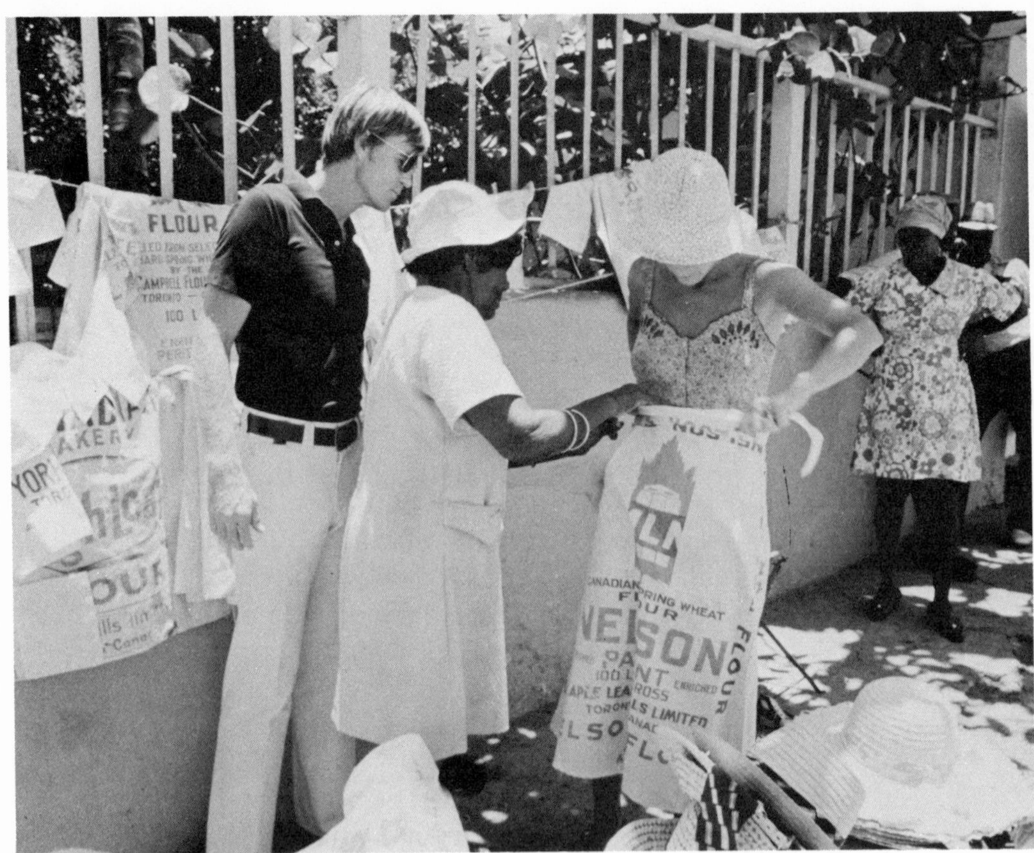

Shopping in St. John's.

island's capital, for a change of pace, including *Brother B's* on Long Street (soul and local fare), the *China Garden* on Newgate Street, the *Kensington* on St. Mary's Street, *Maurice's* on Market Street, and the *Spanish Main Inn* on East Street, which can be an inexpensive place to stay if you've business in town and aren't interested in beaches.*

Also on St. Mary's Street is *Darcy's Restaurant and Bar,* which serves potent rum punch and where steel bands play during the lunch hour. Out of town, the *Admiral's Inn* is worth the visit, also good to stay at. *The Catamaran,* just outside of Falmouth, is good

*Recommended locally are the *Gaiety High* and the *Golden Peanut,* where lobster is a specialty of the house.

for barbecues, fish, and good simple West Indian Food—popular with the beachcombing set and visiting sailors.

Golfers will find three courses in the island, two 9-hole courses at *Half Moon Bay* and at the *Antigua Beach Hotel,* plus an 18-hole professional course at Cedar Valley. You don't need to bring your own clubs with you to Antigua since clubs can be rented locally.

Horseback riding is available at *Galley Bay Surf Club, Hyatt Halcyon Cove* (Dickenson Bay) and at the *Atlantic Beach* at Cosbies. If you're at a different hotel your hotel can make arrangements for you.

Spectator sports include cricket ("lovely cricket") and soccer, plus netball (a cousin of basketball) and horse racing, which takes place most public holidays at the *Cassada Garden Turf Club.* Check with the Antigua Department of Tourism for firm dates.

For those who like a different sort of gamble there's a casino at the *Castle Harbor Club* that comes complete with restaurant and nightclub plus a gorgeous view overlooking the deep-water harbor. Sunsets can be magnificent from the terrace here, and lovers young and old will treasure the memories of the colors of the sky and sea, the shimmering of the water, and the cool wind and the stars as the light fades away.

The *Tourist Guide,* published by the Department of Tourism, and your hotel can give details of what's happening where any particular night. The *Admiral's Inn* has a number of highly successful jump-ups (dances) throughout the year, and *The Hideout,* near the Holiday Inn at Marmora Bay, is popular with locals—as is the *Catamaran.* Best to have your own transportation if you plan to stay out late as taxis can be hard to come by in the wee hours of the morning.

Some History and Some Places of Interest

While the island was named after Santa Maria la Antigua de Seville, it was first colonized by another small group from Sir Thomas Warner's early colony in St. Kitts in 1632. The island's name is consequently pronounced with a hard English G as an-TEE-ga.

The following year the island was occupied by the French, but it was finally ceded to England in 1667 by the Treaty of Breda and has remained British ever since. Later that century it was deeded to Sir Christopher Coddrington, then Governor of the Leeward Islands, outright. Its present status, achieved in 1967, is as an independent state in association with the United Kingdom.

In effect, the new constitution provided for a Parliament consisting of a Senate and a House of Representatives under the Crown, in this case represented in Antigua by a Governor appointed by Her Majesty. The principal instrument of government is the Cabinet, consisting of a Premier who is head of Government and other Ministers.

From a historical standpoint, the most interesting area to explore is in the neighborhood of Nelson's Dockyard, for, as one of the safest natural harbors in the world, it was used in the past by such Admirals as Rodney and Hood in addition to Nelson, who from 1784 was Commander of the Leeward Islands fleet. Today it is the temporary home-away-from-home for many world travelers, plus those who prefer island living aboard a boat.

Nearby Clarence House overlooks the Dockyard and was built by English stonemasons as the residence of Prince William Henry when he was in command of the *Pegasus* in 1787. Today it is the home of the Governor and is open to visitors when the Governor is not in residence.

High on the hill at Shirley Heights overlooking the harbor are the ruins of the fortress named after General Shirley, who was Governor of the Leeward Islands in 1781. He later fortified "the Ridge" of hills overlooking the harbor itself. One of the principal buildings—known as the Block House—was built in case of siege by General Matthew in 1787. The nearby cemetery tells a tale other than romantic of deaths from disease and fever, the scourge of Caribbean service for the men of the 54th regiment who never went home again.

Fort Berkeley was built to control the entrance to the harbor, which was closed off during attacks and sieges by a chain and timber boom drawn across the narrow entrance to the harbor itself. Any ship attempting to plunge through the boom would find itself in irons and subject to a hail of shot from the fort and battery. Without any way on her, it would be almost impossible for the attacker to escape—and there are no records of any such foolhardy skipper's having lived to tell the story of such an attack another day.

A number of other forts attest to the excellence of colonial fortification engineering including Fort Charles, Fort Barrington, Fort George (Monks Hill), and Fort James, near St. John's. Fort James was named after James II, and work started here in 1704. The cornerstone of the big enclosing wall was laid with full masonic honors with officers from the recently formed London lodges in attendance on November 15, 1739. The site was originally a lookout point for the city and was known then as St. John's Point.

The first Anglican cathedral in the capital was built in 1683 and replaced by a stone building in 1745. An earthquake just a hundred years later destroyed it. The cornerstone for the present cathedral was laid October 8, 1845, and the cathedral opened for worship two years later. The building is of stone, and the interior is of pitch pine, the idea being to secure the building from earthquake or hurricane.

The Church overlooking Parham Town is worth a visit, although it has been much damaged by the elements. Rebuilt in the Italian style in 1840, the fine ceiling is gone and little of the stucco work remains, but it is well worth the visit despite the damage that occurred during an earthquake in 1843.

Two interesting portraits by Sir Joshua Reynolds, of King George III and Queen Caroline, are to be seen in the Court House. And Government House is occasionally open to visitors.

For more contemporary sightseeing you may want to visit the Industrial School for the Blind, where you can buy unique pieces of straw work including chairs, or the small but attractive Botanical Gardens, featuring native and tropical trees, flowering shrubs, and so forth. The farm run by the Agriculture Department is also of interest in that it produces plants and fruit trees on a commercial scale. And there's Cades Bay Pineapple Cultivation, worth the visit to taste the fabulous Antigua Black pineapple, a delicious toothsome and sweet fruit.

The Ceramic Factory at Coolidge produces a range of pottery figurines, lamps, vases, and souvenirs. You may want to stop by. Tours of the West Indies Oil Refinery can be arranged, and you may want to take a look at the Potswork Dam, an enormous—and before it was built, highly controversial—project with a capacity of one billion gallons of water. Lastly, for pure sightseeing, there's Fig Tree Drive, a delightful tour through lush tropical hills with the occasional clusters of Royal Palm, and numerous picturesque fishing hamlets and villages strung along the southwest coast.

If you've never seen a distillery in action, you may want to visit the home of Cavalier and Old Mill rums—the Antigua Rum Distillery. Best make arrangements before you get to the island as tours are popular, and you have to go to Rat Island.

Where to Stay

Best value for the money when vacationing in Antigua is to take an apartment, cottage, or villa for a week or longer. A number of these are to be found in the environs of the more expensive hotels, which can mean enjoying the hotel's amenities without paying the high room rates. Many of these private quarters come with maid service and/or babysitter if you're taking the family.

Then there are a number of inclusive package arrangements. These can make some hotels much less expensive than advertised room rates, most of which are quoted as Modified American Plan (MAP), which is breakfast plus one meal, usually dinner.

At the top end of the scale is the fabled *Curtain Bluff Hotel* located on beautiful Morris Bay in the southwest part of the island and it lies below Fig Tree Hill and the village of Old Road. It has just about everything you want from a distinguished resort including tennis (4 courts and resident pro), the use of Sunfish sailboats, yacht-chartering for deep-sea fishing, entertainment nightly, an excellent wine cellar, and good food. Each of the 50 rooms has its own private terrace, and the sugar-mill bar serves a number of specialty items.

If you like the beach but prefer more modest rates the *Callaloo Beach* has 16 rooms on the same bay and is within walking distance if you want to savor the food at Curtain Bluff. Good value.

Back at the upper end of the scale is the *Anchorage Hotel*, which offers a variety of accommodations ranging from the earlier cottage rooms to newer air-conditioned rooms with terrace and some beach-side units reminiscent of Little Dix Bay in Virgin Gorda. The entire setting is attractively landscaped and well kept, and the beach at Dickenson Bay—to the north of St. John's—is splendid. All the usual water sports available, plus tennis (resident pro in the high season only), plus an inclusive cruise aboard the yacht *Anchorage.* Steel bands, gift boutiques, excellent service.

Also at Dickenson Bay, but slightly less costly, is the *Hyatt Halcyon Cove Hotel.* There's a central reception area with boutique, and accommodations are spread out through delightfully landscaped gardens. Each unit is air-conditioned with phone, and enormous bathrooms with sumptuously large baths (save water, shower with a friend?) in delicately tiled mosaic. Private patio, pleasantly prompt room service. Lighted tennis courts for night play.

The beach here is fine and the swimming excellent. There's a jetty from which seagoing activities begin; you can get food here during the day (so-so). The hotel's restaurant sits atop a hill above the grounds and is reached by a Leyland diesel jitney. Music is good, service is good, but the food, while the chef tries hard, is not of the excellence to be found elsewhere. For all that, the staff is courteous and attentive and the accommodations are really pleasant.

In the same price range is the fabulous *Half Moon Bay Hotel* just beyond Freetown, in the eastern part of the island and adjacent to the exclusive Mill Reef Club. The 100-room hotel is undergoing a quiet development project that will add more rooms and homestyle accommodations. One of the two 9-hole golf courses is here, and there are water sports, tennis (lighted for night play), swimming pool, and marina. It's one of the Caribbean's more elegant resorts and, while the rates are high, service and accommodations make this worth it if that's what you're looking for.

The *Galley Bay Surf Club* out at Five Islands to the west of St. John's has developed a following. There are a variety of accommodations including duplex-style doubles with bed/sitting room and bathroom/dressing room connected by a breezeway. These come complete with thatched roofs, are pleasantly decorated, and are situated on a lagoon. Usual water sports available, plus tennis, and the food—local and international—is good. There are horses and a donkey on the grounds; a thatched bar and an attractively Bayerischer dining room are the public buildings.

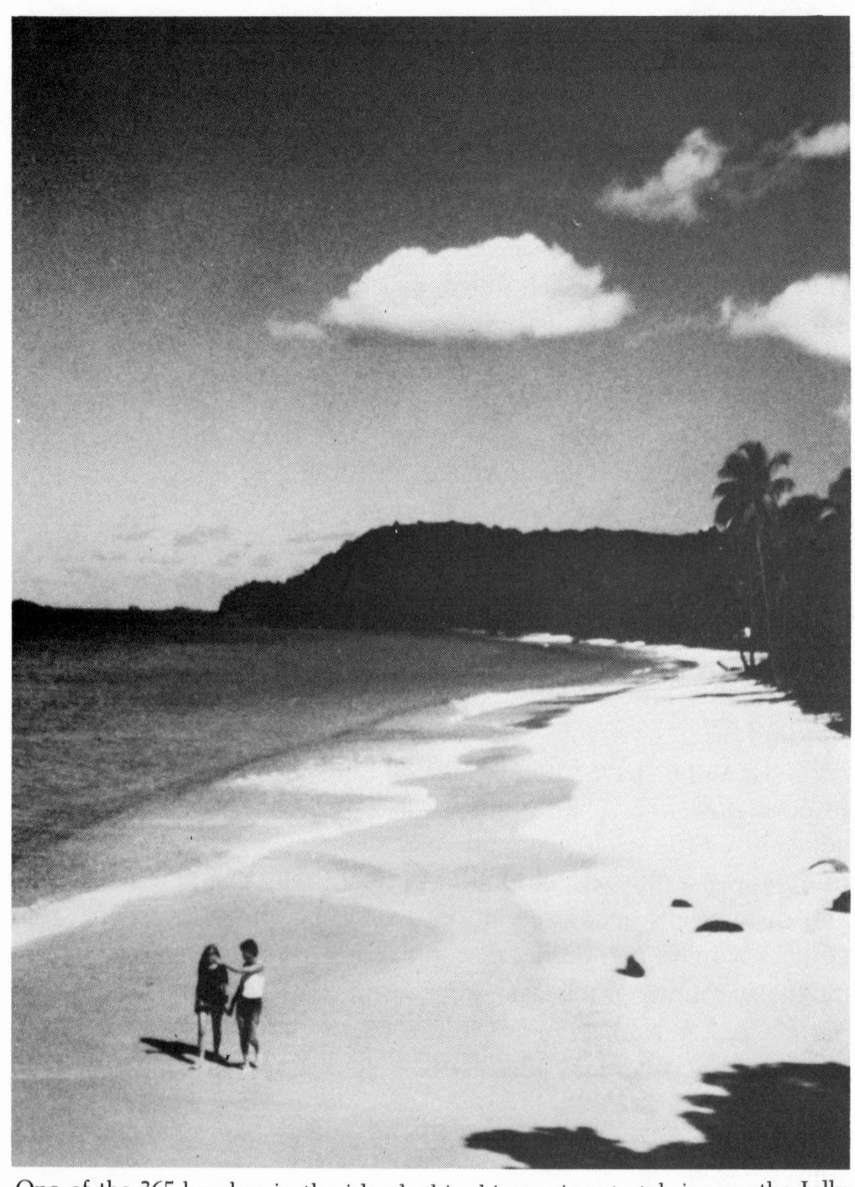

One of the 365 beaches in the island, this shimmering stretch is near the Jolly Beach Hotel.

The *Hawksbill Hotel*, also at Five Islands, has all the usual facilities, with 50 rooms open to the beach, plus a number of cottages of various sizes on the premises for couples or family-size parties. Lounge, bar, dining room, and pool, with a beach house that is the nucleus of daytime activities. Rates slightly lower than Galley Bay Surf Club.

Then there's the *Holiday Inn*, with 100 rooms and the usual amenities that you expect of Holiday Inns around the world. In the southeast of the island, its beach is at Marmora Bay and it's quite close to the missile and moon-rocket tracking station that lies farther down the road. There's a popular marina here, plus swimming pool and tennis, and the evening entertainment is of a sufficiently high standard that even the Antiguans make a point of driving over. Good value for money.

The *Antigua Beach*, the *Blue Waters Beach*, and the *Jolly Beach* are some of the earlier "modern" hotels in the island. The first two are at the north of the island, the Antigua Beach being popular with families. There's golf here, plus horseback riding and tennis. Swimming pool with beach at the bottom of the hill. Special reduced rates for children under 10.

The *Blue Waters* has two 2-bedroom garden apartments in addition to its 50 air-conditioned beach-front rooms. The apartments have cooking facilities and include maid service. Very pleasantly landscaped grounds, swimming pool plus pool bar, tennis (lighted for night play), archery; use of snorkel equipment and fishing rods is free and you can fish from the property. The All Girls Steelband provides regular entertainment, and there are a number of daily activities—some unusual. Some good-natured betting takes place at the crab races, for example, and if you've never seen a West Indian crab race you'd better make the detour here.

The *Jolly Beach Hotel* is now operated by Holiday Inns, and over the years has built a reputation as being a good place for families. In the west of the island at Lignum Vitae Bay, there's a full range of water sports available and a magnificient beach. The hotel itself is set within a palm grove.

Over a lovely Long Bay on the eastern side of the island are *Long Bay Hotel* and the *Antigua Horizons*, both offering good value for money. Long Bay is a charming, informal place and the beach

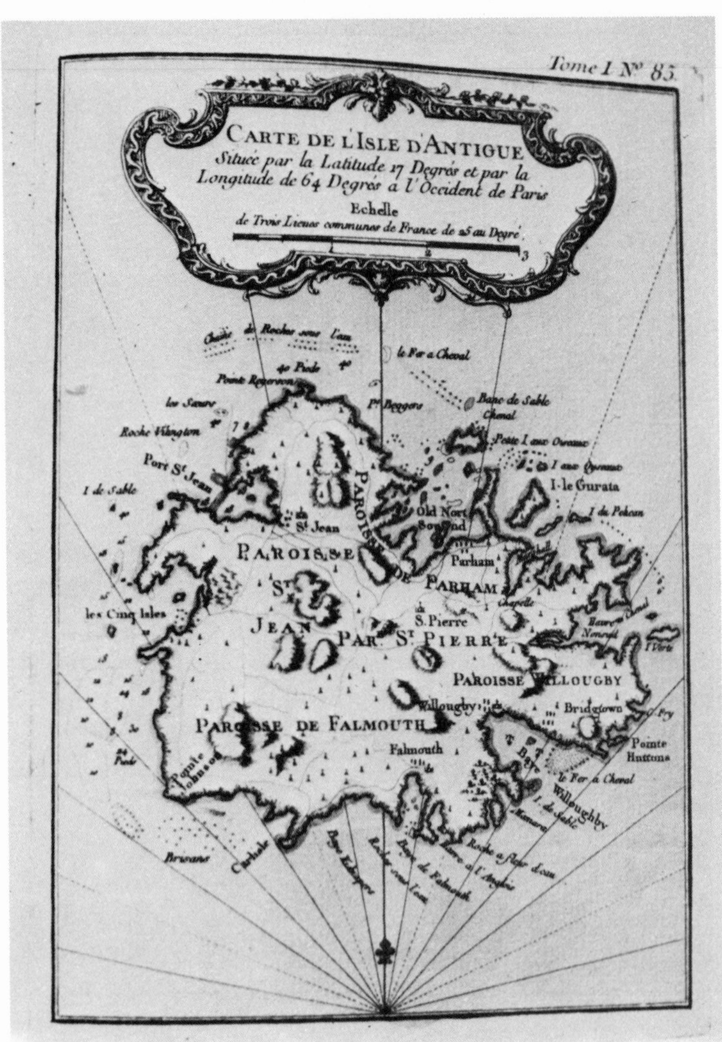

An early French cartographer's version of the island.

house is open to the public. All water sports, including deep-sea fishing, and day trips to islands and islets off shore. There are two efficiency units on the property in addition to 20 rooms.

Antigua Horizons offers excellent food, good entertainment, and pleasing accommodations in any of the 36 rooms—each with patio—in two-story buildings by the sea. Pleasantly informal atmosphere. Rates at both tend toward the high, but the location and atmosphere seem to justify this for both enjoy repeat business. Indian Town Point and the Devil's Bridge are close by.

Down at the south end of the island is English Harbor and in a corner of the sweep of Freeman's Bay is one of the oldest and nicest hotels on the island—*The Inn.* Like an old-fashioned West Country English Inn (the quiet charm of the old English bar with low beams and stone walls adds to your pleasure), the hospitality is olde world while accommodations are extremely comfortable and the excellent food keeps visitors coming back year after year.

Cottage bedrooms either on the hill—for the magnificent view—or at the water's edge emphasize comfort, and a full range of aqua-sports is available. There's a waterski boat, plus yacht for day sailing. Other activities include horseback riding, deck tennis, and croquet. The surroundings, quality of service, and standard of excellence justify the high rates. Good Value.

Less expensive and with a different emphasis in style is the *Admiral's Inn* at Nelson's Dockyard itself. The 200-year-old building has been renovated in such a way that it seems to have enjoyed a continuous existence since it was built, providing an atmosphere redolent of history. Interestingly, the bricks were imported into the island as ships' ballast.

Accommodations are to be found in 9 rooms in the upper 2 storys of the main building, and there are 5 new units in the ground-floor building just across the pillared courtyard. The variety that is available includes a four-poster for those who really want to soak up the historical charm.

Management is unobtrusively good, the menus are varied, the cuisine excellent. Even if you don't stay here, make a point of dropping by for lunch or dinner. The hotel's boat and car are available free of charge for transport to two nearby beaches and there are Sunfish for sailing within the harbor. Popular with the sailing crowd, this is good value for the price.

Just beyond The Inn, below Shirley Heights, is the *Galleon Beach Hotel,* with 16 cottages, including maid service. Accommodations include two twin-bedded rooms with large living area, kitchenette with large freezer, plus balcony. Children are popular here. There are frequent barbecues and rum punch parties at the beach. This, too, could be good value for money, though you may want to include a car if you base yourself here to get around.

Close to the airport one can find more modestly priced accommodations. *White Sands Hotel* (slightly to the north of the *Antigua Beach*) has a definite island atmosphere with a somewhat English emphasis and offers casual tropical living at moderate prices. Some

40 rooms, swimming pool, a step across the road to the beach at Hodges Bay. Occasional entertainment at night. Tennis.

Beachcomber Hotel at Winthrop's Bay has 16 rooms of which not all are air-conditioned at time of writing. Good beach, no entertainment outside of TV, warri (a local game played with pebbles or nuts) and shuffleboard.

Almost next door is the *Lord Nelson Club* hotel with 25 rooms and beach. If you're overnighting in the island, this is the place to be for latest gossip on island and out-island happenings. Good atmosphere.

Low in price is the *Cortsland Hotel,* which is just outside St. John's and provides free transportation to the beach. Good if you've business in town. Also the *Barrymore Hotel,* which also provides free transportation to the beach and offers excellent West Indian food. Swimming pool.

Do It Yourself

Best known are the *Falmouth Harbor Beach Apartment* complex operated by the same management as the *Admiral's Inn.* There are 12 large (twin-sized) studios with maid service and electric kitchen including stove, oven, refrigerator, and freezer. Each studio has its own private full-length terrace for outdoor dining and lounging and the beach is just a few steps from your door. Beach equipment, including sail and power boats, water skis, fishing gear provided at no extra cost. Available for charter is a twin-engined Sportsfisherman.

Also a good value is the *Buccaneer Cove Beach Apartments* on Dickenson Bay (where best hotel entertainment is to be found) in 4- to 6-person efficiency units.

Nelson's Dockyard at English Harbor is being painstakingly restored to its former grandeur. It has already become a place to visit among sailboat adventurers of the world.

Barbuda

Flying In

Coco Point Field is a grass strip, 15 ft elevation, 3,600 ft long. Unicom on 122.8.

Accommodations

Just 30 NM to the north of Antigua is the island of Barbuda, where is to be found that fabled resort of the jet set at Cocoa Point—*Coco Point Lodge.* This is one of the more exclusive resorts in the Caribbean and it's expensive. Still, there's a magnificent beach, the food is excellent, and there are a variety of accommodations. Activities include water skiing, Sunfish sailing, excursions by sailboat, horseback riding, tennis, and snorkeling and scuba. There's also hunting in season—deer and dove.

You can visit for lunch, but it's kept expensive to keep out the hoi-polloi. If you think you'd like to try the high life, book well in advance and mention you'll be arriving in your own aircraft.

The Antigua Department of Tourism is good at answering queries from potential visitors and keeps a listing of available cottages and villas. Alexander Parrish Ltd., whose offices are on St. Mary's Street in St. John's also lists accommodations.

For further information: Antigua Department of Tourism, High Street, St. John's, Antigua (Tel: 20480); in New York at 610 Fifth Avenue, New York, NY 10020 (tel: (212) 541-4117); in Toronto at 21 St. Clair Avenue East, Toronto M4T 1L9 (tel: (416) 961-3085).

Guadeloupe

Flying In

Le Raizet International Airport is some 56 NM almost due south of Coolidge Field, Antigua, and about 40 NM from the north coast of Dominica. There are a number of electronic aids to assist in finding this 584-square-mile island, including VOR DME at 115.1 (PPR) Ch 98 at the field, also an NDB at the field 300 FXG, VHF/DF facility on request, plus ILS, high intensity runway lights, plus another NDB some four miles from the field at 402 AR.

There's plenty of room for jumbos taking off on the long haul to Europe with 11,500 ft on Runway 11 and 10,515 ft on Runway 29. Airport elevation is but 35 ft and radio frequencies are Guadeloupe Radio 128.4 (give them a shout if you're passing through), Le Raizet Approach 121.3 and Tower on 118.4. Hundred-octane fuel and jet fuel available.

Although Le Raizet is the Airport of Entry, Customs and Immigration have become available at Meridien Airport, listed on your chart as St. Francois Field. It's right next door to the hotel of the same name, has 1,800 ft of runway plus full services. A landline connects to Le Raizet for filing flight plans and weather briefing. If you want to fly direct to Meridien be sure to give adequate warning for ADCUS on your flight plan. (Every time you fly overwater, especially VFR you file a flight plan.)

The other island airport at Baillif does not so far have entry facilities and you must first check in at Le Raizet. The out islands with airports include Desirade, 1900 ft of runway at Grandeanse, Marie Galante with 3,100 ft and 2,200 ft at Terre-de-Haut.

For local tourism queries, call 82-09-30.

Background Briefing

The island of Guadeloupe—the Butterfly of the Caribbean—is actually two islands, the wings of this "butterfly" being Basse-Terre and Grande-Terre, which are separated by a body of sea-water known as the Riviere Salee (Salt River). Basse-Terre actually translates as lowland,* somewhat incongruously for Basse-Terre is mountainous with the towering volcano of Soufriere, which looms over a 74,000-acre tropical Parc Naturel of waterfalls and rain forest, mountain lakes and flowers. Even if you are not a lover of natural beauty, the Parc is definitely worth a visit.

Grande-Terre, the eastern wing of the butterfly, is low lying, dotted with windmills and acres of sugar cane, with mile upon mile of shimmering white beaches; it's home to the majority of the island's hotels and restaurants. It's the site of Pointe-a-Pitre, main city of Guadeloupe (Basse-Terre, with a population of around 16,000 on the island of that name, is the actual capital), and a busy commercial center of nearly 90,000 people.

The harbor here is crowded with sailing boats and motor yachts, island schooners and cargo and cruise shipping. The bustle extends into the narrow streets, where you'll find ramshackle shops cheek by jowl with open-air markets and chic boutiques. You'll find everything here, and even though Guadeloupe is not a freeport, there are some excellent bargains in produce and goods from France, much of which is discounted if you're paying by traveler's check.

What makes Guadeloupe such an appealing destination is that it combines the appeal of the French lifestyle with a tropical environment, offering a blend that is both colorful and unique. Some of the most beautiful women in the world are to be seen in Guadeloupe, and the languorous, sensual rhythm of the island's

*The reason for the names goes back to the days of sailing ships. Grande-Terre faces the highest winds, Basse-Terre, thanks to its mountain range, lies in the lee where winds are low.

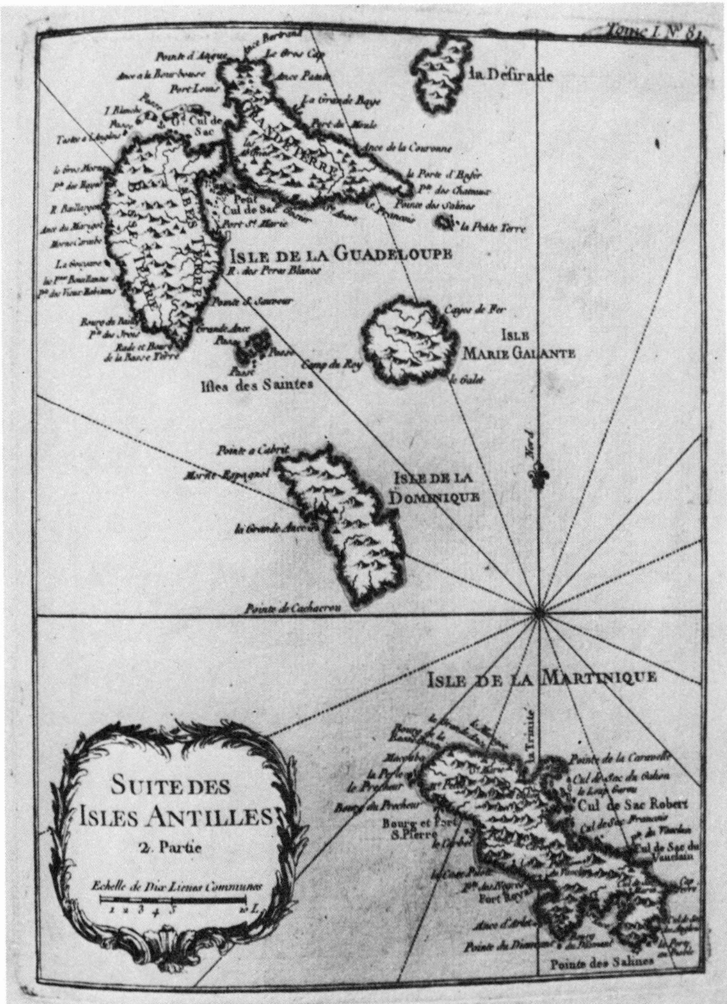

Guadeloupe and its out islands are clearly depicted in this early chart.

beguine will steal your heart away. You can enjoy freshly baked *batons* of crispy bread and the delightful variety of the Creole cuisine. Indeed, the people of Guadeloupe take their food so seriously that each year, during the second week in August, the women cooks on the island declare a busman's holiday to celebrate the Fete des Cuisinieres, or Feast of Cooks.

Highlight of this elaborate occasion is the five-hour banquet of Creole specialities prepared by the female residents, many of whom are owners of the nearly 100 restaurants scattered throughout the island. Invitations are extended to all hotel guests in Guadeloupe at the time, a point you might care to note. More of this festival in a moment.

Scenically, Guadeloupe offers a polarity of views from the flat lands of Grande-Terre to those mountains on Basse-Terre. Along the costal lands you'll find red gum trees, while cabbage palms and mangoes proliferate in the savannahs. On the Out Islands are numerous species of cactus, while several varieties of plantain (or banana) grow almost everywhere. And then there are sugar, cotton, sisal, coffee, numerous tropical fruits, and plump vegetables of almost every sort.

Guadeloupe is actually a *departement* of metropolitan France, and while there were riots inspired by an independence movement back in 1967, a new series of programs of educational, economic, and social developmental import has created a more benign climate. The increasing boom in tourism has created new wealth, which is filtering down to the lower levels of the community in addition to creating work.

Guadeloupe, as mentioned earlier, includes from the point of view of government the islands of St. Barts and, the French half of St. Martin, plus its own nearby dependencies of Marie Galante (named after Columbus' flagship), La Desirade, the Iles des Saints, and the Iles de la Petite Terre. The basic population mix includes people of African origin, descendants of Norman and Breton folk who settled here in the 17th century, and many of racial mixture.

In addition to agriculture and tourism, both fishing and the distilling of rum are significant activities. The island is administered by a Paris-appointed prefect and an elected general council. The departement elects three deputies and two senators to the French parliament.

It's well worthwhile to give yourself an orientation ride, either by public excursion or by driving yourself around the island. One of the best places to begin is at the aforementioned Parc Naturel along the transcostal highway via the Pass of the Two Breasts, so-called because the peaks here are shaped like breasts. Here you'll find lush foliage, richly green tree ferns, and pale yellow-green clumps of bamboo, flowering plants galore and spices. The air is moist, and it rains almost nightly here. To cool off, swim in one of the pools beneath cascading, silvery waterfalls. If you're an amateur botanist, you'll find the names of the plants to be seen at each picnic area in an illustrated guide, with trees identified by name tag. If you want to go off the beaten track, there are a number of interesting trails marked for hikers. Each eventually returns to its point of origin so you don't need to worry about getting lost.

The nearby fishing village of Trois Rivieres is worth the detour. The village itself is quite charming and is also near the site of pre-Columbian rock writings and paintings, of considerable archeological importance. Trois Rivieres is also the start of the sea excursion to the Iles des Saintes. The *Peat du Pischer* (Fisherman's Hut) here is a good small local bistro specializing in Creole-style seafood. At nearby Dole-les-Bains you can soak in the thermal springs, and as you continue farther you'll see the outline of Fort Richepence, which acts as lookout for and guardian to the island's capital.

Basse-Terre is an unusually attractive city with elegant municipal buildings, an attractive 17th-century cathedral, and numerous public gardens and parks. And it's just four miles up a steep and narrow road to St. Claude, once a mountain village, now a suburb of the capital and site of the famous *Relais de la Grand Soufriere*, where lunch is served between noon and 2:00 PM, and where the upper echelons of the local bureaucracy make their homes.

Apart from being an excellent place to lunch, the Relais is a training school for those who want to go into the hotel and restaurant business on the island or elsewhere. It enjoys a reputation as one of the best schools of its kind in the world, as the quality of the meals and standard of service will confirm. Because it is a government venture, it is virtually non-profit, so prices are better than right for the client—which means *you*. Consequently, advance reservations essential.

If you do decide to go to Guadeloupe, you are going to enjoy the food. And if you are a gastronome already, even an amateur, you owe it to yourself to time your visit to coincide with that of the Fete des Cuisinieres, the aforementioned Feast of Cooks.

According to the best hagiographies, St. Laurent is the patron saint of cooks (even as St. Jerome is the patron saint of lost causes).

The Cook's Fete begins with a morning mass celebrated at the Cathedral in Pointe-a-Pitre. Then follows a parade by the women through the streets downtown to the Ecole Amedee Fengarol.

The women are colorfully dressed, wearing traditional Creole costume of full-skirted, multi-petticoated dresses, starched white linen aprons, gold jewelry, silk foulards, and the long, traditional (introduced in the 17th century) madras headresses in which the flair of knots—to those who can read this esoteric language—tells whether the lady is single, engaged to be married, wed, or just merely available. The *madras et foulard* costume is wondrously striking and colorful, and the procession of women, who carry flowers and baskets brimming with utensils and crayfish, lobster and octopus, turtle and conch and other local delicacies, is a truly extraordinary sight to be captured on film and in memory.

As the procession enters the courtyard of the school the bands strike up the *beguine* and in this languorous yet syncopated rhythm the women join their voices to sing of the joys—and occasional miseries—of cooking. A serving of rum all round and some dancing mark that the festival is under way.

In general, food in the island is either classical French, occasionally modified by the types of food that are to be found locally, or else Creole (or Guadeloupian). If you like fish, there are incredible bounties of *fruits de mer*; this includes red snapper—as in Antigua—which is wondrous when created *a la creole*, a casserole of fish, with lime juice, oil and herbs called *blaff*, *Matoutou a Crabes*, which is a form of stuffed crab, plus many more.

The cuisine of the island encompasses the several cultures present, and to the finesse of the traditional French there is added the delicate subtlety of Southeast Asian and Indian fare, where herbs and spices and exotic ingredients can change a ho-hum basic item into something that the palate perceives as vividly original. Then, add, too, that African exuberance, and the original becomes the unique.

Creole cuisine centers around seafood for the most part, tends toward the highly seasoned and usually abounds in herbs. The tropical seas at this point are richer in flavors than even those in the Mediterranean; consequently there's more that can be done, whether it's with crustaceans (shellfish of various sorts), mollusks (of other sorts), or ordinary or not so ordinary fish, as well as such delicacies as octopus and squid.

Wherever you go in the island you'll find an excellence that is unbelievable for those of us who live in fast- and junk-food times here. Whether it's a small fishing village by the seaside or in the heart of the country, you're never very far from this quality. Many restaurants would earn gold rush–type money if they could be transported to the major cities of almost any Western nation.

If you plan to dine out—or lunch out, for that matter—take the trouble to make a reservation. While the local language is French and French patois, English is spoken at all hotels and restaurants, though you'll get better service if you make an attempt to speak French to begin with.* They'll soon know if you're out of your depth and help out.

On Basse-Terre, in addition to the aforementioned Relais de la Grande Souffriere, there are *Chez Paul* at Matouba and *Chez Ragouvin*, where you'll enjoy the *colombo*, a heavenly stew that is a Guadeloupian favorite.

Elsewhere, for excellence in dining note the dining rooms of the *Hotel Salako* and the *Le Saint Charles* at the Meridien, plus *Le Fountainbleau* and *Le Versailles*, both at the *Caraibe Copatel* (candlelit music on the terrace at the latter); at the *Callinago Le Tomaly*. The *Madras* and *Oiseau des Iles* at Le Raizet airport will satisfy your hungers once you've tied down.

There are also good restaurants at the hotels *Frantel*, *Holiday Inn*, and *Novotel*. At the Guadeloupe Holiday Inn you'll see what an American franchise corporation *can* do when it is pushed by its competition.

At the time of writing, in Pointe-a-Pitre, food was also rather outstanding at *Le Bourgainville*, the *L'Eldorado*, and *L'Oasis*. In Gosier, at *Le Chaubette*, *Chez Rosette* (recommended), *La Creole*, *Le Boukarou* (restaurant-cum-night club), *Le Galion* (Ecotel), and *La Parilla*, among several others. For an evening out, *La Creole Chez Violetta* at the end of Gosier boasts one of the best Creole cooks on the island. And at Basida Fort, serving good Creole food at moderate prices, is *Le Cactus* restaurant. In Sainte-Anne are *Au Coquillage* and *Le Bambou Vert du Rivage*, plus the well-known

*E. g., "Une reservation pour deux a trois heures aujourd'hui; je m'appelle John Doe" should get John Doe a table for two at 3:00 PM for lunch.

Food and drink are important parts of the fun in the French islands, where service with a smile is the name of the game.

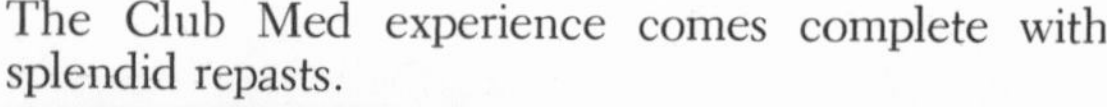

The Club Med experience comes complete with splendid repasts.

At Club Med's Fort Royal village, kids get to have fun on their own at the "mini" Club.

More fun in the sun (opposite page).

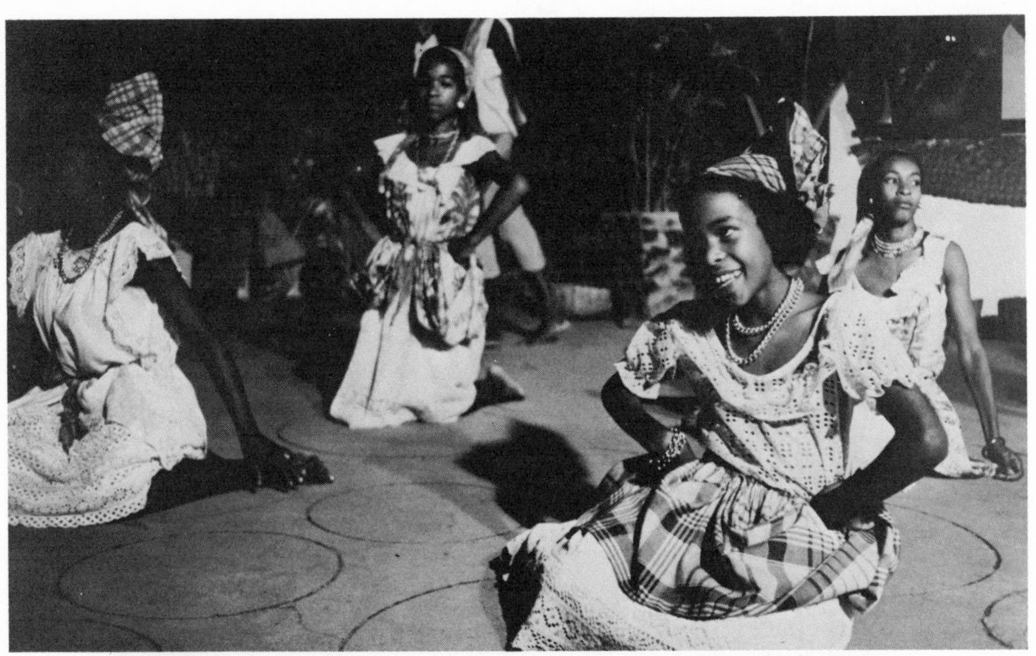

Entertainment is provided nightly at most hotels in the island and includes performances by a Guadeloupe folk troupe—this you should not miss.

L'Auberge du Grand Large. In St. Francois, choose from any of the restaurants toward the Pointe des Chateaux plus *La Cazazoma* at the Meridien, *Chez Madame Jerio's*, and the *Aux Fruits de Mer* and *Aux Raisin Clairs.*

Most menus list so many good things that it can be difficult to know where to begin. Just relax, order an island "Ti-punch" (the local equivalent to the uniquitous planter's potion you'll find offered elsewhere), and then study the list. To nibble on, try some croquettes of codfish, or some ecrevisse (crayfish), or sample the *feroce d'avocats,* an avocado dish whose ferocity lies in its seasoning. Also occasionally available are little mangrove oysters served with a piquant sauce.

For seafood, try the lobster or langouste, the squid, or conch (known in the island as *lambi*) and all delicious. Several varieties of bouillabaisse (fish stew) are to be found, or, if you've never eaten it, try some turtle steak. It's fabulous, delicate, food, and very soon, according to the environmentalists, we'll all have to stop eating it if the turtle is to survive. (Jacques Cousteau has been reported as working on a farming project so that the French and their guests may continue to enjoy this fine fare.)

If you're strictly a meat-and-potatoes person, there are fine beef and lamb available, including tournedos and chateaubriand and even the Creole version of rack of lamb diavolo. (In Gosier, *La Pavillon Grill* serves American steak.) As for the potatoes, pommes frites have never tasted so good, especially when served with an *entrecote garnie* and followed by a selection of cheeses.

Those who have trouble watching their weight should go on a diet *before* leaving for Guadeloupe, in order to enjoy the vacation to its fullest.

Grande-Terre, the eastern wing of the island, is flatter and coral-based and, minutes after you leave Pointe-a-Pitre, you encounter the modern Guadeloupe with sleek homes and apartments, the streamlined university campus, a yacht basin, and a coastline marked by comfortable, medium-sized hotels.

At Bas du Fort, near the historic Fort Fleur d'Epee, are two of the most modern, the *Frantel* and *Novotel.* And then there's Gosier to the east, to all intents the center of Guadeloupe's vacationland with a cluster of hotels including the ever-popular *l'Auberge de la Vieille Tour*, the *PLM Arawak*, and *Holiday Inn*, plus restaurants and discos, numerous tennis courts, and water-sports facilities. A second hotel training program is run here at the *Ecotel-Guadeloupe*, which is also an hotel.

Further along the road at Ste. Anne is a splendid mile-long beach where the *Club Med Caravelle* is to be found, and also here is a rather pleasant ten-room Creole style lodging, the *Auberge du Grand Large*, with an attractive thatch and madras-trimmed bistro.

And the road then brings you to St. Francois, site of the Meridien airport and numerous hotels. To the north on the Atlantic coast is Le Moule, a picturesque and somewhat sleepy fishing village with a contemporary resort nearby; at the opposite end of the village is the *PLM Les Alizes Hotel*.

While you are making your island exploration, don't be shocked if you should turn up some naturists. At present, nude bathing is just short of total government approval. Guadeloupe is one of the few islands in the Caribbean where it is acceptable; you can get a list locally of which beaches these are. (Les Alizes has one.) Pointe Tarare, at the Pointe des Chateaux on the easternmost part of Grande-Terre, where there is an extraordinary rock formation that appears to be the ruins of a castle, is another.* Over on the Ilet Gosier, a tiny cay off Gosier, you'll find them, and at Terre-de-Haut, the beach just over the hill from the *Hotel Le Bois Joli*, is yet another. Both Club Meds have out-of-view, but within easy walking distance, beaches for naturists.

Where to Stay

In Guadeloupe the selection of places to stay covers the gamut from expensive to low budget. At the top end of the scale at the village of Moule is the handsome *Le Caraibe Copatel* with 222 luxury rooms, all air-conditioned and with private balcony, set by the beach in bungalow units of 20 rooms each. (Moule is 17 miles from Pointe-a-Pitre.)

There are two restaurants offering French specialties and a third offering Creole cuisine. There's a convention center, *Le Forum*, with a capacity in excess of 200 persons, plus the usual aqua-sports,

*The view from the Calvary built at the top of a huge rock gives a splendid view of the Islands of Petite Terre and Desirade.

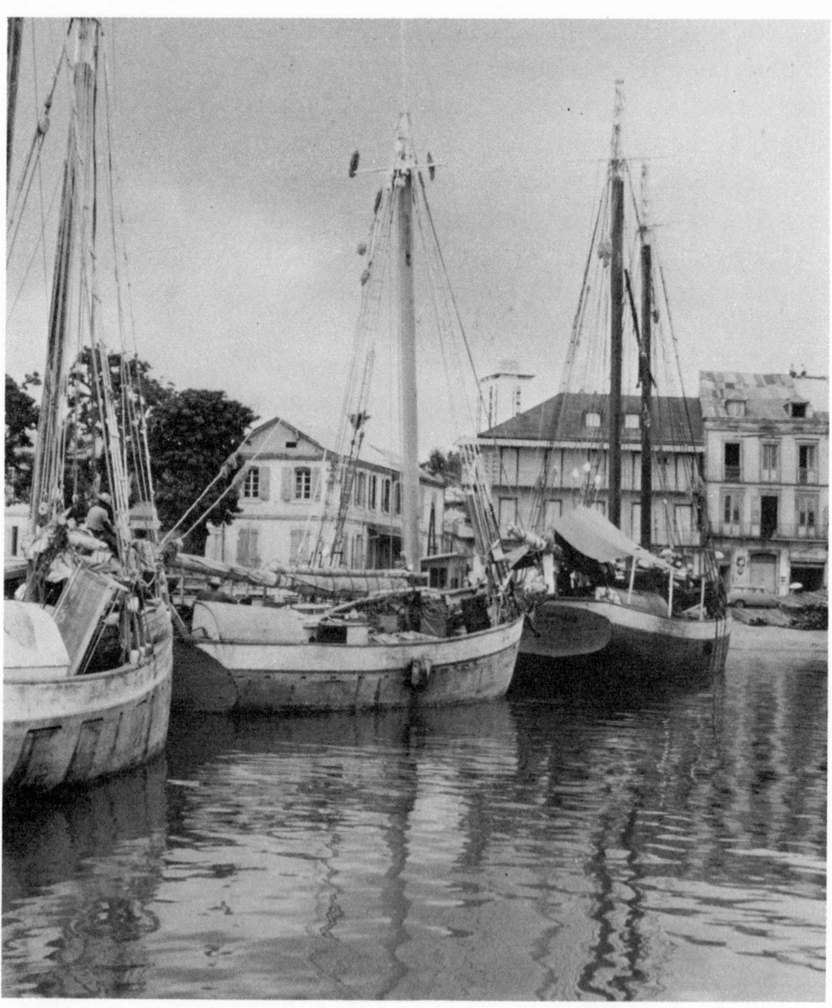

A familiar sight throughout the islands is these sturdy schooners.

volleyball, and tennis. Numerous bars, regular dinner dances, discotheques, boutiques and shops, plus a beauty salon. Very good value if this is your sort of resort.

Le Caraibe Copatel, which is a newcomer to the Caribbean vacation scene, has already been listed as a preferred French West Indies destination resort in the American Express brochure.

Le Meridien, at St. Francois, some 24 miles from Pointe-a-Pitre, was designed as a totally self-contained resort; the hotel originally opened in 1973. It has consistently offered good accommodations and excellent foods and wines ever since.

There are 277 air-conditioned and balconied rooms, three conference rooms, a lagoon, private beach, swimming pool, tennis, and fishing. There are two restaurants, a number of attractively furnished bars, evening entertainment and a discotheque. A number of boutiques and shops off the hotel lobby offer extensive selections of French couture items and fragrances at duty-free prices.

The complex, which includes a marina and the airfield, covers 150 acres, and while the rates are high the quality is good.

The Meridien complex also houses the Hamak villas, for which a number of package arrangements are available. You get the benefit of the resort's amenities, including golf course, wind-surfing and so on, plus the casino, a European-style gamblers' hideaway with three game rooms for boule, roulette, blackjack, baccarat, and chemin-de-fer.

Also at the Meridien complex is the *Trois Mats Hotel,* with studios and duplex apartments with kitchenette and terrace plus the wide range of aqua-sports available. Also *Honore's Hotel.*

For some of the best French food outside of Paris, try *La Marine,* opposite the pier at St. Francois.

Rather different, but internationally renowned for its excellence in comfort, ambiance and cuisine, is *L'Auberge de la Vielle Tour.* Set around an authentic 18th-century sugar mill (the "Vieille Tour" is the old sugar tower) in Gosier, there are 84 air-conditioned rooms with radio and telephone, all with private balcony and separate bathroom. Views of the sea and of the mountains of Basse-Terre. The restaurant has mahogany beams and a romantic atmosphere. At night you can enjoy the excellence of the cuisine in candlelight. Dancing, of course, and within easy walking distance of all the other activities in Gosier.

The Auberge is set within its own 15-acre estate, with swimming pool, lighted tennis courts, L'Ajoupa thatch-roofed outdoor bar/restaurant. There's a private sheltered beach with white sand, occasional barbecue evenings, and overall the quiet and distinguished elegance of a prestige establishment.

One of the things that makes Guadeloupe such a pleasant place to visit is that there are many good quality and *affordable* hotels. This is especially true of Gosier, which has become something of the center of tourism. A typical example is the quiet and comfort-

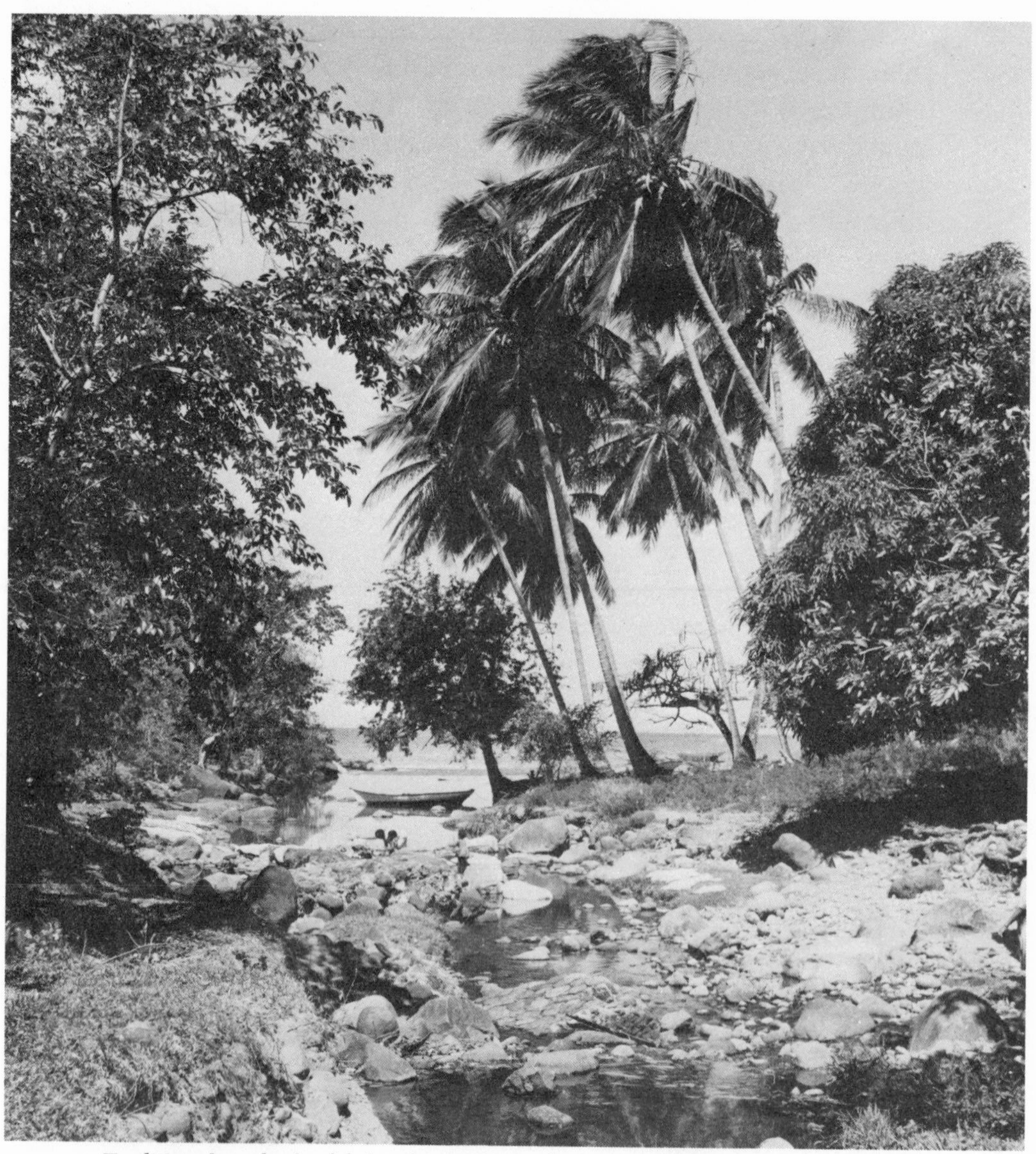

Traditional methods of doing the wash are often employed in the more rural areas of the island.

able *Hotel Callinago*, four miles out from Pointe-a-Pitre (and next door to the Vieille Tour), where you'll find 41 air-conditioned rooms, all with private bathroom, radio and telephone plus balcony, and all overlooking the sea. It's right at the water's edge, yet there's a fresh-water swimming pool and attractive flower gardens, steel band entertainment and outdoor barbecues. Usual water-sport amenities. It's locally owned, and its *Le Tomaly* restaurant is noted for its French and Creole cuisine.

Next door is the *PLM Arawak Hotel*, which, like *Le Meridien*, opened in 1973. Despite its relative newness it has already established a repeat clientele with whom you'll have to vie for accommodations in one of its 160 air-conditioned rooms, which include television. From the upper rooms of this 8-story building are views of the local archipelago, the mountains, Pointe-a-Pitre, and Dominica.

The Arawak's *Jean Lafitte* restaurant features French and Creole fare—uniformly excellent—evening dancing, and the Blue Sky discotheque. Water sports include fishing, and there's tennis, a nice large swimming pool, boutique, and beauty salon.

Le Salako, opened in 1976, and shares dining privileges and leisure activities with Le Calinagro and the Vieille Tour. It is somewhat more European in style, with spectacular views of Les Saintes and the Caribbean sea. There are 120 rooms, with individual balconies, pleasantly landscaped gardens, a large fresh-water swimming pool, and that fine white sandy beach. There are tennis and the usual aqua-sports. French cuisine, nice atmosphere.

The French Frantel hotel chain's to be found on Guadeloupe, at Bas-du-Fort, on the outskirts of Gosier, offering a Gallic ambiance with a tropical accent. *Frantel Guadeloupe*, which opened in 1976, has 200 air-conditioned, balconied rooms, the well-known *Le Grand Gosier* restaurant, its beach restaurant *Le Cicali*, and *Le Wahoo* bar. The rooms are Caribbean modern, studio-style, and there are tennis, swimming pool, and aqua-sports, plus *Le Fou-Fou* discotheque.

The hotel has two conference rooms. Inevitably, *Fort Josephine* and *Fort Napoleon*.

Also at Bas-du-Fort is the *Novotel Fleur d'Epee Caraibe*, rather less than three miles from Pointe-a-Pitre, with 190 air-conditioned rooms, two restaurants offering French and Creole cuisine, two tennis courts (floodlit for night play), large swimming pool, evening entertainment and dancing. Here you can learn some of the more esoteric of the island's rhythms, including *calanda, Bel-Air,* and the *Laghia.* Aqua-sports, a superior planter's punch, and, for the businessmen, convention rooms. Package arrangements may be available.

At Pointe de la Verdure, Gosier, some 5 miles from Pointe-a-Pitre, is the *Holiday Inn.* Although the chain is an American franchise, its Canadian division is responsible for this property, which perhaps explains why its imaginative design is matched by an excellence of service. Or maybe it's because it's up against stiff competition.

Apart from the food, mentioned earlier, there are 156 air-conditioned rooms, including several for invalids. Two beaches—one for waterskiing, one for swimming—two tennis courts, an American bar, plus a coffee shop. Several package arrangements are available—inquire.

Then there's the aforementioned training hotel, *Ecotel-Guadeloupe*, surrounded by luxuriant tropical vegetation and less than half a mile from the Gosier beaches. Its *Le Galion* restaurant is especially worth a visit. On the small side with only 44 air-conditioned rooms, there are a local-handicrafts boutique, telex service, an attractive swimming pool, and lots of students wanting to impress you with the excellence of their work. Much, much better value than it sounds, if you're at all adventurous.

The hotel is the work of the same architect who designed Le Raizet airport, Gilbert Corbin, and consequently there are tasteful decoration and good design—thoughtful and long on creature comfort—all around. Guest beach privileges at La Vieille Tour.

Out to Moule once more for a look at PLM's other hotel in Guadeloupe, the *PLM Alizes*, for casual beachfront relaxation *a la francais.* Situated on an attractively landscaped 45-acre estate on one of the best of the beaches in the island, no fewer than half of the 128 air-conditioned rooms (two double beds) come with kitchenette arrangements, which means you can do-it-yourself-if-you-want-to here. Which means a Hotel/Residence Club. One of the best values on the island.

There are a restaurant, snack bar, and disco, of course, plus swimming pool, tennis, aqua-sports, all set within some 50 acres of coconut plantation. Horseback riding available. Package arrangements when available are an especially good value.

Oh yes, and there's swimming *au naturel* close by.

At Ste. Anne,* just about halfway between Gosier and St.

*For clam soup, turtle steak, and lobster on the Route Ste. Anne, stop at *La Chanbette.*

Francois, lies the *Auberge du Grand Large,* where you'll find accommodations in 10 bungalows and a restaurant that specializes in Creole food. The bar serves potent drinks and attracts a colorful and mostly local clientele. Fun place to be, but rates tend toward high. Very tropical-Mediterranean, pleasantly informal ambiance.

Also in Ste. Anne is the guesthouse *Le Mini Beach Hotel.* There are 8 rooms and 4 thatch-roofed bungalow accommodations, all simply but attractively furnished. This could be a good choice.

In Pointe-a-Pitre, right in the heart of town, is *Le Bougainvillee.* Its rooftop restaurant is one of the best places in town to eat, yet it caters primarily to the business community and those who prefer to stay in town. It's cheap, and good. The *Hotel Normandie,* on place de la Victoire, boasts *le Bacchus* grill room, where specialties include veal, steak, and lamb, plus seafood from the charcoal grill.

At the lower end of the price range in Gosier are *Les Flamboyants,* bungalows with kitchenette; the *Hotel J. J.,* which provides Guyanese specialties from the chef (8 air-conditioned rooms only); and *Serge's Guest House.*

In Basse-Terre, note the *Hotel Relaxe,* with its views of the volcano and sea, bar, restaurant, and night club. The *Hotel Recroy,* some 5 miles from the capital, is the choice of many business people.

So far not too much has been said except peripherally about the two Club Mediterranee resorts. Club Med was originally conceived soon after World War II as an experiment in socialist vacations. The idea was that the worker would buy a package that would include at little extra cost those items on which society sets a premium, such as wines and liqueurs, among the few that have survived within the Club Med philosophy.

Today, the socialist workers' paradise has become a highly profitable capitalistic arrangement with centers around the world. Two are in Guadeloupe, in the French West Indies, with a third in Martinique.

Back in 1973, the Club took over the splendid 300-room *Hotel Caravelle* at Ste. Anne, on one of the most beautiful beaches in the island. Although it's opulently 4-star quality, the same weekly arrangement applies, and the local currency—beads, for purchases within the hotel—still applies. The rooms are enormous, and the twin beds glide around on rails. There's a disco on the premises.

Because this Club Med is almost always sold out you must book well in advance, minimum stay one week.

Fort Royal, Club Med's first Caribbean village, is reportedly better than ever now that it has undergone extensive modernization. It bridges two magnificent golden beaches at Deshaies.* There's an enormous swimming pool—the sea can be difficult for tyro swimmers here.** For the various packages contact Club Med direct. Their address: Club Med, Inc., 40 West 57 St., New York, NY 10019; tel. (212) 977-2170. For further information, contact the French West Indies Tourist Board, French Government Tourist Office, 610 Fifth Avenue, New York, New York 10020; (212) 757-1125.

Enjoy Guadeloupe and its islands.

Bonne chance, bonnes vacances, bonne idee!

*It is the only Club in the Western hemisphere to offer a fully supervised "Mini-Club" for 4-to-12-year-olds who endorse the experience. Meanwhile, *les parents* get to relax.

**A new joint scuba/snorkel and recreation center recently opened at Pigeon Bay, which includes restaurant, shuttle service to the villages and includes water skiing.

Pointe des Chateaux.

Out Islands

LA DESIRADE

La Desirade is only a short hop from Meridien, and a slightly longer one from Le Raizet.*

A former leper colony, it is now a charmingly picturesque spot, and makes an interesting day's excursion. While undeveloped for tourists, the simplicity of the lifestyle of the locals is as good as a rest cure. You'll also be able to see an indigenous iguana, a small land lizard that makes its home here. The iguana, which is also to be found on the island of Anegada in the BVI, is the last surviving living relic of the prehistoric reptilian era.

There's a small, very simple hotel right on the beach, and you can savor just about every delicacy that comes from the sea, including sea snails, clams, sea urchins (*oursin*, as it is known here), plus lambi and numerous fishes.

MARIE GALANTE

Flying In

Open from sunrise to sunset, there's a 3,000-ft strip (Runway 09/27) situated at the south of the island near Pointe des Basses. A

*You should call ahead of your arrival, and someone will meet you at the strip in an old van for the drive to town. It's a very long walk otherwise.

light airplane club is at the field, and transport is available. File at Le Raizet.

The Island

Like Grande-Terre, the island of Marie Galante is dotted with ancient windmills, and the fields are alive with the silvery-green shimmering of the cane in the wind.

Some 27 miles southeast of Pointe-a-Pitre, the island (also like Grande-Terre) is of limestone formation, and with an area of 59 square miles, is the largest of the islands forming the offshore archipelago of Guadeloupe. Because it is circular in shape, Columbus' crew initially nicknamed the island "Sombrero," though the official name was Maria Graciosa. At that time it was inhabited by Carib Indians, and it would later become a refuge to the Caribs who originally lived in Guadeloupe.

The island enjoys the charms of the past (chalky lanes furrowed by ox-carts). Agriculture is still the principal resource. In the 18th-century the island was renowned for the quality of its sugar and rum, and at one time there were 72 Pere Labat sugar mills, named after the French Dominican missionary. Each served to grind the cane and represented an independent family's operation.

Then, in the 19th-century, the older sugar mills and ancient refineries were replaced by 4 factories in the middle of vast plantations: these were at Grand'Anse, Le Robert, Pirogue, and Dorot. Today, only the one at Grand'Anse is in working order, and only 5 distilleries remain of the dozens that used to do business here. Still, the rum is of a remarkable quality, as you'll discover if you care to sample it.

Of the secondary crops for which Marie-Galante was famous in years gone by—indigo and tobacco, cocoa, coffee and cotton—scarcely a trace remains. Today the islanders tend to produce cassava, yams, beans, and pigeon peas. Cattle also are raised.

The island's population is around 16,000 and there are three main communities: at Grand Bourg, the capital (about 8,000) in the southwest; Capesterre in the southeast; and Saint-Louis in the northwest. Just a few miles from Grand Bourg is the Chateau Murat, justly described as a princely domain, though bearing no connection with the famous princes of that name. Rather it was the creation of a lawyer and planter, one Dominique Murat, who had a small coffee plantation in the late 18th century and who lived in nearby Capesterre. The chateau was built in 1832 and its architect was Mademoiselle Murat, who had studied at the Ecole des Beaux-Arts in Paris.

A painstaking restoration program, begun some years ago, is nearing completion. Of particular interest is the estate's original sugar mill with its vanes and machinery restored to working order.

Near the sugar factory of Pirogue toward the island's interior is the punchbowl, or *mare au punch*, which acquired its name just following the permanent abolition of slavery. It seems that the newly freed slaves were so excited that they entered the factory and emptied the entire stock of rum and all the molasses into a nearby pool, drinking all night from their "punchbowl."

Students of windmills will have a field day in the island, where one of the more interesting, outside of Vieux Forts, is the windmill of Agapit, with its unusual vertical shaft.

Also near Vieux-Fort is the *Gueule de Grand Gouffre*—Mouth of the Giant Chasm. Here the swirling tides of the ocean crash against the steep rock, and the fury will take your breath away. A little further on the same game between sea and rock is played at *Caye Plate*.

Potholers and those interested in the mysteries beneath the earth's surface should make the excursion to the *Trou au Diable*, or Devil's Hole, a grotto some 328 feet long that encloses an underground lake and a cavern with stalactites. You should make arrangements ahead of time in order to have a guide and the proper gear.

On the way to Saint Louis you'll pass the Grand'Anse sugar factory and the sugar port of Folle Anse with its silos of sugar.

While there is a public bus service between towns, it's possibly more convenient to rent a car, as there are only a limited number of taxis. Self-drive arrangements can be made through M. Seytor on rue Beaurenom in Grand Bourg (tel. 87-20-56).

Where to Stay

The *Hotel Soledad* has 9 rooms in Grand Bourg and is just a couple of miles from the airport. Also in Grand Bourg is the *Hotel le Quartier Latin* with 5 rooms. Out toward Capesterre is *Le Belvedere*, 5 rooms only but with a nightclub in addition to its restaurant. In Saint-Louis, *Hotel Le Salut*, 15 rooms plus restaurant.

In addition to the restaurants at these hotels, the following offer

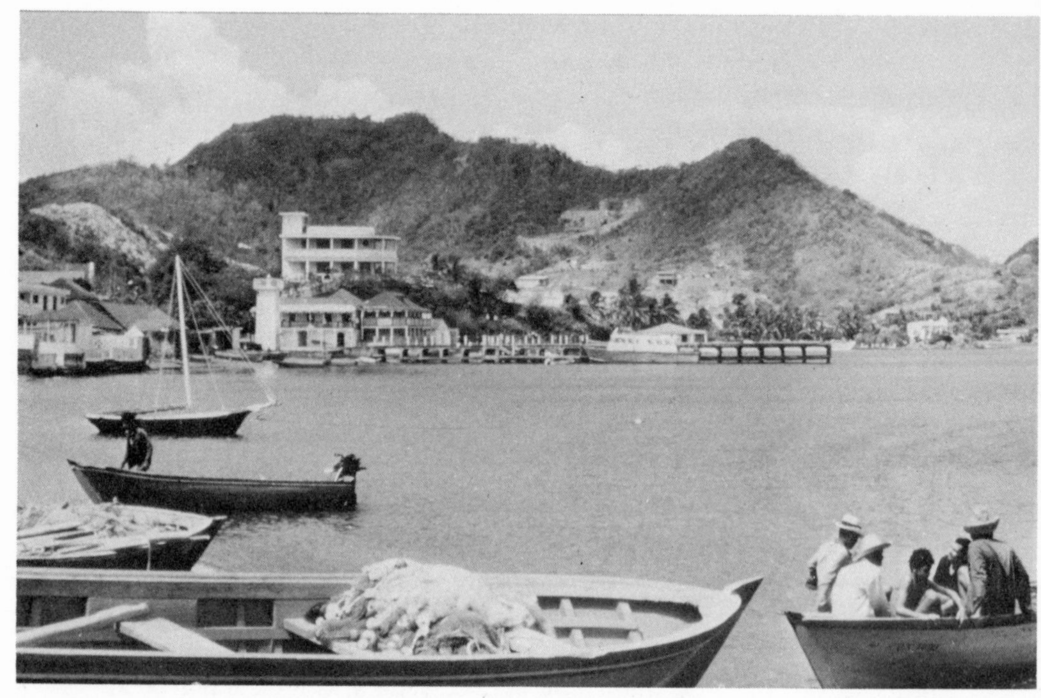

reliable and usually imaginative and tasteful fare. In Grand-Bourg, *Chez Pincel* and *Chez Verin, Au P'tit Pecheur.* In Saint-Louis, *Arc-en-Ciel, Chez Grazielle, Aux Crabes,* and *Au Coquillage.* Also good is *Le Bekeke,* Plage de la Feuillere, and *La Touloulou.*

ILES DES SAINTES

Flying In

Prior permission has been required at the 1,900-ft strip that lies in the center of the Terre de Haut. Flying from Le Raizet or Meridien, you'll come in from the north, make a left downwind and short left base over the water for a touchdown on runway 09. File at Le Raizet.

The Islands

A small archipelago within the larger archipelago, Les Saintes is a grouping of 8 islands some 8 miles from the southern tip of Guadeloupe at Pointe du Vieux-Fort, comprising Terre-de-Haut, Terre-de-Bas, Ilet a Cabrit, le Grand Ilet, la Redonde, la Coche, les Augustins, le Pate, and les Roches Percees. Only Terre-de-

Ruggedly beautiful, the out islands provide a true get-away-from-it-all experience with delightful views. Note airport sited on one of the few relatively flat pieces of land.

Haut, Terre-de-Bas, and the Ilet a Cabrit are inhabited; total population, thirty-five hundred persons. The islands were named Los Santos by Columbus in honor of All Saints Day, which had just passed when he found them, and the French merely translated the name to their language.

Terre-de-Haut (*haut* meaning *high*, with reference to those trade winds) is nearly 4 miles long, a little over a mile wide at its widest point and topped by le Chameau, some 1,014 feet high. It has an irregularly shaped coastline with numerous small and private coves.

Just two miles off lies Terre-de-Bas, smaller, more regularly shaped—almost circular—and richer in vegetation.

During the fierce competition between French and British in the 17th and 18th centuries, Les Saintes proved to be invaluable as a strategic land asset, and what with gun emplacements and other fortifications, Les Saintes acquired the reputation of being the Gibraltar of the Caribbean. The most famous battle took place on April 12, 1782, when Admiral Rodney trounced Admiral Comte de Grasse in a battle in the sea passage between Les Saintes and Dominica. (The islands were restored to France in 1816 following the retirement of Napoleon from the European scene.)

The Saintois fishermen share with those of Saba the reputation of being the best seagoing people in the entire Caribbean. There's a small boat-building industry, which makes boats called *santois* out of local woods. Originally designed for sail, most fishermen today make use of the "iron sail" or engine. Net fishing continues, and since the local waters teem with fish, fishing is the prime economic activity. Red snapper, dorado, tuna, bonito, capitaine, carangue, colat and, of course, langouste and conch are just some of the produce which is marketed most days at Trois Rivieres and Basse-Terre in Guadeloupe.

The boats, which are brightly painted, bear colorful names, such as *Belle Doudou, Apres-Dieu,* and even *Concorde.*

Tourists can camp with a tent or rent a small villa, but those preferring a little more comfort can find a cozy atmosphere in the few small but good hotels in Terre-de-Haut. There's only one street here, which follows the curve of the waterfront and divides the island into two parts. To the north is Le Mouillage, with attractive villas, and to the south Fond de Cure, a fishing village.

Smiles and beauty are not restricted to either the main island or to the lands that make up Guadeloupe's out islands.

There are very few cars in the island so figure on walking. Few beaches are more than ten minutes away. L'Anse Crawen is for swimming *au naturel.*

Where to Stay

Hotel La Saintoise, 10 rooms, in the center of Terre-de-Haut, with a patio restaurant overlooking the water. *Hotel Jeanne d'Arc,* also 10 rooms, on the beach at the Fond de Cure. *La Colline,* with 7 one-bedroom bungalows nestled on the hillside, with all amenities and a spectacular view, Terre-de-Haut.

Famed *Hotel Bois Joli,* with 21 rooms, just ten minutes by boat from the village, fabulous food and one of the best beaches in the world.

Kanaoa, at Pointe Coquelet, just 8 rooms on the water's edge, and a warm and friendly atmosphere and excellent food.

Where to eat

L'Abordage, Le Coq d'Or, and *Le Mouillage* are generally reckoned as the hotels' best competition. Specialties include courtbouillon-style fish stew, steamed clams in their own broth, *burgots* (sea snails), stuffed crab, and much, much more. Try, for dessert, the *tourment d'amour,* an exquisite coconut *tartine.* Simply delicious.

A comparison between early attempts at mapping and the present state of the art navigation today. The island chain, as can be seen, is relatively replete with electronic signposts.

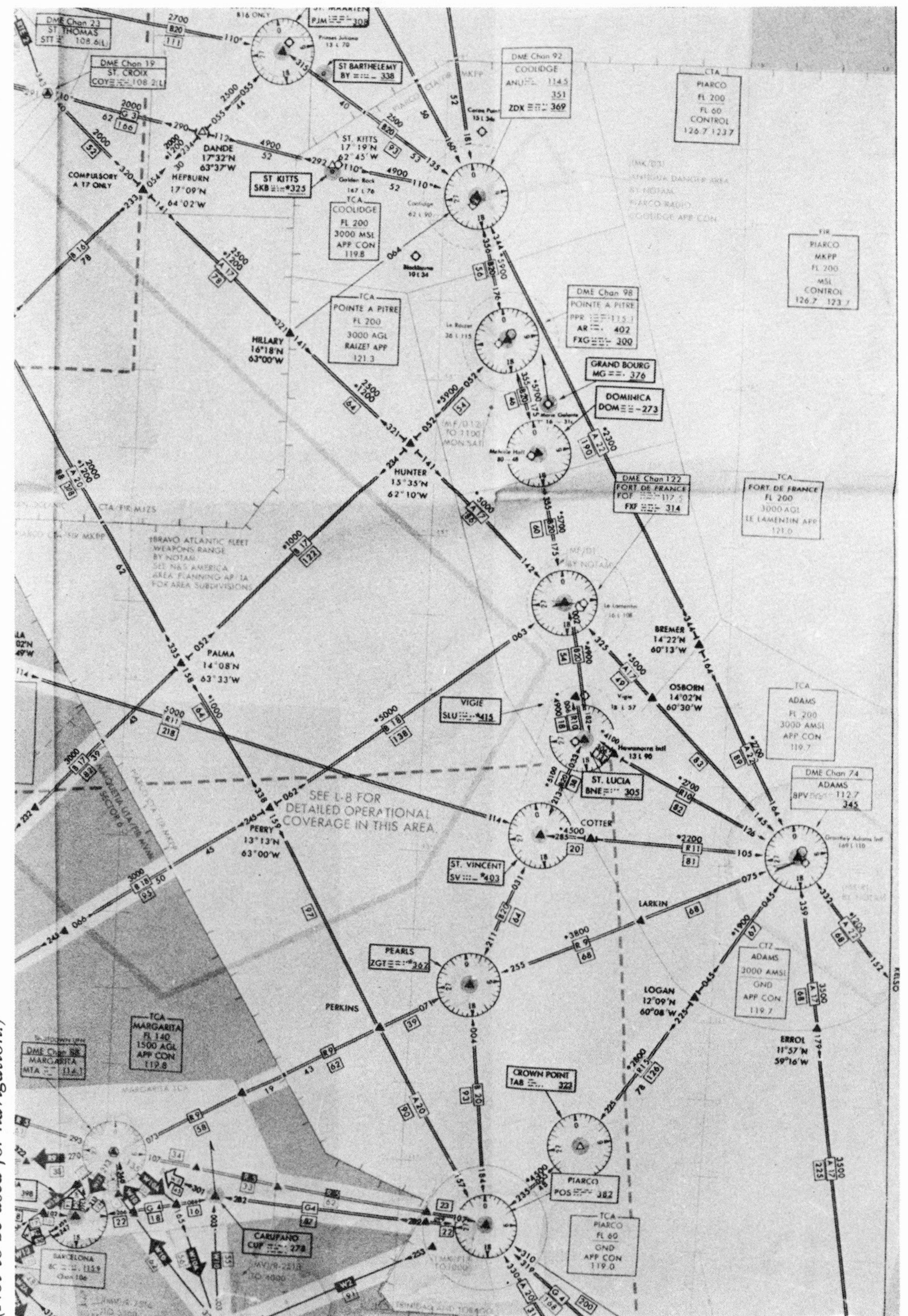

(Not to be used for navigation.)

Dominica

Flying In

Just 46 NM almost due south of Le Raizet is *Melville Hall Airfield.* There's 4,800 ft of runway, but since the main strip faces out into the Atlantic—off which the winds blow into the Venturi funnel of the valley—there are very few days in which it's possible to approach from the sea.

This means some attention must be paid to a correct approach, and you may want to have a look around before you go in because it can be a bit of a pig your very first time.

The LIAT pilots pop their Avro 748s in with great aplomb and their technique is as follows: You climb inland on your downwind—to the north of the field—and then make a short base over the ridge that is one side of the valley. You drop full-flap to give you a steep descent over the tops of the palm trees on the way down the side of the hill, using power all the way down to bring you in. If you're not sure you're going to make it, and it's very easy to find your intended point of contact turning into the far end of the runway, just apply full power and clean up the ship and go around. There's plenty of room since you're going seaward, and you'll gauge it better the next time around.

One visiting pilot in a Mooney—already noted—went around four times before he got it locked up and on the numbers.

Takeoff is seaward and there's nothing special about that. You'll find that on account of the winds off the Atlantic you'll need a shorter takeoff run than usual. On landing, clean up the aircraft immediately the wheels have touched so you don't do any more flying.

Fuel is reported to be available at the field, but best not rely on it.

Background Briefing

At approximately 300 square miles in area, Dominica (pronounced Dom-in-*eek*-ah) is one of the larger of the islands of the Eastern Caribbean. Population is around 80,000 and the two main centers of activity are Roseau, the capital (11,000), and Plymouth, both of which lie on the western side of the island overlooking the Caribbean Sea.

Of volcanic origin, its Mount Diablotin rises to nearly 5,000 ft., and the island is one of the most ruggedly beautiful in the entire region, with a rain forest that shelters some 135 species of native bird. Two endangered species of parrot are to be found only in this island—the Sisserou or Imperial Parrot and the Rednecked Parrot, or *Amazona arausica.*

The population is of mixed descent for the most part, with an emphasis on African-origin. English is the official language of the island and most everyone speaks and understands it, but the chosen language is a musical and lilting French patois that includes a number of transplanted African words and constructions, together with some Portuguese.

The economy is still agricultural, the principal exports being bananas and the famous Rose's Lime Juice. Breadfruit, cassava, corn, and yams are grown locally as basic foodstuff, as is rice. Significant quantities of avocadoes, cocoa, coconuts, and mangoes are also grown, in addition to increasing quantities of lumber for export. Also produced are a strong, robust local rum* from sugar cane; oils and soap from copra; a canning industry specializing in citrus fruits, jams and jellies; bay rum and oil; and a hot spicy peppersauce.

While tourism has grown significantly over the past few years, and while there are investor opportunities in this field, the government is actively looking for further diversification of indus-

*Bagatelle, used as the base for an excellent punch.

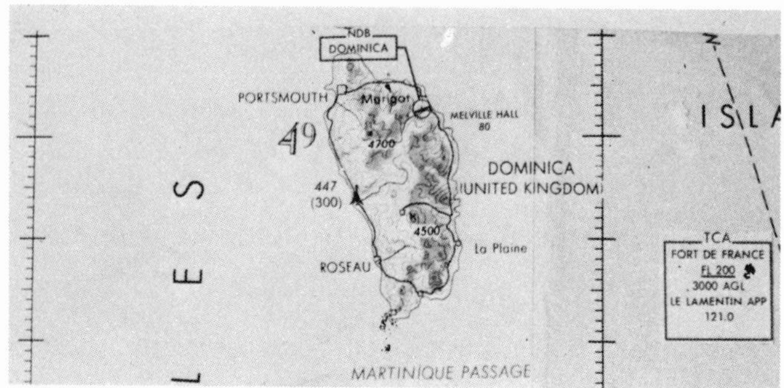

(Not to be used for navigation.)

try. Fields that might interest potential investors include the garment industry, furniture manufacture (the island possesses numerous fine woods including teak), and raising of livestock—a private herd in neighboring St. Lucia did remarkably well, as have two herds in Montserrat.

For the visitor, one of the attractions of the island is the wide range of fruits, including palm hearts, and the exotic delicacy the island shares with Montserrat—the mountain chicken, or *crapaud* as it is called here. Wild pigeon,* known as *ramier*, is delicious, as is the smoked meat of the *agouti*, and *titiri*, a local version of whitebait. Crab backs are also especially good.

The island of Dominica is one of the last refuges of the Carib Indians who fought bloodily against both English and French for their survival. They maintained that French Catholics made better eating than English Protestants and eventually were able to treat with the French for some land they could call their own. The remnants of the tribe live here on a reservation.

But even as the French influence was making its presence felt, the English were readying a turn of the tables, which took place in 1758 as they took this island under their wing. Nevertheless, although Dominica has been British for more than 150 years, French Creole is the favored language of its people.

The island is some 29 miles long by about 16 wide, and at present has only small-scale hotels ranging from 7 to some 40 rooms. It is

*Hunting by visitors is permitted during the season, but for current details inquire of the Dominica Tourist Board.

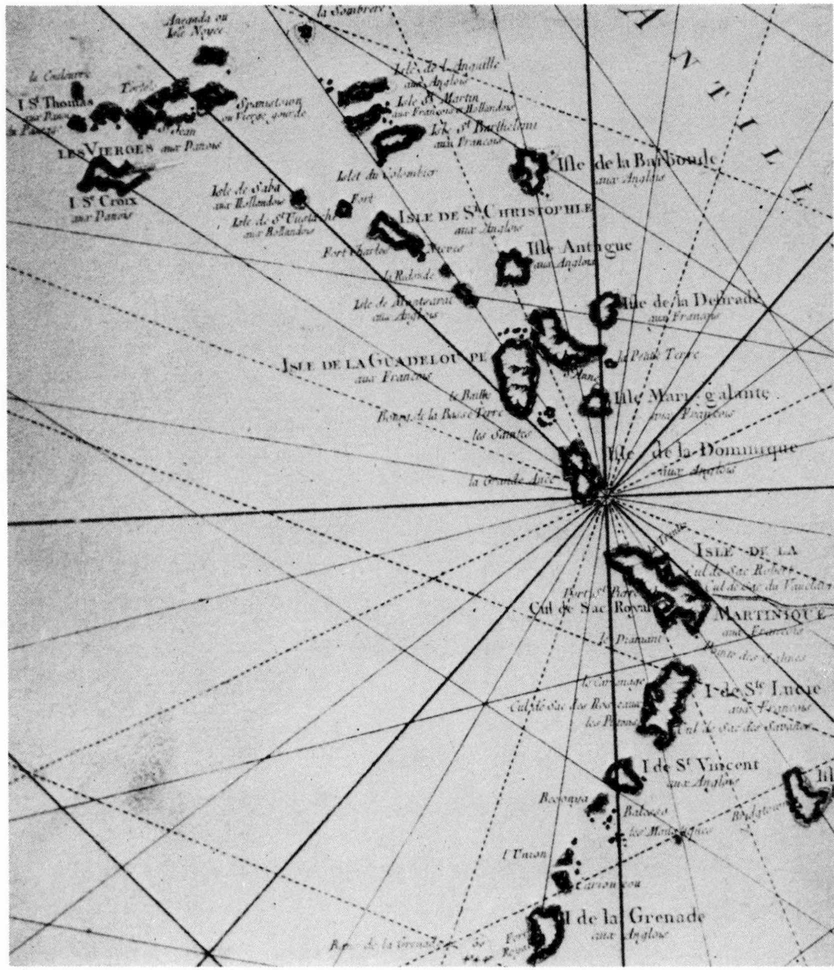

one of the least developed of the islands and you can still see boatmen fashioning the dug-out canoe—according to centuries-old tradition—from the gommier tree.

Because of its rain forest, the island has many streams, cascades and mountain pools—very cool—and rainfall in the mountains can climb to more than 300 inches per year. The rainy season runs from the end of July through November, but on the west coast—where Plymouth and Roseau are situated—it's really not too bad except from an occasional overcast day.

The mountains get very cool at night throughout the year, and temperatures can drop down to the low 40s.

Sightseeing should definitely include a trip into the rain forest; the recently created Morne Trois Pitons National Park of 16,000 acres is a pristine example. Also fascinating is the Emerald Pool Nature Trail in which in a quarter-mile stretch you can see an incredible variety of tropical flora from the most minute and delicate ground ferns to those huge statuesque gommier trees. If you're an amateur field botanist you'll find much to intrigue you, since so much of the island is in its natural state and undisturbed by mankind.

In the center of the island are Boeri Lake, Boiling Lake, Fresh Water Lake, and Trafalgar Falls and the Sulphur Springs. The Carib Reservation is open to visitors and is near the airport. In Roseau is the island's own excellent Botanical Gardens. Mountaineers interested in tackling Morne Diablotin should go with a local guide since the trails are unmarked for the most part and the dense ground cover can conceal a number of treacherous falls.

There are a few self-drive cars available, plus a number of taxis at the airport and in Roseau and Plymouth. Rates are about 35¢ (US) per mile, slightly less if you pay in EC dollars. The Dominica Taxi Association has a number of Land Rovers and Jeeps, and several firms offer the Safari Tour, which is a full-day excursion covering the high spots of the island. The roads are some of the worst in the Caribbean and you may prefer to let someone else do the driving.

Where to stay

The accent at Dominica's hotels is on a pleasant informality and courteous service. At the top end of the scale is the *Anchorage* at Castle Comfort, just half a mile from Roseau. There's a freshwater pool, and there are docking facilities from some dozen or so sailboats.Two wings, one along the shore, the other—three-storied—with sea-view terraces, comprise 26 rooms.

Island House with its 20 rooms is inland, about 5 miles from Roseau, and is built around an attractive spring-fed pool, usually chilly. Some of the rooms have beautifully large tubs, and all are furnished with native woods and island handicrafts. The main

A fumarole, with boiling sulfur.

lounge has a fireplace used to keep out the mountain chills in the evening. Good value if you're looking for something different.

Thirteen miles inland from Roseau is *Riviere La Croix Estate*, some 1,500 ft up in the mountains with spectacular views. There are about a dozen cabins, good food, and a pleasant, informal atmosphere. Swimming pool, river, and a Hemingwayesque hunting-lodge ambiance. The hotel provides free transport to the beach and fishing, and aqua-sports can be arranged. Most guests opt for hikes, and the country here is explorable. (Note that there are *no* poisonous insects or snakes in the island).

On the road north to Plymouth, some 13 miles from Roseau, is the *Castaways Hotel*,* set on 8 acres and overlooking a crisply black sandy beach. This is the nearest you'll get to a resort in the island, and activities include snorkeling, sailing, spear-fishing and game fishing, water skiing and picnics via motor launch. Candlelit dining with as much wine as you can manage. Castaways is also known as the *Club Caribee at Mero Beach*.

Old timers to Dominica will remember *Fort Young*, built into the early stone buildings that overlook the harbor in Roseau. (The deep-water harbor is about a mile to the north of the capital). A new wing has been built, and there are a swimming pool and a courtyard bar area. Food can be good.

New hotels include *Springfield Plantation*, some 6 miles in from Roseau, which offers comfort and good food in a pleasantly tropical setting. The *Kai Papillotte*, just 4 miles inland from Roseau, has begun to develop its following. And in the interior are the *Burundi African Shambas*, which transplant you to a reasonably authentic African-style experience for your island stay.

Inexpensive accommodations at the *Castle Comfort Guesthouse* and at *Asta*, in Roseau.*

Most hotels provide some entertainment during the season and on holiday weekends. *La Robe Creole*, *Seamoon*, and the *Eleven-Eleven Disco Bar and Restaurant* are open nightly, while the *Green Grotto* has dancing at weekends.

Burundi African Shambas has its own *Club Burundi*, which offers soul food and jazz on weekends from noon until midnight, Fridays, Saturdays, and Sundays.

*Sports fishing facilities available here and from Dominica Safaris.

The Green Parrot and the *Calabash* are popular watering holes and good for local gossip.

Sports

Tennis available by arrangement at the Dominica Club in Roseau—2 grass courts; also at the *Anchorage*, where there's a floodlit hard court.

Horseback riding is offered by the *Anchorage* as part of a sports package that includes a half-day tour to a mountain farm.

Shopping

While there's no duty-free shopping, a number of island handicraft stores and boutiques offer a wide range of locally handmade items, including woven products and novelty items made by the Carib Indians, who also make sturdy and ingeniously waterproofed baskets.

Caribana Handcraft and Tropicrafts in Roseau has a range of *khus khus* grass mats, plus fine quality rugs. Dominica Handcraft Company sells a fairly complete range of island produce including jams and juices in addition to handmade wares. Orchid Beauty Shop sells local essences in addition to cosmetics and perfumes.

Further information from Dominica Tourist Board, P.O. Box 73, Roseau, Dominica, WI; from Eastern Caribbean Tourist Association, 220 East 42 Street #411, New York, NY 10017; or from Caribbean Travel Association, 20 East 46 Street, New York, NY 10017.

*CAMPING: There are no official or developed campsites in the island, though camping is generally permitted. You must first obtain a special permit from the Permanent Secretary of Home Affairs at Government Headquarters. You'll have to provide your own tent and equipment. Parts of the National Park are especially beautiful, as are the rugged northeast and east coasts.

Martinique

Flying In

Le Lamartin Airfield, in *Fort de France*, Martinique, is 106 NM due south of Guadeloupe's Le Raizet and 60 NM south of Dominica's Melville Hall.

Navaids include a VOR DME at 177.5 FOF Ch 122 at the field (unusable in the sector 315°–350° beyond 6 NM below 7,500 ft), plus NDB 314 FXF 112° and 4.3 NM to the field. VHF/DF capability plus ILS. Runway lighting includes threshold strobes and VASI. Martinique Radio broadcasts and receives on 128.4, while Approach can be contacted on 121.0. Tower is 118.5

Jet-length runways of more than 10,000 ft, and full fuel (i.e., gasoline and jet).

For local tourism queries, call 71-79-60.

Background Briefing

Like Guadeloupe, Martinique is a full-fledged *departement* of metropolitan France, sending Deputies and Senators to the National Assembly. It has been called the most beautiful of the islands and its name derives from the original Carib name for the island, Madinina, meaning Island of the Flowers. (Columbus, who

Not a mirage, this replica of the famed Paris Sacre-Coeur rises from the palm fronds at suburban Balata, just north of Fort-de-France. (*photo*)

in 1502 landed at Carbet, just south of St. Pierre on the western coast of the island, reportedly received a welcome of burning arrows fired at his ships' sails, and took off in such a hurry that he couldn't think of a name.)

French, the island patois, and English are the languages, and if you do have some French, it is well worth making a point to use it. The islanders always appreciate it when visitors make the attempt, and will come to your rescue in English when they realize you are getting out of your depth linguistically.

Of course, for Air Traffic Control, you'll use English from the beginning, even though you'll hear controllers chattering away in French to local traffic.

Local currency, as in Guadeloupe, St. Martin, and St. Barts, is the French franc, but dollars are accepted—though as with EC currency, you may want to purchase some francs before you leave the US since you'll get a better rate than locally. There are discounts on some items if you pay by traveler's check. At the time of writing the exchange rate was 4.7 FF to $1.00, but with the dollar's poor performance internationally, better check before you leave.

The island is large, being 50 miles long and 22 miles wide with an area of 425 square miles. Highest point is the volcano Mont Pelee, at 4,592 ft. Population is around 350,000, and slightly more than 100,000 live in Fort de France, the capital.

The country has a wide variety of geophysical features, which range from thick, lush rain forest to a desert of petrified wood. The former capital, St. Pierre, was obliterated in minutes the morning of May 8, 1902, when two explosions rocked Mont Pelee. The volcano had been producing ash and smoke for several days earlier, but on account of upcoming elections, no attempt was made by the leadership to evacuate the more than 30,000 inhabitants of the "P'tit Paris des Caraibes." History reports but one survivor of this natural disaster—a prisoner in an underground jail cell.

This modern Pompeii is an incredible place to visit, appealing yet horrifying at the same time. Dr. Franck Perret Musee Volcanologique documents the disaster very thoroughly, with pictures and relics from the former capital, news accounts, and so forth. Check times when it is open.

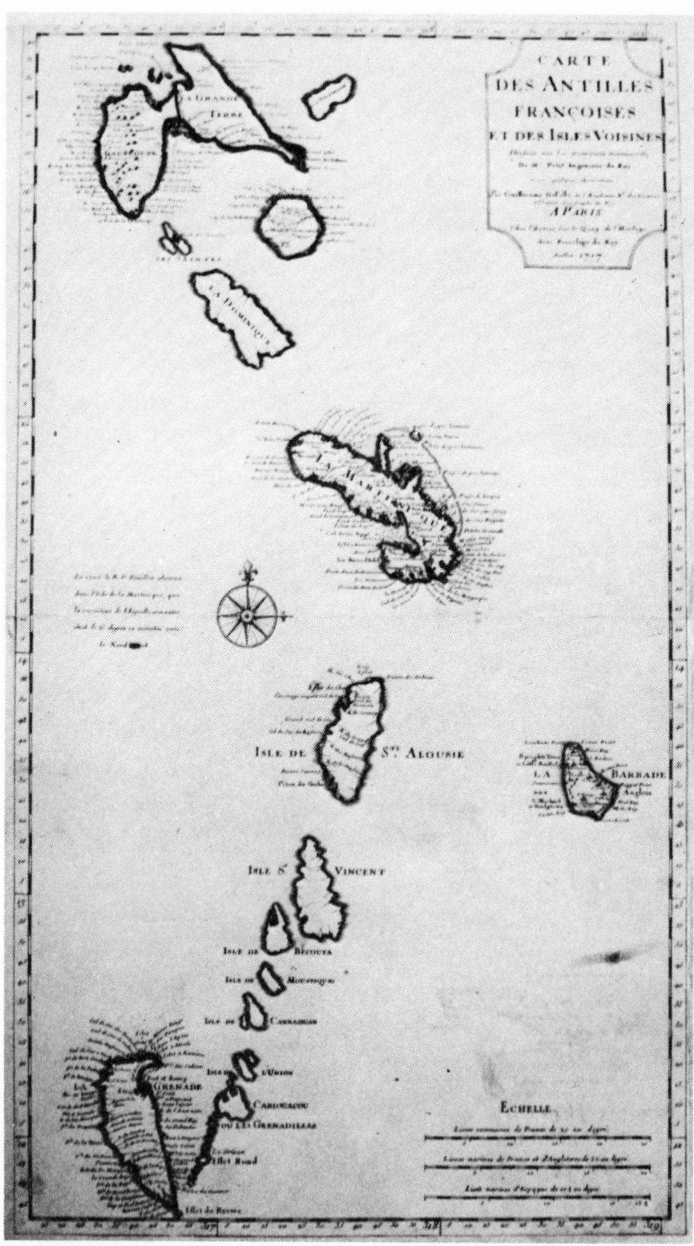

A chart from 1717 shows the French Antilles and their neighboring islands.

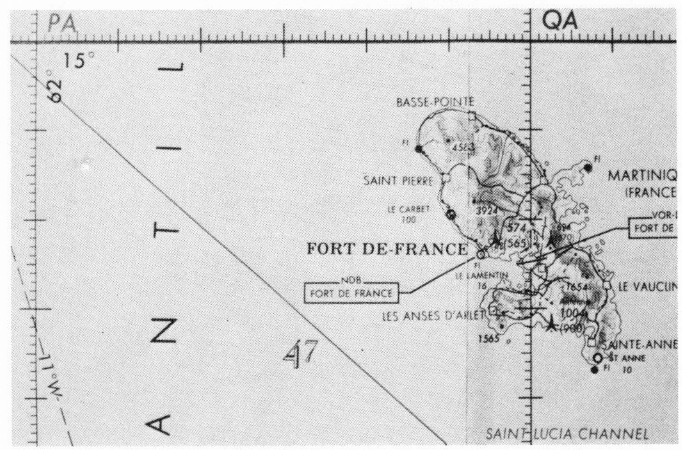

(Not to be used for navigation.)

The disaster at St. Pierre has helped science understand more about how volcanos work. The lava tends to explode through the weaker side, and it was for this reason that when the Soufriere in Guadeloupe was thought to be ready to erupt in recent years, few were worried that Basse-Terre—on its slopes— would suffer the fate of St. Pierre. That capital was fortuitously placed, say the experts, on the safe side of the mountain.

Although tourism is beginning to increase its importance in terms of the island's economy, agriculture is still the mainstay, with bananas and sugar cane being the principal crops. Some livestock is raised, and fishing is important. Several local rums are distilled, some exported. Despite this, the island enjoys subsidies from France and there is still emigration to Europe, a fact that has not cured the problem of un- and under-employment here. Part of the problem is that almost half the population is under 20 years of age.

Martinique has long been popular as a cruise-ship port of call and consequently you'll find a sophisticated approach to the needs of visitors. There's an inexpensive bus service throughout most of the island, though taxis are mostly used by visitors. There's also self-drive car hire through a gamut of agencies, and occasionally a dollar deposit is required.

In addition to the French and Creole cuisine you'll also find Chinese, Italian, and Middle-Eastern fare available. The Martinique Tourist Office can advise you about the numerous excur-

Empress Josephine—Napoleon's first wife—gazes serenely over her territory, while a contemporary *demoiselle* finds her way through the cane.

sions available and provide a list of operators. Apart from St. Pierre, Morne Rouge—the rain forest, Trois Ilets—birthplace of the Empress Josephine, and Les Salines—the petrified forest are featured on most lists. There's also the famous HMS *Diamond Rock*, commissioned by the Royal Navy in 1804 when a 120-man crew held it for some eighteen months. Known locally as the Rocher du Diamont, the French resorted to a ruse when it became apparent that their continual bombardment was a failure. They floated some kegs of rum across the water—soon after, the inebriated British were overcome.

France's original settlement of the island dates back to 1635, and for the first couple of hundred years it was one of the focal points in the struggle between them and the British for a West Indian empire. Fort de France, the capital, is a delight to explore, and the

cathedral and the library are both worth a visit. The Savane is a centrally located mini-park where the locals gather to stroll and sport* and where, on the rue de la Liberte, you'll find the Musee Departementale de la Martinique, which has quite a number of Arawak and Carib artifacts, including a partial Arawak skeleton that was discovered in 1972. (The Arawaks were, of course, the forerunners of the Caribs in the islands.)

A pleasant excursion can be enjoyed by taking one of the ferries which ply between Fort de France and Trois Ilets, and its neighboring hotels, the Bakoua, Meridien, and Hotel de la Marina; another ferry provides services to Anse Mitan and Anse a l'Ane. The views from the sea are great, and the cost is small.

At Trois Ilets there's a small museum on the grounds of the Empress Josephine's childhood home. It features a number of interesting items from her life and times, and she is still highly regarded. The women of Martinique have been irresistible to men all over the world and interestingly enough, Louis XIV's famed mistress Mme. de Maintenon was also from Martinique.

Food in the island is as special an occasion as in Guadeloupe. Some of the seafood is outstanding and if you are up to it, try stuffed baby crabs or the *soudans* (small clams) or *oursins* (sea urchins). The *colombo,* here in Martinique an almost South American dish of spiced meat and rice, is excellent.

There are a number of first-class restaurants in the island of which *La Grande Voile* at Pointe Simon, Fort de France is generally reckoned to be the best—and most expensive. *The Restaurant de l'Europe,* in the hotel of the same name, is outstanding on special occasions such as La Noel (Christmas Eve), and very good indeed at other times. *Escalier, Le Gommier,* and *Typic Bellevue* all offer excellent Creole and seafood dishes—Typic Bellevue is an extraordinarily good value (it is also a guesthouse—with just 4 rooms).

The hotel restaurants are almost all uniformly good.

The two best known—and inexpensive—island rums are Bally and Clement. Other liquor tends to be more costly, especially Scotch. If you're drinking out, keep to rum or to French *biere.*

*Visiting Lotharios can also try their luck here for an island *liaison amoureuse.*

Nightly entertainment is provided by the hotels and there are a number of *boites* and discotheques. Gamblers can enjoy the casinos at the Hotel Meridien and La Bataliere.

Le Tamtam and the *Manoir* are good night spots, and disco enthusiasts should check in at the *St. George's* and at *Sweety's*.

Carnival takes place at the traditional time, just before Ash Wednesday, in Martinique. It's a uniquely colorful occasion and not to be missed. Island music includes the *beguine*, the *merengue*, and the graceful *mazurka*, and on the night of Mardi Gras the island is jumping. On Ash Wednesday *les diablesses* take over town, and there is a protacted wake for King Vaval, which culminates in a funeral pyre lighted at dusk. *Le Fete de la Diablesse* should not be missed; it's the spectacle of a lifetime.

Where to stay

Martinique offers an extremely good range of accommodations of just about every type in hotel, villa, apartment, studio and guesthouse. Camping is also possible in the island but bring your own gear.

The three main centers are Fort de France itself, Pointe du Boute, and the neighboring Anse Mitan and Anse a l'Ane. Elsewhere the only significant cluster to be found is in the southeastern corner of the island around Ste. Anne, where you'll find *La Dunette*, the *Manoir de Beauregard*, and the famous Club Med's *Buccaneer's Creek* resort on its own 48-acre estate.

But it's beneath the mountains of Trois Ilets at the Pointe du Boute, that the main action is to be found, in recent years a success story that has delighted tourists from almost all over the world. You'll find just about every type of service and activity you could possibly want on your vacation, plus some of the more unusual ones—ever wanted to make an island sightseeing tour by helicopter? Here's your chance; at Pointe du Boute almost all things are possible.

Golf enthusiasts will find the new Robert Trent Jones 18-hole (71-par) championship course pleasantly challenging—and there are a pro shop, a bar, and special green fees for hotel guests. Tennis buffs can play on any of 6 lighted courts, and there's the full range of aqua-sports including scuba (lessons, too), deep-sea fishing, charter yachts, day cruises with steel band accompaniment, and beach barbecues, even cocktail-hour cruises and so on. There are also horseback riding and some duty-free shopping.

The hotels here are *Le Bakoua,* 100 rooms, long-time favorite with old Caribbean hands and reportedly making a comeback after slightly hasty expansion some years ago; the 300-room *Meridien,* another in the Air France chain and popular with American visitors; the recently opened *Frantel* (200 rooms) and the *De la Marina,* 175 rooms. This last is extraordinarily good value for the money, but more in a moment.

The *Bakoua Beach* originated as a small inn and has grown to accommodate an increasing number of patrons who've heard of its quality by word of mouth. Inevitably, there have been growing pains and some complaints. However, the rooms *are* spacious (with two enormous beds), there's air-conditioning, private terrace, radio (TV on request), room and valet service, and baby sitting. It has its own marina and more than 70 selections on a Cordon Bleu menu. The French Ministry of Tourism has awarded the hotel four stars, while Britain's Thomas Cook organisation has listed it as one of the 300 best properties in the world.

The *Meridien-Martinique,* which lies farther up the point from the Bakoua, is one of the finer resort hotels in the Caribbean. It has almost everything, and even if the beach is occasionally washed away, it gets put back fast. Everything else about the hotel is better than fine. It's also worthwhile checking whether any package arrangements are available since the standard rate is high.

The *Hotel de la Marina* lies on the further side of the marina from the Meridien. This PLM hotel offers extraordinarily good value in that accommodations are 240 attractive studios and suites, all with pullman kitchen, and with full hotel service. De la Marina is, as they say, a true French brasserie, which looks out over the boat basin and where you can dine in splendid leisure—or save enormously by doing your cooking *chez vous.* There's a well-stocked commissary on the premises, plus an excellent Creole and a Chinese restaurant. Usual boutiques, laundry, aqua-sports, and splendid pool.

Out on the other point just beyond the Hotel de la Marina lies *Frantel Martinique* with 200 air-conditioned rooms laid out in individual pavilions of 6 to 9 rooms each, each unit with its own

Fishing remains an important part of the island's economy, and is one of the important items in the Creole (and French) *cuisine.*

balcony facing the sea or the marina. Popular with package-tour people, you may want to check whether you can qualify for a special arrangement.

Le Boucat, an air-conditioned restaurant, offers local specialties such as stuffed crab and creole sausage. There are convention facilities with a capacity of up to 300 persons. *Le Vesou,* the Frantel's discotheque, is very much one of the "in" places to hang out at nights.

For something very different within walking distance of this *confrerie,* check the *Hotel* (actually an Auberge) *Madinia* and one of the more splendid of the flowers this island produces. Frequently confused—on account of its excellent restaurant, *Chez Sidonie*—as being a part of the De la Marina complex, it offers simple, basic single rooms, spotless and comfortable at low, low prices. Because its restaurant rates, it helps if you speak French when you reserve your table.

At nearby Anse Mitan and Anse a l'Ane are a number of other hotels including the *Calalou*, the *Auberge Anse Mitan, Bambou, Caraibe Auberge*, and the *Eden Beach*.

The *Auberge Anse Mitan* has developed an American following on account of the first-rate Creole cuisine. Accommodations are simple and adequate and the inn is much improved. There are 20 air-conditioned rooms with private facilities, plus 2 one-bedroom cottages on the beach. Some rooms with sea view. Within easy walking distance of Pointe du Boute.

The *Bambou* is similar in style to the Anse Mitan Auberge, and again it helps if you have some French. Cuisine can be first rate, and accommodations—some 26 rooms—are again adequate and simple. Cockfighting is to be found here, and while not for the squeamish, it's as exciting as a bullfight. Aficionados of the sport will explain that while the last minutes of the defeated bird's life are unpleasant, up to that point in time he has enjoyed the best of everything: food, special drinks, regular medical checkups, exercise programs, even a flock of females to keep him company. And if he's an alpha plus, he'll keep on going and be put to breed. Betting can be heavy on matches.

The *Caraibe Auberge*, a two-story building with 12 air-conditioned rooms, all with private bath, started life as the home of Mme. Guatel, its proprietor. It offers a simple, comfortable and French ambiance, more like a Mediterranean inn, and is very very clean. It's a "fait comme chez vous" sort of place and you'll enjoy it all the more if you can speak some French.

The *Eden Beach* has 14 rooms and is also reasonably priced.

Just a step further from Pointe-du-Boute is the *Hotel Calalou*, a 30-room inn that offers a Modified American Plan (two meals plus accommodation) option. Nothing very special here, just honest value for the money.

The hotels in Fort de France are primarily for businesspeople but offer good value. The *Hotel Bristol*, a former private home, is one of the Relais de la Martinique, but with only 10 rooms. It's reasonably priced. The *Imperatrice* overlooks the statue of Josephine (after whom the hotel takes its name) on the Savane. There are 24 rooms (with private bath). The *L'Europe* and *Malmaison* are next to one another, offering 21 and 19 rooms respectively. The Malmaison shares L'Europe's restaurant. Simple accommodations, but a good value if you want to be in the heart of town.

To the north of Fort de France, just outside Schoelcher, is the *PLM La Bateliere Hotel*, priced toward the middle-upper-range but reportedly worth the money. At Case Pilote is the *Vetiver* village, a local enterprise with thatched beach-hut accommodations, good swimming (and fishing), and a "fais ce que voudras" atmosphere. At Carbet, still farther north, is the 96-unit beach complex of *L'Hotel Latitude*. All accommodations are air-conditioned, with twin beds, private bath, plus radio and telephone. Units are attractively furnished, and while the clientele in the past has been mostly European, more and more North Americans (Canadians and US) are discovering its excellent value. There's disco dancing three or four nights a week and other entertainment during the season. This is one of the points of call of the singularly attractive *Ballets Martiniquais*, a 30-member troupe who have traveled almost world-wide to bring audiences the lively,

Sumptuous Imperial Suite at the Hotel Bakoua.

sensuous, and unique charms of the music and dance of this happy island people.

Plantation de Leyritz in the mountains at the north of the island near Basse-Pointe is worth the visit just to see this attractive spot. Unfortunately, like all too many other gems in the Caribbean, it has been spoiled by its own success and at last visit was pandering to group tourist business. *Tant pis pour nous!* The 200-year-old manor house has been beautifully restored and gives one the feeling of what gracious island living could have been all about.

On the Atlantic coast is the *Madras,* with 14 rooms, inexpensively priced. If you like the sound of the sea, this could be for you, for there's not too much else to do.

At the far south of the island at Ste. Anne is the famed *Manoir de Beauregard.* It's another of the Relais de la Martinique, and it's but a few minutes drive to one of the finest beaches in the island, La Plage des Salines.

The main stone building here dates back to the 18th century, and while restored is still beautifully furnished with antique tables and chairs, and the accoutrements of style that belong to an elegant plantation home: high ceilings, polished mahogany beams, marble floors. Fifteen of the 25 air-conditioned rooms are in a newer building behind the main house, all with air-conditioning, tiled baths, and telephone. Numerous antiques included in the furnishings plus some original four-poster beds. There are several places to eat out in the relatively near neighborhood if you want a change.

La Dunette has 11 air-conditioned rooms in a new building just five minutes from the beach at Ste. Anne. The good Creole cuisine has built a following for this inexpensively priced hostelry. Al fresco dining *dans le jardin.* It helps if you speak French.

A popular excursion for those with their own transport from this area is to take a drive along the coast through the village of Vauclin. There's a fishermen's market most days, and you can either purchase some of their catch for a picnic—cooked traditionally on charcoals in the sand, the fish wrapped in banana leaf and everything covered with sand and left for an hour or two; or eaten raw—or you can take your photographs and drive farther on, up the Atlantic coast.

At Les Brisants, near Le Francois, you can enjoy fresh local lobster with a glass of *jeune acajou* (light rum) or punch.

Driving north on the Caribbean side one comes to Diamont and Rocher du Diamont, better known as HMS *Diamond Rock*. Here the *Diamont les Bains* offers 20 rooms very modestly priced.

Not mentioned in most tourist material about the island is one of its best-kept secrets, the hotel training school known as the *Hotel Martinique*. Two miles out of Fort de France, the only problem is that it closes during students' vacation—otherwise it's a terrific value for money. The food is generally an outstanding value. The only difficulty for those wishing to enjoy the restaurant is that they must be guests of persons staying there. Accommodations are air-conditioned with private bath—reservations in advance a must—and there's a small swimming pool.

For further information, contact the French West Indies Tourist Board, French Government Tourist Office, 610 Fifth Avenue, New York, New York 10020; [212]. 757-1125.

St. Lucia

Flying In

Vigie Field is the airport for Castries, capital of the island, and nearest to the majority of this attractive island's hotels. The other airport, *Hewanorra International* (formerly the USAF's Bean Field) is where jet services land from points north and south. It's located at the southern end of the island, near the town of Vieux Fort. Both operate from sunrise to sunset (earlier or later on request). Vigie has 5,700 ft of runway (BWIA's small jets land here) and strip lighting with an NDB 415 SLU at the field. In neighboring Port Castries, seaplanes can land and dock, though facilities have not been checked recently. Fuel is usually available at Vigie, though occasionally the pumps have been known to be turned off at about 4:00 PM.

As might be expected from an airport that recently enjoyed a $1 million facelift, Hewanorra includes VASI and approach lighting and there's an NDB 305 BNE at the field.

St. Lucia Approach operates on 119.8, with Vigie Tower at 118.0, and Hewanorra Tower on 118.3, with Ground at 121.9. Jet fuels available at both.

There is another field in the island at Grand Anse over on the eastern side of the island. It is private, however, though should you need some place to land there are 1,500 ft available (elevation 450 ft). No facilities.

For local tourism queries, call 2479 from 0830 through 1600 and 2596 until 1900.

Background Briefing

Although traditionalists (and Italians) continue to insist that Columbus discovered the island, naming it for St. Lucy on whose day it was discovered, others—the English—suggest that crewmen from the *Oliph Blossome* were responsible for the name, while yet others—notably Francophiles—prefer the claims of certain shipwrecked mariners who apparently were washed ashore to safety on December 13, 1502, and who in gratitude named it after the Virgin Martyr of Syracuse (St. Lucy, of course).

Regardless of where the real honors belong, it was the French and British who scrapped bloodily for land rights here. The Spanish had other matters to occupy them. The result has been interesting: Islanders speak English, sing and cook in French (they also speak the patois amongst themselves). And in Castries, just recently made a freeport, you'll find splendid bargains in French perfumes and English porcelain and silks. Interestingly, the Castries City Council is the oldest wholly elected body in the entire British West Indies. (The Brits won permanent title in 1794, ratified in 1816 following Napoleon's exile.)

With 238 square miles, St. Lucia is the second largest of the formerly British Windward Islands* and population is approximately 125,000. Of obviously volcanic origin—there's a well-known "drive-in" volcano that was used as *les bains* by the soldiers of Louis XVI and later Napoleon—the harbor at Castries has been an important factor in recent times in the export of agricultural produce, especially bananas. Another harbor, at Marigot Bay, was popular with pirates, and Dudley Pope, a British naval historian turned novelist, used this site for his *roman a clef* of the islands.**

Today, Marigot is much in fashion with the yachting crowd, as is a less-fortunate development at Rodney Bay, which seems likely to become a classic argument by ecologists against careless entrepreneurial activities.

Because this is a large island it is usually worth getting a self-drive car if only for part of the time you spend here. The roads are still not the best, and in the more rugged parts you'll find

*It is now an independent nation within the Commonwealth of Nations.
***Ramage and the Freebooters,* by Dudley Pope. Ballantine Books, N.Y.

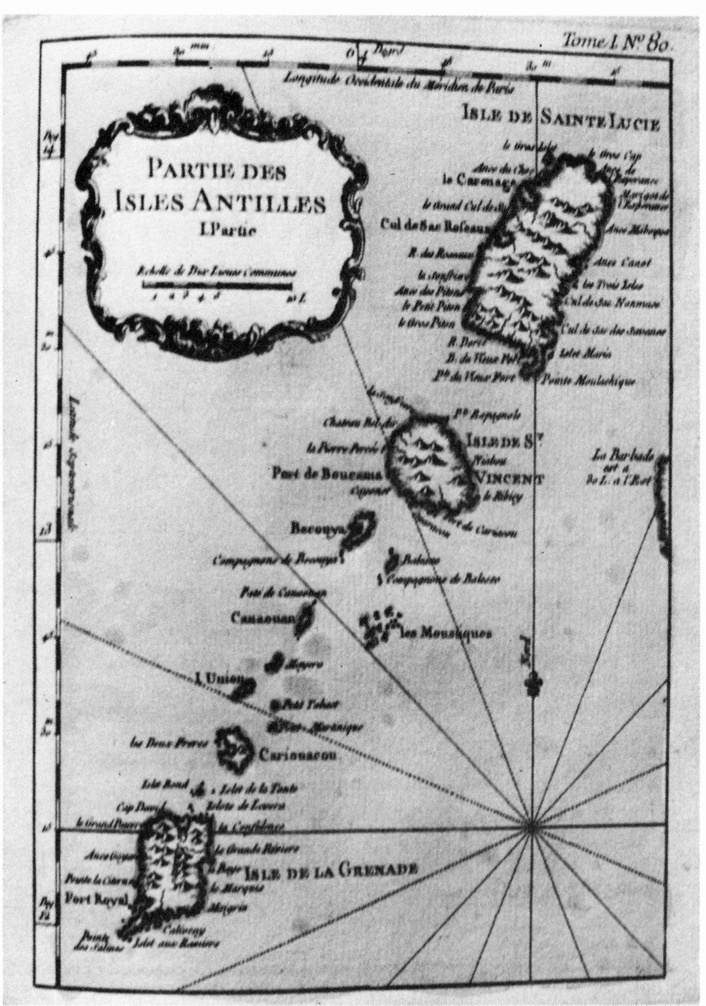

yourself weaving your way through broken coconut-palm fronds and potholes, though efforts are being made to improve things. And taxis, even though there are more of them than there used to be, are an expensive means of transport on a daily—and long-distance—basis.

There are numerous beaches, more than 100, and many are deserted, despite the burgeoning sail-in crowd.

Of interest to visitors—and islanders, for that matter—is the research work that has been done in the study of an exceptionally unpleasant flat-worm parasite known as *bilharzia* (after T. Bilharz,

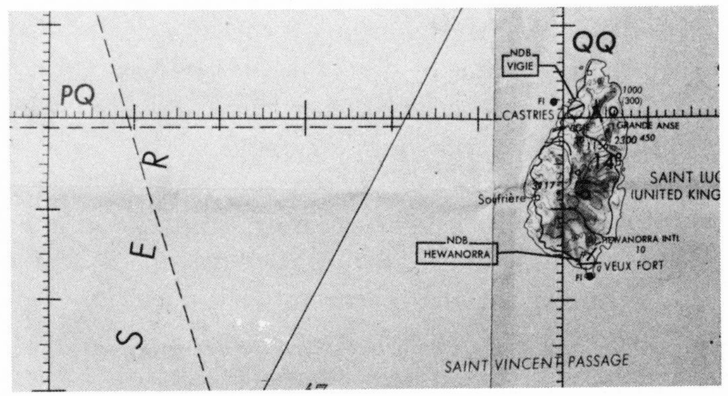

(Not to be used for navigation.)

its discoverer). With financial and scientific assistance from the Rockefeller Institute, the St. Lucian government has been running a program for the past 12 years or so, researching this creature that has been one of the more recent plagues of Egypt and other tropical countries. The results have provided successful methods for its control and eradication around the world.

The city of Castries, population around 50,000, is a curious blend of tacky modern with a few eye-cheering buildings of stone (former French) and brick (early Brit). It keeps getting burned—literally—and underwent a major rebuild after an extensive fire in 1948. Morne Fortune, where the local hospital has provided facilities to the *bilharzia* researchers, is also the site of Fort Charlotte, one of the several prides of the local Archeological and Historical Society. The view is splendid, recommended as a trysting spot at sundown, when you may be fortunate enough to view the incredible, and almost infinitesimally brief "green flash" of a tropical sunset. There's also a batik design and production group here, plus a local pottery.

Interestingly enough, the British once wanted to name Castries after Queen Charlotte, but the islanders refused.* They—the British—had to be content to name their fortification after the queen consort of infamous George III. The UWI (University of

*Eighteenth-century France is remembered in many of this island's place names. Comte d'Ennery, noted as a colonialist who actually improved conditions in his lifetime, is remembered at Dennery. Marechal de Castries was a local hero for whom the capital is named.

the West Indies, already establishing for itself a reputation as one of the leading universities of the Third World) has outposts here too. Its main campuses are at St. Augustine, Trinidad & Tobago; Bridgetown, Barbados; and Kingston, Jamaica.

Castries, because of its natural harbor, features high on the cruise-ship port-of-call list, and when the ships are in town it's a good place to stay away from. The local tourist office—an extremely helpful organization that owes much of its drive to Peter Bergasse, who helped lay the modern foundations of St. Lucia's approach to the tourism industry—can provide a list of dates when you might feel inconvenienced.

Among the main beaches is the Vigie Beach, literally walking distance from the airfield, where you can sneak a dip before moving on to your chosen hostelry. To the north of Castries there is a series of beaches, mostly settled with hotels, of which more shortly. La Brellotte Bay, site of the *East Winds Inn,* has one of the better beaches in the island and a reputation for fine dining at the inn itself. Farther south, there's the aforementioned Marigot Bay where the Yacht Haven hotel of former years has had a change of name and management and now is more appropriately known as the *Hurricane Hole.** Managed by sailor Nick Bowden, it is a home away from home for the sailing people.

A number of other, more or less deserted beaches are to be discovered journeying south toward Soufriere and the Pitons. Largest in the island lies near Vieux Fort at the front of the *Halcyon Days Hotel* at the southern end of the island near Vieux Fort: it's 5 miles long.

The Pitons are to be seen on just about every piece of promotional literature emanating from the island; these two volcanic cones are unique, as more experienced world travelers will tell you. Situated near the fishing village of Soufriere, they may be inspected most easily from seaward, for the land shelves abruptly at this point, and deep anchorage is available literally within yards of the shore.

**Hurricane Hole* is a term applied to any safe anchorage in which a sailing vessel can ride out one of these tyranical tropical storms. Prerequisites include good geophysical shelter (hills, etc., to provide storm brakes with trees and mangroves down to the water). The boat deploys a number of lines both ashore and to seaward to take care of any local (storm-induced) tidal variation.

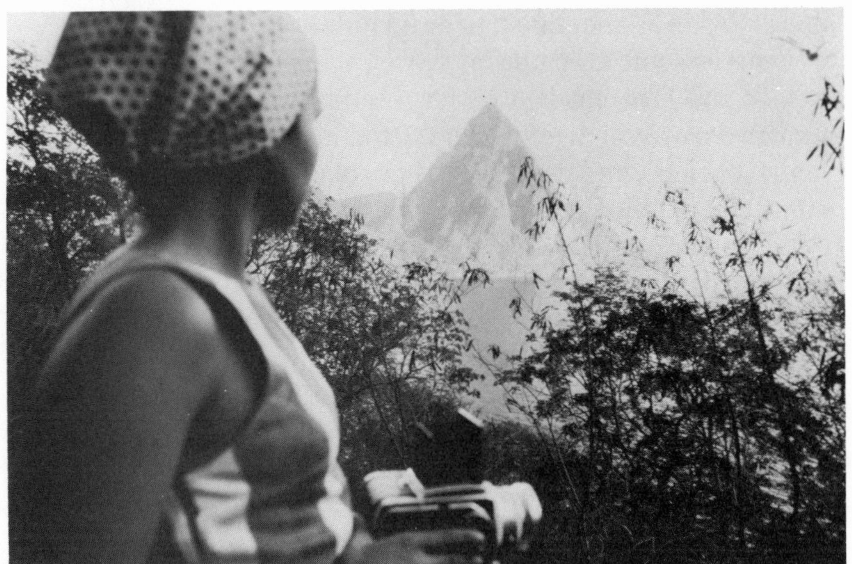

One of the two *pitons* for which St. Lucia is famous attracts photographers from all over the world.

Both are climbable, although they look impossibly steep. The taller is 2,619 ft, the other 2,461 ft. Suggestion: If you want to do the Sir Edmund bit, remember this is rock climbing and take one of the local boys—yes, boys. They've been known to go up barefoot. Unless your own feet are sufficiently adjusted to this mode of walking, use sneakers.

Cap Estate to the north of the island is one of the more intelligent developments in the Caribbean, and elsewhere. Begun in the early 1960s, it first made the headlines for its herd of Santa Gertrudis cattle, which thrived here. Next came a series of home-condominia, again intelligently planned with provisos on acreage and the amount to be spent on construction, including appropriate landscaping.

The South West German Steigenberger* Frankfurt hotel chain has chosen to set its first Caribbean operation on one of the nicer beaches at the Estate, and is one of the showcase operations in the area.

For the more adventurous, there are a number of interesting excursions to be made, either by jeep or on horseback. The

*Steigenberger, loosely translated, means mountain guide, as in *Sherpa*.

interior of the island, much of it still unknown to all but a very few, is home to some magnificent flora, including numerous tropical orchids and bromeliads, tree ferns, and so on. Fauna include an attractive parrot, indigenous to the island (and protected: there are hardly any left), and the less than popular fer-de-lance snake, with a deadly reputation and an occasionally lethal bite.*

It is highly unlikely that you'll come across this unpleasant creature or its close relative, a reddish-colored snake of similar size. Almost all the reptiles have taken refuge in the deep bush since word has spread that they are likely to lose their heads if found by a machete-wielding human—or a mongoose.

If you are unfortunate enough to get bitten, DON'T panic. Make yourself icy calm as if all your instruments had failed in an incipient thundercloud. First, you don't want your heart speeding up the blood-stream. Second, you want to move quickly and efficiently to isolate the place of the bite, using a tourniquet. Put it on tightly some way up from the bite—that poison can spread quickly. Next, open up the wound and use an extractor or have someone suck on the wound. You'll have to release the tourniquet after some ten or fifteen minutes, but this should provide sufficient time to provide local treatment. The tourniquet can be reapplied as soon as the blood has begun to flow again—if you leave it on too long you could lose the limb.

Snakeproof boots are one answer to the problem, or heavy chaparejos (chaps) or gaiters, if you really cannot resist the interior. Only problem, you could get rather warm.

Where to Stay

La Toc Resort Complex, which lies about ten minutes' drive from Vigie Field, has to be one of the better designed Caribbean resorts. *La Toc Village*, an attractive series of cottage villa units within the complex, consists of individual homes-away-from-home, all within 200 yards of the beach, set on gently rising slopes. These provide private, informal, and relaxed tropical living with the use of all the

*Obviously it's best not to get bitten by this snake. In full venom—that is, when it is exceedingly hungry—it is highly poisonous and will kill a human being within two minutes of striking unless appropriate measures are taken. If it has fed recently, while the bite may cause severe reactions, the patient will usually live if given prompt first aid. Not a very large snake, it seldom grows to more than 6 feet in length.

hotel's amenities, and are especially suited to those who prefer to stay longer, who want to entertain friends, and obviously for families.

Accommodations include 1- or 2-bedroom cottages (air-conditioned, each with bath), with sun terrace, living room, and fully equipped kitchen. Many of the 2-bedroom units have their own mini-plunge pools. The sun terrace provides a natural outdoors extension of the living area enhancing that space. Oh, yes: babysitters are available.

The Village Center has its own fresh-water swimming pool with adjacent bar and restaurant for when you don't feel up to doing-it-yourself. At *La Toc Hotel* you can dine more grandly in the elegant restaurant, and there's also a grill room that's less formal.

Villa rates are in the reasonable range considering the numerous advantages of being able to do what you want. They're especially favorable for groups of four or more, which means families for the most part.

Those preferring more traditional hotel life can settle in at the hotel itself, where you've a choice of any of the 164 air-conditioned, balconied ocean-front rooms. Amenities at this attractive beach resort include its own 9-hole golf course, 3 floodlit, championship Har-Tru tennis courts (pros for both sports on hand year around), plus the usual range of aqua-sports, including deep-sea fishing. There's also twice-daily free transportation into town.

This attractively landscaped and well-run resort has to list high with its Caribbean competition. Recommended.

If La Toc Resort Complex represents a modern British approach to tourism (it's owned and operated by the Cunard Trafalgar people), the *Cariblue Hotel* carries a slightly more Teutonic spirit. On one of Cap Estate's more beautiful beaches, it offers superior international comfort all around, and attentive and considerate service.

There are 102 comfortable rooms and apartments all with bath, air-conditioned, and with sea-view terraces. There are a 9-hole golf course, horseback riding, tennis courts (floodlit, of course), plus sailing, water-skiing, scuba, and so on.

In addition to the local specialties, you'll find featured some

The drive-in volcano is one of the island's big attractions, and you can still bathe where Napoleon's soldiers used to. More recent is the introduction of sailing, and St. Lucia is bidding big to become an important center for Caribbean yachting.

European dishes on the menu—exquisitely cooked and served. Packed lunches for excursions are some of the best anywhere in the world, according to a well-known travel magazine.

For something totally different, yet still at the beach, try the *Anse Chastanet* at Soufriere. It's where many St. Lucians go for their own weekend vacations out of the hurly-burly of Castries, and has—since its inception in the late 1960s—developed a small but fairly devoted following of Out-Islanders.

Up above a fine curve of brilliant white sand are a series of octagonal chalets perched on the hillside overlooking the bay. There's a total of 38 rooms, some in the main building, some 1-bedroom suites and two 2-bedroom suites, all with kitchen. Two villas, ideal for families, comprise four bedrooms and (count 'em) 4 bathrooms, making them ideal for families or larger groups.

There's a beachside bar and restaurant area where the decor is somewhat cute (fishing boats double as buffet tables), but the food is island-excellent. Besides the swimming and snorkeling—good—there are a number of interesting walks, including the nearby botanical gardens, where there's a truly fascinating collection of native West Indian trees.

This is a good buy, though you'll probably appreciate having your own transportation to get around and about. Soufriere, the nearest town, now has two rather pleasant restaurants plus *Allains' Guest House* (excellent local cuisine, especially lobster). *The Ruins*—one of the two restaurants—should by publication date have activated a series of condominia for visitors, which will include kitchen plus maid service and use of pool for a modest daily fee. Main building is a restaurant/bar built into the ruins (hence the name, natch) of a one-time handsome homestead. For authentic island food *The Still* has developed its own following and is recommended by many islanders as one of the better places to get acquainted with the unique features of St. Lucia's flair at *haute cuisine creole.*

East Winds Inn, mentioned earlier and just to the north of Castries at La Brelotte Bay, is a super-attractive place to stay, but like Marina Cay in the BVI, tends to be at the upper end of the scale in terms of price for what is offered. The beach is really great, not too large, but especially nice for early-morning or late-evening dips. Accommodations are non-air-conditioned, kitchen provided, beachside cottages, and West Indian (and continental American) cuisine is available at the informal beach bar.

A commissary provides a good range of provisions for those who prefer to do it themselves (or you can shop in Castries), and hospitality is the genuine article. This is strictly a place in which to unwind for there's almost nothing to do, outside of swimming, snorkeling, or sailing in Sunfish—well, that's fun, too. There are lots of books and some hammocks.

About fifteen to twenty minutes from Castries, depending on where you want to go in the city.

Back to the "city" for a moment to include the *Villa Hotel,* a pleasantly old-styled West Indian manor overlooking the Vigie Peninsula and Castries Bay. The main building has a genuine—and quaint—olde worlde colonial charm that reminds of Britannia's more easterly outposts. There are 28 air-conditioned rooms, many with fine balconies, and the airy dining room offers continental, European, and local dishes.

The hotel has a wonderful potential yet tends to settle for the "cheap in August" syndrome. Free transportation to the Choc beach just north of town.

If you stay for any length of time in St. Lucia—or for that matter, in most other English-speaking places in the Caribbean—you'll hear talk of Court Line and the effects on the Third World of the "so-called" Arab oil embargo. Be warned: This is as touchy a subject as the moon landing, which many Caribbean natives believe was filmed in Hollywood. Equally, many believe the oil embargo was created in Washington, DC, in order to effect greater American control over Third World nations as a direct result of (a) the Third World nations' inability to pay for increased prices in energy and (b) as a direct result of US banks' abilities to provide soft loans to help buy oil at increased cost. Factor (c), the increasing attacks on the credibility of the US dollar, is the direct result of such manipulation—and it is going to hurt you, too, in your pocket, when you travel here. Not much, but sufficient to let you know you'll be smarter to change your money at your hotel or at a bank.

You will find surprisingly sophisticated discussion on this subject, for the failure of Court Line was perceived as a direct threat to many local enterprises, even though Court Line was nominally British. What hurt most was the near jeopardy of LIAT, the home-grown airline, and a number of St. Lucia's choice hotels. Fortunately, means have been found to save *Halcyon Beach Club*—88 cabana-style rooms with private patio just outside Castries and with its own discotheque. There's swimming pool plus poolside dancing and barbecue parties, floodlit tennis courts, the usual aqua-sports, and terrace dining. A splendid beach is divided in the middle by a rather less than splendid hotel pier and Fisherman's Wharf restaurant, which features both Creole and modified continental cuisine.

Halcyon Sands Hotel, formerly Vigie Beach, Halcyon Days, has 47 air-conditioned rooms, each with private beachfront balconies. There are a fresh-water swimming pool and the usual aqua-sports operation.

Another hotel—would you believe, the *Holiday Inn*?—also experienced some trauma. While there are 190 air-conditioned units at Reduit Beach, with fresh-water pool, floodlit tennis courts, and so forth, plus nightly entertainment, it seems to have opted for a future as one of those sales-personnel incentive programs.

The *Malabar Beach Hotel*, also at Vigie Beach, is now enjoying a well-earned revival. It offers 30 poolside garden rooms plus 20 air-conditioned beachside cottages and has a regular clientele of repeat visitors and businesspeople. Usual activities, comfortable ambiance, and good food. Rates slightly high.

Down at the far end of the island is a relatively new venture, the *Kimatrai Hotel* at Vieux Fort with 14 self-contained rooms plus some apartments. The restaurant is supposed to offer good-quality local Creole food, and this hotel is quoted as offering "good family atmosphere." Reports welcomed.

Eating Out

While seafood Creole is one of the gastronomic highlights of this Pearl of the Antilles, you'll also enjoy *callalou*, the local crabmeat and dashene stew.

In Castries, some of the best *callalou* is to be found at the *Coal Pot*, just down the main runway—on a parallel road by the water—at Vigie Field. Also good are their flying fish, dolphin, and lobster. It's small, expensive, good for gossip, and popular with the sailing crowd. Local pilots also. Bob and Sonia Elliot are your hosts.

The *Green Parrot*—ideal choice of name for its locale on Red Tape Lane—has had its name suggested for the panoramic restaurant atop the latest Senatorial folly in Washington, DC . . . as *the Green Parrot on Red Tape Lane.* (You read it here first, folks). Up on Morne Fortune, the St. Lucian Green Parrot has languished under a rather chequered career, but is the place to go for a genuine island evening out. The food is mostly very good, the price is mostly modest.

The *Calabash*, the local upstairs-over-the-downstairs type eatery, features a large bar and excellent fare. It's a real value-for-money place and worth your patronage. You can, on occasion, find here the type of *objets d'arts* at prices you can afford.

And then there's *Rain*.

A nice old-fashioned camp-styled place,* with punkahs slowly revolving, a genuine RCA–His Master's Voice gramophone, oil

*"All Under One Tin Roof" is the slogan.

lamps, it has been genteelly described as "pure Somerset Maugham" in breathless voices after certain drinks purloined from Po's locker: "the Reverend's Downfall" and especially "Sadie's Sin."

Not surprisingly, the food is good, the booze is reasonable, and while there've been complaints about the company that has sometimes been kept, management has readjusted the focus (or the clientele have adjusted theirs).

East Winds has earned itself a good reputation for its food and they do accept guests for dinner. The *Kimatrai* at Vieux Fort has a similarly good reputation. At *Cloud Nest Hotel* reports are mixed, but generally good, and the *Far East Restaurant* in Castries enjoys generally good reviews for its Chinese food.

There's entertainment at the Green Parrot several nights each week. Most hotels offer something, including the occasional discotheque.

Clearly opportunities for the adventuresome.

And the prices are right.

For further information, contact Eastern Caribbean Travel Association, 220 East 42nd Street, New York City 10017; [212]. 986-9370.

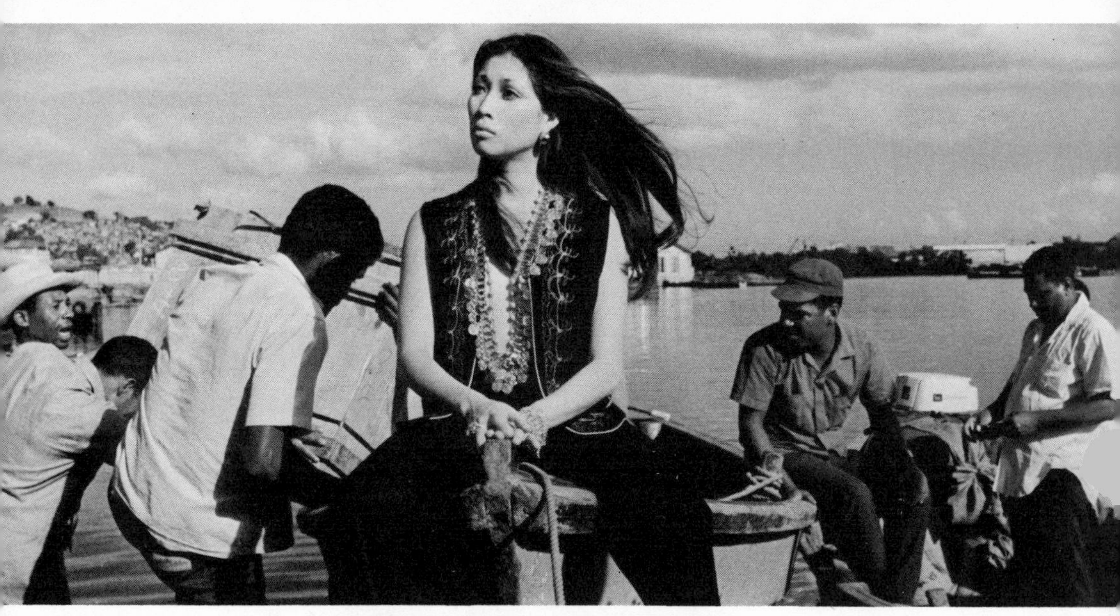

St. Vincent

Flying In

A brief hop of 38 NM brings you from Hewanorra International, St. Lucia, down the Atlantic coastline of St. Vincent to the airfield *Arnos Vale.* There's 4,800 ft of runway and fuel is usually available. Construction has been taking place as of the time of writing, but should be completed by publication. Nevertheless, it's advisable to contact the Tower (118.8) immediately you take off (if coming from St. Lucia) or when you're but fifteen minutes from arrival.

Query Tower for landing instructions, since provided the winds are right you can make a straight-in approach from seaward onto runway 07/25.

The airport takes its name from a small river that lies about a hundred yards east of the strip. Interestingly, it was a trash dump for Carib and Arawak Indians, and artifacts have been discovered here for some years.

Avgas 100 usually available.

Background Briefing

St. Vincent and its Grenadines have perhaps even more charm than those fabled Virgin Islands to the north. Like the BVI, there's been no rush for "instant tourism" and the emphasis is on courtesy and personal attention. St. Vincent itself is a beautiful island, with mountain uplands and numerous beaches, many of fine black sand. It's approximately 150 square miles in size, and population is around 125,000. It's volcanic in origin, and recent activity within its Soufriere in 1979 caused serious concern locally and the temporary evacuation of many settlements in its neighborhood, while producing a light dusting of volcanic ash as far away as Barbados. West Indian and other scientists are closely monitoring the mountain.

The island is approximately 18 miles long on its north/south axis and about 11 miles wide. Soufriere rises to more than 4,000 ft. and is an interesting excursion for the reasonably fit.

If you decide to pass on the excursion to the mountain, the Atlantic road—you follow directions for Calliaqua and Georgetown—will eventually take you to the north of the island to the village of Fancy and will tell you more about the St. Vincentian and *their* island than you could learn elsewhere in a week.

It is at Fancy that you'll find the last descendants of the original Caribs. Although there has been much intermarrying, some of the natives here have that exquisitely defined coloring and features that the original Sun Kings of the southern continent gave to the world. The expedition will take but an afternoon in a self-drive car and is definitely worth it if only for the many incredible scenic—and occasionally cliff-hanging—views.

The Caribs here were some of the fiercest that the Europeans were to encounter, to the extent that the French and British agreed that the island should remain neutral territory in an agreement in 1748. This, after initial attempts at settlement as early as 1627. The island was ceded to Britian in 1763, recaptured by the French in 1779, and finally restored to the British in 1783 at the Treaty of Versailles. It has remained British ever since.

If the Caribs fought the white men, they opened their arms to a group of black men and women who were shipwrecked in the mid-1600s. In fact the Carib welcome was so overwhelming that a new sub-group formed of Black Caribs, who eventually came to

*Volcanologists describe the St. Vincent Soufriere as semi-dormant. Last major eruption was May 6, 1902, just two days ahead of the catastrophic explosion of Mt. Pelee, Martinique. St. Vincentians got off lightly with only 2,000 dead. Most recent rumblings were in 1971, when the new island appeared.

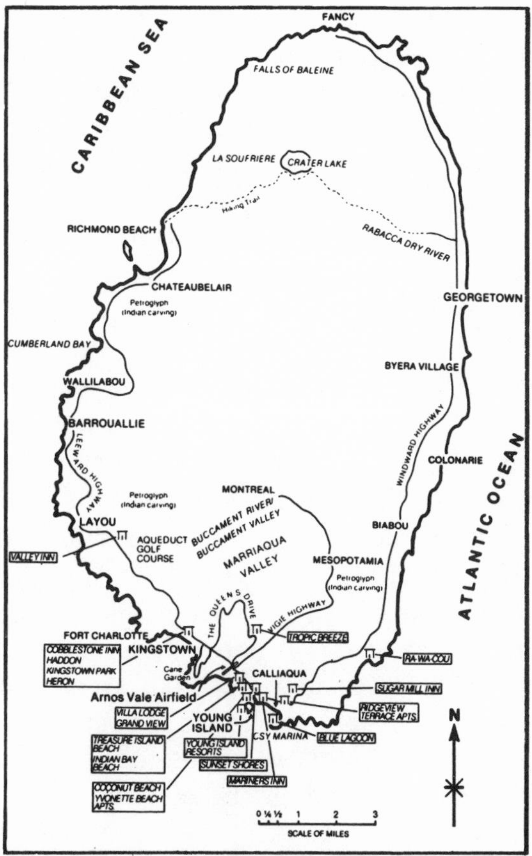

(Not to be used for navigation.)

dominate the originals. In 1795, these Black Caribs, in association with the French, turned on the British planters, and a massive bloodbath ensued. The following year, sufficient reinforcements arrived, order was restored, and some 5,000 of the remaining Black Caribs were shipped off to Honduras to work in plantations.

Emancipation of slaves took place here in 1838, and indentured labor became the norm, with Portuguese and East Indians tilling the soil. Most returned to their homeland, but St. Vincent possesses a remarkable ethnic mix including the predominantly East Indian group in Mesopotamia Valley, the raugetts (pronounced *raw-guess*)—Afro-albinos—and the redlegs, the descendants of protesting English and Irishmen, shipped out in the 17th century, who have intermarried to a degree that makes them resemble some of the earlier Norman settlers in the Caribbean (in St. Barts) and elsewhere. A truly fascinating group of people are the St. Vincentians, staunchly independent, wonderfully warm and friendly when they get to know you. And even if they don't know you, they're liable to strike up a conversation, as you can easily discover if you should make time to take in the weekly Saturday market.

It's a colorful occasion throughout the year, best from April through the summer months when the finest of crops come to town, fruits—soursop, breadfruit, papaya, mangoes and coconuts—and vegetables, and giant stalks of banana and plantain. There are some 13 different species of the banana grown in the island, with different flavors and different methods of cooking. But perhaps St. Vincent is best known for its arrowroot, used in almost all baby foods, and also in the production of paper.* The island also produces Sea Island cotton, and the batik and tie-dye prints produced by the local Caribbee Studios is of such good quality that Harrods of London and Buenos Aires stocks it—check it out.

Fort Charlotte, some 600 ft above Kingstown, capital of the island with a population of around 25,000, is a great place to begin your orientation. From here you have a signal panorama overlooking city and deep-water harbor, and on to the Grenadine islands beyond. (Although the islands are called Grenadines, the majority are administered by St. Vincent.)

Next you should include the Botanical Gardens, the oldest in the Western Hemisphere, originally opened in 1765. Their chief claim to fame is the breadfruit tree grown from a seed from Tahiti by Captain "Mutiny on the Bounty" Bligh. There's a stunning collection of West Indian flora here in the 10 acres, including *spachea perforata*, of prehistoric origin and indigenous to St. Vincent. The island also has two types of parrot, also indigenous and heavily protected.

Kingstown is not exactly fun city, but it is attractive and some of the architecture is reminiscent of late Georgian England. One of the more eccentric buildings is St. Mary's Roman Catholic Presbytery and Church, which features an almost Islamic minaret along with Norman arches and battlements and pseudo-Gothic spires.

*You can arrange to inspect the local Central Arrowroot Factory at Belle Vue.

Even if architecture leaves you cold, it's worth a look. Surprisingly, it was built in the 1930s.

Although there are only about 500 miles of road, of which about 25 per cent only are paved, it's still worth hiring a car for a day or two to make excursions out of town. The road up the Caribbean coast takes you through a number of interesting fishing villages, including the whaling station at Barrouallie.* Whale hunting is mostly from late January to early April and is conducted in the old-fashioned style using open boats and harpoons. Visitors can arrange to go with the fishermen.

Also at Barrouallie is the Arawak *kiborion*, with two of the finest petroglyphs in the entire West Indies.

At Layou is the so-called Carib Rock, with its carving of a human face which dates back to around 600 AD.

Taking the road up to Chateaubelair allows you to approach Soufriere by car. Only the final stages must be done on foot. There's also the Rabacca Dry River, its source in the mountain, whose river bed reveals the congealed and weathered patterns of the lava flow.

The farm country in Marriaqua Valley (Mesopotamia or Mesopotamia Valley, locally, though Mesopotamia is only one of its villages) is beautiful and reminiscent in its terracing of parts of Nepal. It is also highly fertile and crops include banana plantations, nutmeg, cocoa, coconut, root crops, and breadfruit.

Nightlife is pretty much limited to the hotels, although the Aquatic Club—a recreational center patronized by Vincentians—has a dance floor and music, though not every night. The same goes for dining out. Your best bet is to stay with hotels.

Where to Stay

There are some 20 hotels in St. Vincent and another 10 or so in the neighboring Grenadines. They range from the modest yet pleasurable guesthouses to small and sometimes charming hotels.

For a genuine taste of the island, try the *Heron Hotel*, just across from the boat-loading docks in the heart of Kingstown. This is truly a West Indian experience, and inexpensive. There are 15

*The other whaling stations are at Petit Nevis and Bequia.

rooms of varying shapes and sizes, most with bath, and overhead fans or air-conditioning to keep you cool. All are on the second floor, as are Reception and the dining room. Especially good value if you're just passing through.

Somewhat different is the *Cobblestone Inn*, an extensively and expensively remodeled former sugar warehouse brought—at a cost of $250,000-plus—the 200 years to the present. Only 18 rooms, but all with air-conditioning, bath, and telephone. The restoration has been painstakingly done. Another good place to stay if you're passing through.

The Mariners Inn, situated on the mainland just opposite Young Island, has expanded its operation and now has some 15 rooms and baths on the waterfront. The popular bar is a center for news of sailing folks around the planet and a good place for local gossip. Comfortable and reasonable prices, and on Friday nights there's a barbecue feast and steel-band music.

Young Island, just a couple of hundred yards across the water, was the dream creation of a former American Express VP who wanted to get away from it all. Originally opened in the mid-sixties, the project changed hands but the Edenic dream survived. The 24 units are discreetly tucked away behind oleanders and hibiscus on a hillside with a central meeting area that is an attractive, almost Polynesian building down near the water. Most of the staff, courteous and attentive to your every need, have been there since the operation began. New is a tennis court, up and over the hill the far side of which was formerly used by bathers in the buff. There's also a resort-owned yacht for occasional cruising. The island is on slightly more than 20 acres, and rates are high.

Grand View Beach Hotel, about half a mile from Arnos Vale field, lives up to its name with one of the best views in the island as well as one of the nicer beaches. This typically West Indian hotel sits on a point about twenty minutes from Kingstown. There are 12 rooms with bath, most air-conditioned, 4 of which have spectacular views over the water.

Better yet, the food is good, and for authentic (British) West Indies fare it's hard to beat. The hotel is settled in an attractively landscaped 10-acre spot and offers good value for your money. For golfers an additional attraction is that it's right next door to one of the most scenic courses in the Caribbean.

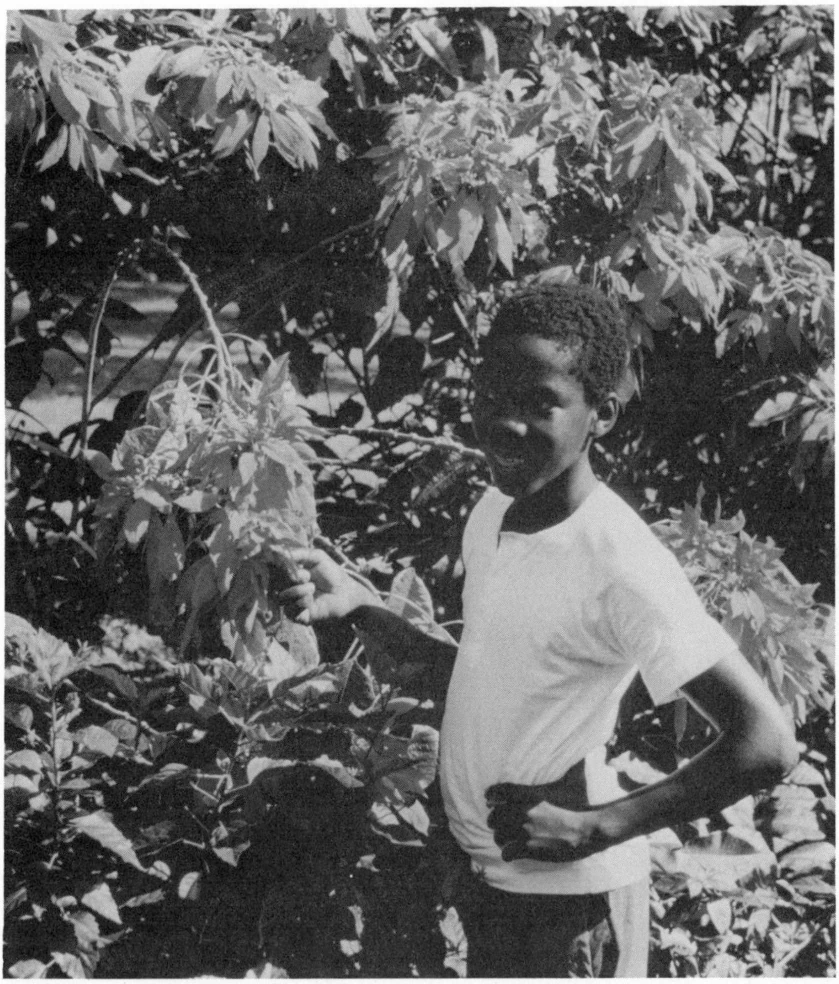

Founded in 1765 by Governor George Melville, the Botanic Garden covers some 20 acres, and is the oldest in the Western Hemisphere. Well worth the detour, if only for passing the time with one of the young and always congenial local guides.

The Sugar Mill Inn is an old plantation house on a thoughtfully gardened promontory some 4 miles from town. There's a newish swimming pool and the hotel provides transport to and from the beach. Food tends to be good and the hotel has developed an island following. Accomodations are okay, the newer ones more modernly furnished. Rates moderate.

The Blue Lagoon at Ratho Mill promontory was originally a private home and has been turned into a pleasing hostelry with 12 rooms. Food is good, the view spectacular. Rates reasonable. Small swimming pool, beach down the hill.

The *Coconut Beach* has developed a devoted following among Nord Americanos seeking sun and relaxation in the island. It's got a super casual atmosphere, there are 10 air-conditioned rooms, and it's a value-for-money spot. It's on the beach just a ways down the road from the *Grand View*.

There are a number of villas available for rent and several self-efficiencies including *Ra-Wa-Cou*, with 10 cottage units with kitchens, located on the Atlantic side of the island by two black-sand beaches. Maid service included, and while there's food, you can hire a cook should *you* need help. Reasonable rates but you'll need a car.

At Indian Bay, just beyond the Grand View Beach, are the *Yvonette Beach Apartments*, a series of efficiencies near the,

Chatoyer, the Chief of the Black Caraibes of St. Vincent, with his five wives (1773).

Downtown Kingstown offers surprisingly good shopping.

Mariners' Inn. Rates are reasonable in winter and low during the summer. All are with kitchen, and all overlook Young Island.

The St. Vincent Tourist Board can give you a complete listing of hotels in the island. The ones listed above are the author's choices.

Villa Lodge, which is in the same neighborhood, has accommodations and is the site of the Crow's Nest nightclub.

For further information, contact Eastern Caribbean Travel Association, 220 East 42nd Street, New York City 10017; [212]. 986-9370.

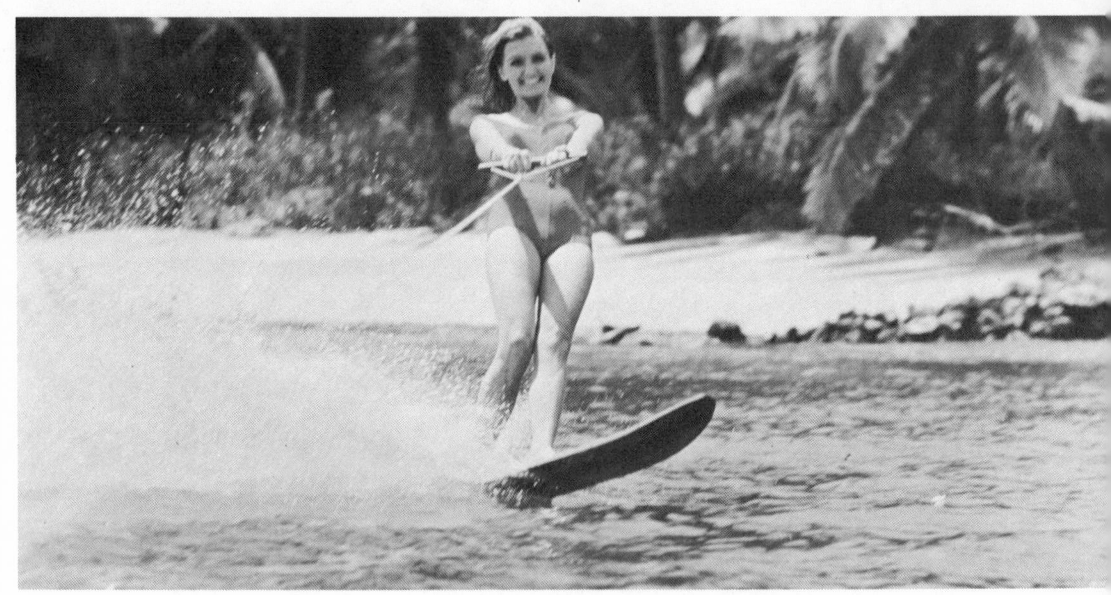

The Grenadines

BEQUIA

Bequia (pronounced Bek-wee) is the nearest of the Grenadines to St. Vincent and can be explored on a full-day excursion using local transportation, i.e., a boat. There are a number of boats that ply this 9-mile channel between the two and on occasion, when the Atlantic and Caribbean currents get out of phase, the water can be surprisingly rough away from the shore.

Bequia is the largest of the Grenadines, and was once an important whaling port. It's also been used for smuggling. Today it's best known for fishing and swimming, and is used as a base by a number of sailboats in the region. When the time is right, a handful of whalers still set out from Friendship Bay and if you're of a mind—and they are—you can go for a ride. *The Whaleboner Bar* (the bar was once the jawbone of a humpbacked whale) has to be one of the best-known watering holes in the Caribbean. Salts and tourists and islanders gather here for refreshment and food, which includes fish and chips, lime pie, and banana-bread sandwiches.

Friendship Bay Hotel is across the island from Admiralty Bay, where the boats come in, and a 10-minute taxi ride over Bequia's bumpy and pot-holed roads. Over the years it has built up an enduring New England clientele who enjoy its privacy and splendid beach. There are 30 double rooms, some in the main building, others in separate cottages; don't expect luxury here, for the air-conditioning is by trade wind. However, the food is first rate, many of the vegetables are grown right on the property, and the fish is fresh right out of the bay. Rates are high in season, for this Shangri-la dreamed up by Coast Guard Captain N. Thomsen, and better value off season, but check that the hotel is open as the skipper occasionally takes a vacation for himself.

Frangipani is another of those delightful homes-turned-hotel in West Indian manner with 6 rooms in the main building and 4 more units up the hill in a newer building. If you're a privacy freak you'll prefer the rooms on the hill (and they also have private bathrooms).

Located by the shore at Port Elizabeth, overlooking Admiralty Bay, it's the property of one of the youngest premiers St. Vincent has known. It's also a popular gathering place during the day with the sailing crowd and serves first-rate food. The fact that it is a home first and hotel second (inn, might be a better choice of word) gives this place an ambiance that soothes tired souls. As at Friendship Bay, rates are high in season, better value off season.

Spring Estate is an attractive working plantation that produces its own vegetables plus the usual bananas and coconuts, mangoes and pawpaw. It also serves as a focus for careful condominium-type development and has room for about 30 guests. The Greathouse has 6 units; the others are away in buildings named Fortress, Hawksnest, and Sea Gull. A remote and secluded mini-resort, there's a swimming pool and the beach at Spring Bay is one of this island's finest. The road to civilization is long and winding and paved with pot-holes and bumps. Rates moderate high, lower off season. Fresh lobster is a regular feature on the menu.

Sunny Caribee at Admiralty Bay now has 17 individual beach cabanas plus 8 rooms in the main house. This is a good place to stay if you want to snorkel or scuba—and Bequia is definitely for those who enjoy the sea. There are informal barbeques and music, usually a couple of nights a week, and the food rates high. There's an attractive beach bar, which keeps you out of the sun at high noon and which provides snacking in addition to cooling libations. Rates moderately high in season, moderate otherwise. The scented orchard adjacent to the property makes this an unusually attractive spot.

Just behind the hotel is a private house called *Bequia Breezes* that is occasionally available for rent. It's suitable for two couples or a family with children.

Julie's Guest House, just off the main jetty in Port Elizabeth, is the best buy on the island. The food is excellent and rates are low. Check *well in advance* for availability.

MUSTIQUE

Flying In

Mustique is a short, not-quite-20-NM hop from Arnos Vale. There's an airstrip of around 2,000 ft—elevation 10 ft—and the entire island is little more than 3 miles long by about a mile-and-a-half at the widest.

The Island

The Mustique (pronounced Moose-teak) Company, Ltd., runs the island—shades of the islands' earlier history—paying for the police, Immigration, and Customs officials provided by St. Vincent, and taking care of the health, education, and welfare of the islanders in addition to maintaining the airstrip.

Mustique used to be an island favorite of Princess Margaret; she and her former spouse built a house here.

The only place to stay is *Cotton House Hotel*, but what a place it is. Owned by the Hon. Colin Tennant (of the English brewing family), the hotel consists of an 18th-century-style Great-house with louvered doors, arches, and balcony. Several small cottages provide elegant accomodations around the main building (11 suites) or, if you want to be completely on your own, there's a 2-bedroom beach cottage at l'Ansecoy Bay, some 400 yards off, which comes with its own staff.

Part of the attraction of Cotton House is that no expense was spared in its construction, furnishing, and decoration. International designer Oliver Messel was brought in for this, and for its first two years, Cotton House was virtually a private club.

Colin Tennant has since moved on to other projects and the hotel is being run by the owner of Martinique's Bakoua Hotel. Rates are high. There are several sports activities for the energetic: there's a pool if you're too tired to go down to the beach, and

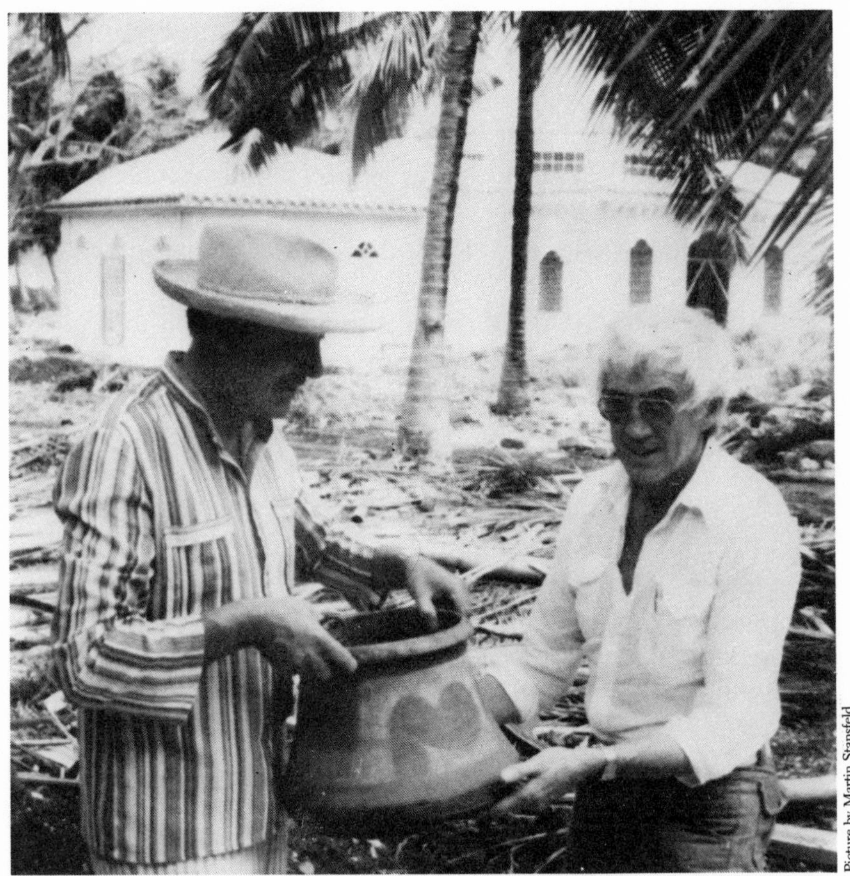

Picture by Martin Stansfeld.

The Hon. Colin Tennant (left)—original founder of the Mustique Company—seen here with Venezuelan industrialist Hans Neumann (now a major stockholder in the venture) with recently discovered Barrancoid artifacts.*

tennis, scuba, sailing, deep-sea fishing, water skiing, and snorkeling. The pier at Britannia Bay has some small shops.

CANOUAN

Flying In

The airstrip on this island is so new it hasn't yet made it to the aeronautical charts. The island itself lies about 15 NM just west of south from Mustique on your way to Prune and Union Islands.

The Island

It's still a perfectly splendid, totally away-from-it-all sort of place,

*The Barrancoid culture was the highly civilized forerunner of the Arawak & Carib settlers in the island chain. Culture peaked around 600 C.E.

though plans are underway for a development program to include homes and rental villas here. Still, it is comparatively big for a Grenadine and there should be room enough to hide most of these proposed buildings.

One spot that needs no hiding (indeed, it has been providing genuine out-island hospitality to visitors since it opened in '77 and has since developed a loyal following) is the *Crystal Sands Beach Hotel*. Developed by the De Roche family, Canouan natives, it offers basic comforts in 10 doubles in 5 villas. Each unit has its own private entrance plus bathroom.

Because Canouan is off the beaten track its existence as a potential destination is known mainly to the sailboat fraternity—and not too many of those—and a few knowledgeable outsiders. For the ultimate in getting away from it all, this has to be it—at least for the next couple of years or so, until that development program swings into action. Don't look for luxury here; what you get are basic comforts and an emphasis on seaside activities, mostly of the do-it-yourself variety.

The main building houses reception and dining area plus recreation for whatever evening activities may be at hand. A tennis court should be completed by pub date, and scuba and snorkeling are available.

Good West Indian fare. Rates moderate. Good value.

PRUNE/PALM ISLAND

Flying In

There's 1,500 ft of airstrip, and if it's closed, you can land just across the channel on the 1,600-ft airstrip at Union Island, where a boat will pick you up. Elevation at Prune/Palm Island is 25 ft while at Union it's a bare 6 ft above sea level.

The Island

John Caldwell's name is pretty familiar to anyone who's done much sailing and Palm Island is where he and his wife Mary have chosen to swallow the anchor—for the time being, at any rate.

The island is listed on nautical and aviation charts as Prune Island, but the Caldwells have busied themselves with the planting of more than 8,000 palm trees and they feel that the name should now change. In fact, they've done such a convincing job that

Palm Island Beach Club is now one of the better-known international out-island resorts.

Palm Island is roughly 110 acres in area; in addition to the 20-unit cottage colony (with private baths) there are a dozen or so homes that are available for rent (when the owners aren't there, of course). These include maid service for most of 'em, and there's a commissary for provisioning.

Meals are available at the main house or at the beach club if you don't feel like cooking.

There's a pleasant bar, and the nautical crowd stop over from time to time, which leads to spontaneous partying. There's also a tennis court, and the swimming is out of this world.

Food is mostly very good indeed. Rates are high, but overall, worth it.

UNION ISLAND

Flying In

At time of writing, prior permission was required from St. Vincent and from the owner, M. Andre Beaufrand in order to land here. Local tower 130.7 and Unicom on 122.8, and fuel is usually available.

There's 2,000 ft of concrete, but the approach to runway 08 is somewhat tricky with wind shear and telephone wires on final. Radios are manned 0700–1800 local time.

Two small hotels here, the *Sunny Grenadines* with 7 rooms and the *Clifton Beach* with 10. Both are strictly no frills and rates are accordingly low.

In addition there are two groups of cottages available for rent and a scuba operation has recently started. For latest details contact the St. Vincent Tourist Board.

PETIT ST. VINCENT

Let them know whether you're landing at Union or at Palm Island, and when, and the *Petit St. Vincent Resort* people will have a boat standing by for the twenty-minute or so ride to their island.

The name of the game here is understated island chic, at least in the evenings, and while management suggests that a fresh sports

Snorkeling is just fine in the waters of the Grenadine Islands.

shirt for the gentlemen is about as formal as anyone gets, it won't hurt your standing if your shirt is by Dior or Cardin or Puccini di Roma, while your smart Top Sider moccasins will show you're at ease with the boating crowd that makes this a point of call for fresh water and ice and fresh bread.

The island is 113 acres and the luxury cottages have been carefully sited in hillside and beach settings. There are 22 of them, designed by Swedish architect Arne Hasselquist, each with large living room and outdoor patio, 2 queen-sized beds in the bedroom, plus a private bath with its own dressing room. Couches in the living area make into daybeds, though in some cottages, where the partitioning is not roof high, privacy might be a problem.

The cottages are made of native stone, with *khuskhus* matting over tiled floors and wooden beams supporting the wooden roof. Wall decorations include the same khuskhus-made rondels, and there are 2 basins in each tiled bathroom, enormous bathsheets to dry oneself, and comfortable chairs. It's island deluxe.

No telephones, but room service is provided by a unique motorized driver who passes each cottage at thirty-minute intervals between the hours of 7:30 AM and 7:30 PM. The trick is to place your order in the mailbox outside your cottage and run up the red signal flag. Pegasus will be right along to pick up your order. No charge for service—it's included.

Meals are served in the main building, which repeats the same stone motif of the cottages on a grander scale, with a large lounge and dining room and an attractive bar. Your room rate includes all meals, including a delightfully authentic English afternoon tea. Food is mostly excellent.

There's no formal entertainment save for an occasional evening with a steel band, and those visiting yachtsmen, of course. There's an excellent tennis court. Rackets and tennis balls are available, but bring your own sneakers. Snorkeling equipment and half a dozen Sunfish plus a larger sailboat are all available courtesy the management. Or you can go off on a day's charter to neighboring Carriacou. Deep-sea fishing is especially good in May, June and July around here.

Children are welcomed and babysitters are available.

Rates are high, but so is the quality, and for out-island chic, Petit St. Vincent is pretty hard to beat.

Grenada

Flying In

Pearls Airport is the gateway to the Spice Island of the Caribbean and it lies a short 64 NM ride from Arnos Vale in St. Vincent, bringing you down the colorful chain of the Grenadine Islands. Pearls is also to be found on the 255° radial of the Barbados VOR/DME at 112.7/8PB at 68 NM. There's an NDB at the field, 362 ZGT. Tower is 118.2.

Pearls has enjoyed a number of facelifts over the years, the most recent extending the runway to 5,800 ft. Elevation is 30 ft; there's strip lighting in case you'll be late, but if so, be sure to get prior permission. Airport hours are normally 0800 through 1800 local time, and gasoline and jet fuel are usually available. However, if you're flying up-island from Trinidad and simply stopping off, better start with full tanks in Trinidad where it's cheaper. While Grenada is actively prospecting for petroleum (and some experts believe that the Eastern Caribbean may be sitting on the largest undiscovered reserves in the world), so far there's been nothing to report.

For local tourism queries, call 2001 or 2778. Emergencies only, 2603.

St. George, now known as St. George's, capital of the Island of Spice. (*photo*)

Background Briefing

If the name Grenada (pronounced Grenn-ayd-ah) rings somewhat doubtful bells in your mind, you're right. There was some unrest here around independence time in 1974 with a lot of infighting of an unpleasant kind. It was all highly unusual on an island that has won world respect for the genuine kindness of its people; it was mostly a family-type quarrel.

Even the nicest of people can't afford this type of struggle and tourism almost came to a full stop, as did investment. However, although there are occasional rumbles of discontent, common sense and good order have been restored since tourism is an important item in the island's economy, and will be for the foreseeable future (until they discover that offshore oil).

The fallout from all this has included changes in ownership of some of the properties, and a number of local improvements of the showcase variety, such as the National Convention Center. This recently hosted the Seventh Regular Session of the General Assembly of the Organization of American States. Grenada has won admission to the UN, and has been able to negotiate a treaty with the EEC.

These are very real achievements for an island with an area of 133 square miles and a population of around 125,000. In addition to its mainland, its outside territories include a number of small islets, rocks, and cays, plus the islands of Carriacou* (largest of the Grenadines) and Petit Martinique, and Ronde Island. Grenada's other occupied off-shore islands include Calivigny, Glover (a former whaling station), Green, Sandy, and Sugar Loaf.

The territories are administered from the capital, St. George, now known as St. George's through one of those accidents of language, even though the parish in which it is situated is still called St. George. English is the basic language, with a typical Grenadian lilt, and use of the French patois is almost extinct. Currency is the EC dollar known here as the Grenadian dollar. The island is a member of the British Commonwealth with a parliamentary system of government; US and British citizens need

*Carriacou is the only one with its own airstrip, at Lauriston Field: it's 2,100 ft long, elevation 15 ft.

only proof of citizenship and onward tickets for stays up to three months. West Germans no longer require visas.

The people of the island are mainly of African descent, mixed with Carib—the original settlers following the Arawaks—and white settlers and traders. The result is large numbers of good-looking people of both sexes.

While the economy is still agricultural, it has been only quite recently that the effects of hurricane Donna, which razed a central portion of the island in the 1950s, almost killing the nutmeg industry, have been erased. The ineffable nutmeg—*Myristica fragrens*—has long been used to enhance food flavors. It's a doubly useful little nut, for its outer coat is used to make mace, while the inner kernel is the nutmeg. Grenada is responsible for one-third of the world's current supply of these spices; before that hurricane, the world market share was even greater.

Chief exports include cocoa and coconuts, bananas and sugar. The island also produces numerous vegetables and avocados, many of which are also available for export to less fortunate territories. It's also an important producer of cinnamon, another reason why it's called the island of spice. Indeed, driving through the farming regions and in the hills, the air seems curiously scented in a manner that's a mixture of puzzle and delight.

Around 40 percent of the available working population is still employed in agriculture, fishing, and forestry. And while unemployment and inflation are bones of contention between rival politicians, union demands have inflated hotel rates, though not seriously enough to keep satisfied tourists away.

One of the reasons may be that Grenada does know how to show its visitors a good time. The taxi drivers who will seek your business at the airport are for the most part excellent guides to their island, will give thoughtful and penetrating answers to your questions and surprise you with the amount of detailed statistics they can provide. One person who deserves recognition for this local raising of consciousness has to be—forgive me, Gert—Mrs. Gertrude Protain, who over more years than either she or I care to remember, has been mostly at the helm of Grenada's tourism industry and development and who has actively encouraged an enlightened approach elsewhere. The results in Grenada have been fair shakes for the tourist and a massive repeat business that has mostly survived the toils of political change.

The Hopkin's of Ross Point have also been active in this field. Curtis and Audrey Hopkin originally opened their Inn back in the early 1950s, and their son, Royston—who is in real estate and car rental—is now general manager and gourmet in residence. What the Hopkin family has done is raise the standard of West Indian cuisine to a point where it begins to approach the art of the classical Chinese, French, and Indian. No small achievement even in an island of spice. Their influence has spun off by word of mouth—in the happiest sense of all—elsewhere in the island and to the other islands of the former British West Indies. The result, here in Grenada, is that one must make reservations for meals at Ross Point well in advance.

Of volcanic origin, Grenada has a marvelous harmonious blend of scenery from the highlands in the island's center—Mount Saint Catherine rises to 2,757 ft—with its lakes and waterfalls, to the innumerable creeks and inlets, bays and harbors that play along its shores. Then there are the beaches. One of the finest is on the

(Not to be used for navigation.)

northwest tip of the island, just across from Levera Island at Levera Bay and Beach, with its Pirate bar-lounge. A Canadian consortium has plans for hotel development here to include a golf course and country club, plus cottage and villas (condominia-type operation), plus a shopping center. The government of Grenada, like most other Caribbean governments, provides tax holidays and incentives to investors interested in developments that will be beneficial to the island. These are not necessarily touristic.

The largest beach within easy reach of the capital is the famous Grand Anse *plage*, which, in turn, has served as a nucleus for the bulk of the hotels in the island. It's a public beach, as are all beaches in the island, however, even though hotels have been built almost down to the water.

Just down from Grand Anse is Morne Rouge, which has become an overflow area, with its attractive bay. Still farther down (though not on the same road—you have to backtrack) you will come to Grenada's only lighthouse, at Pointe Saline, and the incredible juxtaposition of a black beach and a white beach separated solely by the narrow track. This is one of the most beautiful spots in the island, and definitely for your list of "must see" things.

Nearby is the almost equally well known L'Ance aux Epines (pronounced Lanse-syoo-peen), also with an attractive beach, and just farther on, yet another delightful beach at Mt. Hartman Estate opposite Hog Island. Inland from here is the village of Woburn, featured in that all-time classic Caribbean movie, *Island in the Sun*. Farther on from there is the Westerhall Development, one of the classiest real estate developments in the Caribbean, with numerous trees and shrubs, many of them rarely to be found in the Caribbean. This hundred-acre peninsula has many delightful properties, some of which are available for rent. Beach activities are nice here, too.

In the interior, worth making tracks to, is the beautiful crater lake at Grand Etang. There's a government guesthouse nearby, which provides modest accommodations for those who would stay overnight. Better bring a sweater along because those nights are delightfully cool, and you'll want to take a walk when the moon is up for the incredible views and the stars that seem so brilliantly close your hand could capture them.

Nearby are the Annendale Falls, while a little to the north is the site of Fedon's camp, which, as history buffs will know, was where Fedon plotted to oust the English from the island on behalf of the French. There's also a waterfall between Concord and Concord Valley.

Two good places to see how nutmeg and mace are prepared are at the spice factories at Douggleston Estate, just inland from the fishing village of Gouyave on the west coast of the island, and at Grenville, just south of Telescope Point—and immediately south of Pearls Airport—which you'll have seen on your approach.

St. George itself is one of the most delightful capital cities anywhere in the world. It exudes olde worlde charm, despite the busy little mini-mokes and other vehicles (and occasional donkeys) that all want space in the narrow streets.

The harbor and the careenage (where local residents only can haul their boats for repair) are among the safest in the entire Caribbean, its only rival English Harbor in Antigua. A relatively new deep-water jetty permits cruise ships to land their passengers just across the way from the original old town. The Lagoon, which

The old French chart shows St. George as the City of Port Royale.

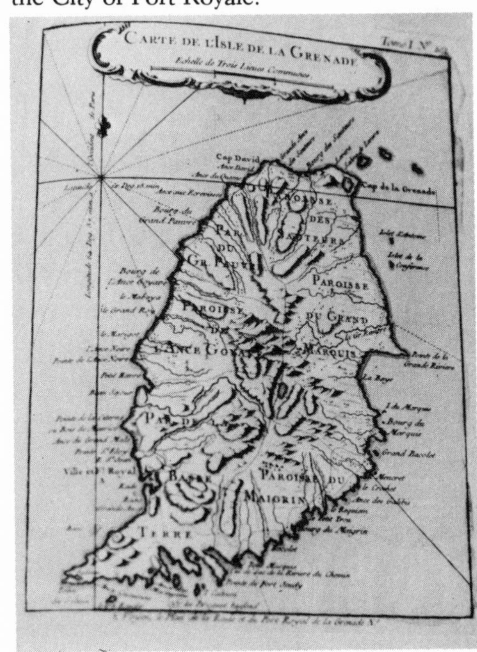

lies just to the south, is now home to several charter operations, and numerous visiting sailboats who seem, quite rightly, in no hurry to move on. (If you sail, the Grenadines equals the best of the Virgin Islands and is, in the opinion of many, even nicer on account of fewer people. However, the waters can kick up, and there's less immediate shelter available if your crew is looking for an out.)

Grenada was originally called Concepcion by Columbus, who sighted it but did not land on August 15, 1498. First attempts to colonize came in 1609, when a group of Britons attempted a settlement but were driven off by the Caribs—who were apparently as fierce as those in St. Vincent. Some fifty years later, through bribery (rum and trinkets), the French were able to persuade the Caribs to treat with them, which unluckily—for the Caribs, that is—they did. The French then proceeded to wipe out the Caribs with the sword; the last to survive made their way to the north of the island, perhaps hoping to escape to the Grenadines. But they'd been encircled up near Sauteurs—now the third-largest town in the island—and escape was impossible. Rather than surrender, they threw themselves down toward the sea from the rocky promontory known as Caribs' Leap. Few, if any, can have survived the rocks beneath.

Sauteurs, incidently, takes its name from this hill, known in French as Le Morne des Sauteurs, or Leapers' Hill. About 100 years later the British moved back, their West Indian fleet and army having grown in size. There followed a series of power struggles for sovereignty, which was finally established by the French in 1779. Just four years later, by the Treaty of Versailles, the island was returned to England. A famous uprising in 1795, instigated by the French and in which Fedon was involved, saw the massacre of a number of planters and the island's Lieutenant Governor. Serious reprisals followed and it was not until emancipation in 1838 that tempers cooled.

The island became an Associated State in 1967 and independent in 1974.

Apart from excursions, there's a surprising amount to see and do around St. George. And the government has exempted a number of items that are available duty-free at certain stores. Typical are: cameras, Swiss watches and clocks, French perfumes and essences, items of gold, 14 kt and over, sterling silver, warranted fine

porcelain or bone china, and liquor, supposedly the cheapest in the Eastern Caribbean.

Charles of Grenada, in a fine new building on the corner of Cross Street just the far side of the Sendall Tunnel, which helps connect the two halves of the city, has scarves and other fine products from Liberty of London, cashmere and wool items from Pringle, a range of Daks slacks and shorts. Veronica's Tropical Fashions features a number of good locally made items, or will custom-make something tropical (or not so tropical) to your fancy at short notice. The Granby Stores Ltd. has a good range of souvenirs, in addition to English silks and cottons—they're at the corner of Granby and Melville—while at Huggins, on Young Street, you'll find records, sporting goods, and appliances, in addition to their numerous other items.

The Nutmeg is a bar and restaurant known the world over to sailing folk and others who've visited this island. It continues its gracious tradition of honest food and drink in its second-story location overlooking the careenage and inner harbor. Food includes delicious turtle steak, lobster (thermidor, or however you fancy), lambi (conch), fish and chips, chicken, or regular steak for the meat eaters. Rum punch is the traditional cooler, and for males*—in the evening—this is a good spot to reconnoiter for an evening's amatory dalliance. (You'll usually be politely accosted, so politely you may not even notice, as you leave.)

Rudolf's stays open later than *The Nutmeg*; it's just a block down

*Women looking for amusement in the Caribbean have problems that men don't experience. Unlike the all-too-shy women of the islands, the indigenous males know only too well what they want and how to get it.

the road and has developed its own following. Other possibilities for refreshment and food are *Peebles* and *Aboo's the Cubby Hole*, and the *Turtle Back* at the harbor entrance. *Jane's Roti Shop* and *Soul City* are in the shopping center.

For more serious dining, many of the hotels' restaurants offer excellent food, the aforementioned *Ross Point* being a leader in West Indian cuisine. (Good also for lunch. Reservations a must!) For curry, try the *Cinnamon Hill* hotel restaurant for Sunday lunch. For Italian, *Casa Mia* (also in the Grand Anse area) offers pizza in addition to several other delicious Italian specialties. Chinese enthusiasts can find good (mainly Cantonese) fare at *Yin Wo* (the Bird's Nest) or the *Golden Dragon*.

The Red Crab, out on the L'Anse aux Epines road, and as hospitable a place as you'll find in the island (it describes itself as "An English 'Pub' with a tropical flavor where there are no strangers, only friends you haven't met yet") provides real pints of draught English beers, plus an eclectic menu, which nevertheless includes such staples as steak and fish.

If the thrill of catching your own fish appeals to you, the deep-sea fishing season here runs from November through March and boats with experienced skippers are available by the half-day, day, or week. You'll have a chance to do battle with both blue and white marlin, with sailfish and dolphin, and the rich grounds aren't too far offshore.

Other activities include tennis, played widely in the island. Both the Richmond Hill and the Tanteen Tennis Clubs welcome visitors as temporary members. But proper tennis whites are preferred. A number of hotels have tennis courts and more are being built.

There's golf at the Woodlands Golf Club, with low green fees. Scuba enthusiasts will want to visit the wreck of the *Bianca C*, which lies just off Pointe Saline in about 100 ft of water.

Spectator sports include cricket and soccer, and horse-racing at Easter and in August.

There are a number of regattas throughout the year, the number-one choice being the Carriacou event held during the first weekend in August, which attracts a larger following each year.

Where to Stay

In Grenada there is a very definite choice between staying on your own—and there are numerous accommodations from deluxe country villas to small-sized apartments—or the hotel life.

The Caribs' method of fighting in the seventeenth century.

Your next decision must be whether you want to be close to the capital, or whether you'll accept being just a little farther out of town. Essentially, this means a choice of being near that wondrous *plage* Grand Anse or at L'Anse aux Epines.

If it's simply a lazy good time you're after, with a certain amount of convivial company, you'll probably choose Grand Anse, where it's easy to move around on foot, and where taxis are always available if you want to go someplace else.

While it's possible to adopt the same philosophy at L'Anse aux Epines, it's really more convenient to have a rental car. For while taxis (and rides) are available, you're just that much more independent.

Even if you're on island for business, there's not too much point settling in the heart of town for the occasion. You might as well enjoy this enchanting place, since you'll stand a far better chance of an informal meeting with the political VIPs you came to meet at somewhere like the *Evening Palace* (*Terese's Beer Garden* is a sometimes popular haunt, here) in the Morne Rouge/Grand Anse area than in town.

On the other hand, if you're after the real island life, then you'll find superb informality, plus good cooking, at a number of the inns and guesthouses in and around St. George. Rates are super low, accommodations basic, and hospitality warm year-round.

At Grand Anse there's a pleasing cluster of hotels including the *Spice Island Inn*, the *Holiday Inn* (formerly the Grenada Beach Hotel), *Blue Horizons, Silver Sands*, the newer *Cinnamon Hill Hotel and Beach Club*, plus *Tropical Inn* and the *Flamboyant*, just off the beach.

The *Spice Island Inn* has offered good comfort and value since it first opened. It continues to do so even though it is now operated by a Grenadian-Canadian corporation. There are 30 air-conditioned units—20 beach-front and 10 pool-side suites—landscaped to ensure privacy and simply but comfortably furnished.

Thoughtfulness abounds, from the local and contemporary art in each suite and in the lobby to the pleasant mix of the menu, which tries to satisfy your hunger in the most pleasant of ways possible while educating the tyro's palate to some of the more delicious foods the island has to offer. Recommended is the restaurant's green turtle soup, still made to a recipe conceived by the original owner, and the soursop ice cream. Both delicious. Expensive, but enjoys repeat business.

A Holiday Inn is a Holiday Inn is a Holiday Inn—well, the *Grenada Holiday Inn* is just a bit different, and not only on account of the glorious beach. Service is extremely good, for a start, and that old West Indian magic is beginning to be found in the menu. The grounds are attractively landscaped and kept in trim. All in all, this Holiday Inn makes an effort.*

There's the usual swimming pool (fresh water), and a concessionary shopping area, and there's evening entertainment. Rates are island-modest, for this sort of thing.

Blue Horizons sits a short distance in back of the Spice Island Inn and, while not *on* the beach, is so close that it scarcely matters. It is also one of the better buys on this stretch of strand, offering 16 duplex suites with private patio, 8 units around a swimming pool. What's good is that you can prepare your own food if you prefer to, and there is dining available at the outfit's own restaurants. Rates extremely reasonable.

Silversands Hotel and Beach Resort offers comfortable and relaxed West Indian-style living right at the beach with simple comforts. It's a combination of main building and cottages in a mostly landscaped plot fronting the beach. All accommodations with private bath and balcony, and the rates are reasonable considering the location and the genuine hospitality of mine host, Grenadian Owner-Manager Earle Gittens. Interestingly, this is one place in the island where massage and chiropody are available. Rates reasonable.

The *Cinnamon Hill Hotel and Beach Club* started life as an ambitious condominium project that never quite got off the ground. Visitors today are fortunate, for it offers near-luxury apartment and hacienda-style suites with a fresh-water pool. Rates with meals are high, but for those who prefer self-sufficiency, this is a reasonable buy given the setting and comfort. Restaurant and bar, of course.

At the other end of the scale is *Tropical Inn,* 10 rooms in air-conditioned duplex apartments, cottage-style, with its own fresh-water pool. Rates are super low.

Also near Grand Anse is the well-furnished hillside cottage

*It has still a way to go though, before it can match its Guadeloupe counterpart.

development of Jim Needham; rates vary according to how high up the hill you are. This is mostly do-it-yourself, though there's food when the cruise ships come to town. The name of this particular game just four miles from town is *The Flamboyant.*

To get to *L'Anse aux Epines* when leaving St. George you take exactly the same road as you would were you going to Grand Anse. Before you get to the turnoff you will come to two other establishments, the *Crescent Inn* and the *Ross Point Inn.*

The *Crescent Inn* overlooks the yacht basin and offers excellent West Indian food, and simple but adequate accommodations in 14 rooms in the main building and annex.

Ross Point Inn has 12 rooms with private facilities plus 5 other cabanas, and really needs no further note. It's what you've always wanted for a genuine West Indian vacation, even though it's not on a beach (they provide free transport). Graceful and spontaneous hospitality.

Back on the road toward L'Anse aux Epines: There are a couple of turnoffs to the right before you come to a T-junction on your way to L'Anse aux Epines. Make a left, and then take the first right, and you're on track. Very shortly you'll pass the factory of Carib Breweries, which makes a very fine local beer.*

In the L'Anse aux Epines area you'll discover *Horse Shoe Bay Hotel* (and a little beyond, at Mount Hartmann Bay, the *Secret Harbor*) plus the good old *Calabash*—a long-time favorite with friends from all over the world. The *Hibiscus House* offers 2 units for do-it-yourselfers and is an excellent value, as is the *Twelve Degrees North* project, which eschews children.

Horse Shoe Bay Hotel is one of the more delightful of island residencies with 12 attractive hillside units furnished with considerable charm, including antiques and four-posters. Main building is Spanish airy stucco and the grounds are almost perpetually aflame with blazing tropical flowers, muted only by the bourgainvillea. Although sensible informality is the order of the day, chances are you'll feel more comfortable with a tie and jacket at dinner. Many of the island's elite drop by and dressing up is one of the tropics' diversions, so be warned. This doesn't mean you

*They used to offer excursions to visitors who were interested in the brewing process. A telephone call will elicit whether they still do.

should pack your tropical dinner jacket; only that should His Excellency drop by for some late backgammon you'll feel better if you're appropriately dressed.

There's a swimming pool, and a handsome beach at the bottom of the hill. Out of season there are occasional bargains, since some cottages have kitchen units with maid included. Even during high season this has to be one of the best values in the island. As they say, check it out. Good value, especially the food, which can be Spice Island superior.

Sports include use of Sunfish or Windsurfer, and a rowboat. Scuba can be arranged, as can deep-sea fishing and yacht chartering. Local snorkeling is just fine. More sedentary folks will prefer bridge, poker, and other card games, snooker or billiards, darts, or just plain sunning. West Indian elegance.

The Calabash has made many friends over the years. Now under new management, it has managed to maintain most of its old friends with the hospitality that it was famed for. Accommodations are again cottage-elegant, with an abundance of tropical plants and fauna.

Tennis, billards room. Food good. Self-sufficiency available off season. Otherwise, rates high.

Secret Harbor is one of the newer of the island's hotels, yet has already managed to build up its own select group of repeaters who return year after year. The four-poster theme is repeated in the 20 suites atop the slope that runs down to Mt. Hartman Bay, and the suites are bigger than you'd believe. This is sumptuary comfort, each suite with privacy and splendid view, plus a swimming pool—beach below—plus tennis courts and putting green for those who feel itchy without some sort of club in their hands.

Nicely landscaped surroundings, but you'll probably feel more comfortable if you have your own wheels: much better for beach-hopping. Rates highish in season, good value off season.

The aforementioned *Hibiscus House* comprises the *Maxi-Hibiscus* (4 beds) and *Mini-Hibiscus* (1 bed) just a short walk to the sea. These cottages are surrounded by flowers and tropical growth of the nicest kind, and rates are rare value, especially for those intent on staying awhile.

Also in the same area is *Twelve Degrees North*, which has a number of fully equipped 1- and 2-bedroom housekeeping apartments. For couples this one is an especially good value for the money, since it includes maid service (yes, laundry too) and the beach is at hand.

OUT ISLANDS/CARRIACOU

From a visitor's point of view, "out islands" must mean the island of Carriacou unless he or she is arriving by boat, in which case there's no problem with accommodation (or backpack).

The Mermaid Inn in Hillsborough is the place to stay here—unless you're camping—with 10 rooms. There's a premium to be paid if you want private bath, and you'd better let them know when you make your reservation or you could lose out. Still, rates are modest and include both breakfast and dinner.

Friendly intimacy is the story here, and a taxi drive around the island—it's bigger than you'd think—will show you a delightful amalgam of farming allotments, hillside hamlets, large stretches of sand.

Camp Carriacou is where the marine biologists hang out and it's a barefoot kind of place, for a totally informal vacation. A tropical bamboo-hut vacation camp, it offers scuba diving, cruising, and seaplay. Rates low.

Not yet noted in the Grenada Government's "Where to Stay" listings are the *Modern Guest House*, in Hillsborough, the *Amigo Guest House*, and the *Silver Beach Holiday Resort*.

The Modern is right across the beach with 5 rooms in Hillsborough and modest rates. *Amigo* has 8 rooms and equally modest rates, while the *Silver Beach* resort provides duplex apartments to be rented hotel-style or on your own. Still modest.

Carriacou: you'll either adore it or loathe it. There are few in-betweens.

Places to eat out, to cool off, include the *Blue Tropicana* and the *Tip Top*.

For further information: Grenada Tourist Board, PO Box 293, St. George, Grenada, West Indies.

For further information, contact the Grenada Tourism Information Office 866 Second Avenue, New York City, 10017; [212]. 759-9675.

Barbados

Flying In

Barbados is the easternmost of the islands of the Lesser Antilles, about 100 NM almost due east of St. Vincent and around 82 NM southeast of Hewanorra International in St. Lucia. There is one airfield, at the southern end of the island, formerly known as Seawell, now as *Grantley Adams International* after the island's leading elder statesman.*

Eleven thousand ft of runway are available. Main runway has approach lights and VASI and the field is well signposted electronically. There's VOR/DME (112.7/8PV Ch 74) and NDB 345 8PV and ILS. There is a TCA—marked on the chart as Seawell TCA—and the island is in a restricted area, (MK) R1, so check latest NOTAM. Approach Control is at 119.7 while the Tower is 118.7; Ground Control is at 121.9.

Grantley Adams also has radar, frequencies for which are 120.2, 120.7, and 121.2, should you need an assist. Fuel for both jet and regular aircraft is usually available, as is maintenance, mechanical and electronic. No landing fee or parking charges for aircraft 6,000 lbs or less, at time of writing.

*Sir Grantley Adams, an Afro-Barbadian and founder of the Barbados Labor Party, became the island's first premier in 1954 and was the person primarily responsible for the smooth impetus toward independence. He was also an uncle of the present premier, the Hon. John Michael Geoffrey ("Tom") Adams, who was born in 1932.

Because Barbados is the first piece of land this side of the Atlantic, many long-distance transatlantic sailboats look to it as the landfall of choice in the islands. The reason is that during the day puffs of cumulus build up which appear to reflect the green of the land beneath, marking the spot, as it were to confirm the navigator's work. This build-up becomes quite impressive as the day lengthens, with tops going up to 20,000 ft and more some days. VFR pilots are recommended to make an early-morning departure in order to avoid this phenomenon, since the distance flown will presumably be short.

Background Briefing

The island of Barbados is approximately 21 miles by 14 and is shaped like an avocado. Its area is 166 square miles, much of it extensively cultivated, though sugar, the main crop for centuries and until very recently its prime export, has declined to about third place in an increasingly modern economy, which now includes light industry.

The first inhabitants of the island appear to have been the Arawaks, though when in 1536 Pedro a Campos, a Portuguese sailor, landed on the island, he and his companions found it deserted. (On his way to Brazil, he marked the existence of the island in his chart and named it *Los Barbados*, supposedly for the beardlike appendages that hung from the fig trees.)

Not quite a hundred years later, a group of British privateers landed for water near Holetown on the west coast and claimed the island in the name of King James. Their reports were of sufficient interest in London that a new expedition was funded and financed by a syndicate headed by Sir William Courteen: objective, a settlement to be constructed and to be called Jamestown.

The economy quickly prospered, though at the beginning there had been near-disaster, with settlers quarreling over boundaries and titles, and neglect of the crops, their *raison d'etre*. By 1631 there were some 5,000 new settlers growing mostly maize and tobacco. Most of these people were indentured laborers. It was a scheme that appealed to the newly displaced generations of Britons, for in return for a contract in which the laborer agreed to work without pay for from 3 to 7 years (depending on terms), he was provided with his ocean passage, clothing, accommodations, and food. At the end of his term he'd receive land of his own.

The overthrow of the feudal system and the increasing power of the monarchy, which began with Henry Tudor of Wales (King Henry VII), had continued apace. Laborers who had found purpose under the overlordship of the monasteries were now hard put under their new masters. While the conditions were nowhere near so bad as that which would occur two centuries later with the onset of the industrial revolution and the enclosure of land, it was a beginning.

By 1640, the population of Barbados had leapt to 30,000 souls and there was already a system of government. One of the island's more illustrious citizens, a Welsh lad called Harry Morgan, started his fabled career in this island, where he worked for a plantation owner whose business failed. Harry fell in with a rough crew, and together they heisted a Spanish ship that had stopped off for water and wild pig. It was the beginning of an archetypical robber baron's career that was to conclude with a Lieutenant Governorship of Jamaica, his own estate, and a knighthood from Charles II.

Because the island was somewhat off the beaten track, and because two of its closest neighbors were Carib redoubts, Barbados was spared the internecine strife that developed elsewhere. The result was that when Virginian tobacco began to drive out the Caribbean product—held by men of the time to be of inferior quality—the Bajans looked around for a new product and found it in cane.*

The early plantings yielded better than any expected, but they were low, and the cost of an *ingenio*—the Spanish term still held—seemed outrageous to the London merchant bankers who were still financing the operations. Here the Dutch Jews came in. They'd already experienced the marketing of sugar from plant to finished product in Brazil before their Iberian competitors had driven them off. They offered lines of credit and technical assistance in the form of agricultural expertise and equipment, which included large-scale vats for boiling and crystalizing and crushing rollers to get the juice from the stalk (which might be powered by wind or water, animal, or—at a pinch—a team of men).

It was an offer that couldn't be refused. And the results held up.

*The Spanish had understood the importance of sugar cane as a crop from the earliest days. Within 15 years of Columbus' discovery of Hispaniola, a mill had been established.

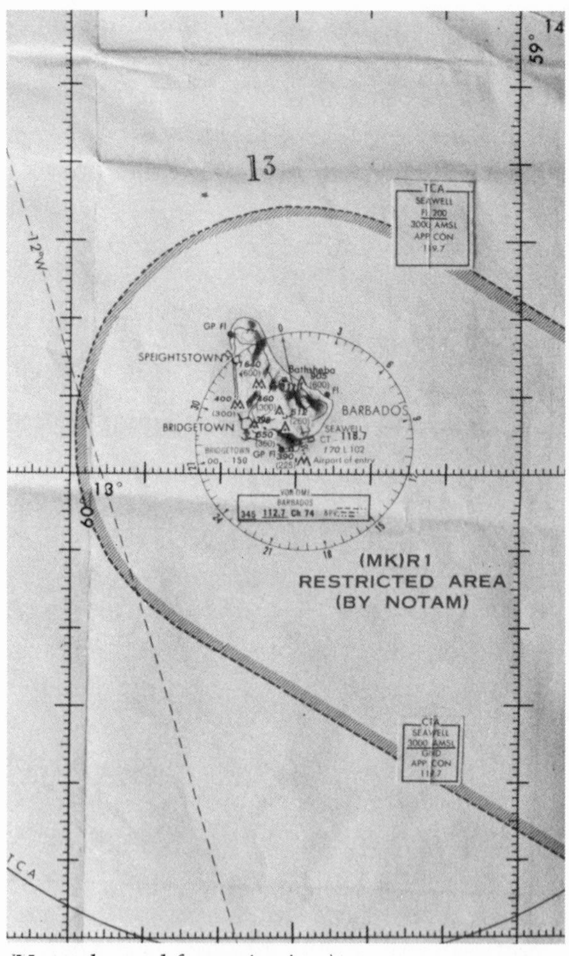

(Not to be used for navigation.)

A synagogue was built and by the mid-1650s profitability per acre was—according to one report—around $80 per acre, so that a modest plantation of, say, 500 acres could produce a profit of $40,000. In terms of our own currency those were high earnings and led to the term "as rich as an Indies planter."

Like Morgan, Tom Modyford also had ideas when he decided to plant in Barbados. (He had become Lt. Governor of the island by Harry Morgan's time, with a knighthood. He would later become Governor of Jamaica.) He wrote friends: "I vow to return to

England a rich man." By rich, he felt he ought to be able to turn at least a half million dollars one way or another.*

In any event, the island quickly became a thriving colony, with shipping and trade and a *laissez faire* attitude toward business of almost every sort. One important precept emerged from all of this (from these same Dutchmen, the Jews) and it was the right of settlers "to be as free as they were born in England." A direct result was that indentured men were worked harder than slaves, for whom the owners provided wives and rum, and toward whom the owners practiced a much more Roman attitude than elsewhere—manumission according to Leviticus in some examples, or on the death of the owner. The indentured person had a much rougher time of it. He was there to be worked for a certain period. Better if he died on the job, as it were, for his land would be forfeit.

The slaves remembered the oppression the white man had undergone. The result is that while rivalry between black and white remains in the island in terms of contemporary success, there was never a slave uprising here, and the islanders have seen "fair play" while producing such cultural heroes in the field as the fabulous Gary Sobers, a world renowned cricketer. The former prime minister, Errol Barrow, is an accomplished pilot. And Bajans today are providing a nucleus of Third World teachers the likes of which have never been seen before. It is possibly in the field of education that Barbados will make its greatest contribution to the human family.

While the official language is English, an interesting English-based patois has developed which is occasionally heard. It is relatively easy for foreigners to understand, compared with the French equivalents.

More than just a tourism destination point, Barbados is a thriving mini-nation that is currently providing some of the best brainpower in Third World studies.

*While *pieces-of-eight* were a system of dividing a gold or silver coin into small pieces—still preserved in our own times as in "two bits"—sugar was frequently used as currency at the rate of one penny per pound. Consider the price of sugar today, at 49¢ per pound, to get some idea of the ratio. Then consider this: A pair of shoes cost 16 pounds of sugar, and Osnaburg white linen—clothing for slaves & indentured workers—cost just 6 pounds a yard; 3½ yards made a suit.

It is really unfair to talk of Barbados in these times as "Little England" because the Bajans have added their own sparkling sheen to the English tradition. For something a little different in vacationing, visit the local courts to see bewigged judges and barristers; then appreciate the typical Bajan repartee between bench and advocate. It scintillates much of the time, and could rarely be heard in the dryer tones of London Town, or any US urban area.

And if afternoon tea and lawn tennis seem unfashionable pursuits of leisure, treat yourself at least once to cucumber and watercress sandwiches, sliced thin, and thickly spread with butter, plus the experience of a choice Darjeeling or Ceylon tea. And tennis is much more fun when played on real grass rather than on the several modern substitutes, though these too are available.

Currency can be a problem.

The Bajans finally dismissed the EC currency, which was linked with the British pound sterling, to link their own dollar with that of the United States: a par ratio of two Bajan dollars to one US was established, new coins were milled, and the system went into effect in 1975. What is hurting right now in Barbados—apart from union demands for higher wages in the trades and services industries (which means tourism)—is the fact that the US dollar, on which Barbados' own is based, is crumbling like a drunken person in the world markets.

Already, Barbados has passed the $200-a-day rate in hotels for accommodations and meals. And while the platinum coast *is* beautiful, and one of the best resort areas in the entire Caribbean, you can get a whole lot more service and worth for your dollar if you spend it somewhere else—especially in the smaller islands. (What you won't be able to buy is the super independence of almost every Bajan you meet, in terms of treating you as just another individual. Bajans are especially good at that.)

On the other hand, you don't have to stay at the most expensive hotels even if you want to be on the platinum coast. *The Swiss Chalet*, for example, has its own fine—if small—beach; its upper-level accommodations are spacious and comfortable and are not too costly. Better book in advance, however, for more and more people are hearing the word-of-mouth recommendations that have made this one of the more popular places to stay.

One of the questions that the prospective vacationer invariably asks after the first few glorious days in the sun is: "What else is there to do?" Fortunately, Barbados has a host of things to offer, possibly more than most islands. There are a number of great houses to be visited whose owners have very kindly agreed to let the public in. There are numerous gardens and parks, and at Turner's Hall Woods—a beautiful stand of some 45 acres in St. Andrew—you can find a forest complete with rare birds and a boiling spring. Inevitably, the continuity of the European tradition for more than 300 years means that there's plenty of history to be found.

To begin at the beginning, a good point to start is at the Careenage in Bridgetown, where inter-island schooners still ply their trade and where the harbor police patrol in the colorful *HMS Pinafore*-type uniforms. Nearby is the original Trafalgar Square, which predates its London, England, counterpart by some 27 years and where the Public Buildings—which date back to 1748—house Parliament.

Just out of town is the Barbados Museum, housed within a military detention center built by the Royal Engineers in 1853. You'll find furniture, glassware, models, and library, plus a really fine collection of West Indian prints, which date back to about 1690. There's a children's gallery with dollhouses. The Jubilee Gallery has collections of silver, glass, and china from plantation days, plus geological specimens and archeological finds.

In St. Andrew the Morgan Lewis Mill was the setting for scenes in the movie *Island in the Sun* (see also Grenada), and is now the property of the National Trust. Numerous old mills are to be found around the island, and show that in earlier times, wind power was an extremely potent force for local prosperity. The mill at St. Jude's vicarage in St. George dates back to the 17th century.

High point—literally—in the island is Mount Hillabilly, which just makes it as a mountain, albeit small, with a height of 1,115 feet. There's some fine country bordering the Atlantic Ocean to the north and east, much of which is worth exploring by foot. The waters are also fascinating, though if you do intend to snorkel, take someone who's experienced in working these swells. They can be tricky and they've come a long long way, so they pack quite a punch if you're unsteady.

In St. Thomas is Cole's Cave, not far from Welchman's Hall Gully (acquired by the National Trust and now a botanical garden). It is a large cavern hidden by lush foliage. Inside are running streams and ponds in which blind crayfish live. In places the cave reaches up to 16 ft and there are numerous stalagmite and stalactite formations.*

There are caves, too, at Welchman's Hall Gully, together with spice trees and a tropical garden of fruit. There's a four-foot-diameter natural pillar formed by the joining of a stalagmite and a stalactite, which appears to hold up a rock cliff. This is one of the largest known such formations in the world.

There are more than 150 different species of trees and shrub, which house a small group of wild monkeys.

The serious horticulturist will delight in the profusion of flowers and shrubs at *Andromeda Garden* at Tent Bay, Bathsheba, in the parish of St. Joseph and set on a cliff through which a small stream falls between tropical flora. Owned by John and Iris Bannochie, there's a splendid variety of palms and ferns, oleanders, jade plants, and hiliconiums, plus hibiscus, philodendron, and bougainvillea. There's a small charge for admission, and for plant lovers it's a bargain.

Mentioned earlier were those stately homes available for inspection by the public; these include *Bay Mansion,* supposedly a haunted house with an aristocratic ghost in the form of Sir John Beckles, who died hereabouts in 1840. The mansion, which is on Bay Street in Bridgetown, has a receiving hall and a dining hall, a gazebo with fountain, and no fewer than 13 bedrooms. Numerous antiques include furniture and furnishings, glass, silver, chinaware, and needlepoint.

Byde Mill was a 19th-century plantation in the southeastern section of the island, overlapping the parishes of St. John, St. Philip, and St. George. There's an old mill wall and garden here. More interesting is *Farley Hill,*** which was almost totally destroyed by fire some years ago. A two-story building with arched

*Deposits of carbonate of lime, usually forming like a huge icicle, stalagmites are the ones that grow up from the floor, while stalactites are the ones that hang down from the roof.

**You can still see how the Greathouse appeared in *Island in the Sun* which was filmed here.

windows, it is still visited for the apparent grandeur in which the West Indies planters lived.

Holders House in St. James dates from the 17th century and is partly restored. Existing foundation work and the arched basement of the original storehouse give some idea of the strength of these buildings. There's a family gravesite, too. Also in St. James is *Porters,* former property of the Alleyne family, the structure of which is also believed to date from the 17th century.

Mullins Mill in St. Philip dates back to at least the early 1700s, though the bulk of the present structure dates only to 1831, the original having been demolished in a hurricane of that year. Restoration here includes the kitchen, bake ovens, and boiling house, and the servants quarters, contained in an attractive garden house that overlooks the sea. *Coddrington College,* which was founded in 1745, is located on the site of an estate dating back to 1703. Worth the visit.

Barbados has a number of attractive old buildings and the National Trust is doing its best on extremely small funds to restore these priceless works. It's too bad the hotel association and the government cannot get together to seek outside assistance (from a foundation, perhaps) to bring these relics of a fascinating past into use again, because, unless a large-scale program is worked out in the relatively near future, further decay will mean an impossible task once nature takes back these artifacts of earlier times.

There are numerous picturesque spots in which to stroll; Archer's Bay in the north, parish of St. Lucy, is charming, while Tent Bay—St. Joseph, and just under Newcastle Coral Stone Gates (built by 20th Century Fox as the entrance to the film home of young Fleury*), with its avenue of Royal Palms—is an archetypcal West Indian fishing village. Also lovely is Cherry Tree Hill, St. Peter, reached by a double avenue of sweeping casuarina and bold mahogany trees with a scenic outlook over the Scotland district. Wild monkeys are found here.

For something just a shade different you might consider a visit to the Mount Gay distillery. Reckoned by many to be one of the finest rums in the world, Mount Gay now produces six different varieties of grog, including their Sugar Cane Brandy—more than

**Island in the Sun* again.

10 years old—and as smooth as fine armagnac. Banks Brewers produce an excellent beer, which locals insist is every bit as tasty a brew as Jamaican Red Stripe.

Interestingly, there is quite a bit of duty-free shopping, including liquor—reckoned to be one of the best buys in the Lesser Antilles. There's also some remarkably good tailoring available here, but check on arrival to see what the latest state of play is.

No mention has been made so far, of *Sam Lord's Castle* or the *Villa Nova* as places to see. As a hotel, *Sam Lord's Castle* has always been somewhat heavy on its historical connection with its so-called murdering longshoreman creator, Sam Lord. No one today knows for sure where he originally hailed from, for the way he made his loot was common from Cornwall and Scilly, Guernsey and Ushant to the Carolinas and Hatteras. The trick worked thusly: at night, lights were strung up along on the shoreline to resemble ships at anchor. Vessels approached the lure thinking it safe harbor. A nearby reef did the rest. It used to be alleged that Sam and his slaves got the loot from the grounded wreck and co-opted or dispatched the remaining hands.

The place is nevertheless furnished with some fabulous antiques and the grounds have been superbly landscaped under the thoughtful eye of the Marriott Hotel group who now own this delightful resort. The main house—source of the attraction—though beautifully equipped, seems, say some visitors, to reflect the aura of this murdering thief even on the sunniest of days. Which is strange, for Sam Lord, once he'd made his pile, returned to England in time to see a favorite niece (with whom he was reputed to have been romantically involved) marry a title.

As for *Villa Nova,* this is smaller. A coral limestone building erected in the 1830s, the furnishings are local mahogany antiques, with nearly six acres of gardens with attractive views. At one time the property of the late Sir Anthony Eden, guests have included HM Queen Elizabeth and HRH Prince Philip. It is now the charming home of the Hunte family.

Food & Drink

Although it's a tourism destination, Barbados is also an island nation of uncommonly literate and sophisticated people. Not surprisingly, there are plenty of good places to wine and dine, and the fare at most hotels is better than average with a pleasant mix of West Indian, international, and French cuisine supported by fine and also less expensive but drinkable wines.

First of all, the island boasts two or three quite exceptional delicacies from the sea, *numero uno* being the flying fish. Of a quite indescribably delicious flavor (regardless of how it is served), the flying fish rates high among gourmets. Possibly the fact that it is so highly valued as food by its relatives encouraged this particular family of fish to develop their fins into wings. And they really can fly!

Almost all sailboat navigators of the Atlantic will testify to having found flying fish on deck at some point of their voyage. These silvery blue creatures use their flying ability to track out of the way of underwater predators, smoothly erupting out of the water like Polaris rockets, cruising for a short way, then altering course before returning themselves to the deep. They are capable of performing quite complicated maneuvers, and when a barracuda or shark is feeding near a shoal the activity is riveting as these sparkles of silver rise out of the waves and cavort.

As food in Barbados they have few rivals. Try it: you'll love it.

The *oursin*, or green sea urchin, which grows to about the size of your fist, is the second delight you'll find here. The islanders open up this crustacean and scoop out its golden-colored innards, which are mixed with lime and can be served on Hovis bread and butter as hors d'oeuvres. A more popular version is a saute with onion and butter: delicious!

Numerous other fish dishes are to be found in the island, including the ubiquitous (and highly tasty) dolphin, the crane chubb, and kingfish—surprisingly sporty, fishermen note—plus crabs (of both land and sea). For meat eaters Barbados has a new flavor, its own breed of sheep—the Black Belly—which is becoming an increasingly important export while producing plentiful quantities of wool, lamb, and mutton for islanders and guests alike. The biggest plus, say farmers, is not so much its resistance to tropical disease (it's stolid), but the fact that ewes produce litters of three at each breeding, with very high rates of survival. There are also generous quantities of fine suckling pig for those who enjoy the crackling.

Neither fish nor fowl is green turtle steak, still available here despite diminishing quantities throughout the world. Crab soup (*calaloo* also) is frequently found and delicious, as are the local banana and coconut breads.

The islanders manage to produce prodigious amounts of vegetables and fruits, including northern favorites such as green and red peppers, zucchini, okra, tomato, avocado, coconut, banana, yam and sweet potato, and the less familiar such as breadfruit, plantain, mango, and pawpaw (as papaya is called here).

Hotel restaurants are good, and many offer reciprocal dining, which gives you a chance to go and check out another place's operation. Still, prices are high if you can't do that. It's also important to make reservations, especially during the season; otherwise you could miss out completely.

There are, not surprisingly, a goodly number of regular restaurants and, while quality and price vary, the overall standard tends to be good. Some of the more chic places are not all that they seem, however, so be warned. Being fashionable as a hangout for the jet-set will not necessarily bring good food in its wake.

For seafood, the *Pisces Restaurant* in St. Laurence still seems to be top spot to try out. Martin Donawa, whose *Island Inn* and *Brown Sugar Restaurant* have earned him a number of accolades from the tourism industry, is the owner. The food is excellent and the restaurant is patronized by islanders and visitors alike. *Crane Beach* also serves fish; their chubb and lobster are excellent (near Sam Lord's Castle).

Alexandra's (Disco) also offers dining and is where Londoner Nick Hudson—Nick's Diner, remember?—is offering superior and costly nosh in the island. Named for the "parent" operation in Scandinavia, it's in St. Michael parish, and food is usually very good. Because this is a *boite de nuit* in the nicest sense it's sometimes better to let them know ahead of time (when you make your reservation) that you are coming there to eat. Pricy.

Nick is also mine host at the *Bagatelle Great House*, which for some years has been top choice of the Baedecker bibliophiles of the Caribbean. Located not far inland from the former toff's posh noshery at Sandy Lane, the building was once the residence of the Governor of the West Indies, and is consequently pleasing in ambiance. Food is expensive, mostly good. You have to reserve. "Cutesy" listings of food, which may amuse.

Luigi's vies with *Ascanio's Italian* for the prize in Mediterranean cuisine. Both are good transplants. The former is popular with the Bajan in-crowd, the latter with their guests.

Le Bistro and *La Bonne Auberge* have both enjoyed good reputations and are owned and operated by the same group of people. The latter moved its operation because of rising taxi fares and is still—at its best—one of the best places to eat in the island. The former has its patrons, and is improving. Latest favorite (again!) is *Greensleeves* in St. James.

For West Indian food there are many new places for aficionados on this island. *Dolly's* got burned out but is reported to be reopening. Meanwhile, the *Coal Pot* still offers superior fare, as does the *Flying Fish Club. The Kingsley Club* still enjoys its well-deserved reputation and you must book ahead. It's in Little Scotland, offers spartan accommodations should you need them, and delicious food. *The Grotto* at Holetown has developed an island following.

Regular Indian fare is to be found at the (what else?) *Taj Mahal,* while Chinese enthusiasts can satisy their cravings at *Chopsticks* and the *China Gardens.*

Pebble's open-air dining spot is a popular hangout with islanders and offers visitors good food and fair prices. It's near the Hilton in Bridgetown.

This little sampler should get you started.

Nightlife

As elsewhere in the Caribbean, much of the nightlife centers around the hotel communities, and again reciprocal arrangements permit you to enjoy the floor shows of others in addition to their dinners.

Alexandra's discotheque is one of the more amusing places to be most nights, while on Mondays Martin Donawa's *Island Inn* is jumping to the music of the steel band and limbo performers who inevitably induce the "Norde Americanos" to try their luck—big laughs all around.

The Merrymen—a pop group that has developed its own following in the US and Canada (and elsewhere)—when not too busy occasionally feature themselves at their own *Caribbean Pepper Pot* on the St. Laurence main highway.

King Sugar no longer reigns supreme in the islands, though it still ranks high in Barbados (below) and is exported and used in the making of rum. Factories are still to be found in country areas (right), with the cane growing around. Barbados offers considerable variety to visitors, ranging from botanical walks (facing page, lower right) to unusual items of street furniture (facing page, lower left).

Barbados

Their *Banana Boat Restaurant* has fun and entertainment on Thursdays and Saturdays in addition to food and grog.

And then there's *Harry's Niterie.*

This boite has had a series of ups and downs and for over twenty years. The original Harry has since been promoted out of this world—natural causes and a certain messianic zeal for island fare, said the coroner—but his widow and friends maintain this unique memorial to his name. *Harry's Niterie* is nothing so much as an old-fashioned, Victorian-styled bawdy romp. And it's unique in an increasingly sterile world of hard-core mechanical porn entertainment. As such, a place like Harry's ought to be protected by law, but politicians and editors being for the most part the hacks that they are tend to denounce such goings-on to be (a) re-elected by the dimwitted, and (b) to sell newsprint to the prurient who will not admit to their ids.

The entertainment here is at a harmless adolescent level with pretty young girls cavorting topless to music, and miming and dancing. A lascivious elder-brother type comments lewdly and amusingly throughout the show, and when comes the moment for the girls to sit on the patrons' laps he encourages the inhibited to live out their longings. To stately matrons he may leeringly suggest, "Madame, wouldn't you like to fondle this young child's breasts?" and to foppish, moustachioed studs, "Sir, just imagine this delightful wench is your daughter." In all, it's a fine night out and one that can be enjoyed by almost everybody, despite what the reviewers tell you.

For the loveless, this is supposed to be a place where you can meet for those *liaisons dangereux,* but chances are if that's what you're after it'll be with one of your co-patrons rather than the delightful people who perform one-on-one for you.

For adults who are up for some light-hearted, risque entertainment, *Harry's Niterie* is to be recommended. It's the ultimate in titillation and it's joyful, despite the occasional sometimes deliberately wooden performance of an entertainer who chooses to tease her favorite guest.*

*At our latest inspection Harry's was closed (it was Sunday), as was the next-door Bel-Air Jazz Club. More ominously, local gossip had it that Harry's was now showing an S&M scene—which seems unlikely—but we quote. We need some reports since this change just doesn't sound very Bajan. If you go, don't spend more than $7.00 BDS to go in and do drink beer—it's cheaper than cola or hard liquor.

Where to Stay

Because of the ever-increasing prices, some of the best money is moving to apartments or studios (or villas) for rent for anything more than a night or two in the island. And while you can cover the island fairly completely in three or four days, if you want time to relax you'll need at least a week to get the flavor.

Choosing Barbados as a temporary base for your Eastern Caribbean vacation is wise because there's a good variety of these types of accommodation, plus hotels from the deluxe class down to some very modest guesthouses. Rates thus range from an incredibly modest $21.75 at *La Tropical* guesthouse in Fontabelle, St. Michael, for *two* MAP (where there's a bus stop almost immediately opposite whence you can get to almost anywhere in the island for 25 cents) to the more than $300-per-day rate for two MAP at the deluxe *Sandy Lane* resort.*

Since there are more than 150 different establishments in the business of providing shelter, it is only possible to list some of them. A note to the very efficient Tourism Department will elicit complete details of what you need. For the purposes of this guide, some of the better and lesser known establishments are included, and some of the less high-priced ports of call in the island.

Before having a look at individual hotels, it will probably be helpful to take a quick look at a map of the island. There are eleven parishes, the southernmost being Christ Church, the most northern, St. Lucy.

Back in the 1930s, tourism, such as it was, centered on the beaches around the capital, and Hastings and Worthing—like their namesakes in Britain—were very fashionable. Seawell Airport was built at that time to specifications laid down by Britain's Air Ministry and the first flight (with passengers) occurred on Wednesday, October 19th, 1938. The carrier was KLM, whose route went via Trinidad to Curacao, and back.

The development of tourism following World War II extended the parameters. It also gradually filled in the area between Hastings and Worthing and so Rockley was born. The logic that led to this development was the fact of the airport, and that these ports of call were all relatively easy to reach on the way to Bridgetown.

*Rates are mentioned here only to show the range available.

Then someone noticed that the now-platinum coast—the St. James beach area—had calmer seas, golden beaches, and Highway 1 running almost all the way up. Today hotels line the coast all the way to Speightstown, some thirteen miles from the capital, and a new resort has been opened on the north shore, just about as far as you can get from the airport.

The Atlantic Coast, with its fragrant breezes, has not been so successfully developed. The waves can be big and, while the snorkeling is beautiful, you do have to watch those waves just a bit. If you do opt for the east coast, take a sweater for evening wear as it can get chilly after a day in the sun.

Since most people today think of Barbados in terms of that platinum coast, let's move northward out of Bridgetown on Highway 1.

First stop is the *Paradise Beach Club*, located on one of the nicer beaches of the island, where nice beaches are the norm. Billing itself as the liveliest resort in Barbados, there are 152 air-conditioned rooms with bath on a 12-acre beach-front property. A recent $1 million improvement has brought the number of tennis courts to 5 (lighted for night play), and generally improved this resort. The entertainment in season is good, and there are an attractive swimming pool and an open-air bar and restaurant. Food okay. Boutique and hairdressing salon on the premises. All aqua-sports, golf, and horseback riding nearby. The hotel offers a number of package arrangements, especially off season. If you can arrange one of these, it becomes a good deal. Pricy in season.

Just a short drive north is the *Swiss Chalet*, which has 20 units in its two-story building on its own beach. This charming hostelry, although small, offers good value for money, and the food can excel. But better book well ahead, for this little treasure has many warm friends from all over the world. No entertainment per se, and not much to do—but you've that beach and the whole island to explore. About 3½ miles from Bridgetown, but don't expect to get to or from the city during rush hour: Highway 1 is slow going. High season only.

Moving north again toward Paynes Bay, there are *Barbados Beach Village* and *Coconut Creek Club Hotel*.

Just five miles from Bridgetown, the *Barbados Beach Village* has 81 villa-type units with pool, restaurant, and bar plus its own discotheque, *The Hippo*. Again, off-season packages apply, making this an extremely good value. Expensive in season, with reason.

Owen and Jean Ellison offer guests a delightful tasteful informality, they say, so no jacket or ties, just casual elegance, at *Coconut Creek*. Accommodations include poolside apartment/suites with bedroom and sitting room (or two bedrooms), all with bathroom, kitchen, and patio. Familes are welcome, babysitters available and early meals for the kids are no problem. Cottage units provide privacy and tranquility in a pleasant tropical garden. The *English Pub* bar enjoys an island clientele (and a sometimes swinging reputation), while evening activities include dancing to three or more local bands, Bajan buffets and barbecues, plus the owners' famous cocktail party. This is a really nice haven, and the owners offer a number of special rates including a Honeymoon Package. Oh yes, you get a complimentary rum punch on arrival, and *Gourmet* magazine wrote up their restaurant.

Continuing north on Highway 1 brings you to the biggest cluster of them all. There's the excellent *Buccaneer Bay*, with free bus to the shops, plus aqua-sports, tennis, golf, and horseback riding available. The 38 units here are excellent, with comfortable beds and chairs, a functional kitchenette and equipment, plus breakfast served in your apartment. Maid service at no extra charge. There's a pleasant bar and dining area plus entertainment from time to time. This Bajan-owned property is one of the nicest of this type of operation in the island and offers excellent value for money—even better value off season. This one won't break your piggy bank.

Almost next door is *Tamarind Cove*, an elegant Iberian-styled resort, which can offer splendid comfort and fare. There are some 50 air-conditioned rooms in hacienda-like buildings and a fresh-water swimming pool. Transport to the city. Rates are high, but some packages available. Pricy in season; can be worth it.

Even if you don't choose to stay there, at least go and ogle *Sandy Lane*, just a little farther to the north from Tamarind Cove. This small area may bring to mind West Palm Beach, except that the elegance factor here seems just a bit more real than some of the more phony of those Florida palaces.

This 380-acre estate provides accommodations for some 230 guests in surroundings of super tropical elegance. It's unbelievable how the place conjures up the low-keyed, luxurious ambiance of an 18th-century plantation, while providing the ultimate in 21st-century comfort. And there's just about everything you'll need for recreation: full aqua-sports; an 18-hole golf course that can be split into two 9-hole course, plus everything you need in terms of clubs and caddies—even a pro is on hand throughout the year, plus two restaurants.

Once again, special package arrangements are available to save you money on stays. Of course, you may prefer to spend your money elsewhere, but for that once-in-a-lifetime occasion, Sandy Lane could be just the thing for you and yours.

The fantastic success of the *Sunset Crest Resort* (set on a 100-acre site just up from Sandy Lane) has tended to eclipse the local *Anchorage Apartments*, which lie next to it. The brainchild of a Frenchman from Nice, Alfred Laforet, Anchorage comprises a host of cottages and apartments with maid service and everything you need to keep your household shipshape. And it's not by the room, since accommodations consist of 2 and 3 bedrooms, so if you're an airplane load this could make extraordinarily good sense. There are more than 700 rooms, swimming pool, private club with games room, 4 tennis courts, 3 swimming pools plus a kiddies' play area with its own little pool, a couple of shopping centers, and—as might be expected from a Frenchman—an incredible selection of good French (and other) wines, plus courteous service. The rates are almost impossible to beat. There's a branch of Cave Shepherd here, a fashion boutique, no fewer than 3 different banks, plus police station and post office and duty-free store.

Moving northward once again one comes to the *Discovery Bay Inn*, the middle part of the triumvirate that also comprises *Tamarind Cove* and the most northerly of the three, the *Colony Club*. At present, Discovery Bay is reckoned to be the leader of the three with 75 deluxe rooms, all comfortably furnished and just a few steps from your private patio to the beach. There's a studied elegant charm about this operation, with such added touches as moonlight sailing and dancing under the stars. There's a smallish pool plus a couple of tennis courts, and aqua-sports obviously available. Packages can be available, which helps. Rates are high.

Palm Beach claims the honors for being at the historical spot where the first settlers landed, and the hotel attempts to provide olde worlde elegance within the modern luxury accommodations.

There are 16 fully self contained, air-conditioned apartments, with modern kitchens, and cook-maids available on request. Restaurant and beach bar. Water-sports enthusiasts will find everything here.

Almost next door are *Settlers Beach* and the *Sandpiper Inn*. These belong to another triumvirate, which also includes the Coral Reef.

Accommodations at *Settlers Beach*—actually named for the first arrivals in the island who landed right about here—are excellent, and there are pool, bar, and restaurant. This is a pleasantly small operation with luxury villas and apartments comprising 1- and 2-bedroom units, each with private bath, lounge, and dining area plus kitchen. Package arrangements are sometimes available, making this extremely good value, in season.

The *Sandpiper Inn* is a delightful small ocean-front luxury inn with 32 rooms set in 8 two-story structures, each housing 4, set around a fresh-water pool. Expensive and good.

The *Coral Reef Club* sets its cottages down in one of the more interestingly landscaped beach areas on this coastline. The food is sumptuous, there's a fresh-water swimming pool, and, of course, the continuation of that perfect white sand beach that runs up this coast. There are nearby reefs for snorkelers, plus water skiing and fishing, and beauty salon and boutique on the premises.

Care was taken with the construction of this resort and accommodations are in air-conditioned cottages or suites, either in the tropical gardens or at the beach. There's real privacy here and some suites include separate dressing rooms. Can be outstanding value.

The *Colony Club* has 75 deluxe accommodations on the beach and around the pool. This has been a long-time favorite with regular visitors to the island and if the rates are high, the quality of service and food tends to match. The accommodations are all air-conditioned—though you'll seldom need it—and all have telephone.

Still, there was some grumbling by the regulars on account of the package business that this hotel—like almost every other operation in these islands that cost-accounted to the last pat of butter—was obliged to introduce to keep the overhead at an appropriate level. It's not that tourists drive up in buses, of course.

They arrive, just like you or me, in an airplane, but because discounts are offered under the international ITX program, the hotel discounts an airline passenger's rate if he or she buys an arrangement at the same time as the flight ticket.* Consequently, some visitors (and not only here) felt that the hoi polloi, who couldn't really afford it, was treading on their turf.

The password at *Hotel Miramar Beach* is "Casual Elegance," or so says William Young, its resident director, and this is an apt description of the lifestyle available here. This does mean jacket and tie in the evening for men for the most part, though your Studio 54 get-up should be cool in the Gaming Room.

It's not that the hotel is especially decadent; rather the opposite, for it's sited on 7½ acres of attractive tropical real estate with better than a quarter-mile of beach. Dining tends to informal, rather than casual, elegance, and you'll find a number of island dishes available in the mainly continental cuisine. Island entertainment, aqua-sports, fresh-water pool, and night-lighted tennis courts complete this deal. Boutique and beauty salon on the premises.

Accommodations are good: ocean-front choices include both semi and full suites, with pullman kitchens and living rooms. Studios have kitchenettes. All have large terraces, air-conditioning. Less expensive are air-conditioned garden-view and "standard" rooms.

Just across the parish boundary into St. Peter you'll espy a road leading inland to your right. This is the turn to *Eastry House,* which in former years has numbered many of the international *illuminati* among its friends. The Barbados Tourism Department lists it as a guesthouse on its tourist map, though for the money you pay, it's difficult to think quite in those terms. Guesthouse indeed it is—but with a difference. First, the exclusive atmosphere of the Greathouse era; part of the building has been left in relatively pristine condition (this means that not all rooms have air-conditioning). There are suites available, and maid service is *de rigeur.* Second, though there have been problems in the recent past, the food can be outstanding, one of the reasons—says the

*Package arrangements have been mentioned throughout this book. Consult your friendly travel agent since, if you pre-book space and prepay it, discounting is frequently available.

local wire service office*—it's been the favorite watering hole of royalty the world over.

Expensive.

The Pink House is something else again. Originally opened in the late 1950s, this rather special place is like a private club just a few minutes' walk from the water at Gibbs Beach, St. Peter. There are 10 rooms in 4 different units, of which the standard accommodations are to be found (for the most part) in the main house; there are a 2-bedroom and 2- & 3-bedroom villas, and the so-called Pent House. There's considerable repeat business in the winter, but this is one place definitely worth checking out. If they know you're coming—*and* if you request it—they'll have a car at the airport to pick you up.

Cobbler's Cove is a luxurious resort offering outstanding accommodations in efficiency units—in addition to a pullman kitchen in each unit, there's a separate living room, which leads onto its own private terrace. Rooms furnished with twin beds. The gardens are delightful; the beach, superb; there's exchange dining if you want to check out someone else's place; plus usual aqua-sports and a daily service to Bridgetown. Food's international. The manager's cocktail party is quite a special event. For the money, excellent value.

The Tides North Point Surf Resort is a new establishment with apartment accommodations. Big attractions are the surfing at the beach and the enormous swimming pool. Hotel features an aquatic director plus lifeguards.

On the Atlantic coast, the *Kingsley Club Hotel* is very much an in place with the islanders. Rates are low, the five rooms okay for sleeping, but where it excels is as a laid-back, outdoors, weekend sort of place.

Just a bit farther down the coast is the *Edgewater Inn,* offering comfort, a pleasing swimming pool, fine rum punches, plus okay accommodations (with private bath) and reasonable food that sometimes is excellent. Rates medium; you'll need a car.

This side of the island is undersold by the travel brochures and the experts. It's a particularly attractive stretch of seascape with

*Too readily for it to be totally unrehearsed.

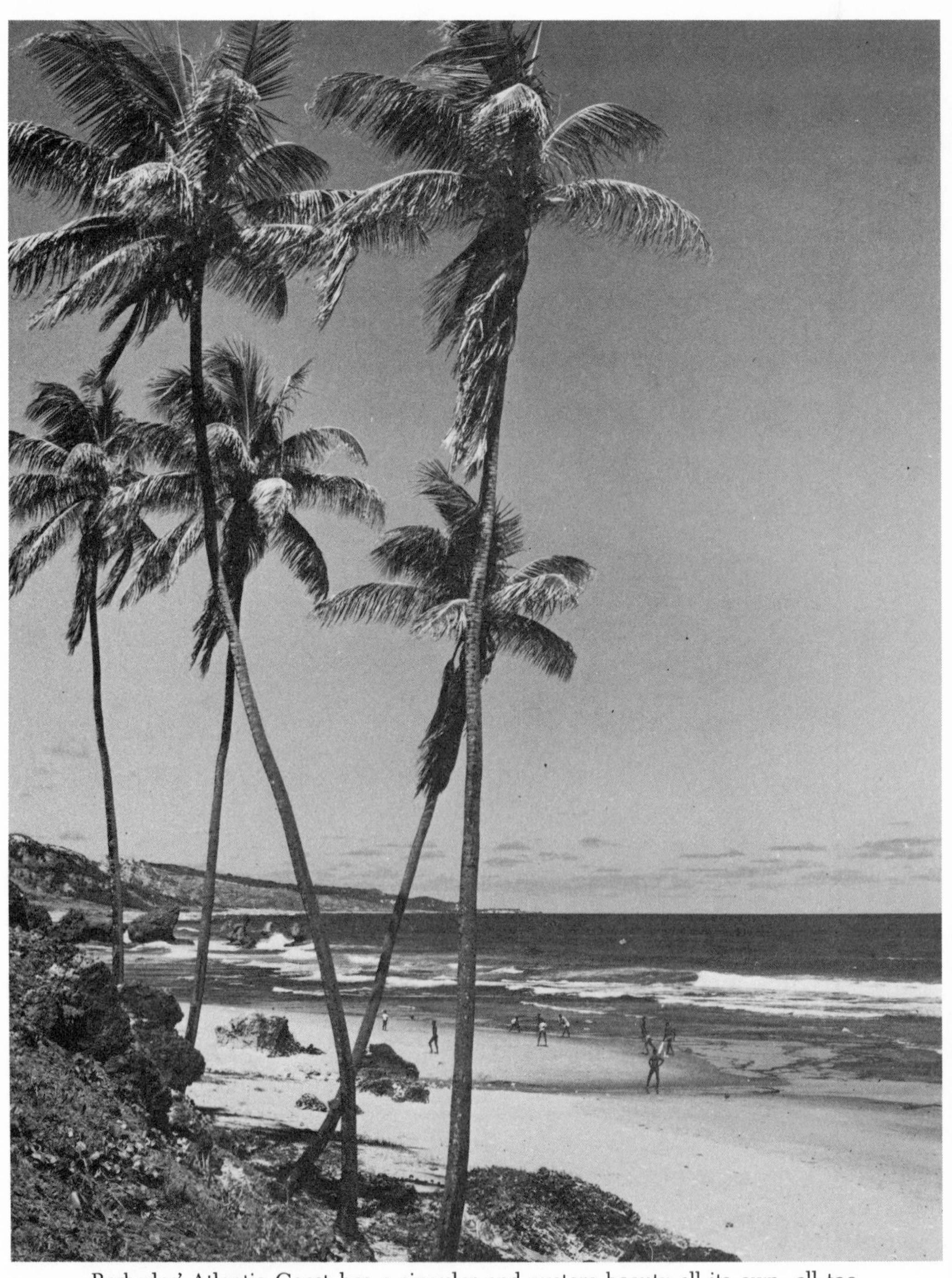

Barbados' Atlantic Coast has a singular and austere beauty all its own, all too often overlooked by visitors.

heaving rollers and a fine breeze and mostly blue skies all day. The Parish of St. Andrew is of special interest—to railroad buffs, at least—in that a railway operated along this coast from 1882 to 1938. Once it shut down, about the only way you could get to many of the places it served was via the right-of-way. (Some entrepreneur should look into the possibility of its restoration, for the scenic ride is better than anything available on the Hythe–Dimchurch line in Britain.)

The Potteries are also to be found in this area and make for a pleasant sightseeing tour, though the wares produced are expensive and—let it be said—not that wonderful. Again, since the basic materials are here, it should be possible for someone to resurrect this area, which once supplied many islands with tableware. (Another entrepreneurial soul is needed here.)

Bathsheba, named for the Biblical rather than the Hardyesque heroine, is the center around here, and was described by Sir Frederick Treves in *Cradle of the Deep* as representative of the Cornish coast in miniature. Also reasonably close are the Andromeda Gardens, aforementioned, and Codrington College.*

Also on this same coast is the *Atlantis*, which is modest, quiet, and which has a pleasant ambiance. Rates, which include meals, are low.

And yes, you'll possibly need that sweater if you're staying on this coast, because after a day in the sun, it really does get a mite chilly here, with the steady tradewind, when the sun goes down.

Accommodations are pretty sparse in this area until you reach Ragged Point—the *Ragged Point Motel*—and the aforementioned Marriott's *Sam Lord's Castle.*

The infusion of Marriott money and know-how has worked several miracles here, while the new—for an American hotel corporation—approach to hiring international talent has helped work wonders, especially in the quality of food now available and the overall standard of service. The grounds, always attractive, have been extensively landscaped and now abound with soaring

*Christopher Codrington was born in Barbados in 1668 and entered Christ Church, Oxford, in 1685. Elected a Fellow of All Souls, Oxford, he succeeded his father as Captain General and Governor of the Leeward Islands when he was 30. He is buried in the Ante-Chapel of All Souls, marked CODRINGTON on a single stone.

purple bougainvillea—plus thickets and hedges of the same with plenty of blossom—plus oleanders, casuarinas, Barbados almond, a profusion of hibiscus and all those other tropical flowers and plants and trees you always wanted to see but never could remember the names of. (Now you can: An ongoing program provides—at the time of writing—names of all major trees and will soon provide name tags for almost everything else.)

There are some 200 rooms and, for very special guests, suites within cottages and in the main Castle building. If you like the resort life, figure on a stay of not less than four days—and, better, one week—to enjoy the extent and variety of pleasures now offered. You'll also want a car for at least a couple of days. Stoute's Car Rental, which is in the local area, has new Datsun 120Vs for about $55 BDS per day, unlimited mileage. They come with automatic shift. You'll need to ride over to Police Station C for a visitor's driving permit, which costs $10 BDS and is good for one year on the basis of your domestic license.

Just around the corner, as it were—the roads get tricky here—you'll find the *Sunrise Beach Apartments* and the *Crane Beach Hotel*. (*The Boxhill Inn* is also here, but it doesn't rate yet with the Tourism Department.)

Crane Beach combines ancient and modern in really delightfully splendid ways. First of all it is small, around 30 beds in toto. But so much love has been lavished in putting the thing together with coral wall stones, antique furnishings, locally woven rugs, that the place screams for attention. Supposedly, it's the first resort hotel in the island in that a property existed here during Victorian times for the pleasures of planters. One wonders for what pleasures it was erected, for it is so sensually right in all directions. While not a lavish resort, the views are extraordinary.

At last count there were nearly a dozen doubles, a studio, and an apartment, plus 4 luxurious suites. Extra-special: they've even some four-poster beds if you've never slept in one, but better specify when you reserve, for reservations at this one tend to be essential.

Moving back to near the Grantley Adams Airport area, we come to the village of Inch Marlowe, where the *Arawak Inn* is the best known outfit. (There are also here the *Silver Sands*, the *Long Beach Resort Apartments*, and *Surf View Apartments*.)

The *Arawak Inn* is supposedly sited on a former Arawak habitation and the mood is exotic. Still, the emphasis is Greek and, while the scent is tropical, it's that tropical labeled especially "for the sybarite." There's no doubt that it's a well-run operation, in all senses of the word, but you may prefer somewhere just a little farther from the airport. Extraordinarily good value for your money.

Long Beach Resort has some 24 ocean-front apartments here, with relatively full kitchenettes. Both adult and children's swimming pools, plus a mini-supermart and restaurant and bar.

Silver Sands offers luxury apartment accommodations and a certain spaciously informal ambiance; still, there's tennis, pool and restaurant plus beach bar. Plus mini-bus service to town.

We move on to Maxwell.

There were nearly 20 potential places to stay here at last counting, for this has long been the Bajan choice of beach.

Benston Beach Hotel offers good value and is nicely landscaped—it gets better every year. There are efficiency rooms, cozy bar and lounge, plus a dining room that has an okay view of the ocean. Nice food; friendly, helpful Bajan-style service.

A converted plantation house (their story, not ours), the *Fairholme Hotel* now also includes one of the nicer apartment operations copying the hacienda-style unit with the usual modern conveniences. Both are good value, and the hotel provides a yet-to-be recognized cuisine of its own. This is one to check out even if only for a meal. Five minutes to their own piece of beach. Rates okay.

Other operations at this end of the scale if you're visiting purely for fun on a budget include *Camarima Flats*, fully furnished 2- and 4-bedroom apartments a couple of minutes from its beach, the *Sheringham Beach Apartments*, with just about every modern convenience; and *Union Villa*, which is a really good buy. There's no service charge, for a start, and there's entertainment.

Moving closer to Bridgetown one comes to St. Lawrence, where a similar number of accommodations are to be found.

Bagshot House has long enjoyed a reputation with its many repeat guests for providing functional accommodations; the 16 rooms all have private bath, some with sea view, and reasonable rates, plus the pleasant clubby atmosphere such places generate over the years. There's plenty of activity at hotels in the neighborhood, though apart from an occasional "owner's" party there's not much on in the evenings. This place is well run, and the food is plain English fare, though if you want a West Indian specialty it'll be provided if you ask.

Sandhurst is an apartment hotel with 21 air-conditioned units, on the beach, each with its own telephone. Rates are moderate and this one's good value. Maid service and pool.

Salt Ash Apartment Hotel is a smaller operation with 9 fully equipped units on the beach.

Andrea-on-the-Sea Hotel is an informal, locally owned operation opposite Dover Beach. There are 40 modern rooms, all with bath, plus an annex of 18 fully equipped self-catering apartments. Bajan cuisine a specialty. Rates reasonable.

Bresmay Apartment Hotel features 50 studios and apartments, fully self-contained and with private sun porches. Air-conditioned. Large fresh-water swimming pool (in case you don't like the sea), *Dinner Bell* restaurant, *Dover Beach Bar*, plus mini-mart for supplies.

Next comes Worthing, with a further selection to chose from.

Super Mare Hotel offers Bajan-style comfort and low rates, though not all rooms are with bath. Most have sea-view verandas. Island food.

A number of locally owned guesthouses offer excellent value for money, and many have rooms with bath.

As you come still closer to Bridgetown, the suburb of Rockley makes its appearance. Here the *Hotel Abbeville* has its following both on and off the island. According to locals ,ou'll drink some of the best rum punch here at the bar, and British and Canadian vacationers who know a bargain when they find one are being joined by US citizens. Twenty rooms, air-conditioned, swimming pool, pleasant informal atmosphere.

The new *Rockley Beach Resort*, with 150 luxurious apartment-style units, set out among the casuarinas and palms by the Rockley golf course, has generated some instant praise. There's a swimming pool just yards from your front door, plus a Beach Club on famous Rockley beach. Five tennis courts, plus pro, to help you with your backhand and your serve; two squash courts; a beachside volleyball court; for the more staid (and adventurous) a lawn for croquet; a sauna; plus a central restaurant. This is one comprehensive resort and good value for the money.

Low rates and a garden setting are the appeal factors of the *Riviera Apartment Hotel.* There are 39 air-conditioned studio units with radio and telephone. Restaurant, pharmacy, boutique, filtered pool, and mini-mart on the premises. This one's just across the road from Rockley Beach.

Southern Surf offers the same theme with 12 air-conditioned apartments, with tub bath and shower, kitchen, and private patio facing the ocean, while *Sunhaven Beach* hotel offers air-conditioned accommodations and pool.

And so into Hastings, which has been receiving visitors for a long, long time.

Time was when the *Hotel Caribee* was the last word in island fashion, but that's all too long ago. The hotel started slipping in the early seventies. Bargain hunters may want to check it out when they're on the island.

The *Windsor Hotel* offers gracious service in comfortable surroundings and the food is good. The grounds are attractive and well cared for and it's been in the Goddard family for years. Good island food in the restaurant—many islanders come here for lunch—and even in winter the rates are reasonable. Just across the road from the sea, there's a pool in the gardens.

Ocean View offers a similar sort of hospitality on the beach and is exceptional value for the money if you enjoy a slightly old-fashioned ambiance with antiques and flower arrangements and even afternoon tea. Even if you don't stay, be sure to have one meal here (reservations a must). There's a swimming pool fashioned out of the coral in front of the hotel, plus a sunning spot and some thatched umbrellas to provide some shade to cool off. The 40 rooms carry the theme of a Plantation Greathouse; and as at the Windsor, there's a lot of repeat business here.

A number of apartment operations around here, also.

And finally to Bridgetown.

There are just 3 hotels in Bridgetown, plus 1 small guesthouse (6 rooms only) at Fontabelle and another small hotel (9 rooms, all with bath) at Brighton.

The 3 hotels include the *Hilton* (currently the most expensive Hilton in the world), the *Holiday Inn,* and the *Island Inn.*

Downtown Bridgetown becomes jammed with traffic and people during rush hours.

From the outside the *Hilton* appears a rather unprepossessing sort of place, lots of grays set amidst the palm trees and dominating the scene with its five storys. Inside, however, is an incredible garden that'll remind you—though it's much better—of the Ford Foundation building in New York. And this really works.

The gardens outside are professionally landscaped, numerous palm trees and shrubs; quality Hilton service (at the price, it ought to be) everywhere. The food is better than average for a Hilton Hotel, though those prices are high. There are a number of package arrangements offered, and if you can get one, you'll do rather better. There are 192 air-conditioned rooms, ocean front, with private balconies, set on this 17-acre peninsula just a mile out of town. There's a thousand-foot beach, and a beach facility serving drinks and snacks.*

*Unfortunately, as detractors are wont to point out, the stench from the adjacent Mobil plant can occasionally overpower one's moments of beauty with an all-too-pervasive, mephitic odor.

The Holiday Inn here had a recent management change and can go nowhere but up. This is where much of the action is some nights, with live shows and nightly entertainment, and full resort beach facilities include yacht cruises. Prices high like the Hilton's.

The Island Inn is small (21 air-conditioned rooms with all facilities), offering friendly hospitality with some of the best in weekly local entertainment in the island. The food is excellent.

Smaller still is *La Tropicale Guest House* but it's the least expensive place to stay on the island. *Brighton-on-Sea* hotel is on the beach with a view of the deep-water harbor. Bajan home cooking. Moderate, nine rooms only, with private facilities.

Where to Find Horses for Riding

Best bets for riding horses include *Brighton Riding Stables* at Black Rock, St. Michael (telephone 04412), where the rates are $10.00 US for an hour and $16.50 for two hours. They'll usually include transport to and from your hotel unless you're in what seems to be

The 72 acres of Sam Lord's Castle has undergone a subtle transformation, with careful landscaping artfully hiding the new wing added by the Marriott hotel group. The Castle remains the center of this luxury resort.

their outback.

Sharon Hill Stables, in St. Thomas Parish, offers the same rate by the hour, but for two hours it's $20.00 US. Similar transportation arrangements.

Where to Play Golf

Sandy Lane Golf Club has an 18-hole course, which can be split into two 9-holers. Temporary members' green fees run $25.00 Baja per day. The pro costs the same, and is available from 8:00 AM through 5:00 PM each day. This one is on the platinum, St. James, Caribbean coast.

At Durants, Christ Church, is the *Barbados Golf and Country Club,* which includes an 18-hole championship course. A letter from your own club will assist in modifying regulations to your advantage. Green fees amount to $18.00 Bajan per day over the 18 holes, or $72.00 weekly. You can also hire electric carts, (a pull trolley costs an awful lot less and a caddie is slightly more though only for 9 holes. Club rentals run $3.00 US per day.)

Most Popular Island Excursion

The Jolly Roger operation, which started back in 1969 with one relatively small island sailboat, has grown like Topsy to two schooners, both of which are comfortable and fairly authentic conversions to resemble pirate ships.

The two 100-ft schooners put out to sea from the Careenage in the heart of Bridgetown each day for a ride up the west coast (depending on wind and sea) to Discovery Bay—or thereabouts—offering non-stop music, a fine buffet luncheon (West Indian-style, with steak and almost as many trimmings as you can manage), plus open bar, which includes a nearly lethal rum punch.

The halfway halt provides opportunities for swimming, and if you still have sufficient energy left from the non-stop dancing, there's para-sailing (great way to see whether you can really fly without wings) and water skiing.

David and Dennis Roach, who run this enterprise, are moving into the restaurant business. Their new Jolly Roger is land-based and seems to be A-okay with the kids.

For further information, contact the Barbados Tourist Board 800 Second Avenue New York City, 10017; [212]. 986-6516.

Trinidad & Tobago

TRINIDAD

Flying In

You can enter this single state with two names at either end, as it were, in Trinidad or Tobago.

In Trinidad, at *Piarco Airport*, you'll find a most hospitable crew—especially if you land on Christmas Day—and an airport that has just about everything you could think of. Superb runway lights (plus VASI), ILS (of course), a VOR/DME (116.9/XE), plus NDB (382/POS) 100° and 4.2 NM from the field, and—because this is an oil-producing state—almost every type of fuel you're likely to need at a reasonable price. Hurray for Trinidad & Tobago!

Approach Control is 126.9 and 119.0, while Tower is heard on 118.1 (and 3023.5) and Ground is the good old 121.9.

Piarco radio finds itself on numerous frequencies, these—at the time of writing—being 126.9, 123.7, and, for Eastern Caribbean traffic, 124.2. On other wave bands you'll find it at 17925, 8847, 5582, 2910 for Northeast South American traffic, and at 11367, 8959, 6540, 5340, plus 2920 for Eastern Caribbean traffic.

The VOR/DME is unusable below 3,000 ft MSL in an arc from

Trinidad's local treasures extend to plentiful supplies of oil and natural gas, making it potentially one of the richer of Third World nations. (*photo*)

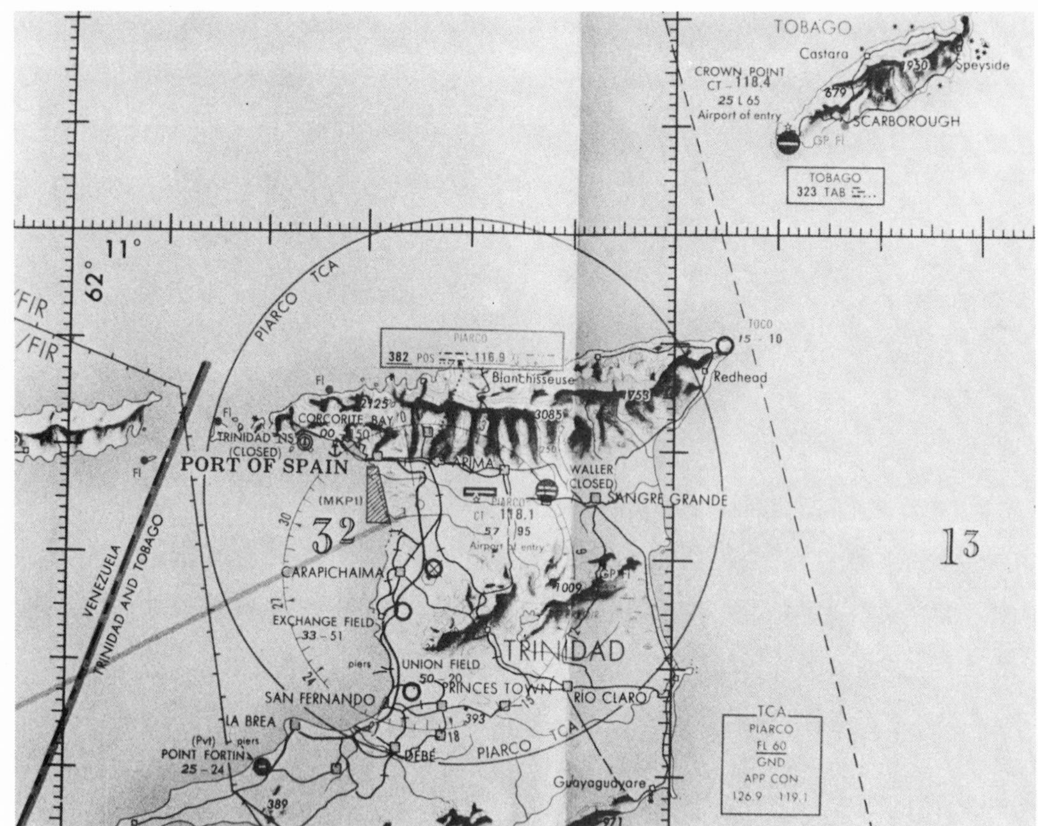

(Not to be used for navigation.)

280° through 070° and below 4,100 ft MSL reciprocally (i.e., 070° through 280°) on account of the mountains.

There are some other fields on your chart, the nearest to Piarco being *Waller,* which is closed. *Exchange Field,* just to the south of Carapchaima, is open, with fuel and a modest FBO operation reported. Still further south is *Union Field,* and just west of La Brea is the private field at *Point Fortin.*

Corcorite Bay, in the bay of Port of Spain, serves seaplanes. Note that there's a restricted area (MKP1) on the waterline just south of the city.

Background Briefing

Trinidad & Tobago is an unusual state in that it has two names and might be said to have two identities—the first of which is an industrialized Third World nation, the second being (in Tobago) the island resort nonpareil.

As a Third World nation, Trinidad is likely to continue its several contributions to the world, which include thus far asphalt (from its famous pitch lake), which covers the roads in most parts of the world, calypso (called kaiso in the island), and the steel band, plus some remarkably fine writings from such natives as Vidiadhar S. Naipaul and the premier, Dr. Eric E. Williams.*

Perhaps the most remarkable achievement of this young nation-state—formed as recently as 1962—is that it has a relatively peaceful population that is about as multiracial as can be imagined, including Indians, Chinese, African, and Carib strains mingled with Spanish, French, Dutch, Jewish, Lebanese, British, and Syrian.

The island became a republic, though remaining a part of the British Commonwealth, in 1977. The head of state is its president, Mr. (formerly Sir) Ellis E. I. Clarke, who was appointed in 1976 and who dropped the title when the nation went republican. The government is run by Premier Williams and his cabinet, and is of the familiar bicameral type.

The nation is almost 2,000 square miles in area with a population of around 1.2 million. English is the official language, though a Trinidadian dialect is popular, as are Indian languages, including Hindi. The islanders are relatively religious, and about 70 percent are Christian, the majority being Roman Catholic and Anglican. Some 20 percent plus are Hindu, and about 8 percent are Moslem. Some African sects also have a following.

Unlike the other islands of the Lesser Antilles, Trinidad started life surfacing from the ocean bed as part of the South American continent. It became separated as an island relatively recently, say scientists, and is a mere eight miles from the Venezuelan coast. The mountains in the north of the island are clearly a former part of those of the Paria Peninsula. Like Tobago, Trinidad is believed to have been first settled by the Ciboneys before the Arawaks came and made their mark here. Then came the Caribs. Extensive finds of artifacts have been made in both islands and it seems certain

*V. S. Naipaul, who now lives in England, became internationally known with his *House for Mr. Biswas*, while Dr. Williams is known for his *From Columbus to Castro*.

there were thriving settlements here as early as 6000 BC. The two narrow channels known as the Dragon's Mouth and the Serpent's Mouth would hardly have deterred primitive canoers.

The island was discovered by Columbus on his third voyage, in 1498, and named for the Trinity after the three mountain peaks he sighted. The "Three Sisters" or the "Trinity Hills" are between Moruga and Galeota Point in the southeast. The Spanish first settled in the island in 1532, and other settlers followed. Principal crops were cocoa and tobacco.

Sir Walter Raleigh turned up in 1595, destroyed the capital city, San Josef de Oruna (now St. Joseph), and caulked his ships with asphalt from Pitch Lake. After that the Spanish settlers were left more or less to themselves except for occasional Dutch, French, and British raiding parties. They were also left pretty much to themselves by the Spanish government, and as late as 1700 there were only about 1,000 settlers here, plus a further 2,000 slaves.

Finally, in 1783, the Spanish agreed to allow immigrants to settle in Trinidad on condition they were Roman Catholic. Soon afterward, they dispatched the very able Jose Maria Chacon, last of the Spanish governors, during whose fourteen years in office the island began to thrive. One reason was that the French Revolution had been exported to Haiti, Martinique, and Guadeloupe. Numerous wealthy emigres and their slaves found a welcome in Trinidad. Sugar quickly became the main crop while the French added their culture and way of living to the predominantly Spanish background. It was in 1783 that the first *Cabildo* (Town Council) was held in Port-of-Spain.

Then, with the Napoleonic Wars, a large British naval and military force, under Sir Ralph Abercromby arrived and the Spanish surrendered without a shot. The first British governor, Sir Thomas Picton, continued the work of his Spanish predecessor, making few changes to the existing way of life. More slaves were imported from Africa and population rose to almost 100,000.

The abolition of slavery in 1834 in the British islands caused problems in Trinidad also. The former slaves retired to the hills to eke out a living from the land. To maintain the agricultural economy, the British were obliged to return to a previous solution and permitted the immigration of indentured workers. These laborers agreed to work for a set period, at the end of which they'd be entitled to a small grant of land or a passage home. In addition, others came voluntarily from China, Madeira, and Portugal. By 1845, East Indians were actively encouraged to emigrate to Trinidad, and continued to arrive right up until 1917, when the Indian government put a stop to the arrangement. (East Indians went in significant numbers to farm plantations in former British Guiana, now the nation-state Guyana.)

During the 19th-century asphalt was added to the list of island exports and drilling for oil began in the 1860s. By the turn of the century, oil was in significant industrial production.

Life was not easy for the workers, and a lack of privacy and sanitation encouraged lawlessness and disease, and led to the famous *canboulay** riots during the carnivals of 1881, 1882, and 1883. The East Indians joined in with another riot during their festival of Hosein the following year. Predictably, the British sent a gunboat, but reforms were introduced in new labor laws, and the stage was set for the development of the trade-union movement, which is now a strong force in the nation.

In 1889, the German discovery of how to make sugar from beets brought the failure of the sugar industry in Tobago. Until that point the island had enjoyed a separate history. Now it requested that it become part of Trinidad and it has remained so since—though for how much longer is uncertain, since there have been rumblings that Tobago is no longer satisfied at being treated as the little sister in the relationship.

During World War II the island was an important military and naval base in the Caribbean, with regular antisubmarine patrols being run to protect Allied shipping from U-boats. (The *Hotel Chagacabana* has arisen phoenix-like from the former US Navy married quarters.)

Then, in 1956, the Peoples National Movement (or PNM), founded by Dr. Eric Williams—an Oxford graduate and historian—was elected as the governing party. By 1961 per capita income had risen to some $580 with a growth rate hovering around 8 percent. The following year on August 31, Trinidad and Tobago became independent.

**Canboulay* comes from the French *cannes brulees*, or burned cane, and was used to describe whites' making their faces black or using blackface during carnival.

The island, because of its industrial (mostly petroleum) successes, is a relative newcomer to tourism. The oil business is, after all, its biggest earner of foreign revenue, and the nation-state is a major exporter in the Western Hemisphere. Recent offshore oil and gas finds make it increasingly likely this will continue. (Output is about 70 million barrels annually.) It is also an important refiner of Mideast oil, and oil from Nigeria and Venezuela. Texaco—which bought out British interests in the 1960s—now has onstream a significant petrochemical and desulphurization complex. The government owns substantial holdings in the industry and has reached an agreement in principle for a 51-percent share of all major oil operations, which might be a model for all governments everywhere in dealing with energy.

An interesting cooperative program is in the making with the Jamaican and Guyanese governments for an aluminum smelter here. Both Jamaica and Guyana are major world exporters of bauxite, the ore from which aluminum is made. Because Trinidad has the supplies of energy needed, the smelter is being built right here. It's expected to go on-line—operational—by 1980. A similar project is planned with Brazil: a sponge-iron plant is to be constructed to be fed by iron ore from South America.

Sugar, while it has declined from its number-one status in the nation's economy, is still the largest employer of labor, and cane is the single most important agricultural crop. Molasses, rum, and bagasse board are byproducts of the industry. Other agricultural production includes cocoa, coffee, citrus fruits, and coconuts, from which copra, oils, and fats are extracted. Rice growing is on the increase and it is expected that Trinidad & Tobago will soon become self-sufficient. Livestock includes beef cattle and excellent milk-fed veal. There's plenty of pork, poultry, eggs, and milk, plus excellent fish.

Other industry includes cement, clay products, textiles, garment manufacture—Trinidad is an excellent place to buy good-quality, inexpensive clothing, and quality tailoring and fine materials can be had almost as quickly as in Hong Kong. Manufacturing includes soap, edible oils, various alcoholic beverages, furniture, engineering products, electronic components (and their assembly), motor vehicles, and domestic appliances including refrigerators, air-conditioners, radios, and TVs.

Tourism has risen to about the third largest source of income, and an important earner of foreign exchange.

Because it is situated just eleven degrees to the north of the equator, and is so close to the South American continent, the island experiences a "rainy" season. (This is not as serious as it sounds.) The dry spell runs from January through May, when rainfall averages a mere 2.3 inches per month. The rainy season runs from June through December, with an average rainfall of about 7.5 inches per month. Usually there occurs a dry spell around October, a sort of Indian Summer known locally as the *Petit Careme* (Little Lent).

You'll find a number of rivers in the island, the most important, rising in the northern range of mountains, being the Caroni, which flows into the Gulf of Paria, and the Oropouche and Matura, which run down to the Atlantic. The Moruga's source is in the Three Sisters, and the Ortoire and the Navet flow from the Montserration Hills. The northern mountain range—a continuation of the Cordilleras—is beautiful; the two highest mountains are El Cerro del Aripo (3,085 ft) and El Tucuche (3,072 ft).

Tobacco is still an important local crop, while the manufacture of fine jewelry is one of the nation's more distinguished arts.

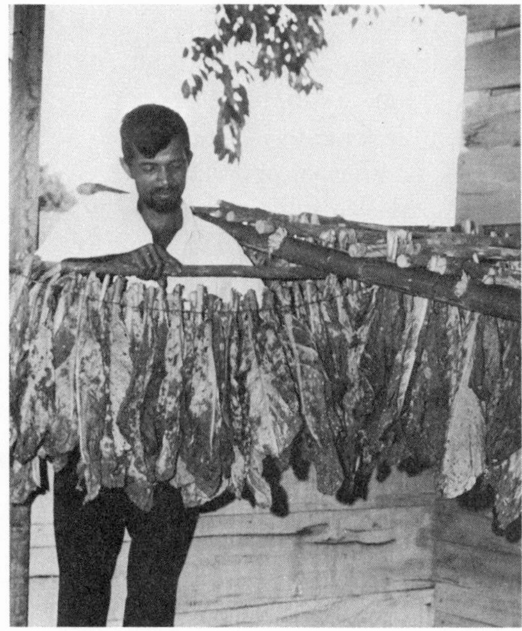

There are two big swamps (you might note in passing that the *aedes aegypti* mosquito is not yet eradicated: you may want to get yellow fever shots): the Caroni, a part of which is a bird sanctuary, and the Nariva swamp on the east coast.

There are a number of mud volcanoes, and there's Pitch Lake, which renews itself each day.

Unusual flora and fauna abound. Hunters interested in rare sport should note that the hunting season for agouti (a rabbit-sized rodent), deer, armadillo, lappe, the spotted paca (which is closely related to agouti and whose meat is favored by connoisseurs), and quenk (peccary or wild hog; it is not a true pig) runs from October 1 through March 31. Animals classified as pests such as squirrels and manicou can be hunted at any time by landowners. Under special protection (and you'd better believe it) are the ocelot, the most beautiful creature of the cat family, and monkeys and porcupines.

There are two species of monkey, the Red Howler and the Trinidad Capuchin. Both keep to themselves in the high forest and are not found in great numbers, hence their protected status. The Howler is so called because of its noise. The Trinidad Capuchin is locally called the white monkey, though its coat is not actually white.

There are at least 60 varieties of bats in the island, including at least three species of true vampire bats, which feed on fresh blood. They range in size from tiny beasts with a wing span of about four inches to near giants with a span of more than a yard and the body of a good-sized rat. Altogether this island has nearly 100 different species of mammals, including several families of opossum (the local manicou closely resembles the species found in the US), armadillo, squirrel, mongoose (originally brought in to kill snakes, now considered a pest on account of its thieving habits), crab-eating raccoons,* brocket (deer), and quenk.

The only member of the crocodile family to be found is the cayman, which grows up to seven feet. It feeds on fish and carrion.

There are large numbers of birds, including the scarlet ibis or flamant (not a flamingo, please), which can be seen at the Caroni Bird Sanctuary; the Crabier or Boat-billed Heron; the Paui—wild

*Crab-Eating Raccoon or *Procyon lancrivorus*: these animals have a highly developed tactile sense and often wash their food before eating it, as do other raccoons.

turkey, type of Guan, and formerly thought to be extinct; Green Amazon Parrots; several varieties of hummingbird, including the colibri and common emerald; the toucan; mockingbird; and the famous flycatcher called Keskidee for its call.*

Likewise numerous flora including cabbage palms and Bamboo Palms, the gru gru (*acrocomia aculeata*), whose yellowy brown fruit has an edible pulp, and the pewa, whose orange-red fruit is also edible. There are large numbers of flowering trees including the flambouyant, cassia, yellow and pink poui, the flame-colored immortelle (known locally as the *madre de cocoa* since it shades young cocoa plants), and the Queen of Flowers, also known here as Pride of India. Wild poinsettia is the national flower of the island and is found on the north coast and in wooded areas.

Those interested in fishing will find an excellent range of fish. Wahoo, bonito, sailfish, marlin, and kingfish are all to be found offshore from Tobago from January through June. Tarpon is to be found year round in the surf at Tobago and around the Caroni and Nariva swamps in Trinidad. Bonefish are found off the north coast of Trinidad from January through June, while fresh-water fly fishermen can enjoy year-round casting for mountain mullet in the streams of the north coast of Trinidad.

Those who prefer to do their hunting in the water will find a full range of fish including parrot fish, snapper, grouper, barracuda—if you insist, though only the smaller ones are good eating—and pargue to point their spearguns at.

Female turtles (200 pounds heavier and 2 feet larger in diameter than males) are also protected, and may not be taken in any way when within a reef, or within one kilometer of a highwater mark of the foreshore when there is no reef.

Because of its multiracial background there are probably more interesting things to see here than on almost any other island in the Eastern Caribbean. In Port-of-Spain, the 200-acre Queen's Park Savannah was formerly part of a sugar estate and today is home to cricket, soccer, horse racing, and hockey. Trinidad provides the English-speaking world with a number of fine cricketers, and Test Match fever runs high. There's an array of architec-

*One of the flycatcher family, *Pitangus Suphuratus*, it was named by the French for its haunting "Qu'est-ce qu'il dit?" ("What does he say?").

ture in the buildings on the west side, ranging from a Rhine-style castle to the gingerbread house in French Second Empire style.

The two cathedrals—Holy Trinity and Immaculate Conception—are both interesting examples of ecclesiastical architecture. For those interested in military architecture there's Fort San Andres, built in 1785 to protect ships in the harbor; it was from here that Don Cosmo Damien de Churruca made the first meridian of longitude in 1792. The Don was astronomer to the Court of Spain and a distinguished naval officer. Fort George was built in 1804 and the cannons mounted on its rampart date from 1797 through 1820. They bear the royal insignia G.R. (George Rex). This building was an important semaphore station in its heyday.*

St. James Barracks (completed in 1827) and the Infirmary are reckoned to be among the handsomest classical buildings in the Caribbean. The elegance of style was poor compensation to the troops who occupied it, and a contemporary writer described the building as "these splendid head-quarters of disease." The building is presently used as a Police Training School. The original Police Headquarters, built in 1877, was burned down—along with much else—in a disastrous fire in 1881. The new Gothic-style building dates from 1884.

Independence Square is undergoing some modernization, bringing it into the 20th century as the earlier colonial buildings give way to some interesting new structures.

North of the Savannah are to be found the Botanical Gardens and the Zoo—both well worth the visit. The Botanical Gardens date back to the early 1800s and contain a profusion of plants and trees. Guides will assist you, pointing out some of the more unusual ones. The Governor-General's House is within the Gardens. At the Emperor Valley Zoo you'll find a number of attractions, including American bison.

The Asa Wright Nature Centre—which also takes guests—is another worthwhile spot to visit. It's about a 50-minute drive from the airport, and—depending on traffic—a little over an hour from Port-of-Spain.

The National Museum and Art Gallery has a number of

*Two forts at Laventvilla are also of interest, Fort Picton and Chacons Fort.

Amerindian artifacts and—for those who think of Trinidad in terms of its Carnival—a collection of costumes. Admission is free.

The northern coast is especially attractive and the drive through Northern Range is extremely popular as an excursion. Maracas Beach is one of the best in the island. The Atlantic coast is rather different, and the turtles come here to lay their eggs.

San Fernando is the second-largest population center in the island, and the trip to the Pitch Lake is short. It's not particularly attractive (if you've seen one you've seen 'em all) but it is certainly unusual. The extent of the oil industry here can be seen by the extensive development in southern part of the island.

Festivals

Everyone has heard of the celebrated Carnival in Trinidad, which rivals the Rhinelanders Fasching and the annual tour de force in Rio de Janeiro. No one is quite sure when Carnival originated, for it seems to have been in existence prior to the arrival of the French emigres. With their arrival it presumably became more decorous, and certainly included masked dancing and music in the streets. Freedmen were allowed to wear masks, though slaves were not.

Following the abolition of slavery, the festival became more lively and contemporaries talked of being shocked by the noise, obscenity, and near-nudity of some of the celebrants. (They sometimes still do.) Eventually the government stepped in, forbidding the start of the celebration until midnight of the Sunday before Lundi Gras. The first *canboulay* riots in 1881 led to a new law: No parades before 6:00 AM Lundi Gras, the moment known as *jouve* to this day.*

Today, preparations for Carnival get under way almost as soon as Christmas is over, and curtain-raisers to the big event include several series of Carnival dances held by restaurants, hotels, and clubs. Also at work are the calypsonians, who have the most extravagant of names to reflect their philosophy. One great favorite still is the Mighty Sparrow (actually a Grenadian), whose work has traveled the world.

Calypso derives from Africa, and the roots seem to be with slave entertainers called "chantwells" who provided court jester–like

*Probably from the French *jour ouvert*, or daybreak.

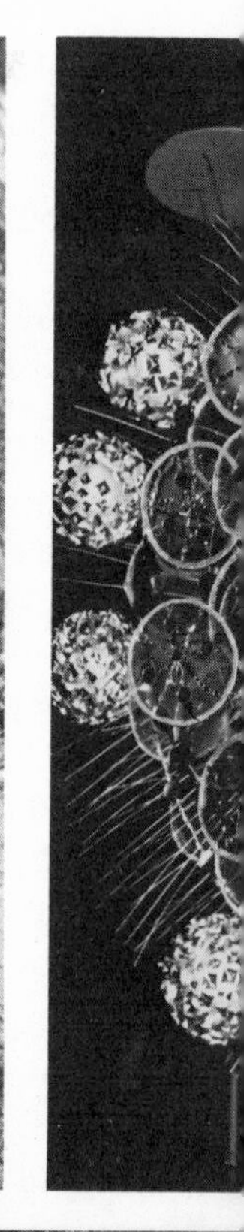

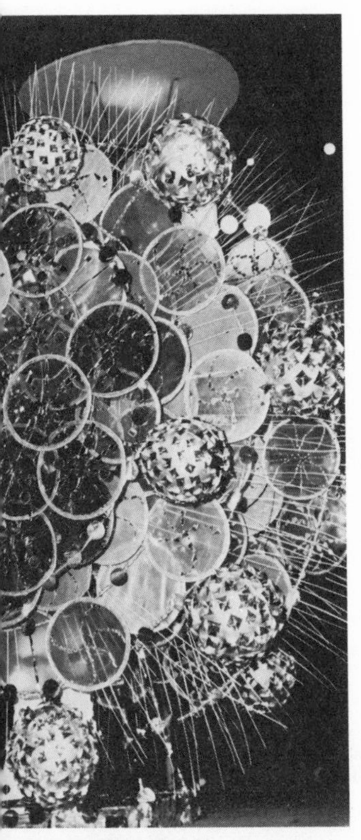

High fashion and some lowdown in carnival wear. (above, and far left below) Providing the music is the job of the pan tuner whose expertise creates the liquid tones of the steel bands.

Feast of Hosay—celebrating the early Muslim martyr Imam Hosein—brings about a different sort of parade. It is celebrated the tenth day of Moharram, the first month in the Moslem calendar.

performances for the amusement of the Plantation boss. Following emancipation, competitions developed among the singers, who involved themselves in all night "wars" against one another. The one who was quickest-witted became leader of the Carnival parade and his song became the theme for the event.

Today calypsonians gather to sing their witty and catchy songs in tents in the city every night, beginning soon after the New Year. It is the latest calypso tunes that provide the rhythm for dancing indoors and on the streets at Carnival, and the steel bands learn the notes.

The steel band is also a Trinidadian invention. These pans, as the instruments are called, are made from oil drums, the tops being heated, note areas inscribed, and then tuned. Depending on the range of the instrument, metal is left to different depths. The music is produced by knocking the tempered areas with valve-grinding sticks, whose rubber ends provide the tunes. Treble pans have only a slight skirt of metal, while tenor pans are more deeply cut. The full bass pans consist of the whole drum.

Tuning a pan is a fine art, and the best tuners are in strong demand. It is also not unheard of for one band to attempt to sabotage another's pans, since prizes are awarded not merely for the best disguised individual and/or the most attractive costumes, but for bands: for the best music, the best calypso, and the most popular road-march. The best places to see Carnival are Port-of-Spain and San Fernando, but you will need to make reservations nearly a year in advance because anyone who's seen the Trinidad Carnival and enjoyed the color (and music) it provides is hooked.

Christmas in Trinidad is very much a family affair, with lots of visiting and eating and drinking and partying. The food is the best that money can buy.

There's more partying—or "feteing," as they say—on the island at New Year's, and Old Year's Night is an occasion for dressing up and attending the numerous public dances around the island.

Easter is a big celebration with divination and *Bobolee*. The divination is performed on Good Friday when you'll see boys place a glass of water in the sun. When it gets lukewarm they pour the albumen of an egg in it; the shapes the albumen forms are used for divination and traditional values are attached to such concepts, so that a church would mean a wedding, a ship would mean travel, while a memorial stone would foretell a death in the family.

Bobolee is also the name given to a Judas-type doll made from straw and grass stuffed into an old pair of pants, shirt, and jacket, set atop with a hat. Bobolee is perched by the side of the road; toward evening, at about five o'clock, the boys who made him and their friends set about him with sticks.

The Indians celebrate several festivals, the Hindus with Ramlilla and Dewali—the Festival of Lights—being held in October. Kartik Nahan occurs in November and Phagwah, which heralds spring, usually occurs in March.

Eid-ul-Fitr marks the end of the month of Ramadan, the ninth month in the Moslem year, during which strict fasting is observed from dawn to dusk. Hosay is the other big Moslem festival, commemorating the martyrdom of Imam Hosein at Mecca in the

A fleet of island schooners load and unload at Port-of-Spain.

early years of that religion. This is a very colorful occasion and occurs on the tenth day of Moharram, the first month in the Moslem lunar calendar.

Some of the smaller Catholic fishing villages observe St. Peter's Day, June 29. The whole nation observes Discovery Day, to commemorate Columbus' find. It's held the first Monday in August and people go either to the beach or the racetrack.

An arts festival and a music festival are held alternate years.

Food and Drink

With its multiracial background it's not too surprising to find such a variety of foods available. You'll be able to enjoy regular American and English fare, together with some fine French (and Creole) foods, plus Indian and Chinese specialities.

If you want to be more adventurous try some of the island's own specialties such as *lappe* or stewed *tatu* (the local name for armadillo) or the delicious (and minature) mangrove oyster. Fish-eaters should try the *cascadura*, a fresh-water fish served stuffed with vegetables. Islanders will tell you that once you've eaten it, you'll return to Trinidad to end your days. And then there's *roti*—an Indian contribution to the island's list of things to eat; everyone makes it, and it's like a *paratha*, or a light dough crepe. (Interestingly, graduates from the St. Augustine campus of UWI have exported roti so successfully to Jamaica and Barbados that you can almost always find someone there who knows how to make roti "as they do in Trinidad.")

Rum is the local drink, but a very satisfying local cooler is gin and coconut water. Trinidad is also home to the Angostura bitters firm, so pink gins and slings are popular. Trinidadians make their rum punches strong: you've been warned.

Nightlife

A number of discos have opened over the past few years and the one currently enjoying top spot is *J.B.'s* at the Valpark Shopping Plaza some 9 miles east of Port-of-Spain off the Churchill Roosevelt Highway. There's split-level seating around the dance floor and strobes. Music is mostly rock and soul with the occasional homegrown product. J.B.'s is so named for its owner, John Boos,

Water buffalo take a break in the noonday sun.

who's the president of the tourist board. An adjoining restaurant serves fine steaks.

The *Hilton Hotel*—the upside-down Hilton—on Lady Young Road has some of the best in live entertainment and is to be relied on. The *Carnival Bar* has mood lighting and music for dancing until 2:00 AM every night except Monday.

The *Calypso Lounge* on the 12th floor of the Holiday Inn on Wrightson Road has a resident trio making music for dancing (or sipping). Attractive waitresses provide friendly service.

More for lonely males is the *Penthouse Club* on Independence Square, providing some of the best in local entertainment outside the hotel circuit. There's a nightly floorshow at 11 PM that occasionally includes off-island performers. By midnight the joint is jumping. Dancing; hostesses.

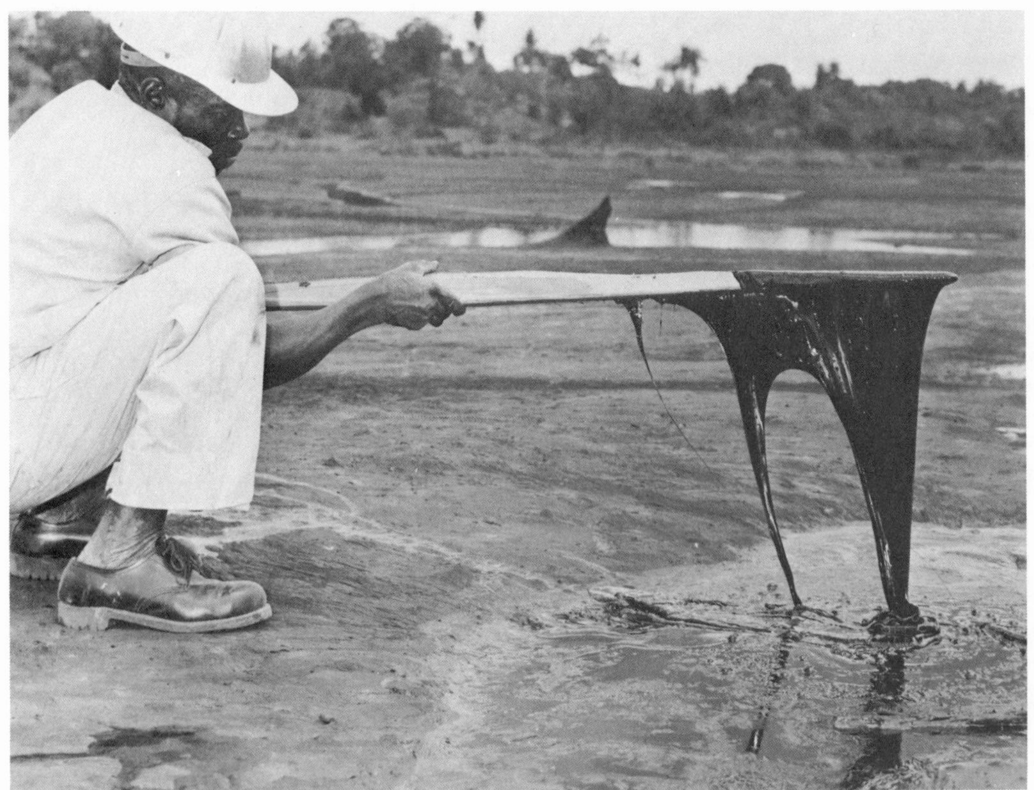

Trinidad's famed asphalt lake renews itself each night. Sir Walter Raleigh caulked his ships with pitch from here.

Restaurants

For West Indian Food the *Bamboo Room* at the Tropical Hotel in the suburb Maraval is rated well, as is *La Boucan* restaurant at the Hilton, which provides both French and Creole cuisine. At lunchtime the *Gourmet* on the first floor of the TATIL building (second largest in the island) provides Creole buffets—delicious—and while evening food is mostly international, the chef will prepare Creole food, including his famed spicy lamb, if given advance notice. The *Errol J. Lau Hotel* also serves island food.

For Indian food, *Mangals* on Queen's Park East is one of the favored places, while for Chinese there's *Kowloon* on St. Vincent Street (Cantonese cooking) or the *Golden Dragon*; and for Polynesian fare, the *Tiki Village* at the Kapok Hotel.

For Italian food try *Luciano's*, about 4 miles out of town on

Ariapita Road, St. Ann's. If the Frederick Street branch is open—same outfit, *Luciano's Hungry I*—that can also be very good.

To dine in the only revolving restaurant in the Caribbean—or to dine in a revolving restaurant, period—go to the *La Ronde* at the Holiday Inn; it offers an international menu with some local goodies included, of which crab back is one. They also serve roast beef and Yorkshire pud if nostalgia gets to you, and a very decent Christmas pudding on Christmas day.

Americans who must have their steaks should check out the *Pan American Guest House*, where the steaks arrive daily from the mainland and the ice cream is superb.

Where to Stay

Until the Hyatt Group decides whether to go ahead with a resort on Maracas Beach, there are no resort hotels on Trinidad per se at

Trinidad has some exotic styles in architecture, including this old favorite—the castle—modeled after a German *Schloss.*

the present time. Meanwhile, the larger hotels are to be found in and around Port-of-Spain.

The upside-down *Hilton* is one of the nicer hotels in the chain, and one has the feeling that they do try to care for their guests, and that the spirit of inn-keeping has been retained. There are more than 400 rooms, and amenities include swimming pool, lighted tennis courts, two restaurants, two bars, and a health club. There's the best in nightly entertainment and captains of industry will be pleased with the meeting rooms and the in-house secretarial service.

The hotel is known as upside-down because reception is at the top instead of the bottom. The building was designed to complement its environment—and does so.

The *Trinidad Holiday Inn* is the only luxury hotel in downtown Port-of-Spain, with some 250 rooms plus 2 suites, all with bath and private terrace. One of the suites is the Presidential (for visiting heads of state?). There are well-thought-out convention facilities, which include special lighting, a complete range of AV equipment, in-house secretarial services, and so on. There's a swimming pool, plus a kiddie's play pool. The main road outside is sometimes noisy.

The Normandie has just completed an expensive facelift operation and reportedly is back in business offering pleasantly large accommodations, all with private bath, patio, radio, telephone, and air-conditioning. Located on St. Ann's Road, it was one of the first of the "modern" hotels in Trinidad, and had begun to show it.

The Queen's Park Hotel is an impressive example of a hotel in an older style. Located at Queen's Park West, it too has been undergoing modernization, though the service is still pleasantly old-fashioned courteous. It's not expensive.

Tops with the younger crowd is the *Kapok Hotel*, Cotton Hill, St. Clair, just a few minutes from the Botanic Gardens and not too far from the *Normandie* (which has long been known for its French food). Small pool at the Kapok: big one at the Normandie.

Out at Maraval is the *Chaconia Inn*, with 48 comfortable guest rooms, which include 10 deluxe two-bedroom suites and 16 deluxe rooms with kitchenettes. Two good restaurants, and *The Baron* is a lively pub with disco music and game room area with dart board and pool table. (Wot? No draught beer?)

Also in Maraval is *Bagshot House,* 15 rooms with bath, and reasonable rates.

One unusual hotel in Port-of-Spain is the *Errol J. Lau.* This inexpensive 17-room hotel used to be a classy brothel.

Out-of-town hotels include the modest *Scarlet Ibis Hotel* in St. Augustine, the *Chagacabana Hotel* at Chaguaramas—St. James at the beach—and in south Trinidad, at Point Fortin, the 15-room *Gulf Coast Hotel* at Clifton Hill.

For apartment accommodations try *Gulf View Apartment Hotel,* at Goodwood Park. And for the complete range of accommodations consult the Trinidad & Tobago Tourist Board.

TOBAGO

Flying In

If you chose the latter, there's an NDB at the field (323/TAB) to guide you to the 6,500 feet of runway which boasts VASI and normal lighting. But that's about where it ends: tower is at 118.4 and ground control at 121.9. So far, at least, no fuel, though the customs and immigration people are some of the most helpful in the world in getting you through without red tape.

Background Briefing

Compared to its bigger sister's, the history of Tobago has been turbulent, with pirates and buccaneers and privateers and would-be colonists fighting it out with each other over a period of

centuries. This may also have been one of the islands Columbus missed, though there is a school of thought that suggests that Tobago is Concepcion, where he did not land, having revittled in Trinidad.

How it came by its present name is also uncertain, but probably—early maps show Tavago, Tobacco, and Tobago—it is derived from "tobacco." The British were first on the scene, and in 1628 Charles I—the Divine-Right-of-Kings fellow who was to lose his head—gave it outright to a court favorite, the Earl of Pembroke. Immediately, the island became a bone of contention among the Dutch, the French, the English, and a group of Baltic seafarers, the Courlanders.

The Courlanders were natives of a small Duchy in what today is Latvia. The Duke of Courland was the head of a small clan of extremely ambitious men and, wanting his share in what seemed like a Caribbean boom, contended for this island—as did his heirs—until they sold their claim to the Swedes.

The squabbling went on despite the Treaty of Nijmegen (1679), which gave the island to the Dutch, and by 1704 it was agreed that it should be a no-man's land (as in the case of St. Vincent, though for different reasons). This suited the privateers and buccaneers just right, and Tobago for a while was used as a base for forays on shipping until the British—who were losing a number of their trading schooners—stepped in with an expedition in 1721. The result was that a Captain Finn, who was unfortunate enough to be recuperating in the island during the attack, was captured and his flotilla destroyed. He was hanged.

On making their purchase of the island the Swedes sent out a small group of families to settle, but their efforts were stymied by a force of Negros and Caribs who joined to put them to flight. Another British force appeared in 1762 and again seized the island, which was formally ceded to Britain the following year at the Treaty of Paris.

Only a few place names recall this turbulent history; for example, Bloody Bay, Courland Bay, Dutch Fort, French Fort, Fort James, Pembroke Village, and Pirates' Bay.

Once the British began to administer the island it was divided into seven parishes and grants of land were made to those who would farm it. Negro slaves provided the labor force and the

Giant waterwheel testifies to alternative forms of energy in earlier times.

principal cash crops were cotton, indigo, and King Sugar. By 1768 a legislative assembly sat for the first time in the island of Studley Park, and an early order of business was to remove the capital to Scarborough for health reasons. The first of a series of slave insurrections took place soon afterward.

A possible reason why John Paul Jones fought for the American colonists is connected with Tobago. It seems that in 1770 he sailed into the roadstead and on complaints by his ship's carpenter was brought before the Admiralty Court. It seems he was fined. Interestingly, in the war which was soon to break out, the colonists thought Tobago an excellent potential prize and instructed privateers to conduct a series of raids In 1778 an American squadron attempted the island's capture, but were driven off by the Royal Navy.

Meanwhile, agriculture flourished. Half a million pounds of cotton were exported in 1780 and nearly 30,000 pounds of indigo. The following year, the French arrived, capturing Tobago and a number of other islands. For a short time Scarborough was known as Port Louis—until the French Revolution broke out and the French troops mutinied, killing their officers and burning Port Louis to the ground. To add to their discomfort, one of the rare hurricanes to hit the island arrived. And so it was that in 1793 the British came back. Then, to the chagrin of the British planters, the island was ceded back to France at the Treaty of Amiens in 1802. Some of the Brits must have made the right noises, however, for the following year the French surrendered, without hurricane or guns, to a British force that landed at Arnos Vale. It is said that they were guided to Scarborough by a slave named George Winchester who was given his freedom and a sum of money for his act.

For the next eighty years Tobago became one of the leaders in world sugar production and that Victorian phrase "as rich as a Tobago planter" was coined. Interestingly, this survived the emancipation of the slaves, but not the monopolistic brokerage of a London firm called Gillespie & Co., which held the financial strings of the planters' wealth. When the firm went bankrupt in 1884, the planters were ruined, and the freed slaves were able to buy up property—and squat on what they could not buy. And so the one crop economy perished. Tobago was joined with Trinidad in 1889 and the islanders learned to grow other crops, such as cocoa and coconuts, its two major exports today.

While it is worthwhile making an excursion over and around this island, chances are you'll want to enjoy the superb John Harris championship 18-hole golf course at Mount Irvine Bay Hotel, or take advantage of the incredibly professional scuba operation run by the Teach Tour Diving people at Speyside.

One item that makes Tobago such a mecca for scuba enthusiasts is the clarity of the water, day in and day out. Underwater visibility of 150 feet is normal, and when you consider that the visibility of our own shores is frequently less than one foot, you'll understand better how divers can go bananas with joy when diving here.

The diver who had the brainwave behind Teach Tour Diving was Roy Morrow, who used to wreck-dive in New Jersey. The operation began simply, but professionally, several years ago, and has grown in size slowly but surely. An example of the forethought of this operation was the acquisition of a recompression chamber, which was formerly used by offshore oil-rig divers in Trinidad. It's

Golf is available throughout the Caribbean but the links at Mount Irving have numerous Stateside fans; for scuba enthusiasts, the waters around Tobago are rated as triple A-1.

primary use is for instructor training, though it's available in case of mishaps.

There are many beautiful reefs around, and these have been graded from *A* through *D*. The *D* here stands for difficult—and, to a tyro, dangerous—where surface swells and surge and oceanic currents are to be found. In fact at some reefs you can take the guided tour courtesy of circular eddies when you know how.

The advantage of scuba equipment compared with snorkeling is that you don't have to keep coming up for air. Depending on your lung capacity, very few can manage more than three minutes beneath the surface just using a tube. With scuba you're not so limited, and if you've never tried it, you may want to check it out. However, a word of warning, since you are a pilot. Using compressed air beneath the water to breathe is not the same as using oxygen in the rarefied atmosphere. This means that just as a regular diver must closely time his dives, so must the user of scuba equipment, returning to the surface in a series of stages to allow the nitrogen in the bloodstream to decompress slowly. Do not plan on any dives below 30 feet within the 36 hours before you plan to fly again, in fact, you may want to skip diving altogether during those hours.

Food and Drink

Pretty much as on Trinidad with more emphasis on seafood. All hotel dining is good, and for authentic island seafare the *Voodoo* in Scarborough, despite its modest appearance, rates very high.

Nightlife

The *Shamrock and Palm* at the Mount Irvine, while modeled on an English pub, offers disco dance and dim lighting. Open most nights until 2:00 AM.

The *Club La Tropicale* at the Della Mira Hotel offers an excellent variety of entertainment in season, with a floor show Fridays and Saturdays. Disco Tuesdays and Thursdays, and live music other nights except Monday when it's closed. Closes around 4:00 AM.

Where to stay

Mount Irvine Bay Hotel with its golf course is generally reckoned to have top accolades in the island. It's a typical well-designed modern hotel complex with fresh-water pool, good accommoda-

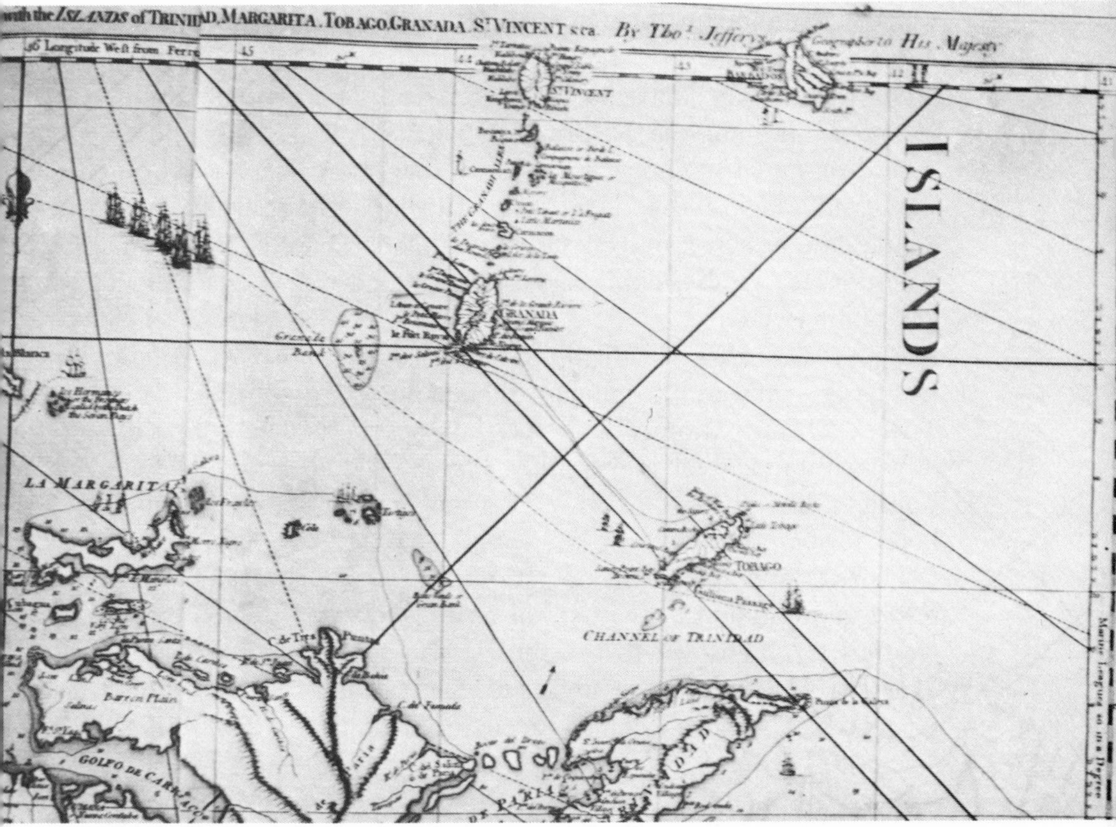

A fond farewell, map by Thos. Jefferys.

tions, babysitters (and medical service), plus beauty parlor and barbershop, boutiques, a conference wing, and so forth. Two floodlit tennis courts, sauna bath, and health club. Rates high, but reduced green fees for guests. All 110 air-conditioned rooms have private patio or balcony.

Radisson Crown Reef at Store Bay offers 115 deluxe rooms and suites overlooking the water. Convention facilities for up to 250. Rates high.

Arnos Vale at Plymouth has experienced downs and ups in recent years. Some nine miles to the north of Scarborough, it is set in a gorgeous 400-acre estate, with a beautiful sandy bay by the sea. Room for 54 guests in comfort. Sunday's Creole buffet luncheon is an island favorite. Reasonable.

Turtle Beach Hotel at Courland Bay near Plymouth is a pleasant small hotel on one of the nicer stretches of sand in the island, where the female turtles come to lay their eggs. Room for just over a hundred guests in attractively furnished two-story cottages; grounds carefully landscaped with tropical foliage, palm trees, oleander, and hibiscus. Reasonable.

Bird of Paradise Inn at Speyside is a spartan haven for ornithologists and would-be bird lovers, run by a charming Chinese couple, the Egbert Laus. It's set in a 700-acre estate that's become a nature reserve. Reservations essential. Good value, especially if you're into wildlife.

The *Della Mira* is a simple West Indian house where the emphasis is on warm hospitality and good food. And it's a bargain. There's a beauty shop and a barbershop on the premises, it has its own swimming pool and is only about 50 yards from the sea. Fourteen bedrooms only, so reservations important for this small hotel at Scarborough.

There is one apartment operation, *Crown Point on the Bay*, a resort condominium set in seven acres of pleasantly landscaped grounds sloping down to the shore. Also at Crown Point is the *Tropikist Beach Hotel*, with 32 fully air-conditioned rooms and separate suites for children connected to parents' rooms at reasonable cost.

For further information contact: Trinidad & Tobago Department of Tourism, 56 Frederick Street, Port-of-Spain, Trinidad & Tobago, W.I. In New York: 400 Madison Avenue, Suite # 712/14, New York, NY 10017; (212) 838-7750. In Florida: 200 East First South Street, Suite #702, Miami, FL 33131; (305) 374-2056. In Canada: 145 King Street West (2nd floor), Toronto, Canada M5H 1J8; (416) 367-0390. In London, 20 Lower Regent Street, London SW 17 4PH.

APPENDICES

Pilots' Briefing

Before making any overwater flight it's vital to your own peace of mind and safety to make sure that your aircraft is in good shape. Also that you, as the pilot, are too.

1.1 As far as the airplane's concerned, this means a thorough check of the engine(s) and related plumbing, electrical and mechanical. Hose and other connections should be checked and, if necessary, safetied.

1.2 You may want to make an oil and filter change. Supervise a ground runup following this since filters have been known to be improperly fitted, resulting in oil spewing everywhere and a spoiled day for everyone.

1.3 Flight controls should be meticulously checked and any unusual friction examined for cause.

1.4 Swing the magnetic compass, and get it to work using the compensating devices provided.

1.5 Check out how fast the DG precesses, and make a note of how often you'll need to reset it. (They do vary; but since you'll be flying over a lot of water without too much to provide guidance, knowing the rate will assist in your making successful landfalls time after time.)

1.6 Make a practical flight test and work out your fuel consumption so that at your usual cruise setting you know how far in time and distance you can expect to travel and at what speed.

1.7 Figure out the time it takes to leave one additional hour's flying time in the tanks.

RADIOS AND NAVIGATION

2.1 This brings us to how your radios and radio navigational equipment work. Check each very closely.

2.2 You'll want to check your own ability to use your VOR and ADF for tracking, and . . .

2.3 . . . since there are an abundance of non-directional beacons plus high-powered radio stations in this little piece of the world, your own tracking abilities and technique.

2.4 Make a flight plan each time you go, and don't be as lackadaisical as you are at home. Know what your checkpoints will be, and make sure you can estimate your position to within one mile of where you are at any time.*

2.5 Before you leave on your trip, practice your navigational technique (the rich guys with those hot-shot DME stuff will probably not bother, but it does go on the blink once in a while, so this is *need-to-know*) so you can get this one right if you have, e.g., a power outage.

EMERGENCY PROCEDURES

3.1 Review engine failure in singles. There's a note later about ditching.

3.2 Review engine failure in twins, bearing in mind that engine-out performance will be critical for most light twins in the tropics.

3.3 Review fire drill.

STANDARD MANEUVERS

4.1 Because many runways are less than ideally located with an almost permanent or semi-permanent crosswind, review takeoff and landing maneuvers.

4.2 Review creative landing techniques that involve a climb on base leg and a steep, full-flaps descent to the numbers, and the milking off of flap for a go-around.

4.3 Review slipping, and how to use the slip with flaps and yet maintain flight if a go-around proves necessary.

4.4 Check your stall and spin technique, especially departure stalls where you are spiraling upward to a small hole in the cloud cover.

*This way, if you should experience a malfunction, the people who come to pick you up will know rather exactly where to look for you.

WEIGHT AND BALANCE

5.1 Four spare cans of oil plus your safety equipment for overwater flight are more useful than your own personally inscribed Jack Nicklaus set of golf clubs.

5.2 Regard full fuel plus safety equipment as being more useful to you than an additional passenger and his or her luggage. It's hot and humid in these tropical climes, and an overloaded Cessna 172 takes forever to reach a decent cruise altitude; you'll wonder if you'll ever make it.

5.3 Be very circumspect about giving lifts or rides to people who are hanging out at an airport. Check their credentials rather thoroughly, and look for firearms. Piracy is alive and well in the Caribbean and your airplane may be needed to ship some dope into the United States.

THE BUREAUCRACY

6.1 The most important items you'll need are:

i Aircraft's Log.

ii Your own Log, plus license, plus health record, plus the Yellow International Vaccination form, which is still looked for: your FAA doctor can usually supply same though he (or she) will probably tell you it isn't needed any more. Get it. The news simply hasn't filtered through in some places.

iii General Declaration Forms. In some places you'll need just one—in and out; in others it can go up to six, and since the number required depends on who's number one at a particular time, get a couple of pads and some carbon paper and reckon on two for in and one for out. Even the local Flight Service Stations are usually unsure of what the current required number is.

iv You'll be filing ICAO flight plans rather than the FAA type. Be sure to file a flight plan, and be sure to close it, either at your destination or at some reasonable time before you get to it.

GENERAL DECLARATION
(Outward/Inward)

Owner or Operator

Marks of Nationality
and Registration ________ Flight No.: ________ Date: ________

Departure from ________ Arrive at ________
(Place and Country) (Place and Country)

FLIGHT ROUTING

(PLACE column always to list origin, plus all en-route stops and final destination)

PLACE	1) TOTAL NUMBER OF CREW	2) NUMBER OF PASSENGERS	CARGO
		DEPARTURE PLACE Embarking Through on same flight ARRIVAL PLACE Disembarking Through on same flight	CARGO Manifest attached

DECLARATION OF HEALTH

Persons on board known to be suffering from illness other than airsickness or the effects of accidents, as well as those cases of illness disembarked during the flight.

____

____

____

For Official Use only

Any other condition on board which may lead to the spread of disease

Details of each disinfecting or sanitary treatment (place, date, time, method) during the flight. If no disinfecting has been carried out during the flight give details of most recent disinfecting.

Sign if required ________
Crew Member Concerned

I declare that all statements and particulars contained in this Declaration, and in any supplementary forms required to be presented with this General Declaration are complete, exact and true to the best of my knowledge and that all through passengers will continue/have continued on the flight.

SIGNATURE ________
Authorised Agent or
Pilot-in-Command.

1) To be completed only when required by State.
2) Not to be completed when passenger manifests are presented and to be completed only when required by State.

v The US ADIZ and how to fly through it. PLEASE CHECK FOR THE CURRENT INFORMATION. This changes from month to month, and from Navy to Air Force to FAA, all of whom tend to monitor it. Current standard is below 10,000 ft, plus below 180 knots ("a good ballpark figure," said the Navy), plus a DVFR or IFR flight plan.

vi Further note on ADIZ: re-entering the US, you'd better note the time, your position, and altitude at which you expect to be re-entering, and let them know ahead, of that time and position.

vii If you do, they can provide you with 24-hour service, on a frequency of 122.2, which is advisory when available (i.e., not tied up by the military) but which can give you almost anything you want to know including current track and ground speed and the nearest airport. Blip in and ask for Radar Advisory.

6.2 IFR: As a general rule avoid it, not so much because it's almost exclusively airline business down here, but also because VFR allows just that much extra flexibility in sometimes downright rotten weather.

6.3 A secondary reason for avoiding IFR unless you are an ace is that there are relatively few locations at which you can practice your skill. Just 3 in the Bahamas chain, and a total of 13 (with no fewer than 5 of them in Puerto Rico) in the Eastern Caribbean.

6.4 Clouds down here are extremely turbulent, and even a brief encounter of the closest kind can turn you topsy-turvy.

6.5 Low cloud and squall-type showers have been known to conceal islands from the unwary.

WEATHER

7.1 The weather is mostly good.

7.2 Chief disturbances are cumulus buildup during the day, with occasional thunderstorms, and haze.

7.3 Occasional disturbances include hurricanes and waterspouts. Both

ICAO TYPE

FLIGHT PLAN

Date:..........

1. Type of Flight	2. Flight Rules	3. Aircraft Identification	4. Aircraft Type/ Special Equipment
International Inter-Island	IFR / VFR / DVFR		
5. True Airspeed knots	6. Radio Equipment Comm/ Nav/	7. Departure time (GMT) Proposed / Actual	8. Point of Departure
9. Cruise level	10. Route of Flight		11. Destination
12. Estimate Time En Route Hours / Minutes	13. Alternate Airport(s)	14. Other Information (Adiz, Closure, etc)	
15. Fuel on Board hours / Minutes	16. Persons on board	17. Emergency/Survival Gear Portable Radio / Life Jackets / Dinghies/color	
18. Color of Aircraft	19. Name of Pilot	20. Aircraft home base or pilot's address	
21. Other equipment/remarks.		22. Signature of Pilot or designated representative	

are to be avoided, but since both travel at far slower speeds than the average airplane, it is possible for the pilot to outfly them.

7.4 Weather briefings in the Caribbean are surprisingly (for US and Canadian pilots) sophisticated. Most islands will give you the sort of weather briefing you can expect within most European states or China and Japan. It's all ICAO and we provide a typical reading card for you.

7.5 Best time to fly is early morning, or after 1530 local time, when the violence has gotten out of the atmosphere. The clouds begin to disperse in the middle afternoon, and they are few and far between at early morning tide.

DITCHING TECHNIQUE

8.1 According to those who had to do it in combat, basic technique means slowing the aircraft down to just above stall and making sure there is some exit already open, since non-floatable aircraft sink swiftly.

8.2 Before you think of having to ditch, check magnetos, fuel tanks, and any electrical failures that could possibly have occurred to make you think that you ought to ditch.

8.3 Review Section 3 (Emergency Procedures)—thoroughly.

8.4 If you have to ditch:-

i Get your MAYDAY out early, clearly, WITH NO PANIC, and state exactly where you think you are situated and where you will go in.

ii Announce that you have marker dye aboard and that you will also be dropping same to mark the area.

iii Now look how the waves are moving. Tests have shown that if you can land in a trough between the waves you will have extra seconds of flotation from your aircraft in which to get your survival equipment working.

iv The technique is to land in a trough, which means a cross-wind

ICAO WEATHER SYMBOLS AND PRESENTATION

Symbol	Meaning	Symbol	Meaning
	Thunderstorm		Cold front at surface
	Tropical revolving storm		Warm front at surface
	Moderate turbulence		Occluded front
	Severe turbulence		Stationary front
	Moderate icing		Inter-tropical convergence
	Severe icing		

Nota Bene: heights for clouds, icing and turbulence are given by flight levels.

CLOUD COVER

Cloud cover is denoted in oktas before type.
FEW denotes less than one-eighth cover.

Types:

CI	= Cirrus	AS	=	Altostratus	CU	=	Cumulus
CC	= Cirrocumulus	NS	=	Nimbostratus	TCU	=	Towering Cumulus
CS	= Cirrostratus	SC	=	Stratocumulus	CB	=	Cumulonimbus
AC	= Altocumulus	ST	=	Stratus	LYR	=	Layer(s)

Standard Heights of Isobaric Surfaces

700 mb = 9,900 ft; 500 mb = 18,300 ft; 450 mb = 20,800 ft; 400 mb = 23.600 ft.

4-Letter Airport Code

KMIA	Miami	MKPN	Nevis
KPBI	West Palm Beach	MKPM	Montserrat
MYGF	Freeport	MKPA	Antigua
MYNN	Nassau	MFFR	Le Raizet, Guadeloupe
MJIG	Isla Grande, San Juan	MFFM	Marie Galante
MJPS	Ponce, P.R.	MFFS	Iles des Saintes
MJMZ	Mayaguez, P.R.	MKPD	Dominica
MJSJ	San Juan	MFFF	Le Lamentin, Martinique
MKSC	South Caicos	MKPC	Castries, ST. Lucia
MKJT	Grand Turk	MKPV	St. Vincent
MIST	St. Thomas	MKPE	Grenada
MISX	St. Croix	MKPB	Barbados
MACM	St. Maarten	MKPT	Tobago
MFFJ	St. Barts	MKPP	Piarco, Trinidad
MKPK	St. Kitts		

* * * * *

Weather info begins with 4-letter international airport code, followed by a 4-digit number. The first two digits indicate the time the forecast begins, the last two, when it ends and both are GMT. Remainder is the forecast. This is given as Wind, Visibility, Weather, Clouds. The latter only appear if significant weather is forecast. CAVOK is used if visibility is better than 10 kilometers (6.2 miles). Wind is given as a 5-digit group, first three showing true direction, last two, speed in knots. Visibility is given in meters (i.e. 0400 = about a quarter mile, 1600 = one miles, 8000 = five miles, etc.)

landing—the idea being to let the wings be supported at least partially by the opposite waves. This gives extra time to bail out.

v Fixed gear equipment should make the approach rather nose high and behind the power-curve on account of the ability of the wheels to flip the aircraft forward on entering the water.

vi Retractable gear should stay where it is, and the pilot should be prepared to bounce.

FLYING THE BAHAMAS

A good tip is to keep Unicom (122.8) tuned in on one radio while you can communicate with Miami Radio, Miami Air Route, and Bahamas Air Traffic control on the other.

You may want to make up an index card to keep in the back of your log book or attached to your sun shield, giving the local frequencies.

As an aid to navigation you may want to know that the Bahamas Ministry of Tourism has an updated Air Navigation Chart which provides complete information on the Bahamas flying area. In addition it lists accommodations, activities, and facilities throughout these islands. It's available from *Bahamas Ministry of Tourism, 255 Alhambra Circle #425, Coral Gables, FL. 33134.*

Entry Requirements:

Aircraft arriving or departing from the Bahamas must first land at or finally depart from an Airport of Entry. Flight plans are required, and flights made between sunset and sunrise must be conducted IFR.

Special Notices:

- Firearms or weapons may not be taken into the Bahamas without prior permission from Customs.
- Exercise caution at all uncontrolled airstrips. Recommended procedure is to overfly at 1,000 ft and observe, before making left pattern downwind. Announce identification, location and intention on 122.8 MHz (and monitor, prior to arrival) before turning final—and before taxiing out for takeoff.
- Use of US military airfields is by prior permission only, except in emergency.
- Flights from Bahamas to Florida must have a flight plan, DVFR flight FAR 99. See DOD, National Security. Bahamian Aeronautical Information Services have an informal agreement to accept, transmit, obtain approval from FAA. File in person or by telephone at least 15 minutes prior to takeoff.

Miami Radio—to open flight plan	122.7
Miami Radio—Grand Bahama Remote	126.9
Miami Radio—Eleuthera Remote	126.9/122.3
Eleuthera Back Up	118.4
Miami Radio—Grand Turk Remote	118.4
All USAF Bases (Grand Bahama, Eleuthera, San Salvador)	126.2

Nassau Radio—Remote at: Bimini, Grand Bahama, Eleuthera, Great Exuma		124.2
Freeport—Approach		126.5
	Tower	118.5
Nassau— Approach		121.0
	Tower	119.5

You can air-file to Nassau Radio on 124.2. For your return, file either with Nassau or Miami, using their remoted stations.

CUSTOMS AND IMMIGRATION

You'll need five (5) copies of the Customs Declaration form if you plan on making a stop-and-hop within the Bahamas, and you'll have to make your entry and exit from a designated airport. On arrival you surrender two copies; the third is then stamped as a cruise permit; and the last two are given up when you leave.

There's a $3 per person exit tax, which you can usually circumvent by providing work titles to your crew—a well-known filmmaker recently went through with pilot and co-pilot, navigator, flight engineer, and three flight attendants. He didn't pay a cent.

INSURANCE:

Usually not a problem, but consult your insurance agent or broker.

CURRENCY:

Cash (US currency) is acceptable throughout the Bahamian islands. Fuel credit cards not necessarily so. One way around this problem is to apply for a *carnet*—an international fuel charge card, available from all major fuel companies.

PROOF OF CITIZENSHIP

You'll presumably have your passport with you, though you will need proof of citizenship in the Bahamian Islands if you've no passport.

US CUSTOMS AND IMMIGRATION

There's no requirement to file with US Customs on departure, but if you've recently bought a new camera or portable radio equipment or suchlike you may want to register it with Customs prior to leaving. This can save hassles on your way back, since there's busy trade in Freeport and Nassau in such items as these and calculators and so forth.

You must clear Customs on your return, and you can check about the best procedure/airport with the FBO who sends you on your way. Do check whether US Customs is still charging an overtime fee for weekend, holiday, or late arrivals before you leave. This overtime charge varies from place to place and can knock a nasty dent in your pocket on occasion. (Why the US Customs continues this anachronistic procedure is known only to them; there have been numerous requests that they drop the requirement, since they are a public service.)

US Customs must be advised in advance of your ETA, which means ADCUS in the Remarks section of the flight plan. It also helps to contact Miami International FSS (126.7 and 126.9) as far out as possible, asking them to forward the ETA to the Airport of Entry you're headed to.

Airports of Entry where fuel Is Usually Available

Andros Island:	San Andros (100—usually)
Berry Islands:	Chub Cay
Eleuthera:	Rock Sound
Grand Bahama:	Freeport
	West End
Great Abaco:	Treasure Cay
	Marsh Harbor
Great Exuma:	George Town

Check Lists

CHARTS

Flight Planning

VFR/IFR Gulf of Mexico and Caribbean Planning Chart.
Scale: 1 : 6,270,551 (1 inch = 86 NM).
On reverse side of Puerto Rico/Virgin Islands LAC, which is extremely useful to have anyway. It provides data of mileages between Airports of Entry, plus a Directory of Airfields with some details of facilities and servicing.
ONC (Operational Navigation Chart) series have the same purpose as the WAC series, but are 42″ × 57½″ as compared to the WACs at 22″ × 30″.
ONC J-27 and K-27 good for flight planning.
Miami Sectional—a good tip. Buy two and tape together, since Bahamian coverage is split across both sides.
WAC CH-25 and CJ-26 cover the entire group of Bahamian Islands.
(DOD) L-5 gives radios, or the Jeppesen Miami Area radio facility chart.

In Flight

Puerto Rico/Virgin Islands Local Aeronautical Chart (reverse side of VFR/IFR Gulf of Mexico & Caribbean Planning Chart)
WAC (World Aeronautical Chart) series CJ-27 and CK-27 provide similar information as ONC series above.
V30-35 BAHAMA ISLANDS-LEEWARD ISLAND North Atlantic Ocean Air Navigation Chart.

Navaids

Enroute Low Altitude Caribbean and South America, published every 56 days:

L-3,
L-5/L-6 (one chart)
A-1/A-2 (one chart)

PUBLICATIONS

Enroute Supplement Caribbean and South America Handbook—Department of Defense publication.

Caribbean and South America Low Altitude Instrument Airproach Procedures—Department of Defense publication.

NB: The people at Jepperson also provide a Caribbean and South American service, on the usual basis.

DOD Supplement can be ordered through your normal chart supplier, or from the Defense Mapping Agency Aerospace Center, St Louis Air Force Station, Missouri 63118. If you are stopping in at Puerto Rico International, the FAA offices—located within the airport—usually have copies available for visiting pilots.

PLUS—*Caribbean Flite Guide* from Caribbean Flite Guide Co., P.O. Box 191, Port of Spain, Trinidad and Tobago. Introduced in 1973, it's a baby Jepp for the islands and amended quarterly.

EMERGENCY GEAR

While an emergency overwater survival pack can be rented at many Florida FBOs, you may want to compile your own.

- Life Preserver (one per person)
- Life raft (load capacity, with canopy)
- Hand inflator (backup for CO_2 inflater)
- ELT (portable)
- Emergency flares
- Marker dye
- Solar still
- Fresh water
- C-rations
- Paddles, sea anchor, rope
- Fishing kit, hooks and line
- Mirror
- Small first-aid kit
- Waterproof flashlight plus spare batteries
- Fort Pierce Flying Service, Inc., at St. Lucia County Airport, Ft. Pierce, FL 33450, has a comprehensive selection of survival gear ranging from life vests to 3-5-person rafts. These are available for rent or purchase, and credit cards are okay. If using cash, a security deposit of half the purchase price (refundable on your return) is required.

ADDITIONAL ITEMS TO TAKE

* Chamois for straining gasoline
* Control locks and sturdy tiedown kit
* Spare quarts of oil (3 or 4) plus opener/pourer and cloth
* Spare set sparkplugs plus sparkplug wrench

* Aircraft-approved aerosol spray for "de-bugging"
* Set of battery jumper cables
* Small tool kit for aircraft
* One roll each of dielectric PVC electrical tape, "gray tape," and masking tape (wide diameter)
* One set of heat-reflecting screens for use when aircraft is parked
* Pocketknife, string, waterproof matches
* Spare pencils, sharpener, erasers (2), and jotting pads

Paperwork

* Personal logbook, current aviation and radio operator's license, medical certificate
* Above for any crew
* Passport* (and visas if required)
* Current driver's license for automobiles (you can use an international driver's license, which is obtainable through the American Automobile Association)
* Current Airworthiness Certificate
* Current Registration Certificate
* Aircraft logbook properly signed up
* Aircraft radio license
* Aircraft insurance policy, with appropriate endorsement to operate in Lesser Antilles
* Energy corporation credit cards for BP, Esso, Mobil (rare), Shell, Texaco, etc.
* Pads of General Declaration forms with carbons

Personal Gear

* Sunscreen lotion.**
* Spare box of tissues
* Light sweater for evening wear, especially if staying in mountains
* Sunshades
* Traveler's checks plus some local currency—EC dollars, French francs, or Dutch guilders—for small local expenses
* Spare set swimming gear, plus waterproof bag for wet gear

* Valid passport is the best ID when traveling in the Eastern Caribbean.

**If you follow the golden rule of not more than thirty minutes each side the first day, before 1000 or after 1530, and half as much again for the next five days you should avoid serious burning. Noxzema cream is good for those spots you missed with the sunscreen lotion.

Tables

AERONAUTICAL CHART SCALES (in statute and nautical miles).
SECTIONAL—8 Statute Miles (SM) or 7 Nautical Miles (NM) per inch
WAC and ONC—16 SM or 14 NM per inch

MILEAGE CONVERSION

1 nautical mile (6,080 feet) = 1.15 statute miles
1 statute mile (5,280 feet) = 0.87 nautical mile
1 kilometer (3,280.8 feet) = .62137 statute mile or .54 nautical mile

SPEED CONVERSIONS

1 foot per second = 60 feet per minute = 3,600 feet per hour
1 mile per hour = 88 feet per minute = 1.46 feet per second
1 knot = 101.288 feet per minute = 1.688 feet per second

US GALLONS

1 US gallon = .83268 imperial gallon
1 gallon = 231 cubic inches = 0.134 cubic feet = 3.785 liters.

MILLIBARS—
INCHES OF MERCURY

MILLIBARS (Mb)		**INCHES OF MERCURY (In Hg)**
1026.1	—	30.30
1022.7	—	30.20
1019.3	—	30.10
1015.9	—	30.00
1013.2	**Standard atmosphere**	29.92
1012.5	—	29.90
1009.1	—	29.80
1005.7	—	29.70
1002.3	—	29.60

ENGLISH TO METRIC

1 inch	25 millimeters or 2.54 centimeters
1 foot	0.3 meter
1 yard	0.9 meter
1 mile	1.6 kilometers or 1,609.3 meters
1 square inch	6.5 square centimeters
1 square foot	0.09 square meter
1 square yard	0.8 square meter
1 acre	0.4 hectare
1 cubic inch	16 cubic centimeters
1 cubic foot	0.03 cubic meter
1 cubic year	0.8 cubic meter
1 quart	0.95 liter
1 gallon	3.79 liters
1 ounce (avdp)	28 grams
1 pound (avdp)	0.45 kilogram
1 horsepower	0.75 kilowatt

METRIC TO ENGLISH

1 millimeter	0.04 inch
1 centimeter	0.39 inch
1 meter	3.3 feet or 1.1 yard
1 kilometer	0.6 mile
1 square centimeter	0.16 square inch
1 square meter	11 square feet or 1.2 square yards
1 hectare	2.5 acres
1 cubic centimeter	0.06 cubic inch
1 cubic meter	35 cubic feet or 1.3 cubic yards
1 liter	1.05 quarts (liquid)
1 cubic meter	35.31 cubic feet
1 gram	0.035 ounce (avdp)
1 kilogram	2.2 pounds (avdp)
1 kilowatt	1.3 horsepower

WEIGHTS

1 gallon of gasoline = 6.0 pounds
1 cubic foot = 7.5 US gallons
1 gallon of oil = 7.5 pounds
1 gallon of kerosene = 6.75 pounds
1 gallon of methanol = 6.62 pounds
1 gallon of water = 8.33 pounds
1 inch of mercury = .491157 pounds per square inch or 70.7266 pounds per square foot

KG	*KG/LB*	*LB*	*KG*	*KG/LB*	*LB*
0.454	1	2.205	9.072	20	44.092
0.907	2	4.409	13.068	30	66.139
1.361	3	6.614	18.144	40	88.185
1.814	4	8.818	22.680	50	110.23
2.268	5	11.023	27.216	60	132.28
2.722	6	13.228	31.751	70	154.32
3.175	7	15.432	36.287	80	176.37
3.629	8	17.637	40.823	90	198.42
4.082	9	19.842	45.359	100	220.46
4.536	10	22.043			

Club Med

Club Mediterranee was originally founded in 1950 as a sports association by Gerard Blitz, a former member of the Belgian Olympic team, and a group of friends. That year the Club opened the vacation village Alcudia, in Majorca, Spain, to some 2,500 members. It was the first of what are now 78 vacation centers around the world.

Life at Alcudia that first year was primitive, with accommodations under canvas and the gentle members sleeping in sleeping bags. They also had to take turns at cooking food and washing dishes, for in those early days the staff numbered just 5 sports instructors.

But Blitz's unusual vacation idea struck a chord with the more adventurous, and Club Med soon became known among Europe's French-speaking population as a place to have fun in the sun. Club Med also developed a significant English following and began to grow; today it is the world's largest vacation village organization with a combined active membership of more than a million.

Ranging in accommodations from traditional thatched-roof housing with minimal furnishings to the more luxurious and modern hotel and bungalow-style units, Club Med's villages are to be found in 24 different countries, ranging from Tahiti to Tunisia, as far away as the Indian Ocean and as near as the French West Indies and Mexico.

There are 19 ski villages, 35 summer villages, 21 year-round villages, and 3 winter seaside villages with a combined total of more than 50,000 beds. The Club provides members with more than 1,000 sports instructors, plus nearly 14,000 staff members. In North America there are approximately 125,000 US and Canadian members, of whom more than 95,000 vacationed at Club facilities in the past twelve months.

Club Med has facilities in the Lesser Antilles at both Guadeloupe and Martinique.

The all-inclusive package that Club Med sells to its members provides—says Jacques Ganin, President of Club Med Inc., who should know—all the elements needed for a complete leisure experience. These include accommodations, unlimited food and wine, extensive sports facilities with free instruction and equipment, together with evening entertainment. There are no hidden extras such as tipping, service charges, or rental fees for sports equipment and beach chairs.

At the *Caravelle* in Guadeloupe, activities take place around the duplex hotel, which contains the dining room, bar, dance floor, cabaret, and lounging areas, plus discotheque. Accommodations are located in wings to either side and in a separate building just a few steps away. The village has its own boutique and beauty salon, plus a French/English language lab and swimming pool.

Sports provided here include tennis (6 courts), scuba (deep dives at Pigeon, where there is a government-protected underwater preserve) for experts and beginners, sailing, snorkeling, swimming, and wind-surfing. Calisthenics, yoga, petanque (similar to bocce), volleyball, and table tennis are also regular items.

Over at *Fort Royal*, where you'll find the only "Mini-Club" in the Western Hemisphere (for children of four to twelve years old), families are housed in hotel rooms where an extra bed can be added for a child, while couples and singles are provided accommodations in bungalow-like buildings, all rooms being air-conditioned with twin beds plus private bathroom.

Amenities include evening restaurant plus bar, nightclub, and discotheque, a boutique and swimming pool. Sports here are similar to the Caravelle—the scuba diving is also at the Pigeon facility—plus archery and basketball.

Buccaneer's Creek in Martinique was supposedly the lair of one of the more bloodthirsty pirates of earlier times. Be that as it may, today this resort is exceedingly popular with the younger set, who enjoy the spacious grounds here.

There's a two-level domed activities building, which houses the bar, dining areas, and entertainment complex with theater, and dance floor. The Cafe du Port, a conically roofed, circular building, is just a few minutes' walk from the center on the Rue du Port (Main Street), overlooking the marina and its sailboats. At the further end of the village is the new combined evening restaurant/discotheque. Beauty salon, boutique, plus French/English language lab.

Accommodations are in double-occupancy, air-conditioned, twin-bedded rooms in bungalows, and the sports provided are similar to those provided at the Guadeloupe villages.

With its French West Indies programs, Club Med also offers island cruising in the famous *Vendredi 13* (*Friday the 13th*), a 128-ft record-setting ocean racing yacht from the Martinique resort, and in the 72-ft schooner *Wally* from its Guadeloupe resorts.

If there's a drawback, it's that vacation plans are booked by the week only, beginning and ending on a specific day. No refund or credit is given for unused days resulting from a premature departure—unless at the request of the Club, or due to illness or death in the family.

As against that, for the money—which is reasonable when you consider it includes full board and lodging plus wine at lunch and dinner, and the use of sporting equipment plus free instruction (horseback riding is extra), plus evening entertainment, no taxes or tipping (tipping is absolutely n-o-t permitted)—you get extraordinarily good value. This is one type of vacation you may want to check out, if you prefer a truly casual atmosphere where a bathing suit, caftan, light slacks or jeans, shorts, sport shirts, and T-shirts are about as formal as you'll get. The ultimate in comfort is the Club Med *pareo*—a colorfully printed length of cloth that in turn can serve as sarong, toga, stole, skirt (kilt, even), and is practically a complete wardrobe in itself. And then, of course, the Club usually has at least one beach where nobody's going to bother you if you want to swim au naturel—another part of the charm.

A word about the staff: they're known as *gentils organisateurs* or GO's for short. It's French for nice organizers, and they're not like other hotel employees. Rather, they're working members of the club, and are employed because of their interest in things you may want to know more about, such as tennis, scuba, and sailing. They're also expert at sharing their knowledge while having fun, so that the experience will be enjoyable to you. They are available so that you will enjoy yourself, and they'll be dining and dancing alongside.

Once you're at a Club Med village, you'll find that you've discovered a virtually classless society—bikinis are great social equalizers. And money isn't used at all—except when you leave. For drinks at the bar, the currency is the Club Med pop-bead, which can be worn as a neckpiece, bracelet or ankle band. They're charged by the strand by signing at the hostess desk. You settle up when you leave.

As for the reason for the weekly unit of booking, the Club has found that it usually takes a few days for its members to unwind from the rat-race before plunging into the full schedule of activities available. So bear with them: they're doing it all for you.

Leeward Islands Air Transport [LIAT]

The tale behind LIAT (Leeward Islands Air Transport) is only worthy of the pen of Nevil Shute or Ernest Gann, because it concerns the efforts of one individual—to start with—to put an idea into practice. As a story it ranges from the bizarre to the crassly commercial and to the effects upon human lives of decisions made by power brokers in far-away places.

West Indians in the know will tell you that the germ of the idea that led to LIAT was a result of the technical obsolescence of a certain carrier pigeon used in those long-ago days to carry dispatches from the island of Montserrat to its then governing body in Antigua. They will add, laconically, that a Kittician, who lived in Montserrat at the time, had a dream. And finally, they will remind you that in the island of Montserrat—where the LIAT story properly began—the Governor's Manse is decorated with a carved wooden shamrock on its roof, and that where the shamrock is found there'll be leprechauns.

In the days of the carrier pigeon, the only way to get around this sector of the archipelago was by boat. And there was a relative plenty of 'em, ranging from those stubby little island-built schooners—mostly cutters with a couple of foresails, a tree trunk for a mast and a mains'l cut from burlap bagging, nicely stitched—to a better class of vessel that more often than not had to drop anchor offshore because deep-water harbors were few and far between.

In those days, if you were an enterprising traveler you could occasionally hitch a ride with a millionnaire in his gin palace or, more simply, with a visiting sailor in need of a pilot or cook. Changes began soon after the cessation of world hostilities. US Air Force teams had flown submarine patrols from many of the islands during the war, leaving behind some quite suitable airfields. And soon after their departure, the British put together a new airline called British West Indian Airways as a sort of Caribbean successor to an earlier Imperial Airways. (The first commercial Caribbean flight was in 1937, when KLM ran a service for business men and visitors among the lower islands of the chain.)

BWIA's task was to provide airborne communications between the more important of the British islands. In effect this meant Trinidad, Barbados, and Jamaica, with occasional stops in Antigua. The other islands were out of the main stream flow of businessmen and politicians. Local services were few and far between and mostly the result not so much of the entrepreneurial business mind as of the aviation enthusiast who wanted to cover the costs of his flights.

It was not until 1956 that anyone thought to replace the apochryphal carrier pigeon whose duty it was to carry local dispatches between Montserrat and its seat of government in Antigua. Up till then, the pigeon—named variously Patrick Malone, O'Reilly, and Kilroy—had been the sole viable commercial link between the two islands (discounting the various ships, of course).

Vernon G. Michael, a West Indian writer who has researched this subject at length, suggests that the pigeon's replacement was determined by three equal factors: (1) lack of payload for the burgeoning of the new industry—tourism; (2) a question of mandatory retirement age—carrier pigeons, even the best of them, do not live forever; (3) the possibility of a major overhaul.

Meanwhile, Frank Delisle—the Kittician who had the dream—firmly discounts the rumor that a leprechaun showed him a pot of gold at a rainbow's end on the site of what is now Blackburne Field in Montserrat. Nevertheless, in 1956 Frank went off and bought himself a Piper Apache and began his modest inter-island service.

The payload in those days was equally modest—though bettering the pigeon's. It numbered exactly three passengers and/or freight. His Montserratian airport was a bare 1,400 ft of turf and not at all aligned to the prevailing trade-wind, as you are likely to discover for yourself when you visit. But Frank is a pilot's pilot and could cope with the escarpment that parallels Runway 14/32, and especially the mountains west and northwest of the field. (The runway today is 3,200 feet.)

Frank quickly discovered that his service was filling a very definite local need and, by early 1957, his routes had been extended to include St. Kitts, St. Eustatius, and St. Maarten. On his twice-weekly schedule, his Apache enjoyed its own progressive maintenance program carried out in San Juan, Puerto Rico, where American-trained mechanics were then available. By the end of his first year—in late 1957—a second aircraft and crew had been acquired, the aircraft being a twin-engine Beech Bonanza, Frank's personal aircraft of choice. And a formal merger between BWIA and LIAT came into being on a 75/25 percent basis.

What the Kittician pilot had proved was simply that he'd invented a better mousetrap, and business was sufficiently good to add a second twin Bonanza the following year. A third and fourth were need by 1959.

Demand continued to outstrip capacity, and so in 1960 a couple of De Havilland Herons were added to the fleet. With 6 aircraft, LIAT had developed the nucleus of its present operations, providing service through all the islands south of Montserrat to Trinidad, and to the north and west to the US Virgin Islands and Puerto Rico. Because of existing politics of international airline operation, the LIAT services into US territories were operated on a wet-lease basis (gasoline included) on behalf of BWIA.*

The early 1960s saw the opening of the tourism potential of the Caribbean islands. Some—Antigua, Martinique, Barbados, for example—had already some pre-World War II experience of what tourism could mean in terms of extra dollars or pounds sterling to the local economy. Some had worked out various plans to encourage investment from outside, but more often it was the outsiders who came and visited and then wanted in.

The result was much discussion between outside businessmen and local politicians, in which all too frequently the local businessmen were given the shaft, and in which all attempted to figure out what opportunities lay ahead for the improvement of economies, and ultimately, the bettering of life for every citizen.

Meanwhile, Frank's original, like Topsy, simply grew.

By now headquartered in Antigua, where a hangar had been built, the growth went on. The Heron Aircraft—originally employed in the Hebrides Islands of Scotland on beach runways for passengers—now serviced the smallest of islands. The Bonanzas were being used almost exclusively for charter work connected with tourism and special services and as occasional backup machinery for scheduled flights.

Finally, in 1964, the corporate decision was reached to equip with an

*An interesting example of how the US government works for its own monopolists against potential Third World competition, despite the fact that that competition is using mostly US equipment and petroleum.

AVRO 748 and move to a bigger league. At the same time, to provide fireproof and foolproof maintenance, a new, modern, fully equipped engineering hangar was designed, with a suite of office on the far side of Coolidge Airport.

Frank's crock of gold continued to prove out like an oil well. Delivery of the first 748 came in February '65 and the Herons left the fleet the next May. A second 748 had to be leased—it arrived in December—and delivery of the second purchased 748 came the following summer.

Outside the office of David Price, LIAT's general manager of marketing, is a sign. It reads: "Samson Killed Ten Thousand Philistines with the Jawbone of an Ass. Twenty Thousand Sales Are Killed Every Day with the Same Weapon."

It is, perhaps, this vigorous approach toward satisfied customers, with which David Price has imbued the company, that has enabled LIAT not merely to survive a series of slings and arrows of outrageous fortune that would have sent most other businesses running for cover, but to renew—as it will no doubt continue to do—a pending application with the CAB to operate flights between Antigua/St. Kitts and Miami, via St. Lucia and St. Maarten in the West Indies, as authorized under the traffic rights agreement between nations that is known as Bermuda Two.

One reason for this cheeky rebuke to the mighty dollar power of government-funded US airlines is that LIAT manages to rack up year after year an incredible 98 percent on-time arrival/departure record. Another is that, apart from very occasional lacerations of baggage, usually in St. Maarten, all luggage that is committed to the baggage section of the airplane arrives with its passenger.

Following the US-arranged Arab oil price hike and the winter of 1973–74, it looked as if LIAT was about to suffer the same fate as those Philistines when, according to local sources, US multinationals combined with Arab princelings to put the peoples of the world in debt when they agreed to escalate the price of oil.

Court Line, a British tourism company that had earlier acquired BWIA's 75 percent interest in LIAT, was forced into bankruptcy the August following these machinations. A large number of resort hotels were bought up by US interests, for the same reason.

Today LIAT (1974) Ltd., as the reorganized corporation is now known, is once again a healthy, profitable, and still expanding operation. And despite the recession, LIAT revenues continue to climb as they continue to serve the Caribbean people.

LIAT's headquarters is in Antigua, and they have some of the best aircraft personnel working with them. They also have an aircraft turnaround crew in Barbados. If you have any sort of mechanical hitch with your airplane, go and talk to them. They don't do servicing themselves on American equipment for obvious reasons, but you'll most likely get a useful reply to solve your problem. Because they are people, and they really *do* care.

In this all-too-brief *histoire* we've overlooked the guiding light in this tale.

Frank moved out when Court Line moved in with its team. He's still established with his new corporation—flying those Bonanzas, of course—out of Coolidge. His new operation is called Carib Aviation. Last time the author called there, there was plenty of business.

As there is for LIAT (1974) Ltd.

FURTHER READING

This is in no way intended as a detailed reading list of material about the Lesser Antilles—for lacunae the reader might start with *Caribbeana, 1900–1965: A Topical Bibliography*, by Comitas Lambros, published by the University of Washington Press, Seattle, Washington (1968); and for matters immediate in socio-economic/politico-commercial spheres refer to the *West Indies and Caribbean Yearbook 1977–78,* 48th edition, published by International Publications Service in New York (1978).

The following is, rather, a personal listing, intended to inform and entertain; and it includes a number of authors native to the region whose works are available in the United States.

Algeria, Ricardo — *History of the Indians of Puerto Rico*. Puerto Rico: Instituto de Cultura Puertorriquena, 1969.

Ayearst, Morley — *The British West Indies*. New York: New York University Press, 1960.

Blair, John M. — *The Control of Oil*. New York: Pantheon Books, 1976.

Bond, James — *Birds of the West Indies*. Boston: Houghton Mifflin, 1971.

Bond, Mary W. — *Far Afield in the Caribbean: Migratory Flights of a Naturalist's Wife*. Wynnewood, Pennsylvania: Livingston Publishing Company, 1971.

Brameld, Theodore — *Remaking of a Culture: Life and Education in Puerto Rico*. New York: Harper & Brothers, 1959.

Carrington, C. E. — *The British Overseas*. Cambridge, England: Cambridge University Press, 1950.

Cesaire, Aime — *Cadastre*, new ed. tr. from French by Gregson Davis. New York: Third Press—Joseph Okpaku Publishing Co., Inc., 1972.

——— *Discourse on Colonialism*, tr. Joan Pinkham. New York: Monthly Review Press, 1972.

——— *Return to My Native Land*, trans. from the French by Emile Snyders. New York: Panther House, Ltd., 1971.

——— *The Tempest*. New York: Third Press—Joseph Okpaku Publishing Co., Inc., 1974.

——— *La Tragedie du Roi Christophe*. New York: French & European Publications, Inc., 1974.

Clark, Sydney — *All the Best in the Caribbean.* New York: Dodd, Mead & Company, 1960.

Connell, Neville — *A Short History of Barbados.* Barbados: Barbados Museum & Historical Society, 1960.

Crouse, Nellis M. — *The French Struggle for the West Indies.* Cambridge, England: Cambridge University Press, 1943.

Davidson, Basil — *Black Mother.* Boston: Atlantic/Little, Brown, 1961.

Deerr, Noel — *The History of Sugar.* London: Chapman, 1950.

Eggleston, George T. — *Orchids on the Calabash Tree.* New York: G. P. Putnam's Sons, 1962.

Fermor, Patrick Leigh — *The Traveller's Tree.* New York: Harper & Row, 1950.

——— *Violins of Saint-Jacques.* New York: St. Martin's Press, 1977.

Forester, C. S. — *Admiral Hornblower in the West Indies.* Boston: Little, Brown & Co., 1958.

——— *Hornblower, No. 5: Beat to Quarters.* Los Angeles: Pinnacle Books, 1974.

——— *Lieutenant Hornblower.* Boston: Little, Brown & Co., 1952.

Gladwin, Ellis — *Living in the Changing Caribbean.* New York: Macmillan Publishing Co., Inc., 1970.

Harris, Wilson — *Ascent to Omai.* London: Faber & Faber, Ltd., 1970.

——— *Caroline Fox.* Philadelphia: Richard West, 1973.

——— *The Whole Armour and the Secret Ladder.* London: Faber & Faber, Ltd., 1973.

James, C. L. R. — *The Future in the Present: Selected Writings of C. L. R. James.* Westport, Ct.: Lawrence Hill and Company, Inc., 1977.

——— *Nkrumah and the Ghana Revolution.* Westport, Ct.: Lawrence Hill and Company, Inc., 1977.

Lamming, George — *Cannon Shot and Glass Beads.* London: Pan Books Ltd., 1974.

——— *The Emigrants.* New York: McGraw-Hill Book Company, 1955.

——— *In the Castle of My Skin,* Charles R. Larson, ed. New York: Macmillan Publishing Company, Inc., 1970.

Lynch, Louis — *The Barbados Book.* New York: Taplinger Publishing Co., Inc., 1964.

Maran, Rene — *Batouala: A True Black Novel*. Tr. from French by Barbara Beck and Alexandre Mboukou. Washington, D.C.: Inscape Corporation, 1972.

——— — *Djogoni*. New York: Panther House, Ltd.

——— — *Le Liure du Souvenir*. New York: Panther House, Ltd.

Mannix, Daniel P. and Cowley, Malcolm — *Black Cargoes*. New York: Penguin Books, 1976.

Naipaul, V. S. — *A House for Mr. Biswas*. New York: Penguin Books, 1976.

——— — *Flag on the Island*. New York: Macmillan Publishing Company, Inc., 1968.

——— — *Guerillas*. New York: Alfred A. Knopf, Inc., 1975.

——— — *Island Voices: Stories from the West Indies*, new ed., Andrew Salkey, editor. New York: Liveright Publishing Corporation, 1970.

——— — *The Middle Passage: The Caribbean Revisited*. London: Andre Deutsch, Ltd., 1962.

——— — *The Mystic Masseur*. New York: Penguin Books, 1977.

Pope, Dudley — *Governor Ramage, R.N.* New York: Simon & Schuster, 1973.

——— — *Ramage and the Freebooters*. London: Weidenfeld & Nicolson, Ltd., 1969.

Proudfoot, Mary — *Britain and the United States in the Caribbean: A Comparative Study in Methods of Development*. Westport, Ct.: Greenwood Press, Inc., 1976.

Roberts, W. Adolphe — *The French in the West Indies*. New York: Cooper Square Publishers, Inc., 1971.

Selvon, Samuel — *A Brighter Sun*. New York: Longman, Inc., 1972.

Sherlock, Philip M. — *West Indies*. New York: Walker & Co., 1966.

Steiner, Stan — *The Islands: The Worlds of the Puerto Ricans*. New York: Harper & Row, Publishers, Inc., 1974.

Wagenheim, Kal — *Puerto Rico: A Profile*, rev. ed. New York: Praeger Publishers, Inc., 1976.

Walcott, Derek — *Another Life*. New York: Farrar, Straus & Giroux, Inc., 1973.

——— — *Dream on Monkey Mountain and Other Plays*. New York: Farrar, Straus & Giroux, Inc., 1971.

———	*The Gulf*. New York: Farrar, Straus & Giroux, Inc., 1970.
———	*Sea Grapes*. New York: Farrar, Straus & Giroux, Inc., 1976.
———	*Selected Poems*. New York: Farrar, Straus & Giroux, Inc., 1964.
Waugh, Alec	*Island in the Sun*. New York: Farrar, Straus & Cudahy, Inc., 1955.
Westlake, Donald E.	*Under an English Heaven*. New York: Simon & Schuster, Inc., 1972.
Wilgus, A. Curtis	*Caribbean at Mid-Century* (Caribbean Conference Series: Vol. 1). Gainesville, Fla.: The University Presses of Florida, 1951. (Also numerous other studies in this series by the same author)
Williams, Eric E.	*Capitalism and Slavery*. New York: G. P. Putnam's Sons, 1966.
———	*From Columbus to Castro: The History of the Caribbean, 1492–1969*. New York: Harper & Row, Publishers, Inc., 1971.
———	*History of the People of Trinidad and Tobago*. Levittown, N.Y.: Transatlantic Arts, Inc., 1962.
———	*Inward Hunger: The Education of a Prime Minister*. Chicago: The University of Chicago Press, 1972.
———	*Negro in the Caribbean*. Brooklyn, N.Y.: Haskell House Publishers, Inc., 1970.

FAA CERTIFIED REPAIR STATIONS, AUTHORIZED INSPECTORS, AND AIR TAXI OPERATORS

Repair Stations

Certificate Number, ***Name & Address***

761–1
Arnold Greene Testing Laboratories
of Puerto Rico, Inc.
167 Quisquiya Avenue
Hato Rey, Puerto Rico 00917

761–3
Puerto Rico Int'l Airlines, Inc.
International Airport
San Juan, Puerto Rico 00913

761–5
Electric Gyro Corporation
P. O. Box 614
Humacao, Puerto Rico 00661

761–7
San Juan Avionics
Q-906 Glaicia Avenue
Urb. Vistamar
Carolina, Puerto Rico 00630

761–9
Eastern Air lines, Inc.
Caribbean Division
P. O. Box 6035, Loiza Station
San Juan, Puerto Rico 00914

761-10
Mr. Jose Hernandez Acosta d/b/a
South Electronics
3 A-16 Alta Vista
Ponce, Puerto Rico 00731

761—11F
British West Indian Airways, Inc.
Kent House Maraval
Port of Spain
Trinidad, West Indies

761-14
Antilles Air Boats, Inc.
Seaplane Ramp, Veterans, Drive
St. Thomas, U.S.V.I. 00801

761-15
Aero Service
International Airport
Box 3309
San Juan Station, Puerto Rico 00930

761-16
Dorado Wings
P. O. Box 50, Dorado Beach Hotel
Puerto Rico 00646

761-17
Liferafts Incorporated
621 Fernandez Juncos
Santurce, Puerto Rico 00901
Mailing Address
P. O. Box 2081
San Juan, Puerto Rico 00903

761-18
Borinquenair Corporation
406 Ponce de Leon Avenue
2nd Floor
San Juan, Puerto Rico 00914
Mailing Address
P. O. Box 12124
Santurce, Puerto Rico 00914

Authorized Inspectors

Albertorio, Ramon E.
Calle H-B-54
Urbanizacion Valle Real
Ponce, Puerto Rico 00731

Aloyo, Oscar
P. O. Box 267
Rio Grande, Puerto Rico 00745

Asbury, Lindell L.
P.O. Box 4232
St. Thomas, U.S. Virgin Islands
00801

Cruz-Figueroa, Rafael
Caribe de Aviacion, Inc.,
Isla Grande Airport
G.P.O. Box 3123
San Juan, Puerto Rico 00936

Delgado, Jose I.
G.P.O. Box 13187
Santurce, Puerto Rico 00909

Donato, Silvestre
West Indies Valve & Machine Works
Tallaboa, Ponce, Puerto Rico 00731

Estrella, Juan Antonio
Santa Elena G-15
Urb. Santa Elvira
Caguas, Puerto Rico 00625

Etten, Gary Albert
Roosevelt Roads Flying Club
Box 875
Ceiba, Puerto Rico 00635

Flanagan, James C.
c/o Antilles Air Boats, Inc.,
West Seaplane Ramp
Christiansted
St. Croix, U.S. Virgin Island 00820

Freehling, Charles R.
P.O. Box 731
Fredericksted
St. Croix, U.S. Virgin Islands 00840

Hernandez, Ruben
Borinquen Airport
P.O. Box 437
Hatillo, Puerto Rico 00659

Kissoonlal, Baldeo
Rhagoonan Road
Enterprises Chaguanas
Trinidad, West Indies

Martinez, Jorge Luis
St. #5, #1124, Villa Nevares
Rio Piedras, Puerto Rico 00927

Nieves Correa, Eliezer
Box 2593
Bayamon, Puerto Rico 00619

Oduber, Harold
Lloyd Smith Bldv. 16
Oranjested, Aruba, Netherland Antilles

Quinones, Luis E.
Urb. Bahia Vista Mar
Calle Marginal D-1
Loiza Station
Santurce, Puerto Rico 00913

Rivera Camacho, Eduvigis
Calle 5, Este P-116
I-8 Bo. Buena Vista
Bayamon, Puerto Rico 00619

Rodriguez, Luis A.
B-5 Llanes St.,
Urb Villa Andalucia
Rio Piedras, Puerto Rico 00926

Ruiz Hernandez, Modesto
Calle 16, Bloque M-7
Castellana Gardens
Carolina, Puerto Rico 00630

Sanchez Landron, Manuel
1174 S. E. 30St.
Caparra Terrace
Rio Piedras, Puerto Rico 00921

Tous Rosa, Jose M.
Calle #14, K-9
Castellana Gardens
Carolina, Puerto Rico 00630

Air Taxi Operators in San Juan and US Virgin Islands

34–SO–1
Dorado Winds, Inc.
Dorado Beach Hotel
Box 50
Dorado, P.R. 00646

AT–761–2
Marvin L. Kirk d/b/a
Aero Caribe
Calle A #36, Apt. 2
Perla Del Sur
Ponce, Puerto Rico 00731
Mailing address
Marvin Kirk
Aero Caribe
Mercedita Airport, Mercedita, P.R. 00715

34–SO–3
Air Best de P.R., Inc.
Calle Alamo BF-15
Valle Arriba Heights
Carolina, P.R. 00630

AT–761–5
Osvaldo Gonzales d/b/a
Vieques Air Link, Inc.
P.O. Box 487
Vieques, P.R. 00765

61–SO–7
Virgin Air, Inc.
Truman Airport
P.O. Box 2788
St. Thomas, USVI 00801

34–SO–9
Ruben Maldonado-Ortiz
d/b/a Mayaguez Air
76 Salvador Brau St.
Cabo Rojo, P.R. 00623
or
P.O. Box 3816
Mayaguez, P.R. 00708

34–SO–10
All Island Air, Inc.
P.O. Box 664
St. Thomas, USVI 00801

AT-761-7
Isle Grande Flying School &
Service Corporation
P.O. Box C
Hato Rey, P.R. 00919

61-SO-78
Francisco Cruz d/b/a
Air Vieques
Box 242
Vieques, P.R. 00765

Angel Luis Perez d/b/a
Ocean Air
P.O. Box 417
Vieques, P.R. 00765

61-SO-88
Old South Air Service, d/b/a
Old South Air Service, Inc., Air
Caribbean
San Juan International Airport
Isla Verde, Puerto Rico 00913

61-SO-89
Manuel Bracete-Ortiz d/b/a
A&B Flying, Inc.
1671 Parana St.
Urb. Rio Piedras Heights
Rio Piedras, P.R. 00926

AT-761-3
Roberto Acevedo Rios d/b/a
Aguadilla Air Service
P.O. Box F- Borinquen Branch
Bldg. 1029 Borinquen Airport
Aguadilla, Puerto Rico 00604

Sky Roads Trading Co.
P.O. Box 5723
Old San Juan Station
San Juan, P.R. 00905

AT-761-11
Air Mont, Inc.
Calle Baldorioty #17
P.O. Box 73
Vieques, P.R. 00765

AT-761-14
Miguel Fernandez
476 Cesar Gonzalez Avenue
Roosevelt, Hato Rey, P.R. 00918

AT-761-15
Beta Equipo, Inc. d/b/a
Betair Co.
P.O. Box 29236
Rio Piedras, P.R. 00929
or
Calle 4 G-12
Colinas Verdes
Rio Piedras, P.R. 00924

61-SO-20
Caribbean Air Services, Inc.
P.O. Box 164, Kigshill
St. Croix, USVI 00850

61-SO-24
Antilles Air Boats, Inc.
Seaplane Ramp, Veterans Drive
St. Thomas, USVI 00801

61-SO-26
Puerto Rico Int'l Airlines, Inc.
(PRINAIR)
Puerto Rico Int'l Airport
San Juan, Puerto Rico 00913

34-SO-33
Dr. Clarence Lloyd d/b/a
Valleyair Service
P.O. Box 3947
St. Thomas, USVI 00801

34-SO-34
Helicopter Rental Co.
P.O. Box 13278
Santurce, Puerto Rico 00908

AT-761-8
Eastern Caribbean Airways
P.O. Box 6981 - Sunny Isle
Christiansted, St. Croix
USVI 00820

34-SO-65
Terry Muniz d/b/a
Universal Aviation Training
Enterprises, Inc.
P.O. Box 5747
Old San Juan Station
San Juan, Puerto Rico 00905

61-SO-72
Trans Commuter Airline
P.O. Box 1856
St. Thomas, USVI 00801

61-SO-76
Pedro Martinez Medina d/b/a
Metro Air Cargo
P.O. Box 10432
Caparra Heights Station
San Juan, P.R. 00922

AT-761-16
Flamenco Airways, Inc.
P.O. Box 214
Culebra, P.R. 00645

AT-761-18
Thomas R. Roed d/b/a
Roed Air
P.O. Box 3368
USVI 00801

AT-761-19
Frederick G. Landon
P.O. Box 4096
St. Thomas, USVI 00801

AT-761-20
Bill N. Willard d/b/a
Air Tropic
P.O. Box 6924 Sunny Isle
Christiansted, St. Croix
USVI 00820

61-SO-67
Manuel Sanchez d/b/a
San Juan Cargo
Calle 30 SE 1174
Caparra Terrace
Rio Piedras, P.R. 00921

61-SO-85
Bernardo Cintron Molinary
Ing. Jose A. Canals 455
Urb. Eleanor Roosevelt
Hato Rey, P.R. 00918

AT-761-23
Alberto Pedreira d/b/a
Air Transit International
Calle 126 BX-6
Valle Arriba Heights
Carolina, P.R. 00630

AT-761-22
Aero Virgin Islands Corp.
Franklin Bldg. Suite 34
P.O. Box 546
St. Thomas, USVI 00801

AT-761-24
Donald J. Heber d/b/a
Island Hopper Air Charter
Ave. Wilson 1414, #405
Condado, Santurce, P.R. 00907

AT-761-21
Juan Ramon Ibern Maldonado d/b/a
Air Culebra
F-1102 Urb. Munoz Rivera
Guaynabo, P.R. 00657

SUPPLEMENTAL CHARTS FOR INFORMATION

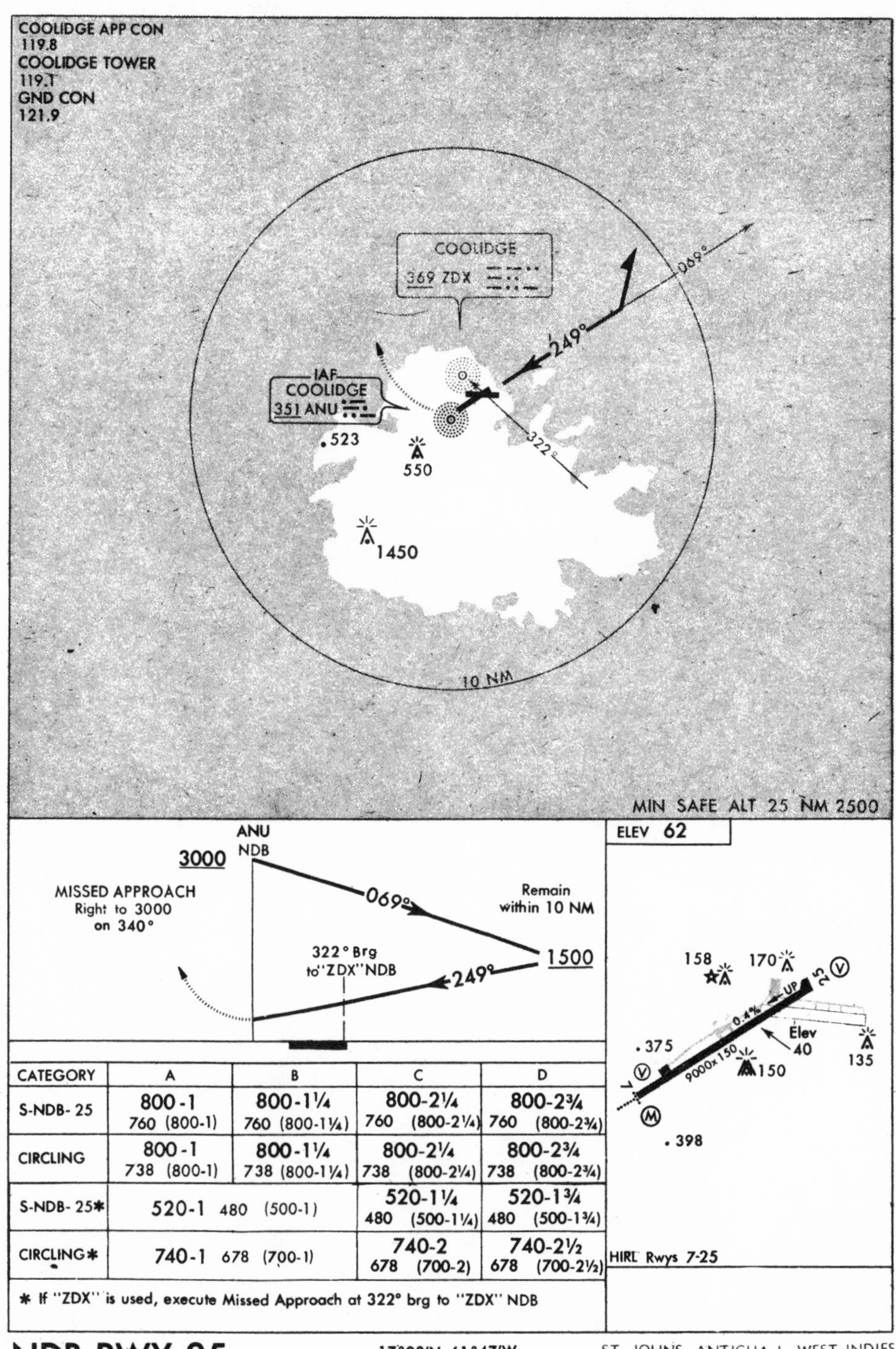

CATEGORY	A	B	C	D
S-NDB-25	800-1 760 (800-1)	800-1¼ 760 (800-1¼)	800-2¼ 760 (800-2¼)	800-2¾ 760 (800-2¾)
CIRCLING	800-1 738 (800-1)	800-1¼ 738 (800-1¼)	800-2¼ 738 (800-2¼)	800-2¾ 738 (800-2¾)
S-NDB-25*	520-1 480 (500-1)		520-1¼ 480 (500-1¼)	520-1¾ 480 (500-1¾)
CIRCLING*	740-1 678 (700-1)		740-2 678 (700-2)	740-2½ 678 (700-2½)

* If "ZDX" is used, execute Missed Approach at 322° brg to "ZDX" NDB

(Not to be used for navigation.)

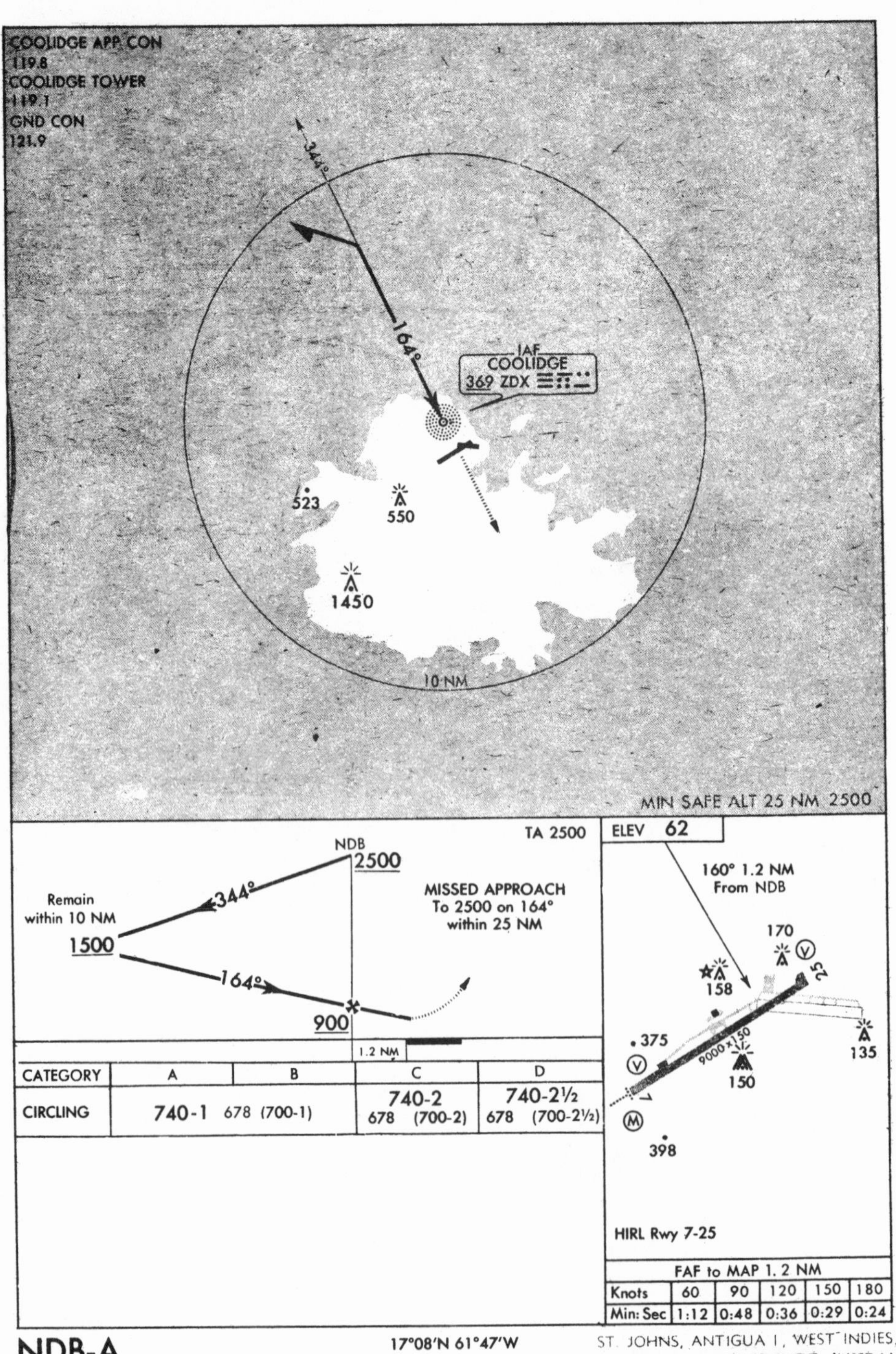

CATEGORY	A	B	C	D
CIRCLING	740-1 678 (700-1)		740-2 678 (700-2)	740-2½ 678 (700-2½)

FAF to MAP 1. 2 NM					
Knots	60	90	120	150	180
Min: Sec	1:12	0:48	0:36	0:29	0:24

NDB-A

17°08'N 61°47'W

31

ST. JOHNS, ANTIGUA I, WEST INDIES,
COOLIDGE (MKPA)

(Not to be used for navigation.)

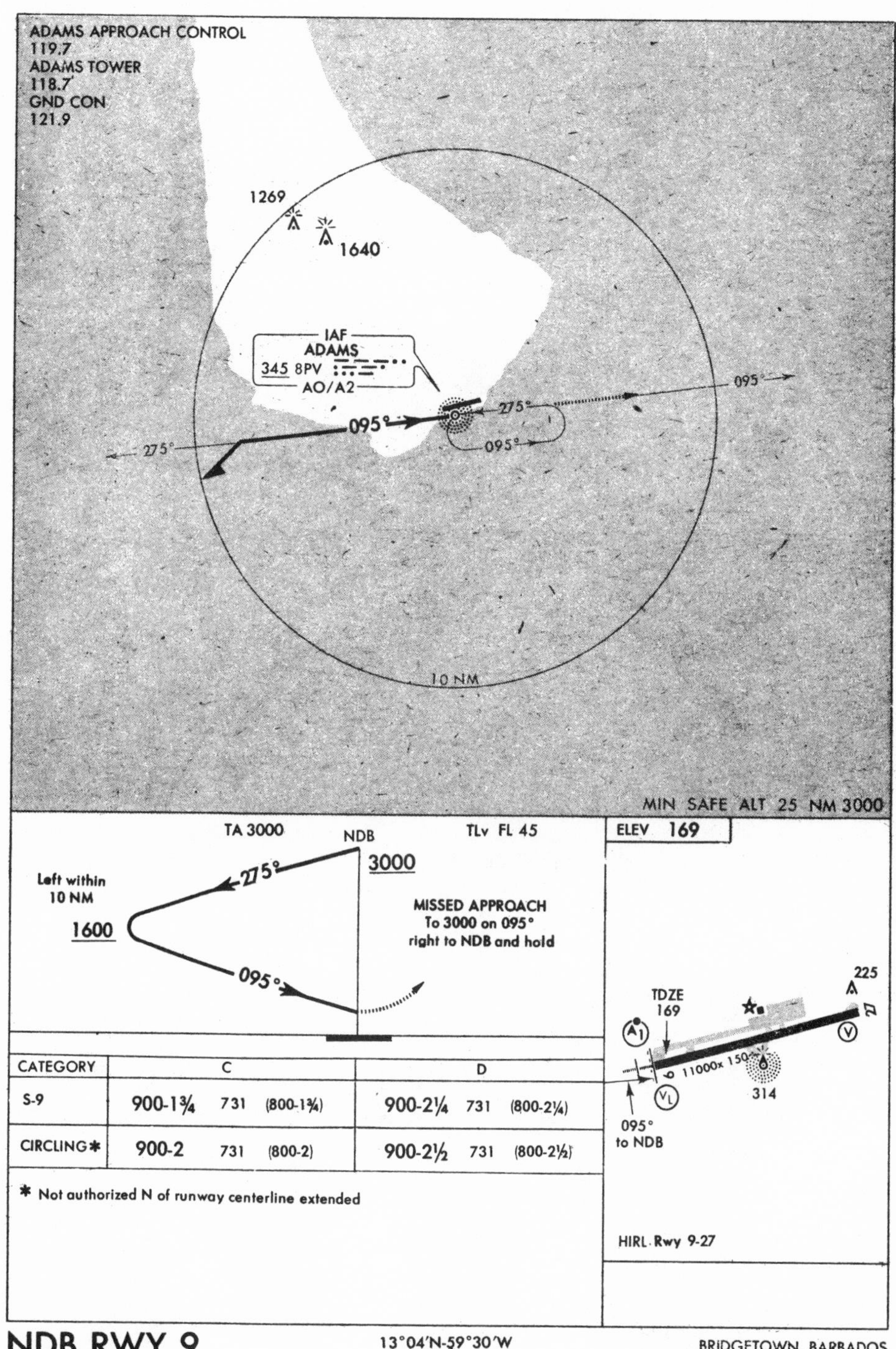

CATEGORY	C			D		
S-9	900-1¾	731	(800-1¾)	900-2¼	731	(800-2¼)
CIRCLING*	900-2	731	(800-2)	900-2½	731	(800-2½)

* Not authorized N of runway centerline extended

NDB RWY 9

13°04′N-59°30′W

66

BRIDGETOWN, BARBADOS

GRANTLEY ADAMS INTL (MKPB)

(Not to be used for navigation.)

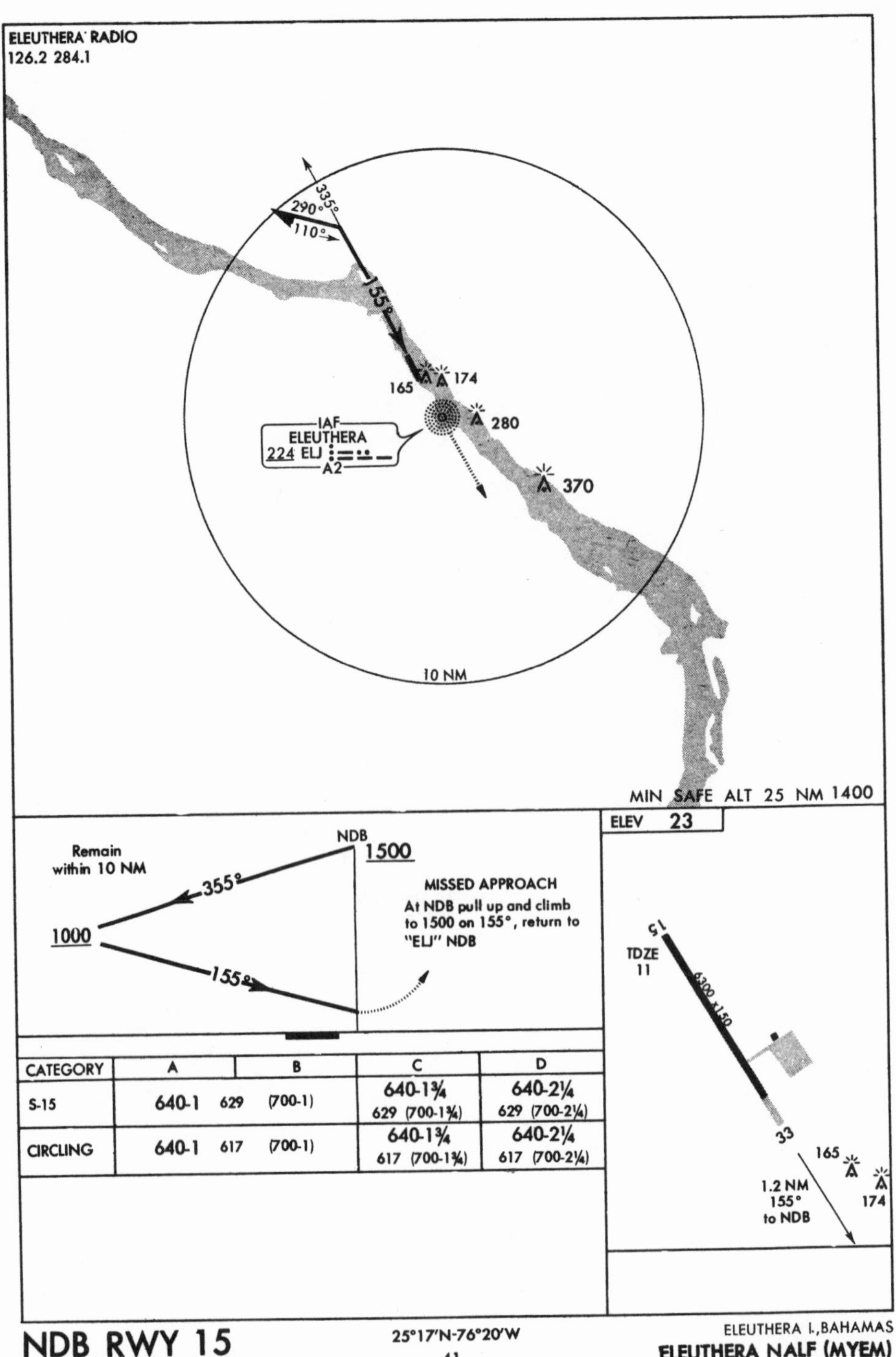

CATEGORY	A	B	C	D
S-15	640-1 629	(700-1)	640-1¾ 629 (700-1¾)	640-2¼ 629 (700-2¼)
CIRCLING	640-1 617	(700-1)	640-1¾ 617 (700-1¾)	640-2¼ 617 (700-2¼)

NDB RWY 15

25°17′N-76°20′W
41

ELEUTHERA I., BAHAMAS
ELEUTHERA NALF (MYEM)

(Not to be used for navigation.)

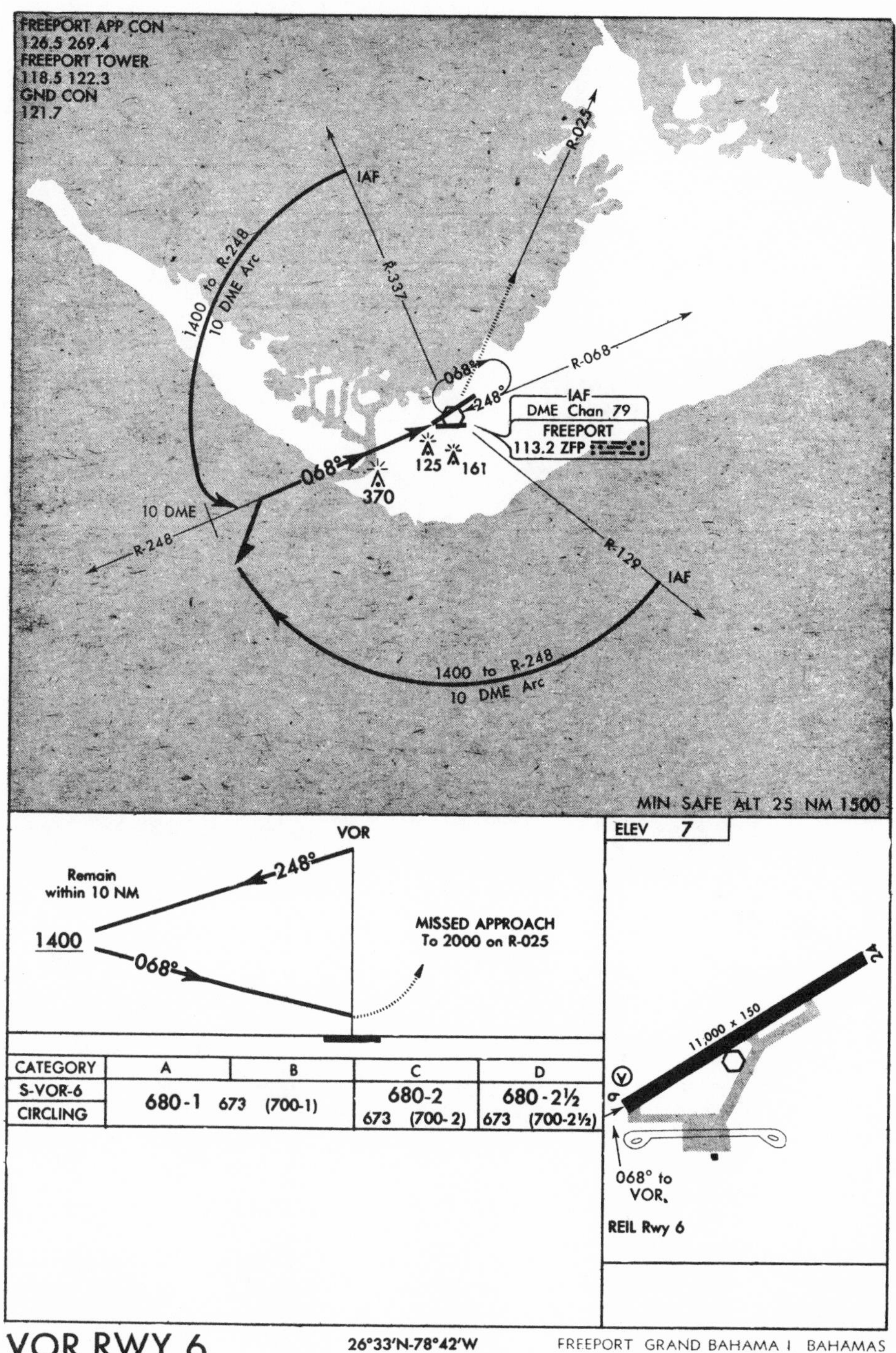

CATEGORY	A	B	C	D
S-VOR-6	680-1		680-2	680-2½
CIRCLING	673 (700-1)		673 (700-2)	673 (700-2½)

(Not to be used for navigation.)

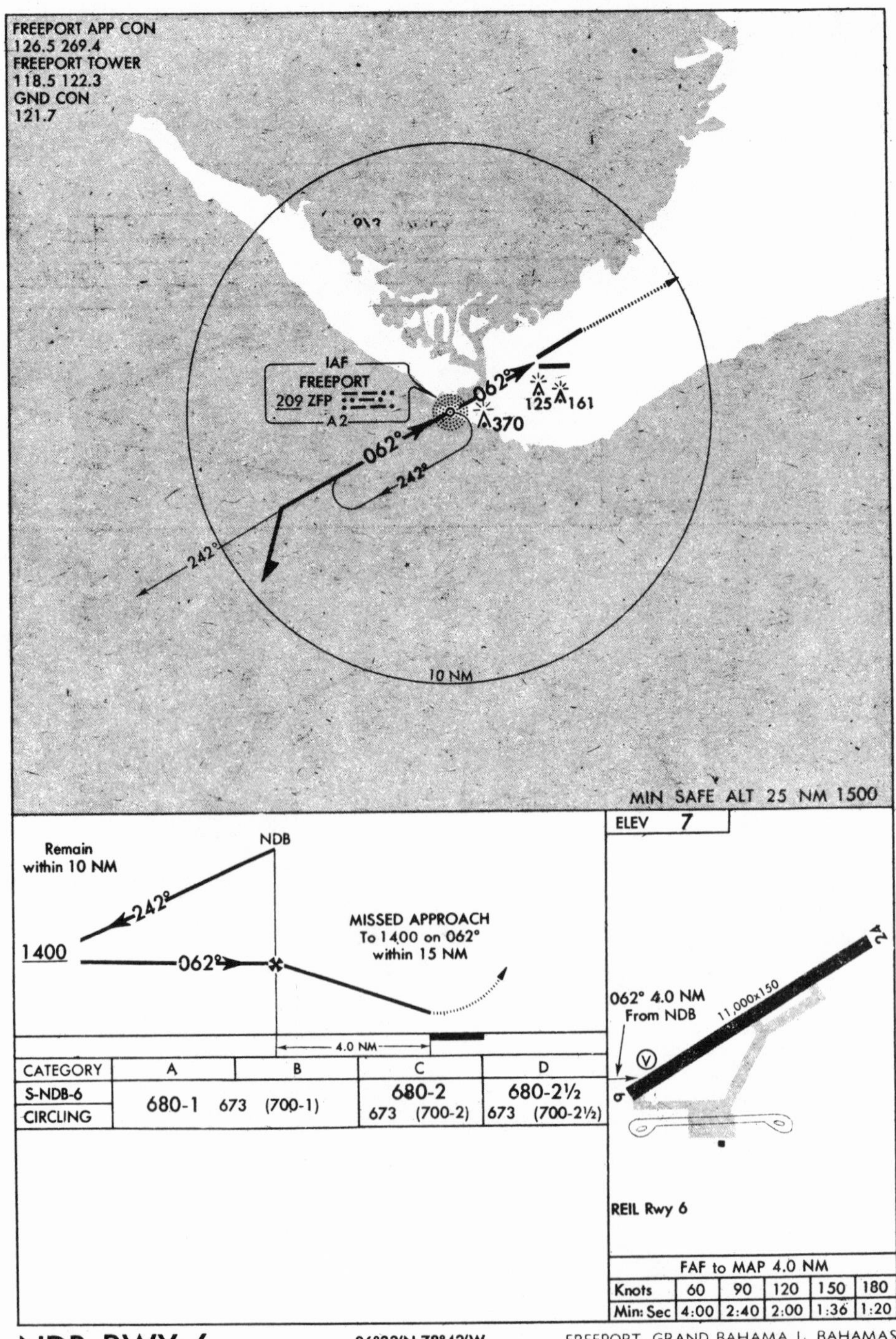
FREEPORT APP CON
126.5 269.4
FREEPORT TOWER
118.5 122.3
GND CON
121.7
IAF
FREEPORT
209 ZFP
A2
062°
242°
125
161
370
10 NM
MIN SAFE ALT 25 NM 1500
Remain within 10 NM
NDB
242°
1400
062°
MISSED APPROACH
To 1400 on 062° within 15 NM
4.0 NM
ELEV 7
062° 4.0 NM From NDB
11,000x150
24
REIL Rwy 6
CATEGORY A B C D
S-NDB-6 680-1 673 (700-1) 680-2 673 (700-2) 680-2½ 673 (700-2½)
CIRCLING
FAF to MAP 4.0 NM
Knots 60 90 120 150 180
Min: Sec 4:00 2:40 2:00 1:36 1:20
NDB RWY 6
26°33'N-78°42'W
55
FREEPORT, GRAND BAHAMA I., BAHAMAS
FREEPORT INTL (MYGF)

(Not to be used for navigation.)

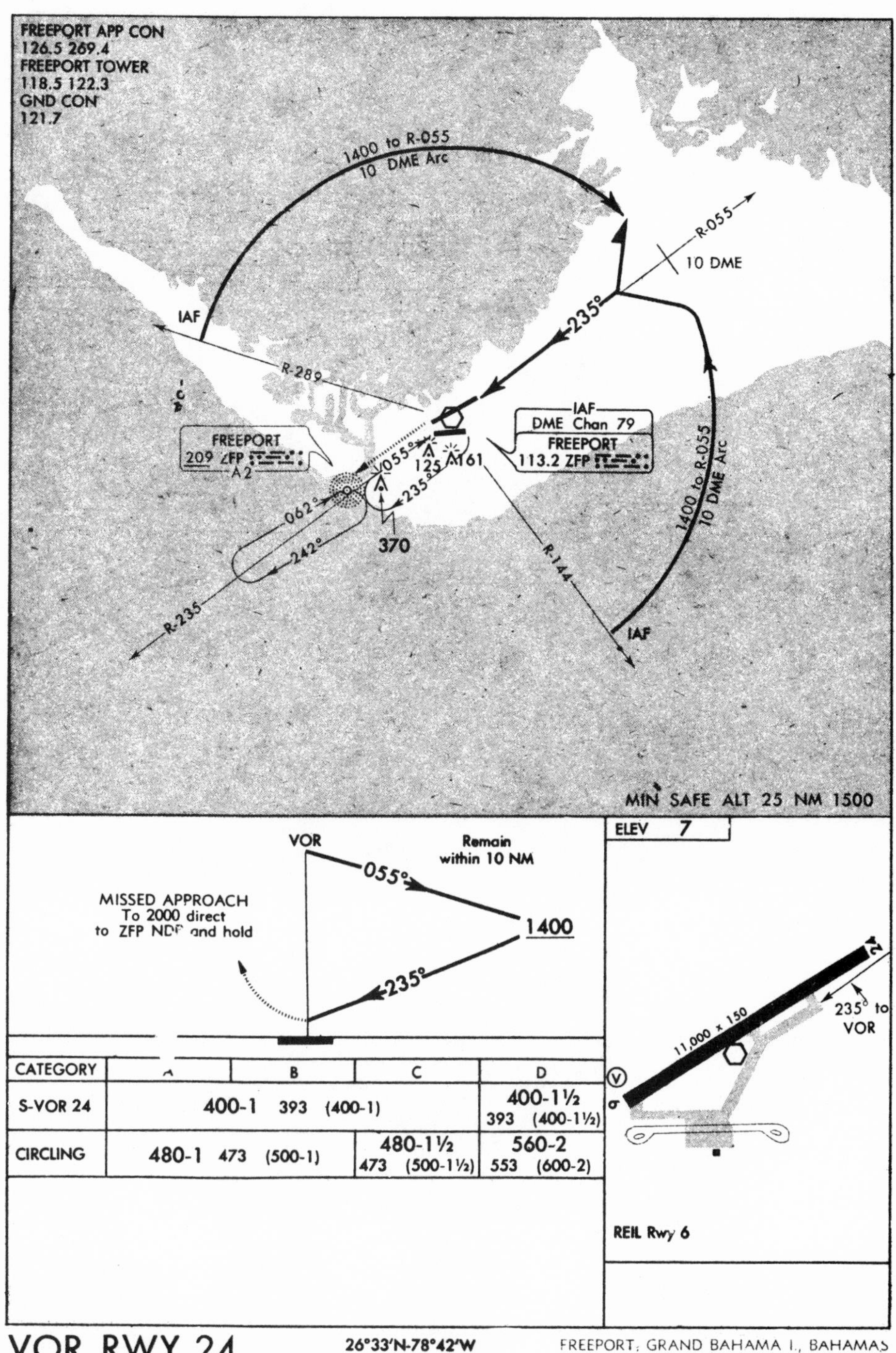

CATEGORY	A	B	C	D
S-VOR 24	400-1 393 (400-1)			400-1½ 393 (400-1½)
CIRCLING	480-1 473 (500-1)		480-1½ 473 (500-1½)	560-2 553 (600-2)

VOR RWY 24

26°33′N-78°42′W
60

FREEPORT, GRAND BAHAMA I., BAHAMAS
FREEPORT INTL (MYGF)

(Not to be used for navigation.)

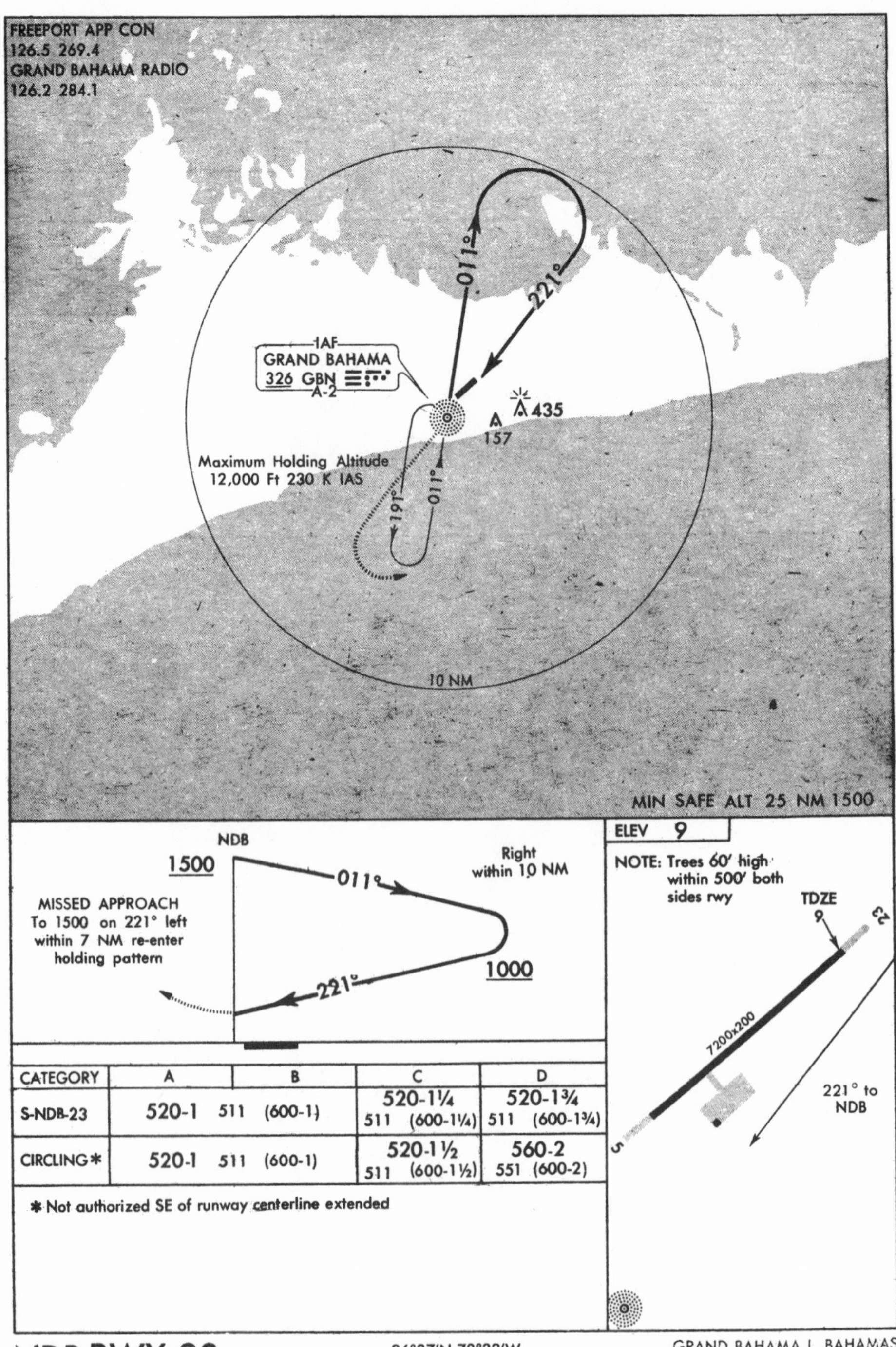

CATEGORY	A	B	C	D
S-NDB-23	520-1	511 (600-1)	520-1¼ 511 (600-1¼)	520-1¾ 511 (600-1¾)
CIRCLING*	520-1	511 (600-1)	520-1½ 511 (600-1½)	560-2 551 (600-2)

* Not authorized SE of runway centerline extended

NDB RWY 23 26°37′N-78°22′W 64 GRAND BAHAMA I., BAHAMAS
GRAND BAHAMA AUX AF (MYGM)

(Not to be used for navigation.)

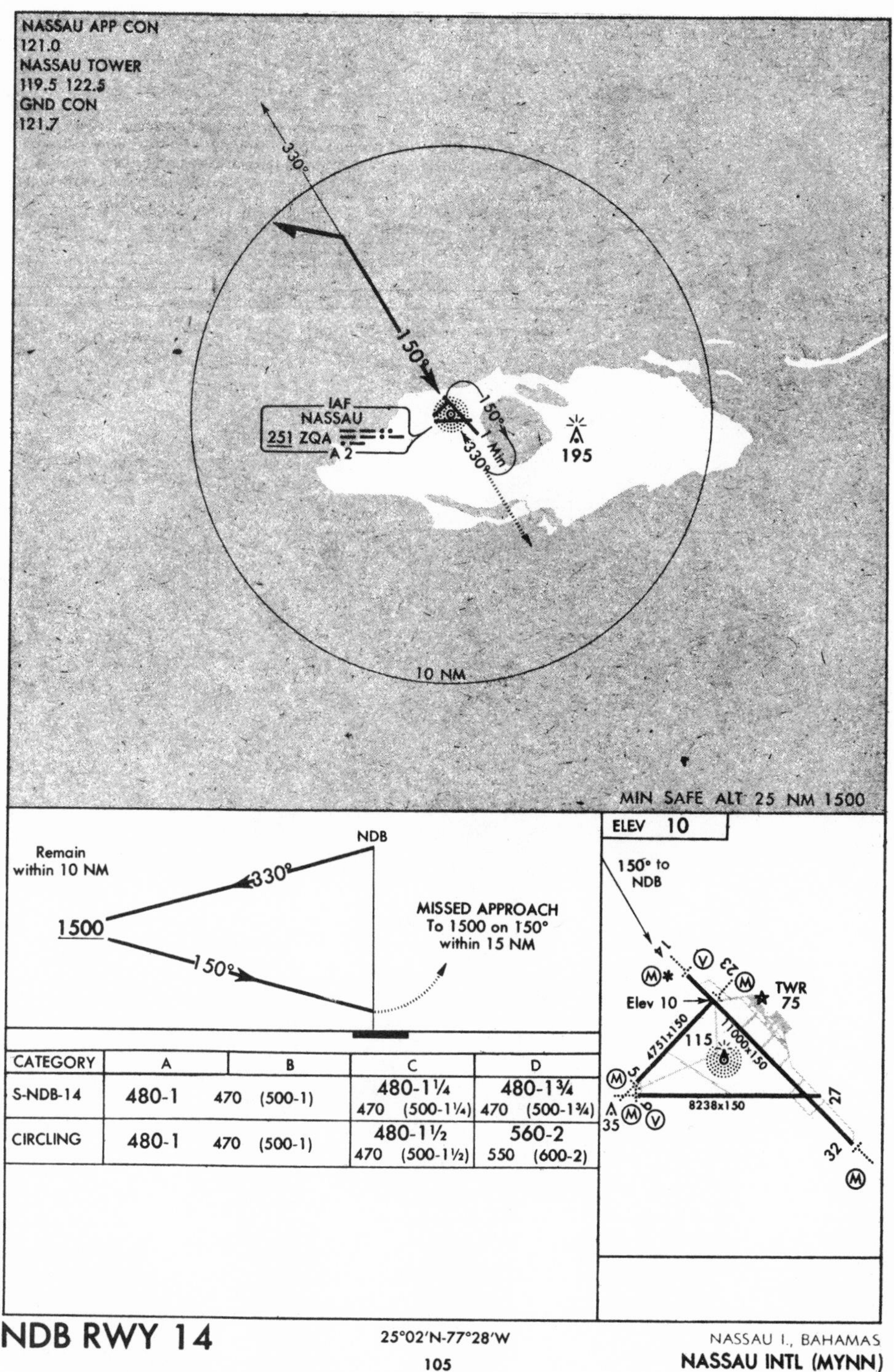

CATEGORY	A	B	C	D
S-NDB-14	480-1 470 (500-1)		480-1¼ 470 (500-1¼)	480-1¾ 470 (500-1¾)
CIRCLING	480-1 470 (500-1)		480-1½ 470 (500-1½)	560-2 550 (600-2)

(Not to be used for navigation.)

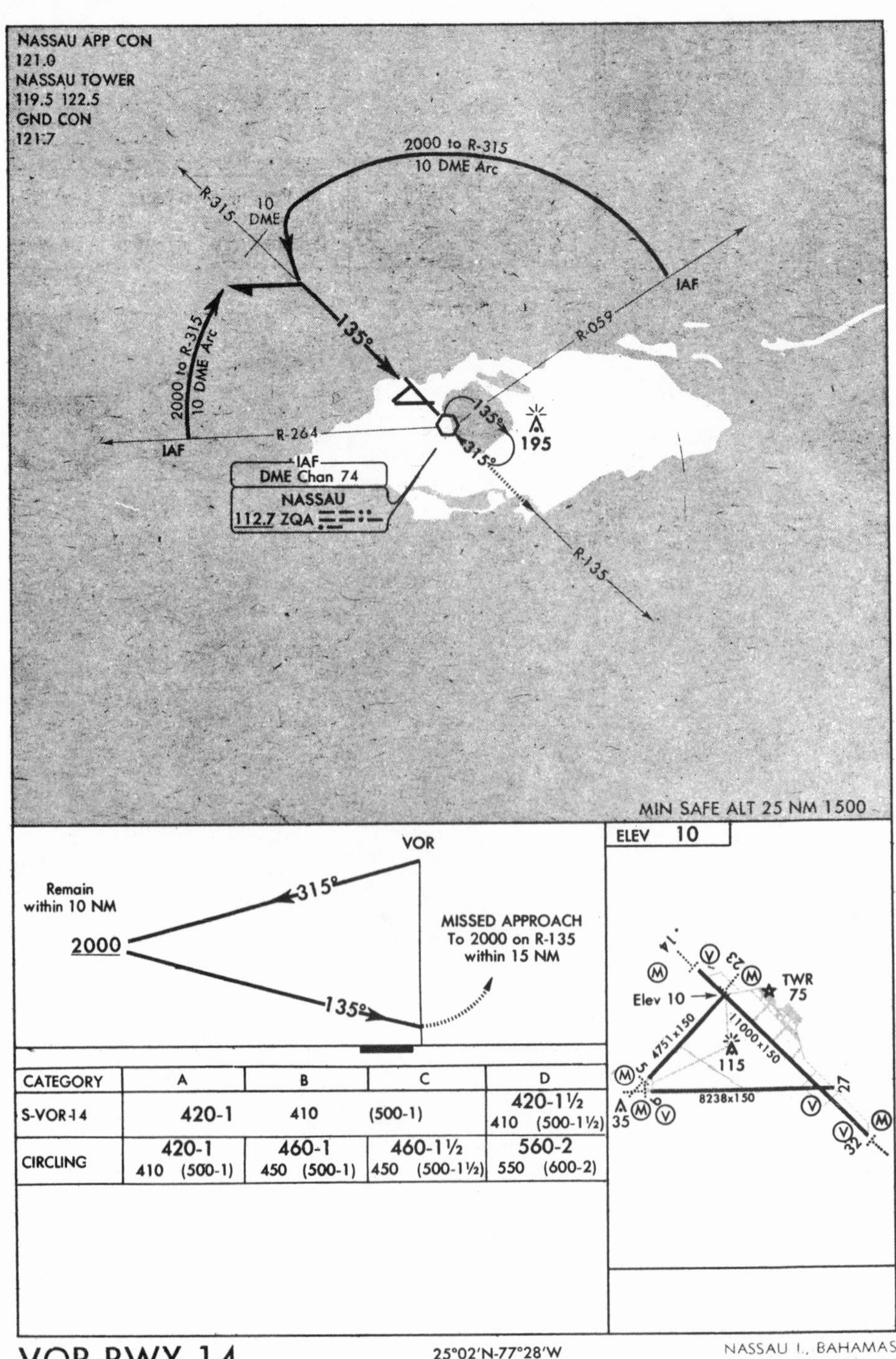

CATEGORY	A	B	C	D
S-VOR-14	420-1	410	(500-1)	420-1½ 410 (500-1½)
CIRCLING	420-1 410 (500-1)	460-1 450 (500-1)	460-1½ 450 (500-1½)	560-2 550 (600-2)

VOR RWY 14

25°02′N-77°28′W

102

NASSAU I., BAHAMAS

NASSAU INTL (MYNN)

(Not to be used for navigation.)

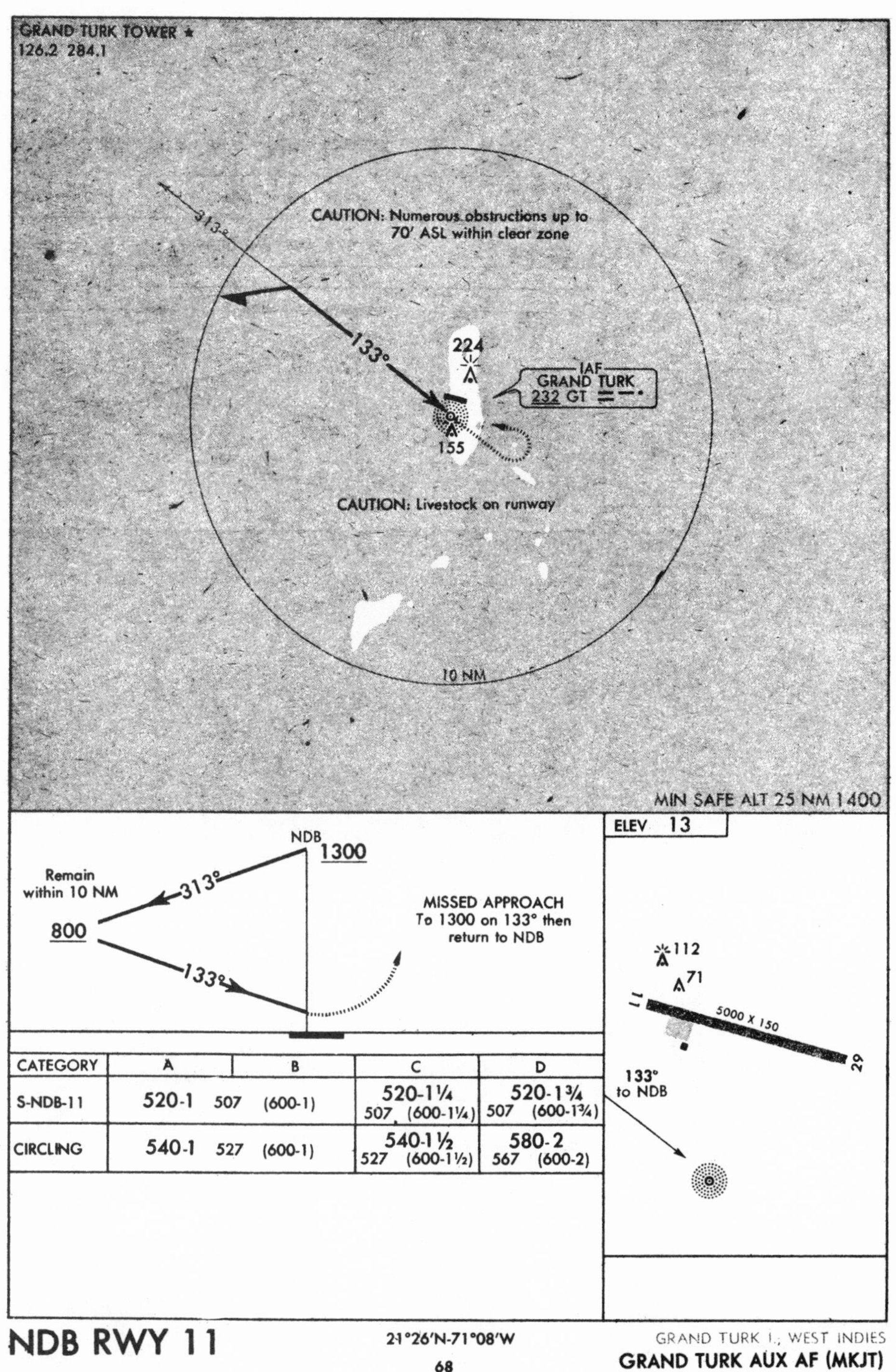

CATEGORY	A	B	C	D
S-NDB-11	520-1 507 (600-1)		520-1¼ 507 (600-1¼)	520-1¾ 507 (600-1¾)
CIRCLING	540-1 527 (600-1)		540-1½ 527 (600-1½)	580-2 567 (600-2)

(Not to be used for navigation.)

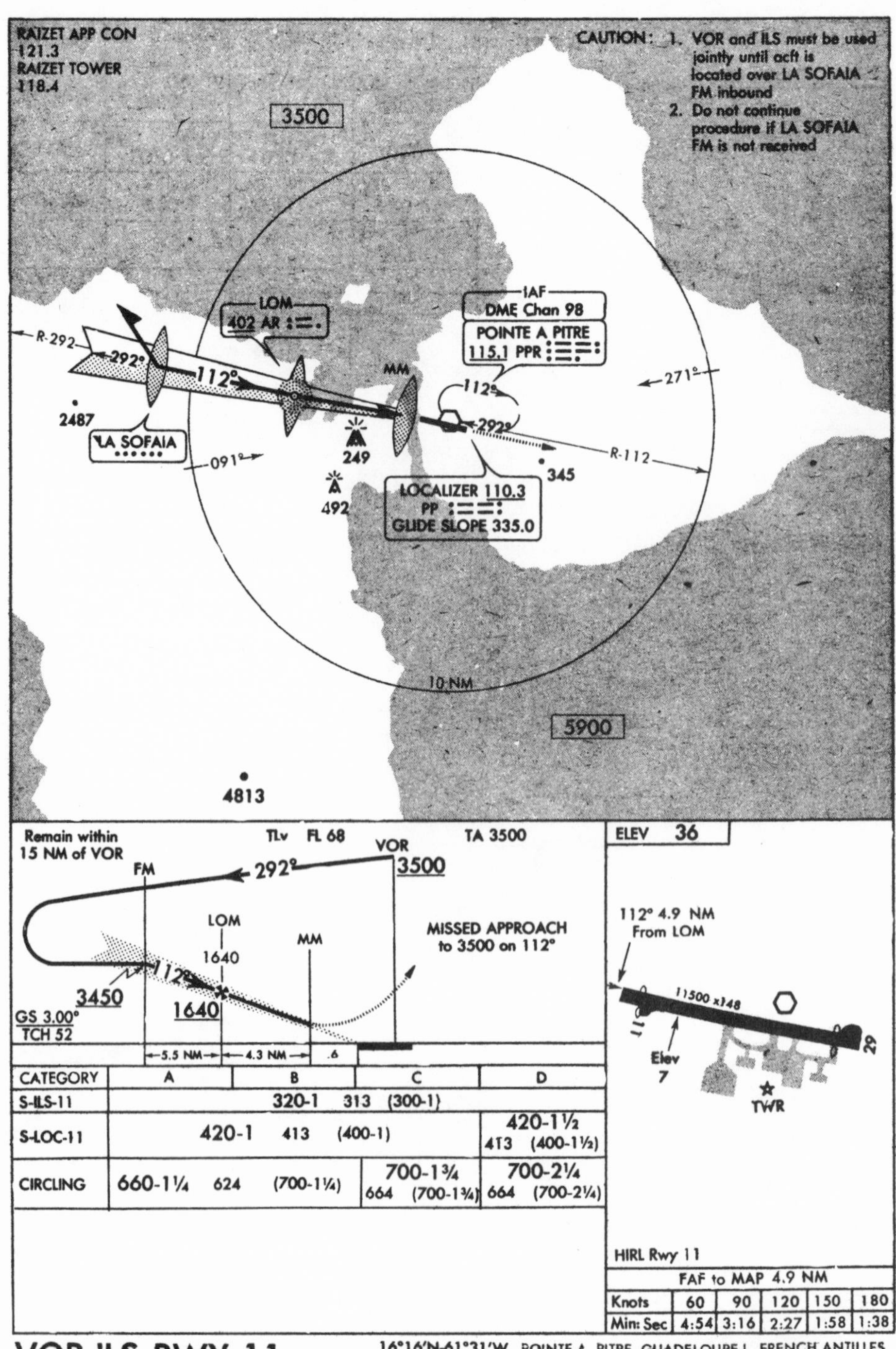

CATEGORY	A	B	C	D
S-ILS-11	320-1 313 (300-1)			
S-LOC-11	420-1 413 (400-1)			420-1½ 413 (400-1½)
CIRCLING	660-1¼ 624 (700-1¼)		700-1¾ 664 (700-1¾)	700-2¼ 664 (700-2¼)

FAF to MAP 4.9 NM					
Knots	60	90	120	150	180
Min:Sec	4:54	3:16	2:27	1:58	1:38

(Not to be used for navigation.)

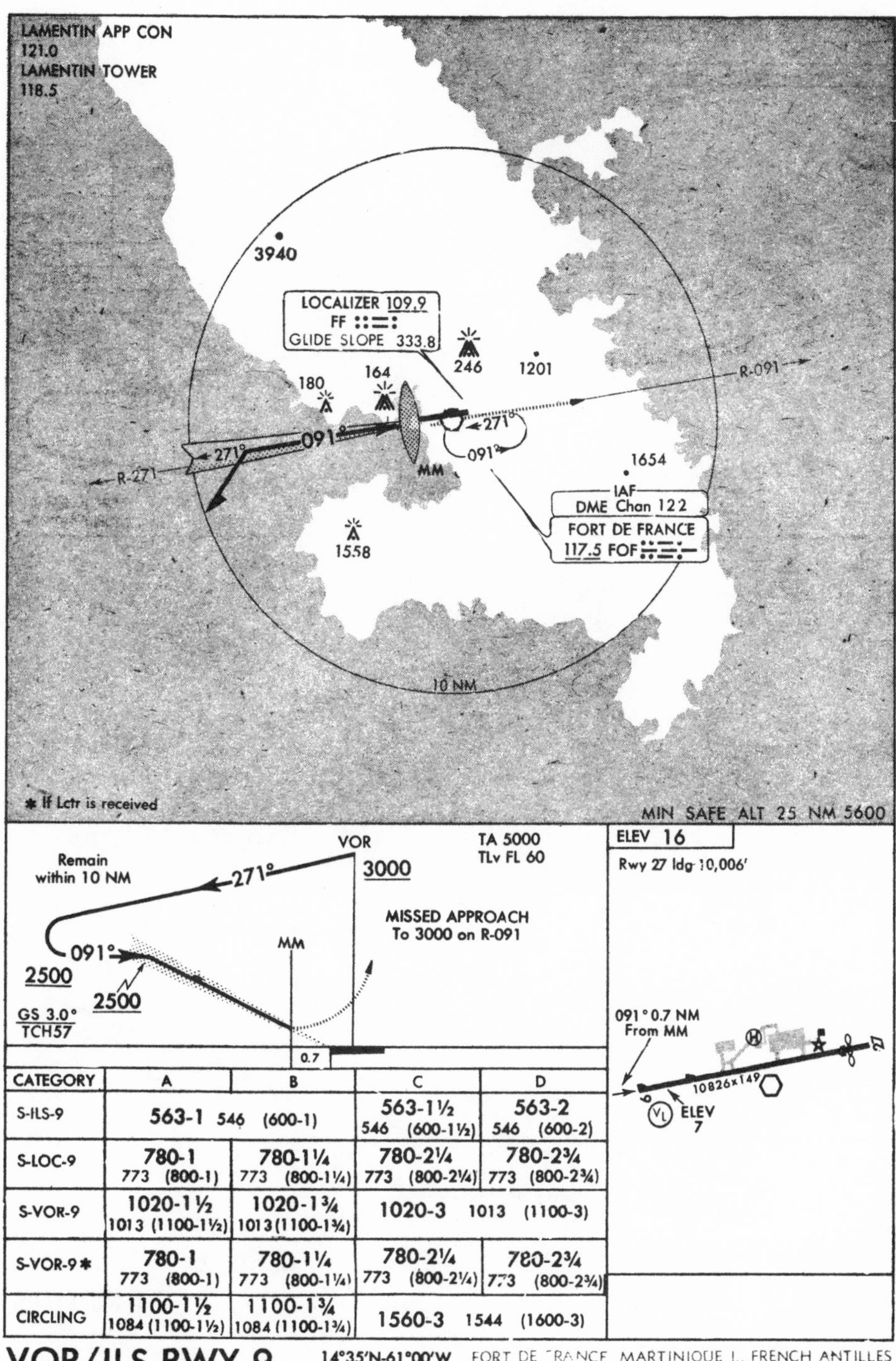

CATEGORY	A	B	C	D
S-ILS-9	563-1 546 (600-1)		563-1½ 546 (600-1½)	563-2 546 (600-2)
S-LOC-9	780-1 773 (800-1)	780-1¼ 773 (800-1¼)	780-2¼ 773 (800-2¼)	780-2¾ 773 (800-2¾)
S-VOR-9	1020-1½ 1013 (1100-1½)	1020-1¾ 1013 (1100-1¾)	1020-3 1013 (1100-3)	
S-VOR-9 *	780-1 773 (800-1)	780-1¼ 773 (800-1¼)	780-2¼ 773 (800-2¼)	780-2¾ 773 (800-2¾)
CIRCLING	1100-1½ 1084 (1100-1½)	1100-1¾ 1084 (1100-1¾)	1560-3 1544 (1600-3)	

(Not to be used for navigation.)

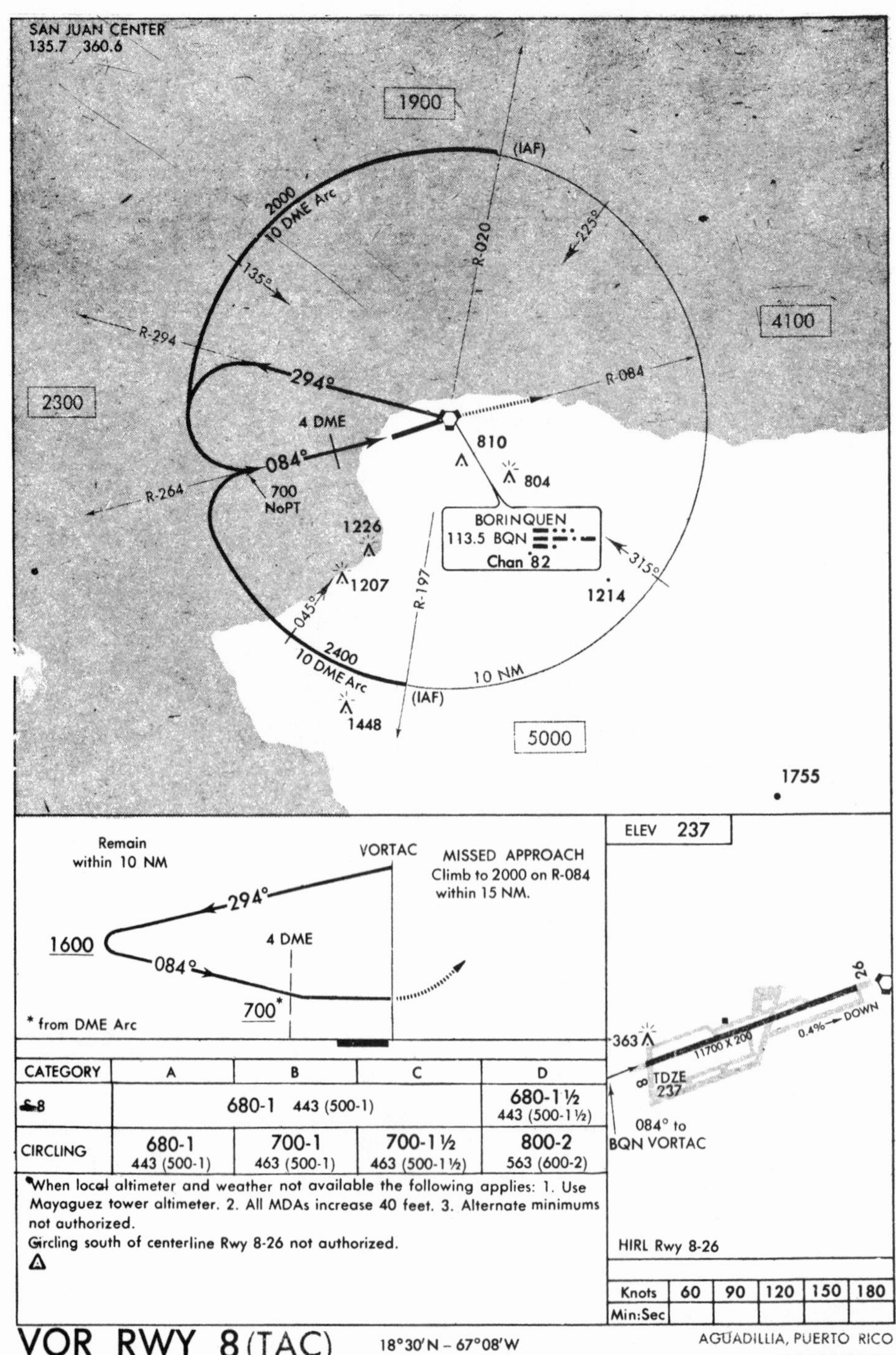

SAN JUAN CENTER
135.7 360.6
1900
(IAF)
2000
10 DME Arc
R-020
225°
135°
4100
R-294
294°
R-084
2300
4 DME
810
084°
804
R-264
700
NoPT
1226
BORINQUEN
113.5 BQN
Chan 82
315°
1207
1214
R-197
045°
2400
10 DME Arc
10 NM
(IAF)
1448
5000
1755
Remain within 10 NM
VORTAC
MISSED APPROACH
Climb to 2000 on R-084 within 15 NM.
294°
1600
4 DME
084°
700*
* from DME Arc
ELEV 237
26
363
11700 X 200
0.4% DOWN
8
TDZE 237
084° to BQN VORTAC
CATEGORY A B C D
8 680-1 443 (500-1)
680-1½ 443 (500-1½)
CIRCLING 680-1 443 (500-1)
700-1 463 (500-1)
700-1½ 463 (500-1½)
800-2 563 (600-2)
When local altimeter and weather not available the following applies: 1. Use Mayaguez tower altimeter. 2. All MDAs increase 40 feet. 3. Alternate minimums not authorized.
Circling south of centerline Rwy 8-26 not authorized.
HIRL Rwy 8-26
Knots 60 90 120 150 180
Min:Sec
VOR RWY 8 (TAC)
18°30′N – 67°08′W
15
AGUADILLIA, PUERTO RICO
BORINQUEN

(Not to be used for navigation.)

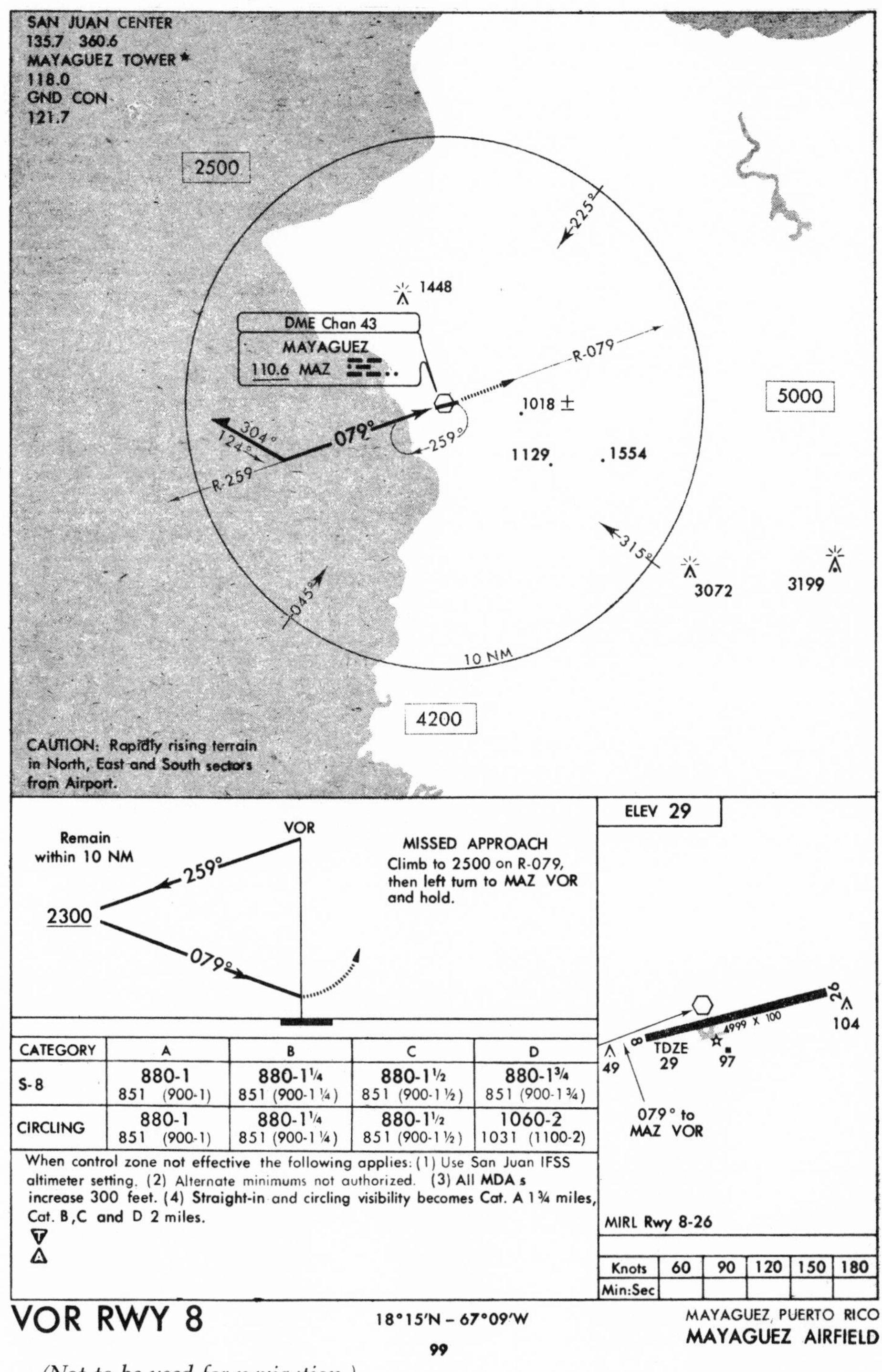

CATEGORY	A	B	C	D
S-8	880-1 851 (900-1)	880-1¼ 851 (900-1¼)	880-1½ 851 (900-1½)	880-1¾ 851 (900-1¾)
CIRCLING	880-1 851 (900-1)	880-1¼ 851 (900-1¼)	880-1½ 851 (900-1½)	1060-2 1031 (1100-2)

When control zone not effective the following applies: (1) Use San Juan IFSS altimeter setting. (2) Alternate minimums not authorized. (3) All MDA s increase 300 feet. (4) Straight-in and circling visibility becomes Cat. A 1¾ miles, Cat. B, C and D 2 miles.

(Not to be used for navigation.)

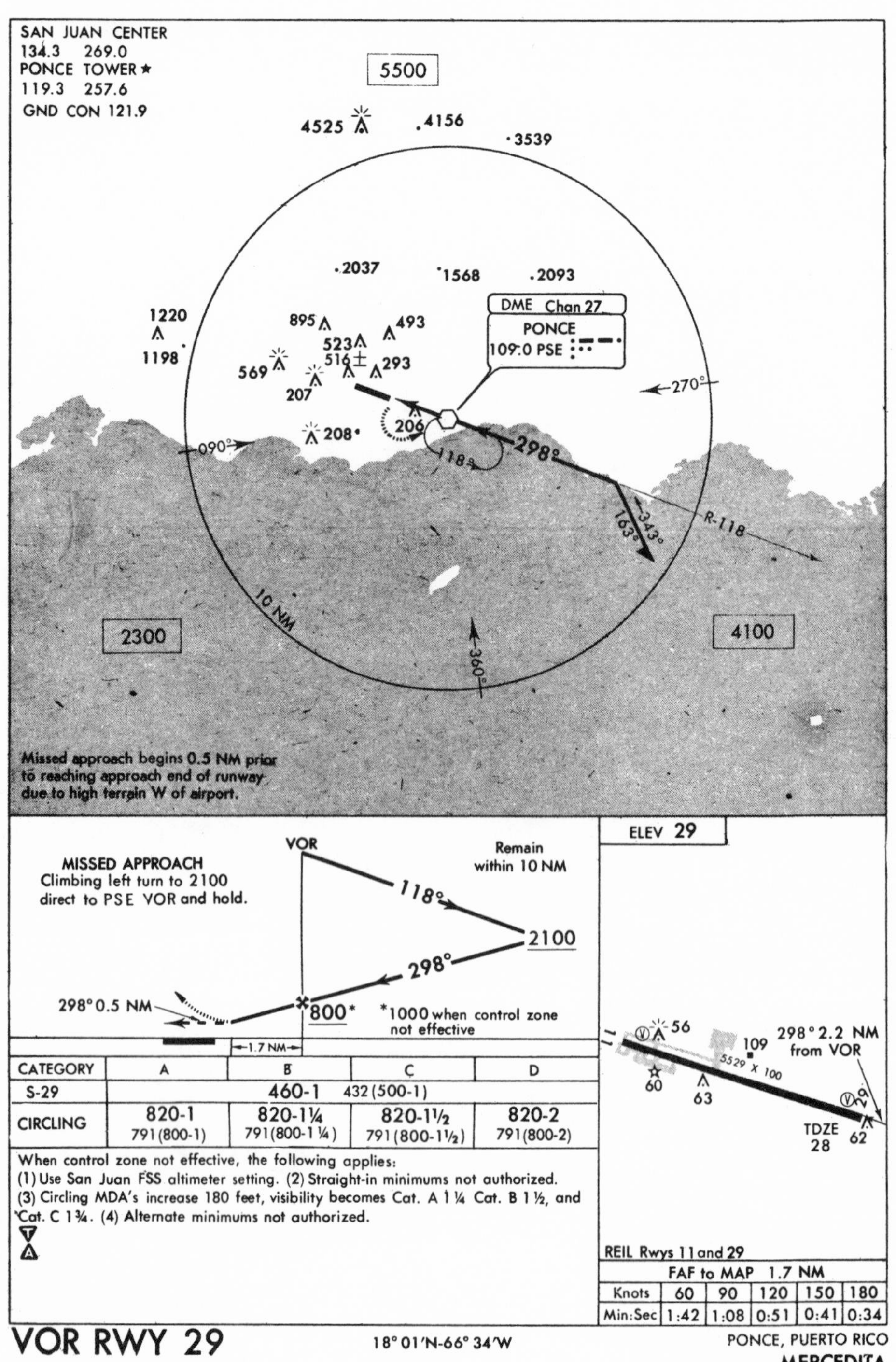
SAN JUAN CENTER
134.3 269.0
PONCE TOWER ★
119.3 257.6
GND CON 121.9
5500
4525
.4156
.3539
.2037
.1568
.2093
DME Chan 27
PONCE
109.0 PSE
1220
1198
895
493
523
516
293
569
207
206
208
270°
090°
298°
118°
163°
343°
R-118
10 NM
360°
2300
4100
Missed approach begins 0.5 NM prior to reaching approach end of runway due to high terrain W of airport.
MISSED APPROACH
Climbing left turn to 2100 direct to PSE VOR and hold.
VOR
Remain within 10 NM
118°
2100
298°
298° 0.5 NM
800*
*1000 when control zone not effective
1.7 NM
ELEV 29
56
109
298° 2.2 NM from VOR
5529 X 100
60
63
TDZE 28
62
CATEGORY | A | B | C | D
S-29 | 460-1 432 (500-1)
CIRCLING | 820-1 791 (800-1) | 820-1¼ 791 (800-1¼) | 820-1½ 791 (800-1½) | 820-2 791 (800-2)
When control zone not effective, the following applies:
(1) Use San Juan FSS altimeter setting. (2) Straight-in minimums not authorized.
(3) Circling MDA's increase 180 feet, visibility becomes Cat. A 1¼ Cat. B 1½, and Cat. C 1¾. (4) Alternate minimums not authorized.
REIL Rwys 11 and 29
FAF to MAP 1.7 NM
Knots | 60 | 90 | 120 | 150 | 180
Min:Sec | 1:42 | 1:08 | 0:51 | 0:41 | 0:34
VOR RWY 29
18° 01'N-66° 34'W
100
PONCE, PUERTO RICO
MERCEDITA

(Not to be used for navigation.)

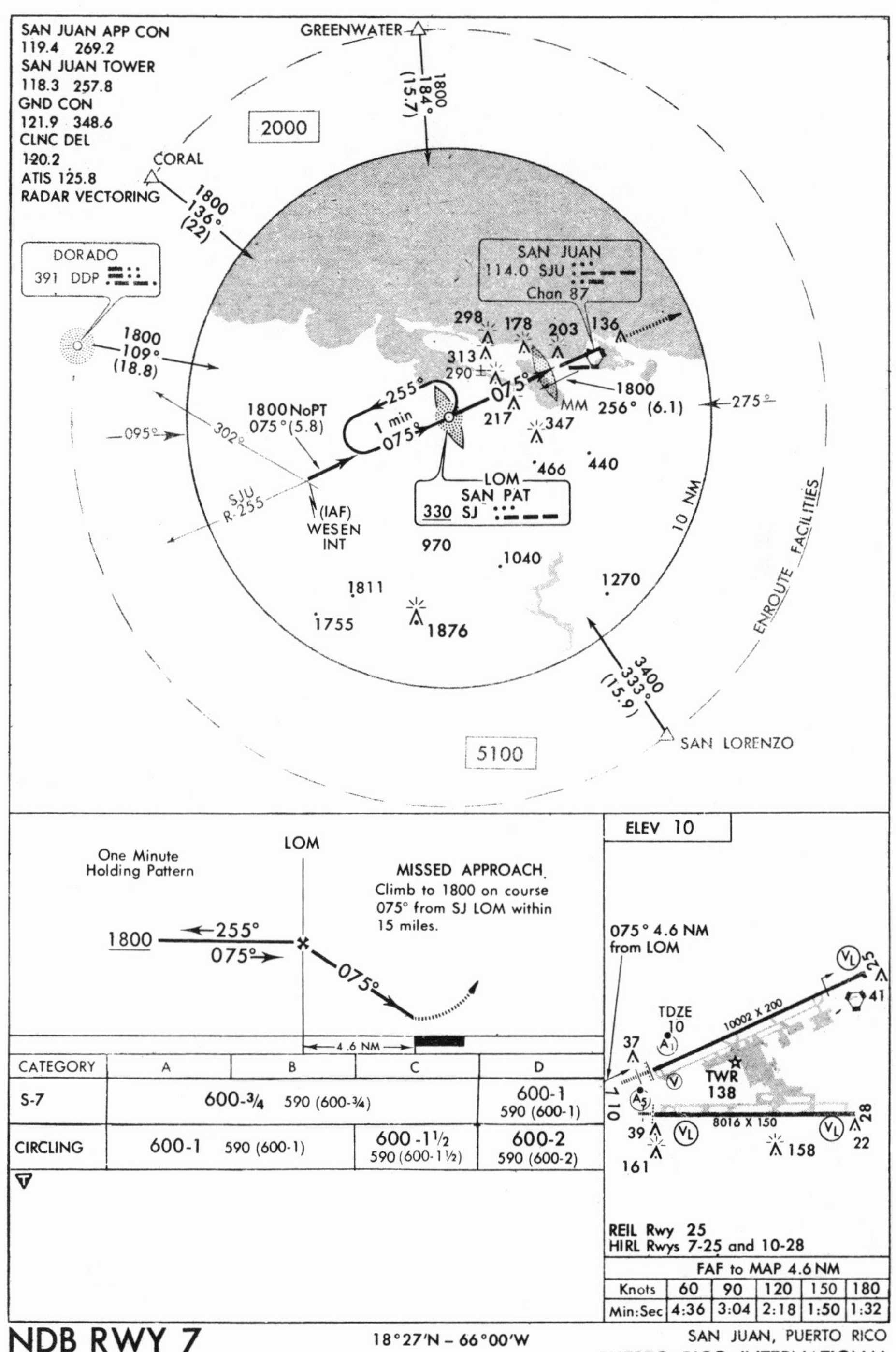
SAN JUAN APP CON
119.4 269.2
SAN JUAN TOWER
118.3 257.8
GND CON
121.9 348.6
CLNC DEL
120.2
ATIS 125.8
RADAR VECTORING
GREENWATER
CORAL
DORADO
391 DDP
SAN JUAN
114.0 SJU
Chan 87
1800NoPT
075°(5.8)
(IAF)
WESEN
INT
LOM
SAN PAT
330 SJ
MM
SAN LORENZO
ENROUTE FACILITIES
10 NM
2000
5100
One Minute
Holding Pattern
MISSED APPROACH
Climb to 1800 on course 075° from SJ LOM within 15 miles.
ELEV 10
075° 4.6 NM
from LOM
TDZE
10
TWR
138
REIL Rwy 25
HIRL Rwys 7-25 and 10-28
CATEGORY A B C D
S-7 600-3/4 590 (600-3/4) 600-1 590 (600-1)
CIRCLING 600-1 590 (600-1) 600-1 1/2 590 (600-1 1/2) 600-2 590 (600-2)
FAF to MAP 4.6 NM
Knots 60 90 120 150 180
Min:Sec 4:36 3:04 2:18 1:50 1:32
NDB RWY 7
18°27'N – 66°00'W
118
SAN JUAN, PUERTO RICO
PUERTO RICO INTERNATIONAL

(Not to be used for navigation.)

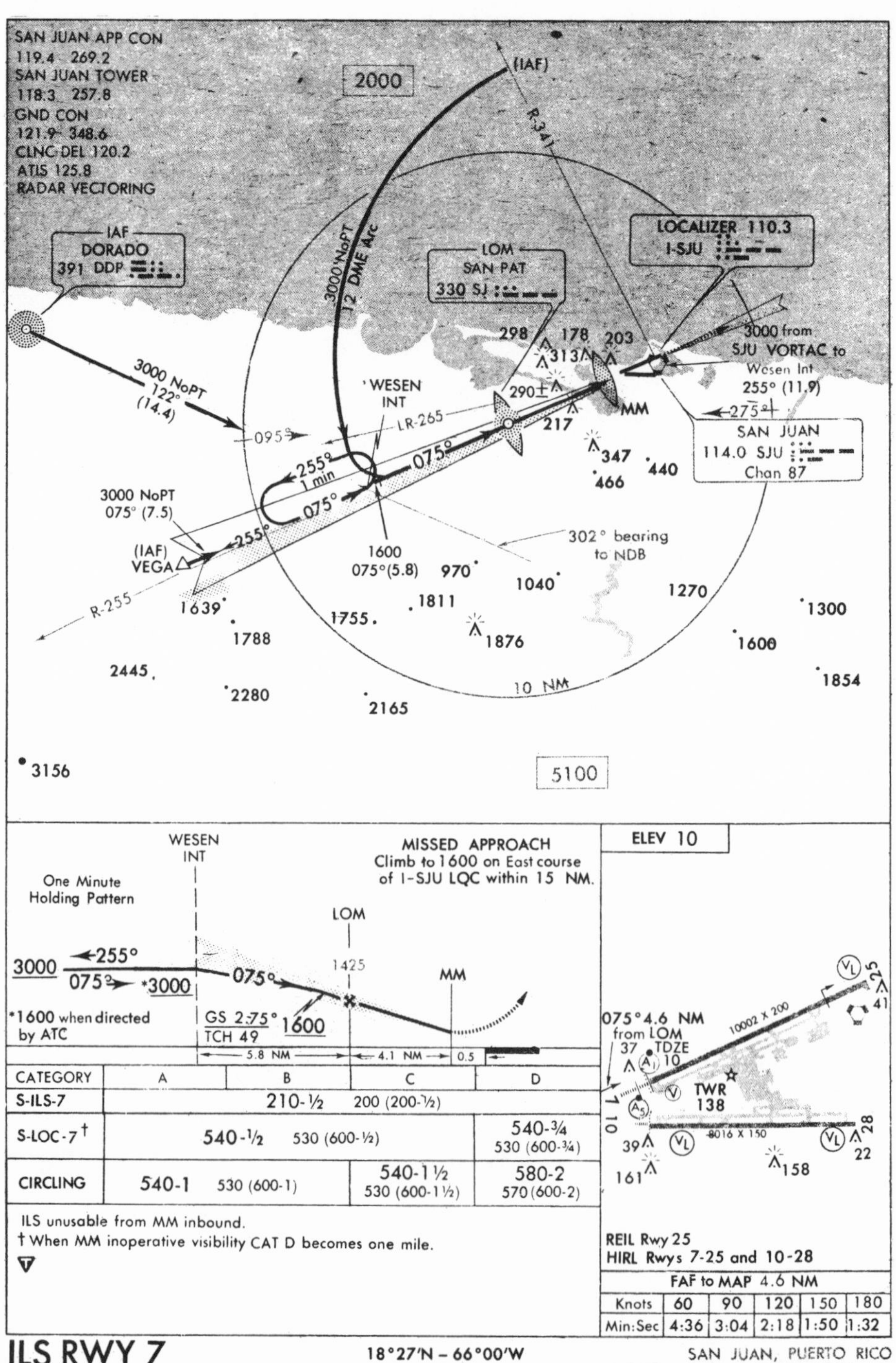
SAN JUAN APP CON
119.4 269.2
SAN JUAN TOWER
118.3 257.8
GND CON
121.9 348.6
CLNC DEL 120.2
ATIS 125.8
RADAR VECTORING
2000
(IAF)
R-341
IAF
DORADO
391 DDP
3000 NoPT
12 DME Arc
LOM
SAN PAT
330 SJ
LOCALIZER 110.3
I-SJU
3000 from
SJU VORTAC to
Wesen Int
255° (11.9)
3000 NoPT
122°
(14.4)
WESEN
INT
LR-265
095°
255°
1 min
075°
298
178
203
313
290
217
MM
275°
SAN JUAN
114.0 SJU
Chan 87
347
440
466
3000 NoPT
075° (7.5)
(IAF)
VEGA
255°
1600
075°(5.8)
970
1040
302° bearing
to NDB
1270
1300
R-255
1639
1788
1755
1811
1876
1600
2445
2280
2165
10 NM
1854
3156
5100
WESEN
INT
MISSED APPROACH
Climb to 1600 on East course
of I-SJU LQC within 15 NM.
ELEV 10
One Minute
Holding Pattern
LOM
1425
MM
3000
255°
075°
*3000
075°
*1600 when directed
by ATC
GS 2.75°
TCH 49
1600
5.8 NM
4.1 NM
0.5
075° 4.6 NM
from LOM
37
TDZE
10
10002 X 200
TWR
138
8016 X 150
25
41
10
28
39
22
161
158
CATEGORY | A | B | C | D
S-ILS-7 | 210-½ 200 (200-½)
S-LOC-7† | 540-½ 530 (600-½) | 540-¾ 530 (600-¾)
CIRCLING | 540-1 530 (600-1) | 540-1½ 530 (600-1½) | 580-2 570 (600-2)
ILS unusable from MM inbound.
† When MM inoperative visibility CAT D becomes one mile.
REIL Rwy 25
HIRL Rwys 7-25 and 10-28
FAF to MAP 4.6 NM
Knots | 60 | 90 | 120 | 150 | 180
Min:Sec | 4:36 | 3:04 | 2:18 | 1:50 | 1:32
ILS RWY 7
18°27'N – 66°00'W
SAN JUAN, PUERTO RICO
PUERTO RICO INTERNATIONAL
120

(Not to be used for navigation.)

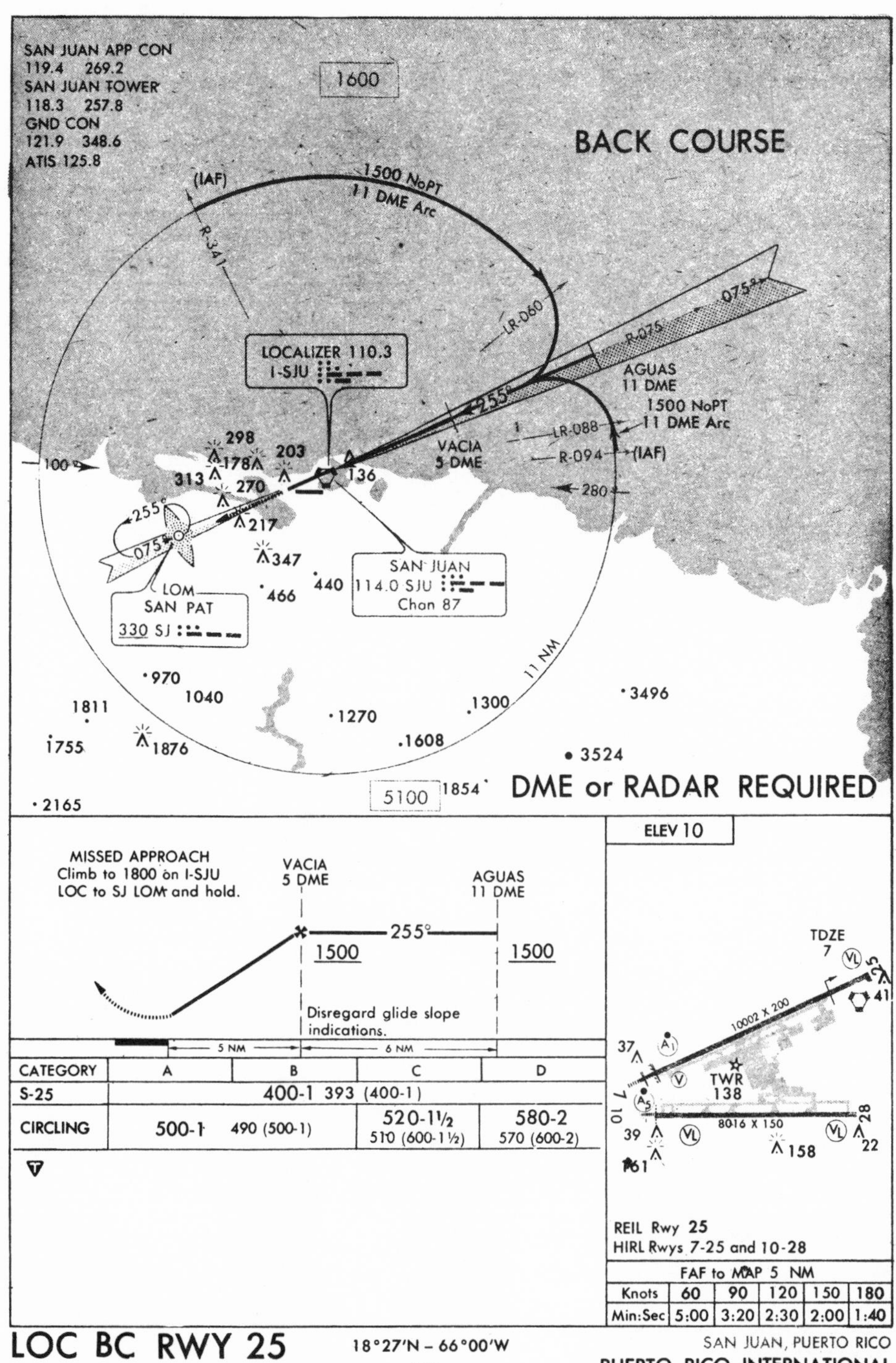

CATEGORY	A	B	C	D
S-25	400-1 393 (400-1)			
CIRCLING	500-1 490 (500-1)		520-1½ 510 (600-1½)	580-2 570 (600-2)

FAF to MAP 5 NM					
Knots	60	90	120	150	180
Min:Sec	5:00	3:20	2:30	2:00	1:40

(Not to be used for navigation.)

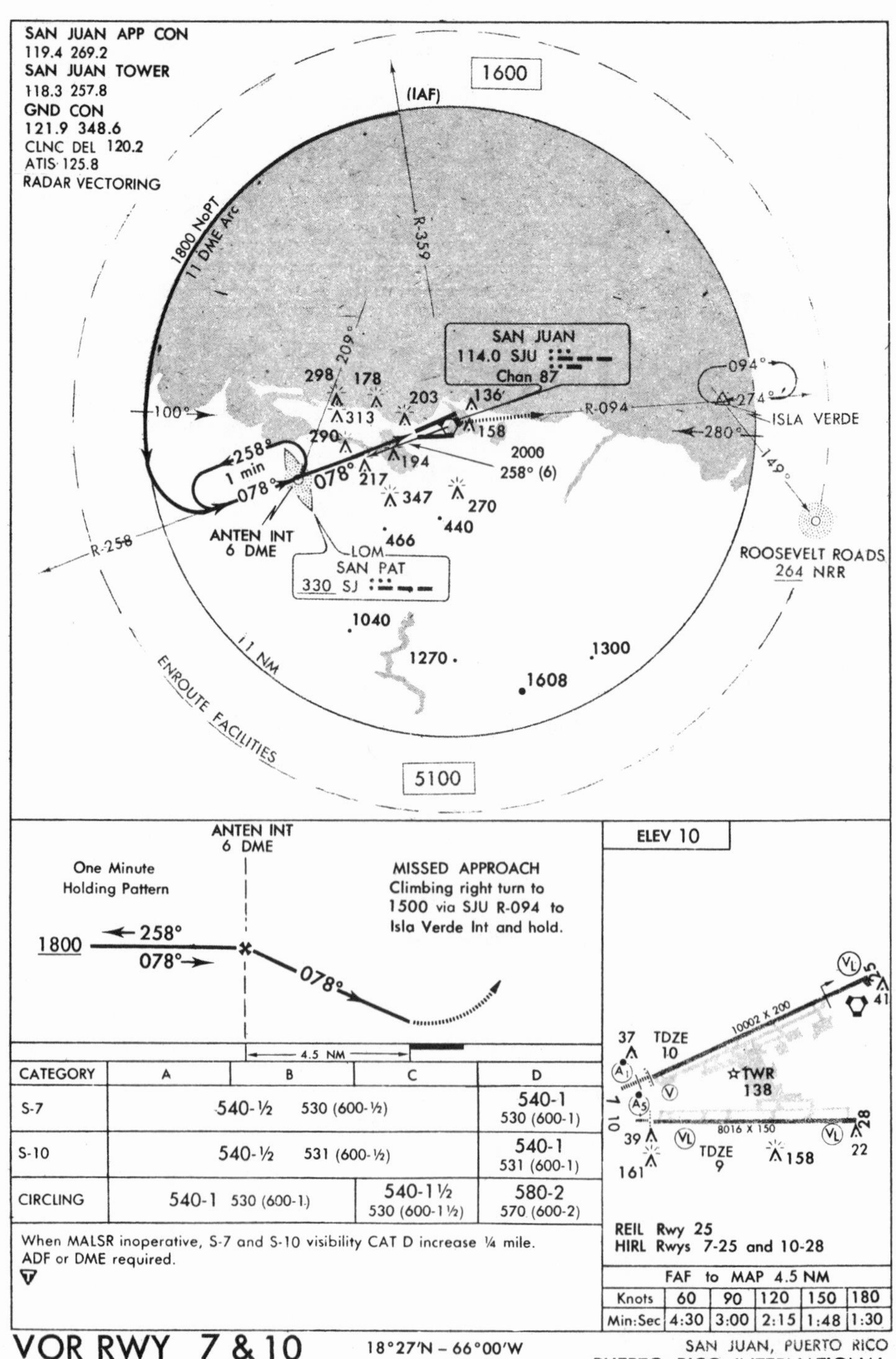

CATEGORY	A	B	C	D
S-7	540-½ 530 (600-½)			540-1 530 (600-1)
S-10	540-½ 531 (600-½)			540-1 531 (600-1)
CIRCLING	540-1 530 (600-1)		540-1½ 530 (600-1½)	580-2 570 (600-2)

FAF to MAP 4.5 NM					
Knots	60	90	120	150	180
Min:Sec	4:30	3:00	2:15	1:48	1:30

(Not to be used for navigation.)

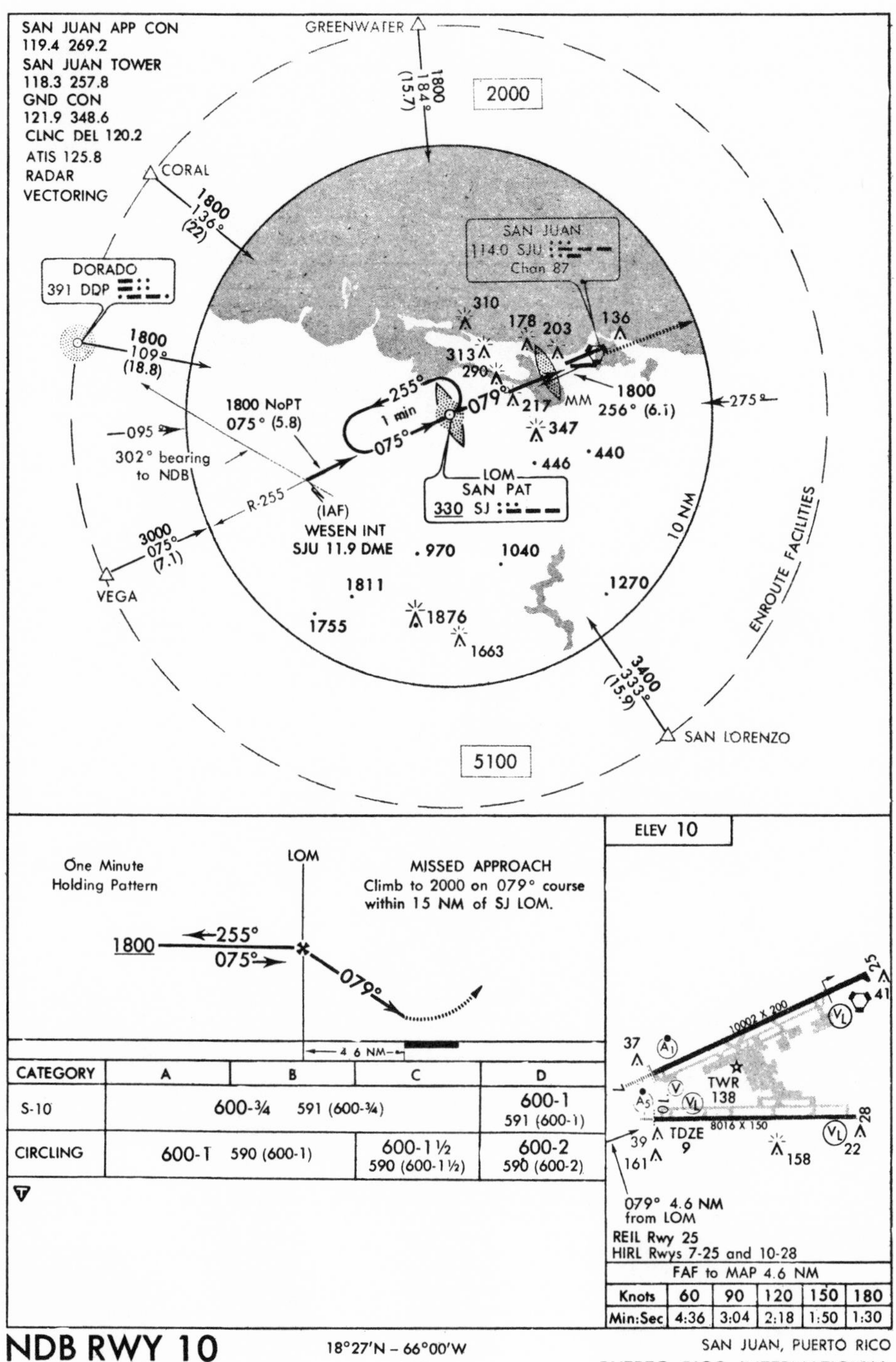
SAN JUAN APP CON
119.4 269.2
SAN JUAN TOWER
118.3 257.8
GND CON
121.9 348.6
CLNC DEL 120.2
ATIS 125.8
RADAR
VECTORING
GREENWATER
1800
184°
(15.7)
2000
CORAL
1800
136°
(22)
SAN JUAN
114.0 SJU
Chan 87
DORADO
391 DDP
1800
109°
(18.8)
310
178
203
136
313
290
1800 NoPT
075° (5.8)
255°
1 min
075°
079°
217
MM
1800
256° (6.1)
275°
347
095°
302° bearing
to NDB
446
440
LOM
SAN PAT
330 SJ
R-255
(IAF)
WESEN INT
SJU 11.9 DME
3000
075°
(7.1)
VEGA
970
1040
1811
1270
10 NM
ENROUTE FACILITIES
1876
1755
1663
3400
333°
(15.9)
SAN LORENZO
5100
One Minute
Holding Pattern
LOM
MISSED APPROACH
Climb to 2000 on 079° course
within 15 NM of SJ LOM.
1800
255°
075°
079°
4.6 NM
ELEV 10
37
41
10002 X 200
TWR
138
8016 X 150
39
TDZE
9
161
158
22
079° 4.6 NM
from LOM
REIL Rwy 25
HIRL Rwys 7-25 and 10-28
CATEGORY | A | B | C | D
S-10 | 600-¾ 591 (600-¾) | 600-1 591 (600-1)
CIRCLING | 600-1 590 (600-1) | 600-1½ 590 (600-1½) | 600-2 590 (600-2)
FAF to MAP 4.6 NM
Knots | 60 | 90 | 120 | 150 | 180
Min:Sec | 4:36 | 3:04 | 2:18 | 1:50 | 1:30
NDB RWY 10
18°27'N – 66°00'W
125
SAN JUAN, PUERTO RICO
PUERTO RICO INTERNATIONAL

(Not to be used for navigation.)

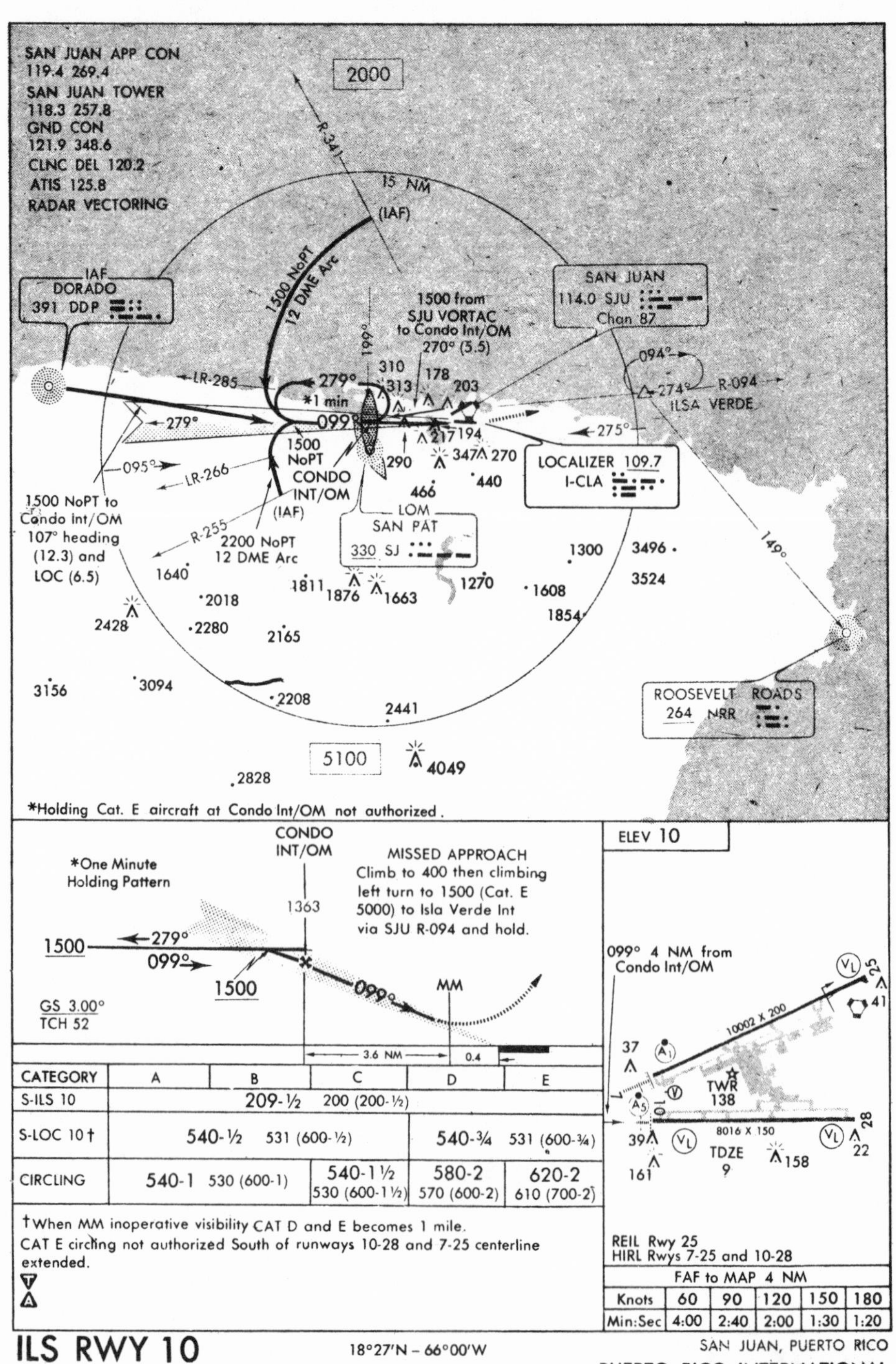

CATEGORY	A	B	C	D	E
S-ILS 10	209-½ 200 (200-½)				
S-LOC 10†	540-½ 531 (600-½)			540-¾ 531 (600-¾)	
CIRCLING	540-1 530 (600-1)		540-1½ 530 (600-1½)	580-2 570 (600-2)	620-2 610 (700-2)

†When MM inoperative visibility CAT D and E becomes 1 mile.
CAT E circling not authorized South of runways 10-28 and 7-25 centerline extended.

FAF to MAP 4 NM					
Knots	60	90	120	150	180
Min:Sec	4:00	2:40	2:00	1:30	1:20

(Not to be used for navigation.)

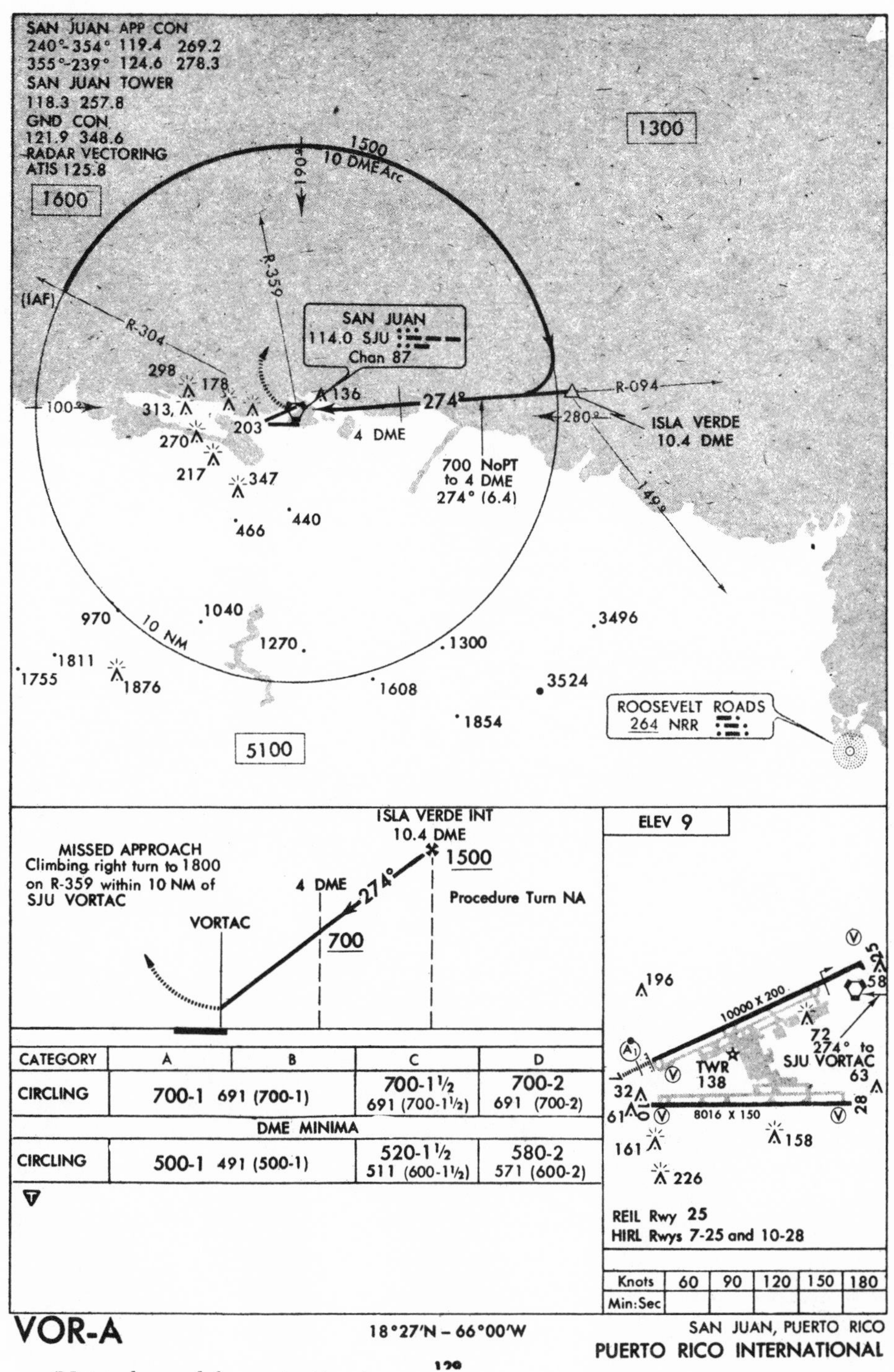
SAN JUAN APP CON
240°-354° 119.4 269.2
355°-239° 124.6 278.3
SAN JUAN TOWER
118.3 257.8
GND CON
121.9 348.6
RADAR VECTORING
ATIS 125.8
1600
1300
1500
10 DME Arc
190°
R-359
(IAF)
R-304
SAN JUAN
114.0 SJU
Chan 87
298
178
313
270
203
136
217
347
466
440
100°
274°
4 DME
R-094
280°
ISLA VERDE
10.4 DME
700 NoPT
to 4 DME
274° (6.4)
149°
970
10 NM
1040
1270
1300
3496
1811
1755
1876
1608
3524
1854
5100
ROOSEVELT ROADS
264 NRR
ISLA VERDE INT
10.4 DME
1500
MISSED APPROACH
Climbing right turn to 1800
on R-359 within 10 NM of
SJU VORTAC
4 DME
274°
Procedure Turn NA
VORTAC
700
ELEV 9
196
10000 X 200
72
274° to
SJU VORTAC
TWR
138
63
32
61
8016 X 150
28
158
161
226
REIL Rwy 25
HIRL Rwys 7-25 and 10-28
CATEGORY | A | B | C | D
CIRCLING | 700-1 691 (700-1) | 700-1½ 691 (700-1½) | 700-2 691 (700-2)
DME MINIMA
CIRCLING | 500-1 491 (500-1) | 520-1½ 511 (600-1½) | 580-2 571 (600-2)
Knots | 60 | 90 | 120 | 150 | 180
Min:Sec
VOR-A
18°27'N – 66°00'W
SAN JUAN, PUERTO RICO
PUERTO RICO INTERNATIONAL
129

(Not to be used for navigation.)

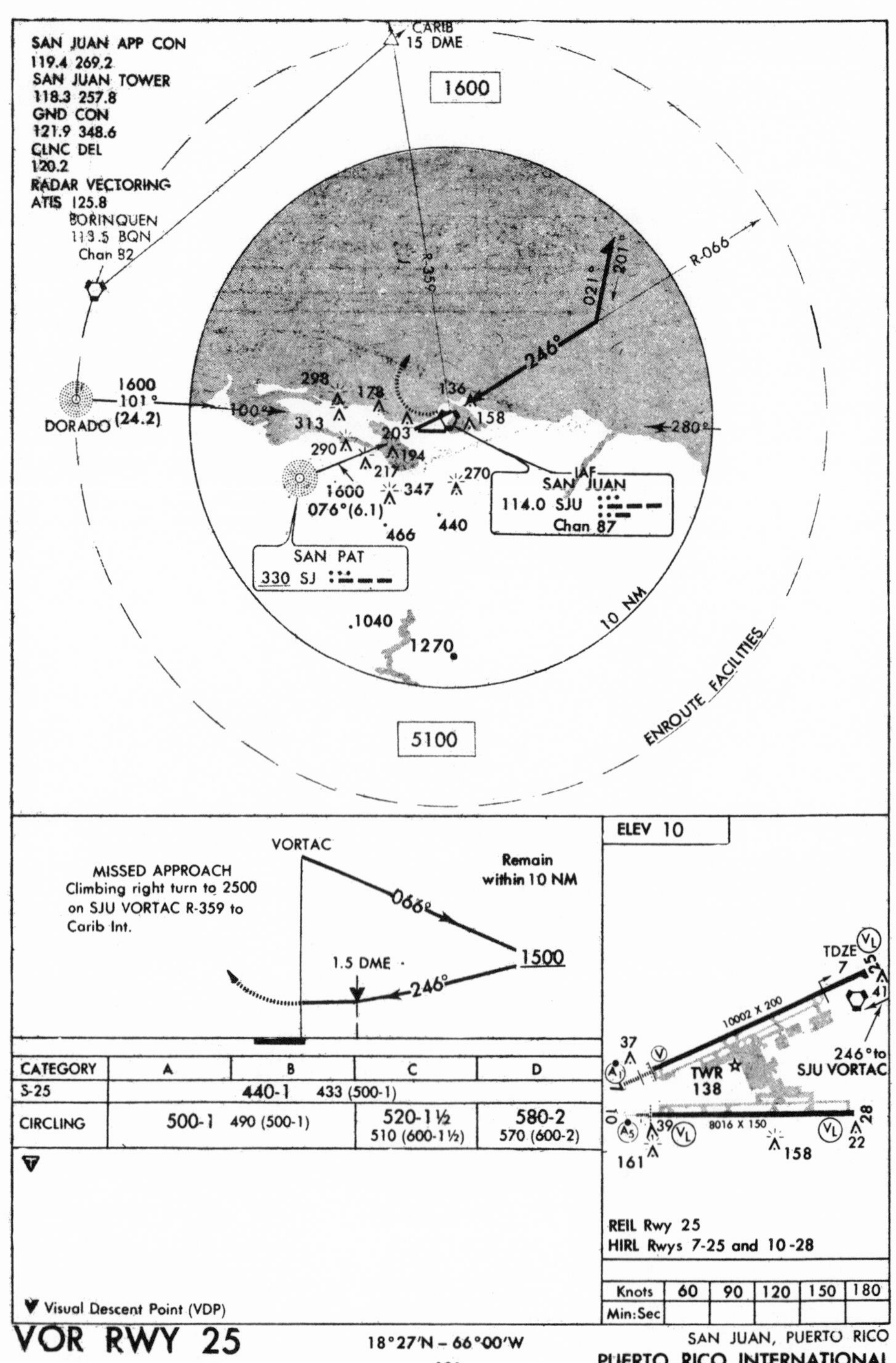
SAN JUAN APP CON
119.4 269.2
SAN JUAN TOWER
118.3 257.8
GND CON
121.9 348.6
CLNC DEL
120.2
RADAR VECTORING
ATIS 125.8
BORINQUEN
113.5 BQN
Chan 82
CARIB
15 DME
1600
R-359
R-066
021°
201°
246°
1600
101°
(24.2)
DORADO
100°
298
178
136
313
158
203
290
194
217
270
280°
1600
076°(6.1)
347
440
466
IAF
SAN JUAN
114.0 SJU
Chan 87
SAN PAT
330 SJ
10 NM
.1040
1270
ENROUTE FACILITIES
5100
MISSED APPROACH
Climbing right turn to 2500
on SJU VORTAC R-359 to
Carib Int.
VORTAC
Remain
within 10 NM
066°
1500
1.5 DME
246°
ELEV 10
TDZE
7
25
41
10002 X 200
246° to
SJU VORTAC
37
TWR
138
10
8016 X 150
28
39
22
161
158
CATEGORY
A
B
C
D
S-25
440-1 433 (500-1)
CIRCLING
500-1 490 (500-1)
520-1½ 510 (600-1½)
580-2 570 (600-2)
REIL Rwy 25
HIRL Rwys 7-25 and 10-28
Knots 60 90 120 150 180
Min:Sec
Visual Descent Point (VDP)
VOR RWY 25
18°27'N – 66°00'W
131
SAN JUAN, PUERTO RICO
PUERTO RICO INTERNATIONAL

(Not to be used for navigation.)

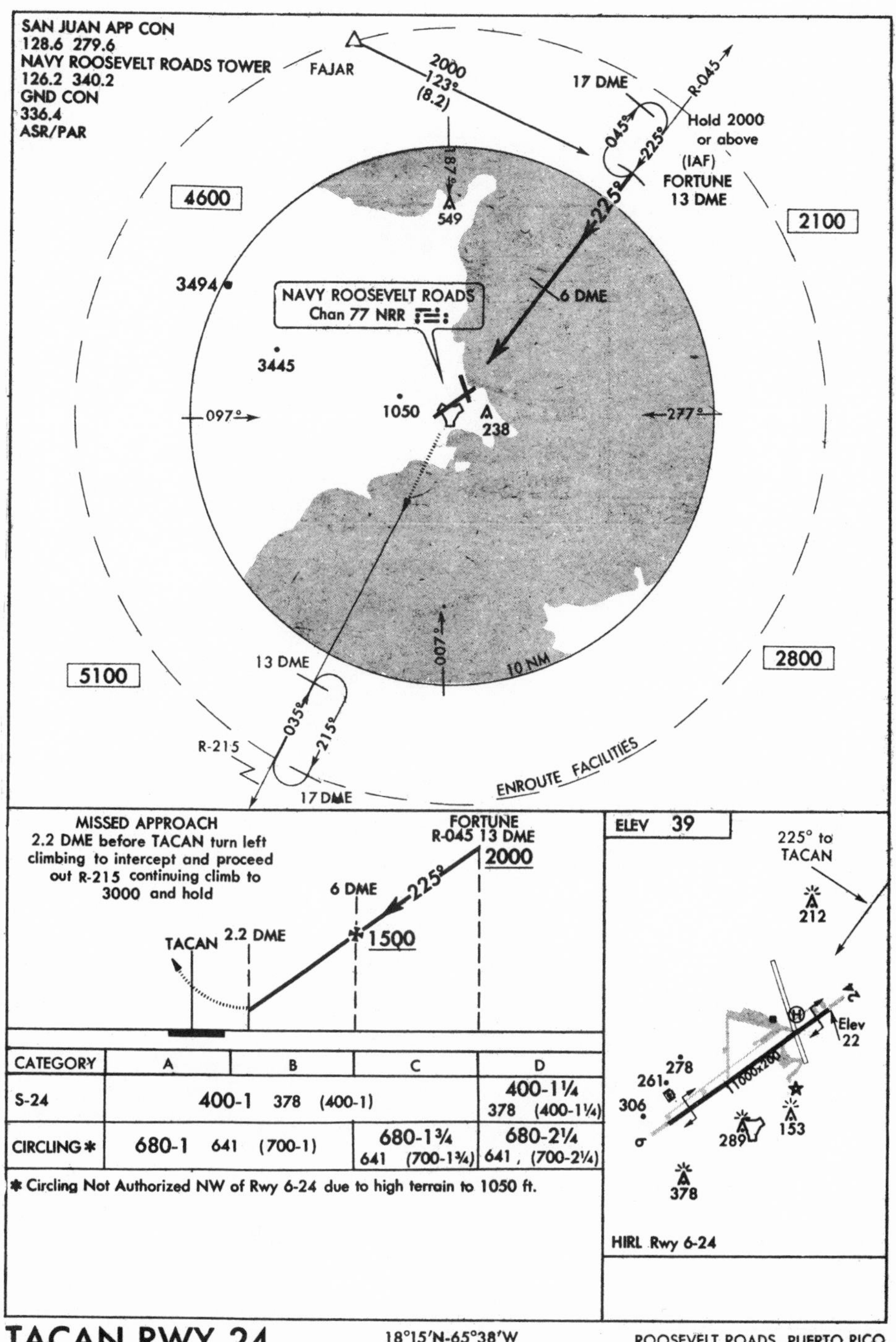

CATEGORY	A	B	C	D
S-24	400-1 378 (400-1)			400-1¼ 378 (400-1¼)
CIRCLING*	680-1 641 (700-1)		680-1¾ 641 (700-1¾)	680-2¼ 641, (700-2¼)

* Circling Not Authorized NW of Rwy 6-24 due to high terrain to 1050 ft.

(Not to be used for navigation.)

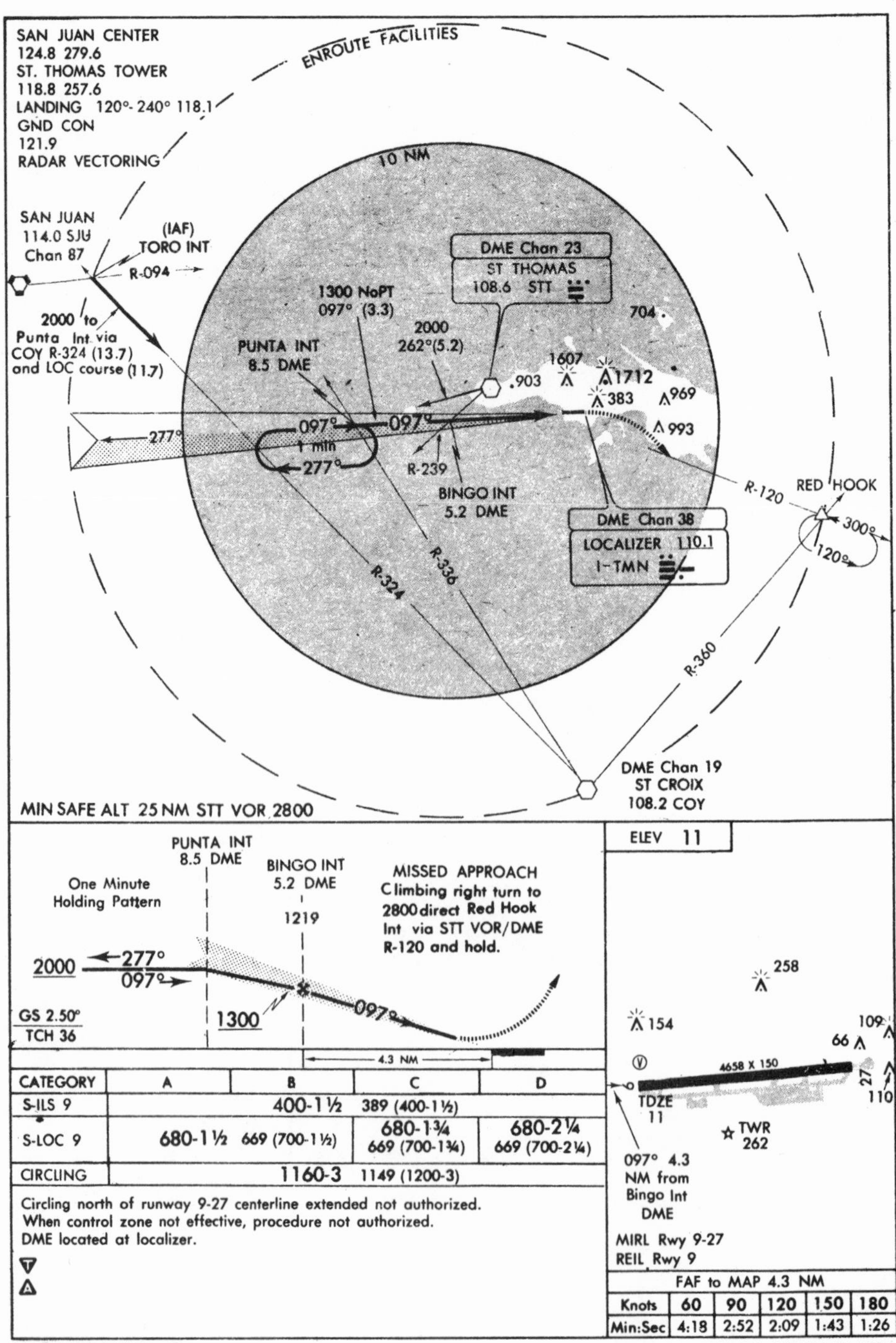

CATEGORY	A	B	C	D
S-ILS 9	400-1½ 389 (400-1½)			
S-LOC 9	680-1½ 669 (700-1½)		680-1¾ 669 (700-1¾)	680-2¼ 669 (700-2¼)
CIRCLING	1160-3 1149 (1200-3)			

Circling north of runway 9-27 centerline extended not authorized.
When control zone not effective, procedure not authorized.
DME located at localizer.

FAF to MAP 4.3 NM					
Knots	60	90	120	150	180
Min:Sec	4:18	2:52	2:09	1:43	1:26

ILS RWY 9 18°20′N – 64°58′W CHARLOTTE AMALIE, ST. THOMAS, VIRGIN ISLANDS

HARRY S. TRUMAN

(Not to be used for navigation.)

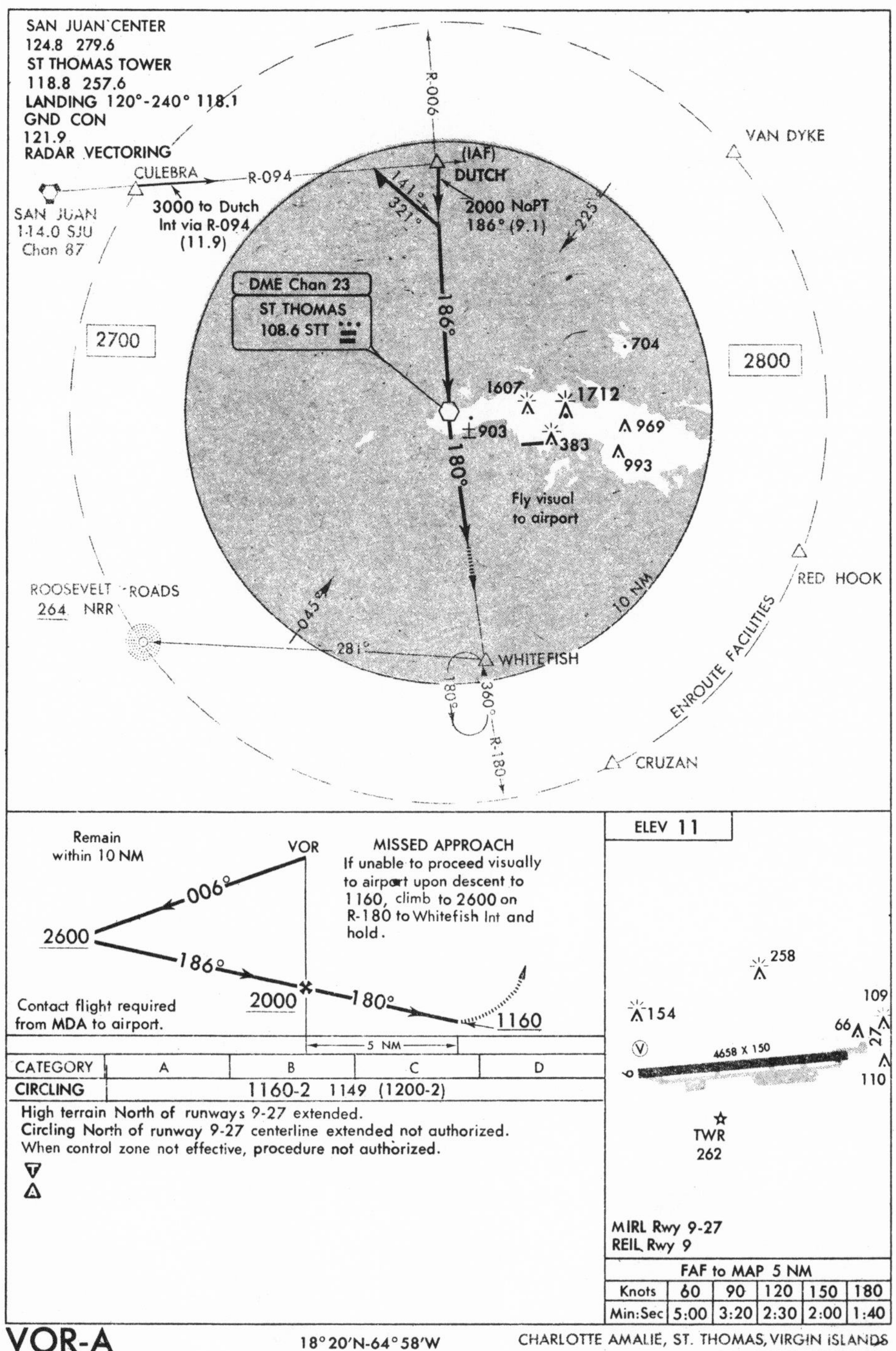
SAN JUAN CENTER
124.8 279.6
ST THOMAS TOWER
118.8 257.6
LANDING 120°-240° 118.1
GND CON
121.9
RADAR VECTORING
CULEBRA
R-094
SAN JUAN
114.0 SJU
Chan 87
3000 to Dutch
Int via R-094
(11.9)
R-006
(IAF)
DUTCH
141°
321°
2000 NoPT
186° (9.1)
225°
DME Chan 23
ST THOMAS
108.6 STT
2700
2800
VAN DYKE
186°
.704
1607
1712
903
383
969
993
180°
Fly visual
to airport
ROOSEVELT ROADS
264 NRR
045°
281°
WHITEFISH
10 NM
RED HOOK
ENROUTE FACILITIES
180°
360°
R-180
CRUZAN
Remain
within 10 NM
VOR
006°
2600
186°
2000
180°
1160
5 NM
Contact flight required
from MDA to airport.
MISSED APPROACH
If unable to proceed visually
to airport upon descent to
1160, climb to 2600 on
R-180 to Whitefish Int and
hold.
ELEV 11
258
154
109
66
4658 X 150
9
27
110
TWR
262
MIRL Rwy 9-27
REIL Rwy 9
CATEGORY A B C D
CIRCLING 1160-2 1149 (1200-2)
High terrain North of runways 9-27 extended.
Circling North of runway 9-27 centerline extended not authorized.
When control zone not effective, procedure not authorized.
FAF to MAP 5 NM
Knots 60 90 120 150 180
Min:Sec 5:00 3:20 2:30 2:00 1:40
VOR-A
18°20'N-64°58'W
CHARLOTTE AMALIE, ST. THOMAS, VIRGIN ISLANDS
HARRY S. TRUMAN
74

(Not to be used for navigation.)

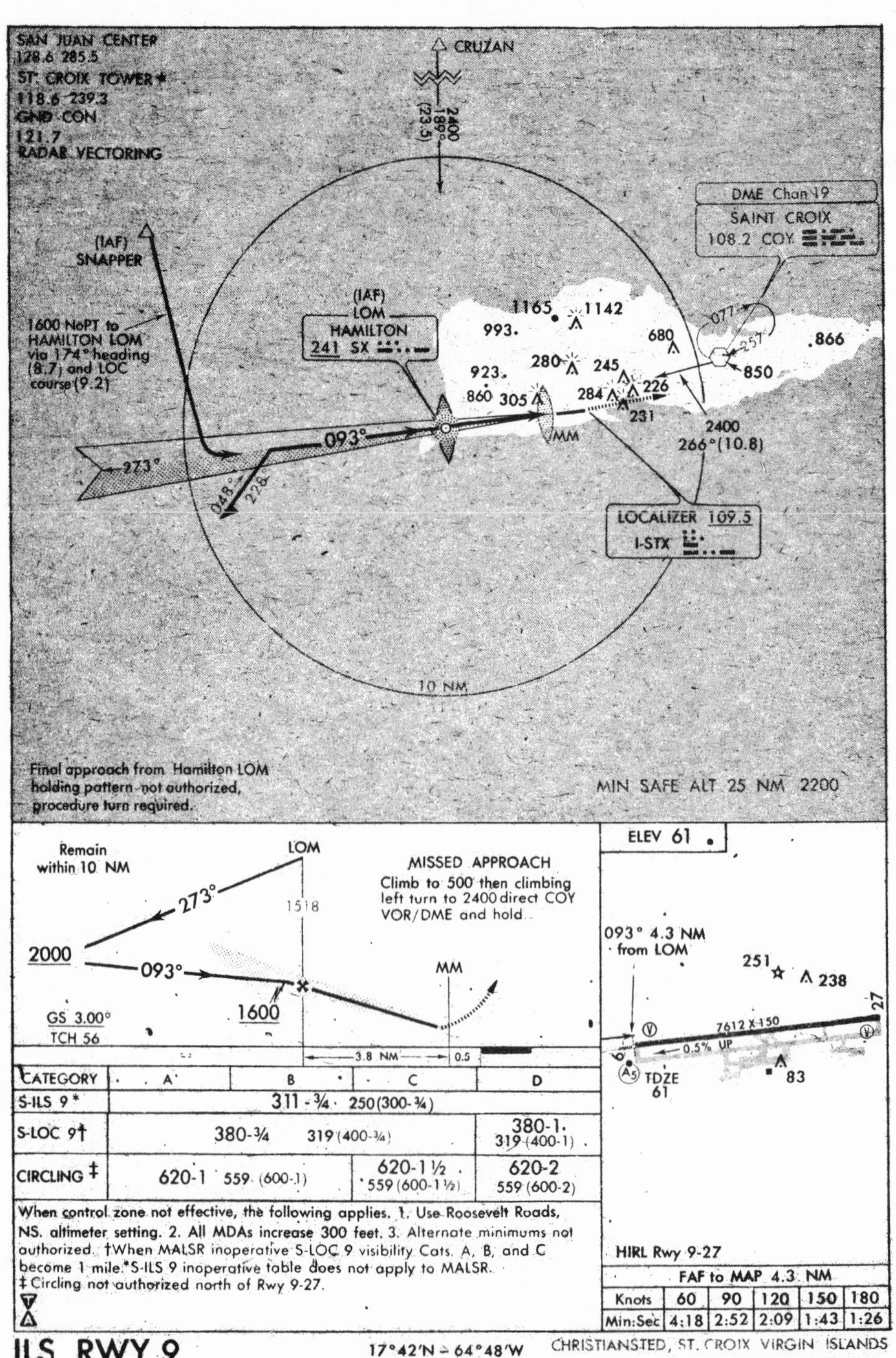

SAN JUAN CENTER
128.6 285.5
ST. CROIX TOWER*
118.6 239.3
GND CON
121.7
RADAR VECTORING
CRUZAN
2400
189°
(23.5)
DME Chan 19
SAINT CROIX
108.2 COY
(IAF)
SNAPPER
1600 NoPT to HAMILTON LOM via 174° heading (8.7) and LOC course (9.2)
(IAF)
LOM
HAMILTON
241 SX
1165
1142
993
680
.866
280
245
850
923
226
860
305
284
231
093°
273°
048°
228°
MM
2400
266°(10.8)
LOCALIZER 109.5
I-STX
10 NM
Final approach from Hamilton LOM holding pattern not authorized, procedure turn required.
MIN SAFE ALT 25 NM 2200
Remain within 10 NM
LOM
1518
MISSED APPROACH
Climb to 500 then climbing left turn to 2400 direct COY VOR/DME and hold
273°
2000
093°
MM
1600
GS 3.00°
TCH 56
3.8 NM
0.5
ELEV 61
093° 4.3 NM from LOM
251
238
27
7612 X 150
0.5% UP
9
TDZE
61
83
CATEGORY | A | B | C | D
S-ILS 9* | 311-¾ 250(300-¾)
S-LOC 9† | 380-¾ 319(400-¾) | 380-1 319(400-1)
CIRCLING ‡ | 620-1 559(600-1) | 620-1½ 559(600-1½) | 620-2 559(600-2)
When control zone not effective, the following applies. 1. Use Roosevelt Roads, NS. altimeter setting. 2. All MDAs increase 300 feet. 3. Alternate minimums not authorized. †When MALSR inoperative S-LOC 9 visibility Cats. A, B, and C become 1 mile.*S-ILS 9 inoperative table does not apply to MALSR.
‡ Circling not authorized north of Rwy 9-27.
HIRL Rwy 9-27
FAF to MAP 4.3 NM
Knots | 60 | 90 | 120 | 150 | 180
Min:Sec | 4:18 | 2:52 | 2:09 | 1:43 | 1:26
ILS RWY 9
17°42'N - 64°48'W
6
CHRISTIANSTED, ST. CROIX VIRGIN ISLANDS
ALEXANDER HAMILTON

(Not to be used for navigation.)

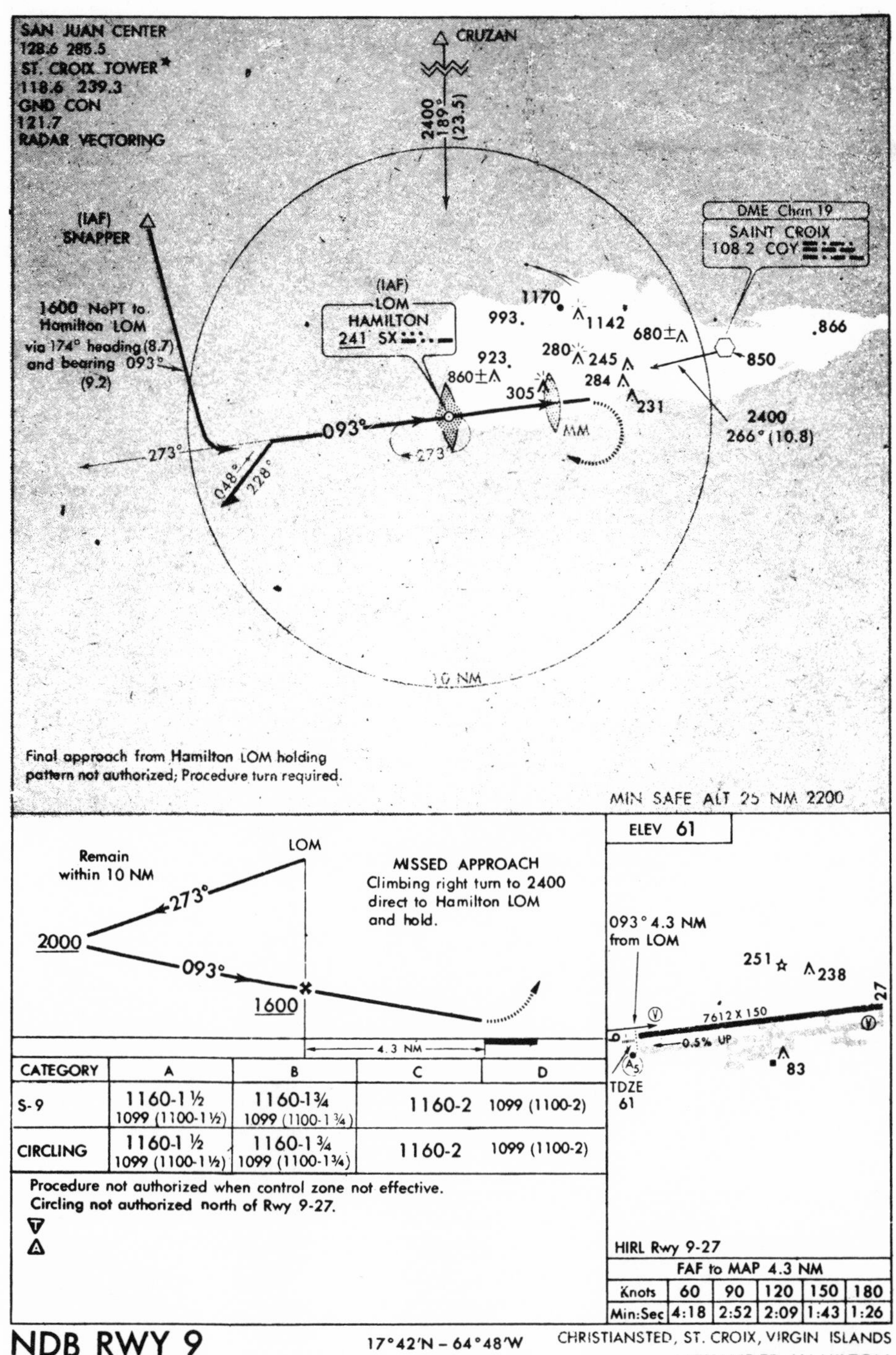
SAN JUAN CENTER
128.6 285.5
ST. CROIX TOWER*
118.6 239.3
GND CON
121.7
RADAR VECTORING
CRUZAN
2400
189°
(23.5)
(IAF)
SNAPPER
1600 NoPT to Hamilton LOM via 174° heading (8.7) and bearing 093° (9.2)
(IAF)
LOM
HAMILTON
241 SX
DME Chan 19
SAINT CROIX
108.2 COY
1170
993
1142
680±
.866
850
923
280
245
860±
284
305
231
2400
266° (10.8)
093°
273°
273°
048°
228°
MM
10 NM
Final approach from Hamilton LOM holding pattern not authorized; Procedure turn required.
MIN SAFE ALT 25 NM 2200
Remain within 10 NM
LOM
273°
2000
093°
1600
4.3 NM
MISSED APPROACH
Climbing right turn to 2400 direct to Hamilton LOM and hold.
ELEV 61
093° 4.3 NM from LOM
251
238
7612 X 150
0.5% UP
27
83
TDZE 61
CATEGORY | A | B | C | D
S-9 | 1160-1½ 1099 (1100-1½) | 1160-1¾ 1099 (1100-1¾) | 1160-2 | 1099 (1100-2)
CIRCLING | 1160-1½ 1099 (1100-1½) | 1160-1¾ 1099 (1100-1¾) | 1160-2 | 1099 (1100-2)
Procedure not authorized when control zone not effective.
Circling not authorized north of Rwy 9-27.
HIRL Rwy 9-27
FAF to MAP 4.3 NM
Knots | 60 | 90 | 120 | 150 | 180
Min:Sec | 4:18 | 2:52 | 2:09 | 1:43 | 1:26
NDB RWY 9
17°42'N – 64°48'W
CHRISTIANSTED, ST. CROIX, VIRGIN ISLANDS
ALEXANDER HAMILTON
5

(Not to be used for navigation.)

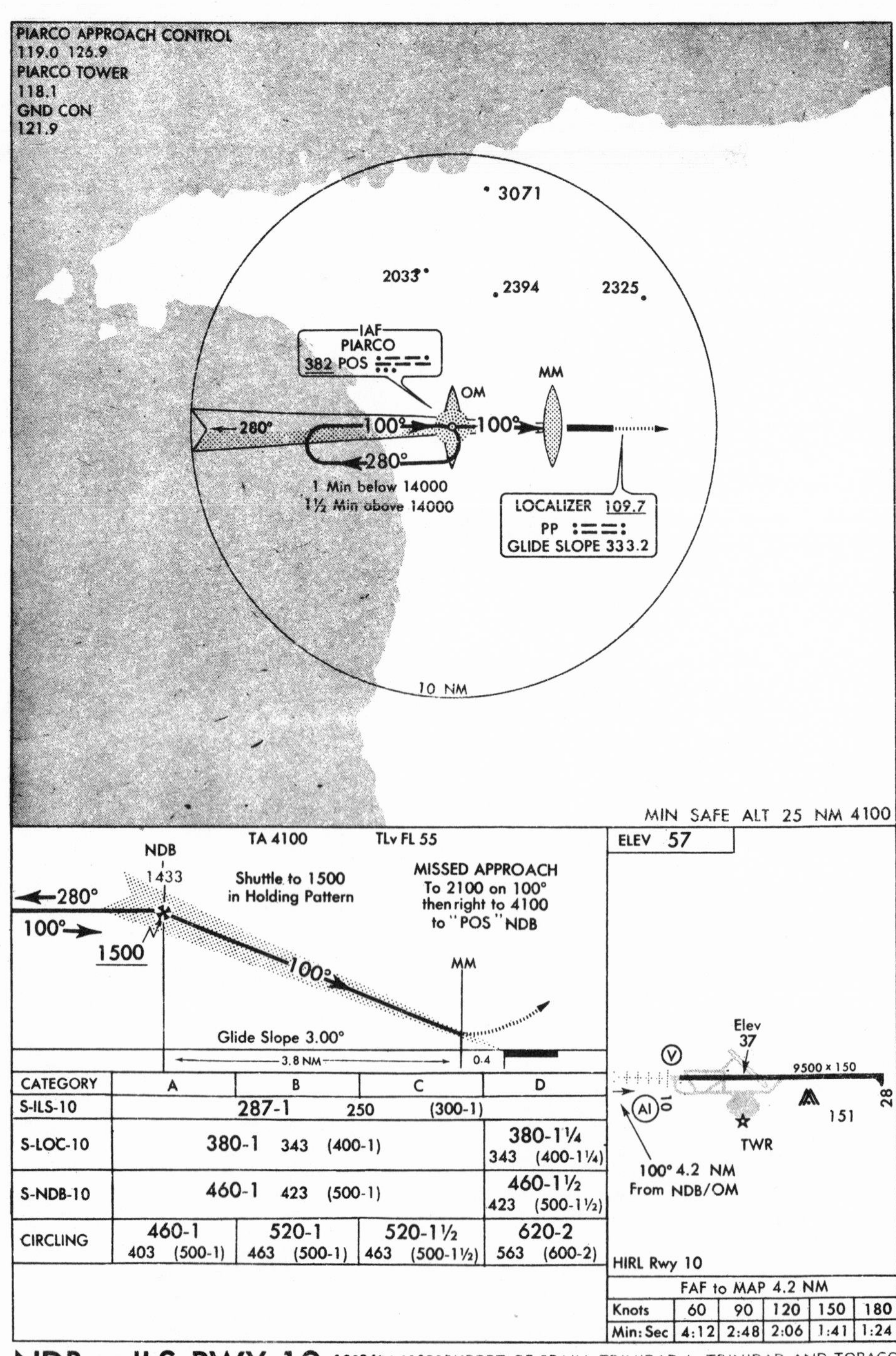

CATEGORY	A	B	C	D
S-ILS-10	287-1 250 (300-1)			
S-LOC-10	380-1 343 (400-1)			380-1¼ 343 (400-1¼)
S-NDB-10	460-1 423 (500-1)			460-1½ 423 (500-1½)
CIRCLING	460-1 403 (500-1)	520-1 463 (500-1)	520-1½ 463 (500-1½)	620-2 563 (600-2)

FAF to MAP 4.2 NM					
Knots	60	90	120	150	180
Min: Sec	4:12	2:48	2:06	1:41	1:24

(Not to be used for navigation.)

Index